THE SPIRIT AND STRUCTURE
OF GERMAN FASCISM

THE SPIRIT AND STRUCTURE OF GERMAN FASCISM

by

ROBERT A. BRADY

ASSOCIATE PROFESSOR OF ECONOMICS
OF THE UNIVERSITY OF CALIFORNIA

with a Foreword by

PROFESSOR H. J. LASKI

If that the heavens do not their visible spirits
Send quickly down to tame these vile offences,
It will come,
Humanity must perforce prey on itself,
Like monsters of the deep.

King Lear

LONDON
VICTOR GOLLANCZ LTD
1937

Printed in Great Britain by
The Camelot Press Ltd., London and Southampton

To

MICHAEL

CONTENTS

CONTENTS

ACKNOWLEDGMENTS

So MANY PEOPLE have assisted with material and have contributed to the clarification of the far-ranging issues discussed in this book that I may not acknowledge them all without reproducing a list resembling a small telephone directory. But the aid and counsel of those who have worked with me directly in the research and writing are of an order which I must at least record though I cannot expect ever to repay. Mr. Norman Bursler, of the University of California, and Professor William H. Taylor, of the University of Hawaii, provided invaluable aid in the collection and first sifting of original source materials. Without their assistance, it would not have been possible either to select intelligently from the vast accumulations of literature available, or to check adequately against the oral expressions of opinion given by the numerous persons interviewed. Even greater is my debt to Rosalind Zoglin, whose systematic and painstaking sifting, checking, and rechecking of literature and opinion from every angle touched upon, made possible the writing in half the time normally required. My obligation to Miss Zoglin is deepened by the high quality of her innumerable suggestions, the keenness of her criticisms, and the almost unbelievable celerity and sureness with which she moved through sheaves of turgid, on the surface endlessly contradictory, and at all times heartbreaking literature.

ROBERT A. BRADY

FOREWORD

PROFESSOR BRADY has written an admirable book. Its value consists, above all, in its careful and detailed analysis of Fascist institutions in Germany—the most complete, to my knowledge, that exists in the English language. As a survey of the mechanisms through which the purpose of Herr Hitler's dictatorship is fulfilled, I know no existing book of comparable value.

What emerges from his study? Above all, I suggest, the conclusion that Fascism is nothing but monopoly-capitalism imposing its will on those masses whom it has deliberately transformed into its slaves. It is fundamental to its understanding that all the organs of working-class defence are destroyed; it is fundamental to its understanding, also, that society has been merged into a state the outstanding characteristic of which is the imposition of its will by coercion. There is no social revolution: the ownership of the instruments of production remain in private hands. There has been a political revolution in the sense that those organs through which, prior to 1933, criticism of the social order might be expressed, have been ruthlessly destroyed. What replaces them is essentially a partnership between monopoly-capitalism and the Nazi Party in which that supreme coercive power which is of the State's essence is used to compel obedience to the new system.

The reader of Professor Brady's book will find here all the material necessary to understand how the apparatus works. What is new in it is less the purpose by which it is informed than the thoroughness with which its purpose is fulfilled. It has replaced capitalist democracy as a form of state because, in the latter, it proved impossible, under German conditions, to achieve that discipline of the working-class which is required to maintain profitability under monopoly-capitalism. Democracy sought to recognise the inherent work of the individual citizen: to capitalism, he has always been a commodity to be bought and sold that profit could be made. Upon the plane of democracy, the resolution of the conflict between the purposes of these two conceptions proved impossible. Freedom meant a possible challenge to the privileges which monopoly-capitalism offered to the owners of the instruments of production. The suppression of freedom was therefore necessary lest, upon some future occasion, the challenge prove successful.

Professor Brady explains in detail the methods by which Herr Hitler and his supporters were able to secure their victory. The lessons implicit in his analysis are of grave importance for ourselves. For wherever capitalism finds itself in the dilemma so ruthlessly solved by Herr Hitler, someone akin to him will arise to act, if he can, on its behalf. There is no reason, I suggest, to suppose that any nation is so inescapably wedded to democracy as to be free from the danger of Fascism. Professor Brady shows how profound are Fascist tendencies in the United States. The experience of Italy and Austria, of Greece and the Balkans, enforce a similar lesson. France and Belgium have so far escaped: but the reality of the danger in each of them needs no emphasis to any well-informed observer. And, as I write, General Franco is seeking, with the aid of Fascist auxiliaries, to impose on Spain a régime which will place its citizens under the unfettered despotism of a capitalist alliance.

There is no logical reason I can see why Great Britain should have a different experience unless we are warned in time. The lesson of all foreign experience is that a governing class will not permit the use of democratic institutions to abrogate its economic privileges. So long as those institutions do not so operate as to interfere with the basic structure of capitalism, they are respected. But so soon as they are used to attempt a fundamental change in the incidence of economic power, faith in the validity of democratic institutions is rapidly undermined. Indeed, the experience of Western Europe makes it plain that the attempt need only be potential; in both Germany and Italy the threat to, rather than the attack upon, capitalism was sufficient to provoke aggression against democracy. To the possibility of a British fascism, the weak reply only is made either that such an experience is wholly alien from our character, or that democratic institutions are here too firmly rooted to be overthrown.

But it was a favourite exercise of German observers before 1933 to explain that Germany was not Italy, and that the German national character would prove toughly resistant to Fascist ideas. In fact, German democracy not only collapsed without a blow; it has since accepted, as Professor Brady here

admirably shows, a mass of pseudo-scientific nonsense which
many of its most vehement exponents would, only five years
ago, have treated as the nonsense it is. Not only that. Its leaders
in thought have accepted with hardly a protest the expulsion
from Germany of writers and men of science whom, before the
Nazi victory, they accepted without question as the ornaments of
contemporary German civilisation. If in so brief a time so startling a transvaluation of all German values can take place, are we
reasonably entitled to assume that, under a similar threat, we
would act so very differently ?

Let us admit that our tradition of democratic institutions is
more firmly rooted than in Germany; that, so far, their resistance
has not been threatened by defeat in war. We have, surely, to
remember two things of importance: first, that the constitutionalism of British capitalists has not been tested by serious
political defeat, and, second, that its benevolent mood has not
yet been subjected to the rigours of such German crises as the
inflation. Even as it is, the post-war years have seen British
legislation intended to school British workers to a proper mood
of obedience: the Trades Disputes Act of 1927, the Incitement
to Disaffection Act of 1934, the Political Uniforms Act of 1936,
are all of them contingently Fascist legislation. The militarisation
of the police, the striking growth in the number of convictions for
seditious utterance, the recent and gravely sinister dismissal of
dockyard workers without a hearing and on the testimony of
unknown spies offered to an unnamed tribunal, the harrying of
the unemployed under the Means Test, the very different
treatment meted out by the Courts to socialist agitators, on the
one hand, and to Fascist agitators, on the other, all point in a
similar direction. The class-character of some of our fundamental institutions, above all of the armed forces of the Crown, is
a significant thing; and though the case for the democratisation
of the Army has been strongly urged by Mr. Lloyd George no
movement towards it has been made. It is notable that, save for
the pre-revolutionary army of Spain, the class-structure of the
British Army is the least democratic of any important State.
After the Ulster mutiny of 1914, a simple faith in its obedience
to the orders of a socialist government which sought to effect
drastic economic changes would be a luxury indeed.

German political democracy perished, above all, for two reasons. As Professor Brady here shows, it left its enemies undisturbed in possession of the main instruments of political and economic power. When, therefore, its formal authority was challenged, those enemies were in possession of all the key positions of the State. For fourteen years they had been left almost unimpeded in their tacit encouragement of the enemies of Weimar: the most striking thing about the character of the Weimar republic, indeed, was the tenderness with which it treated its opponents and the harshness with which it discouraged its friends. And, as Professor Brady again makes clear, that working class which, in a crisis, should have been its natural defender was, in fact, stricken into impotence by its divisions. When the challenge came those divisions were fatal to its ability to defend itself.

A good deal of this analysis could be repeated, without considerable adjustment, of Great Britain. Here, as in Germany, the Labour Party defends a formal democracy as such without attempting to realise the importance of its capitalist context. The Communist doubt of whether capitalism can be peacefully transformed is held by the bulk of the Labour Party leaders to justify the same kind of division as brought Germany to disaster. It is, no doubt, true that the forces of British communism are much smaller than those of its German analogue. But it is, I think, also true that the main reason for the rejection of a unity repeatedly proffered is the fear of British Labour leaders that capitalist respect for constitutionalism would not survive a stirring campaign for power by a united working class which took the political offensive. The main direction of Labour Party thought in this country has a grim resemblance to that of the German Social Democratic Party before the advent of Herr Hitler. Its anxiety seems to be the offer of proof to its opponents that its formal socialism need not be taken too seriously. And, even within its own confines, it seems to lack that clarity about immediate objectives which gives to a party the right to the initiative in the struggle for political power.

There is, I think, involved in this approach the view that the state-power in a democracy is a neutral thing which, in a parliamentary democracy, lies equally at the disposal of that party which obtains a majority at the polls. There is little in the history of the post-war years to support that conclusion—Italy, Germany, Austria, Spain, each of these is, as an experience, a footnote of grave doubt upon its validity. It is notable, also, that M. Blum, after his arrival at power in France, has had to make important changes in the personnel of his administration. It is significant, also, that not the least of President Roosevelt's difficulties has arisen from the need to improvise a personnel upon whom he could rely; and the conflict between his policies, at no point socialist, ànd the attitude to them of the judiciary has raised issues which go to the root of the American system. The adaptation, in a word, of the institutions and habits of capitalist democracy to the needs of a socialist government make the thesis that the state-power is there capable of neutrality at the best a dubious one.

It is, I think, significant that Herr Hitler has from the outset abandoned any such view. In a critical time, explains one of the protagonists of the new order, the bureaucracy must be stuffed " with trustworthy and tried fighters of the national front." So, too, the Bench has been completely subordinated to the purposes of the new regime; an eminent lawyer has even defended the grim massacre of June 30th, 1934, as the supreme embodiment of justice. The High Command of the Army becomes interpenetrated with the leadership of the Nazi Party; and each of these, as Professor Brady shows, is so linked to the leading figures in German industry as effectively to make the former instruments of the end German capitalism seeks to serve in this monopolistic phase of its history.

Professor Brady touches relatively lightly upon the implications of Fascist practice in the international field. But it will be obvious from his discussion that the inescapable outcome of its habits is war; and I think that Englishmen of all parties will be agreed that war is no longer compatible with the successful maintenance of parliamentary democracy. At what stage the war will come is, no doubt, obscure. But it is at least clear that the kind of organisation modern warfare requires necessarily makes an end of the habits associated with a democratic system. War, as Viscount Grey saw, is the mother of inevitable revolution; and the adjustment of institutions to the situation it will

exact will leave little standing of the European pattern to which
we have been historically accustomed.

It is a grim outlook; and there is little on the horizon to make
it look less grim. This only, I think, can be said. Fascism has to
meet the tests to which any system of government is subject;
at some phase of its history it must seek to co-ordinate the relations of production with the potentialities of production. Given
its inherent purposes, I do not see that it is capable of achieving
that co-ordination. I believe, therefore, that it is a phase in the
history of society which is necessarily destined to self-destruction.
Our problem is to prevent it, as it destroys itself, from involving
our fate with its own. To that prevention, knowledge of its nature
is essential. Professor Brady's book is a warning which comes
while there is still time to learn its lesson. I hope it will be learned
quickly and profoundly enough to aid in that unity, national and
international, of the progressive forces which is the one sure
safeguard against the disaster which it threatens.

HAROLD J. LASKI

Chapter I

The Spectre on the Brocken

BETWEEN the great war and the depression which broke in 1929, Germany passed through a twilight zone of peace. Not peace without troubles and gnawing anxieties, but a peace of comparative quiet. The black years of the war were over; the chaos of revolution and inflation were past. Nobody asked for the future. Whether it boded good or evil for the time being did not matter. At last there was a chance to relax a little bit, to sit quietly for a few hours in the garden with friends and a glass of beer, to listen to some half-forgotten music and to laugh.

The period was not long—a short half-dozen years at best. The war swept to a blind and broken halt in late 1918. Revolution and inflation followed in quick succession. Not until 1924 was there a return to "normalcy" and an opportunity to think about living instead of death. Then followed five continuous years of peace-time readjustment and rebuilding.

Late in 1928 there was cause for a certain uneasiness. But, though conditions steadily worsened throughout 1929, it was not until the approach of the new year that people came to realise that the country was once more teetering on the edge of an abyss. The deepening depression opened again the lid of Pandora's box, and by 1933 the furies had swept Hitler into power; with him came again the dull echo of marching feet, domestic terror, and the clutching fear of another world war.

The interlude of peace between these two darknesses restored a certain sense of freedom and well-being. For most there wa now a certain freedom from actual hunger, a freedom to go and come at will, to speak and think more or less at ease. For a short stay of time it was not necessary to behave like a human robot. For the moment, one need not gear one's actions to the pattern of the stiff command, and for a while no one preached openly that servility and meekness to arbitrary authority were the only roads to virtue.

In this somewhat relaxed atmosphere Germany passed through a sort of "Indian Summer," a kind of late autumnal warming before the harshness of another bitter northern winter could set in. The German university once again became the intellectual leader of the world. The brief flowering of German science was so rich in content and varied in scope as to constitute, even in a country with such a glorious scientific past, a renaissance in achievements of the mind. The music and opera of the great German masters were revived on a new and richer level. The German theatre became for a short time the pride of western Europe. German scholars and men of letters began to turn out what seemed almost a tidal wave of books, brochures, and periodicals on every conceivable subject. For a period of time German new-book listings were as great as those of England, France, and the United States combined.

For the bulk of the population much of old German *Gemütlichkeit*—" easy-going-ness "—revived. The German term has a special meaning. It reflects the picture of the ordinary citizen who, after his day in the factory or in the office, returns home to play with his children on the floor, or to work, gently and with loving care, amongst his flowers in the little back-yard garden. In the evening he goes to a near-by park. There are tables, waiters, and an orchestra. He sips his beer, makes love to the waitress or his wife of thirty years, listens to the music, dances a little, and talks—talks about politics, the threatened wage cut, the music of Beethoven, or the decline of the Roman Empire.

Rich and poor alike, *Gemütlichkeit* in some degree or other was a fact of daily experience. In the poorest villages or the most scabrous quarters of the great industrial cities, some measure of the *feeling* for " good living," for enjoyment of food and music, for the slight float of mind that comes with a stein of Bock or— on occasion—a glass of wine, was regarded as the due need of all. In the poorest districts of Berlin or Cologne, Hamburg or Essen, one would see everywhere window-boxes of gaily coloured flowers, and *Bierstuben* where workmen sat of an evening with their wives.

City and country alike never lost the touch of what seemed almost infinite care. Perhaps, during the interlude, there was a certain freshening of the touch. More marked than this, how-ever, was the mounting stream of men, women, and children who trekked to the country on every possible occasion. By train or river boat, by car or bicycle, alone or in especially arranged tours, and by the multiplied thousands they poured out of the cities in the evenings, on holidays and week-ends. Those who could not go far into the country, flocked to the parks, lakes, and near-by forests. The degree of mass participation in the enjoyment of the public facilities and the natural beauties of city and countryside was without parallel in any other European country.

The visitor was welcome in the counting-house or the workman's quarter. There was no embarrassed laughing at mistakes made in German, and no sneers for strange ways and thoughts. Everywhere there was a lively interest in America, in England and France, in Africa and the Orient. Books and tales on adventures in the most distant lands were paced by the almost unbelievable out-pourings of travel books and guides. An increasing number of the children in the lower common schools were learning French, English, Italian, or some other foreign language. There was, amongst the great rank and file, no hatred of the Jews, no hatred of the French, no hatred for the Russians or any other people. It was as easy to talk to a workman or a peasant on almost any conceivable subject as it was to get travel information from a professional guide.

There was, likewise, an almost unbelievable mass participation in the cultural side of life. Nowhere else in Europe could one find either the crowds or the complete representation of all social classes one would meet in the Kaiser Wilhelm Museum of Berlin, the Pinakothek of Munich, or the Zwinger of Dresden. At times the number of visitors to the gigantic industrial arts museum of Munich, the Deutsches Museum, were so great as to resemble organised pilgrimages. The same was true for the theatres and the opera houses. Anyone who has sat or stood in the galleries through the long performances of Wagnerian opera in Berlin or Munich during these years has some idea of the cross section of the population which such audiences represented. Entire galleries would at times have scarcely anyone in them who was not a student or a workman.

The percentage of the German population able to play some musical instrument or other must have been three or four times that of any other nation. Nowhere else were so many concerts given, so much singing and choral music, so much interest in the music of the past and of all other lands. Little theatres, local player troupes, folk dance ensembles and numerous other art forms were to be found in great profusion in the large cities, and represented in nearly every village and hamlet. Workers' clubs meeting in the Communist-controlled Piscator Theatre, or in the Social Democratic-controlled People's Theatre (*Volksbühne*) put on musical evenings and prepared theatrical productions, organised trips into the country, and set up sports clubs. The pattern remained essentially the same for all other groups, ranging from the left towards the right.

This is not a romantic picture, but the Germany as visitors saw and knew it during the years of the interlude. True, none of what there was to see or know along these lines was new—unless, perhaps, it be the great interest in the subject of sports. All of it would have been found there before the war. The war and its aftermath had merely covered it over, submerged it under drifts of hatred, worry, and privation. What one saw was, rather, that during this brief " Indian Summer " a gifted people came back into its own, and took up where it had left off before with the advancement and enjoyment of a rich, multi-coloured and vividly alive cultural heritage.

Nor is this to deny the seamy side of that tradition. There had been much heel-clicking and military truculence in the days of the Kaiser, and this had left its stamp on much that survived the war. Even more significant, was the fact that the poverty of the peasantry, of the rural and urban proletariat, and of the unemployed was never lightened after the war. But in the face of the tragedy which has preceded the interlude, the extent and the quality of the resurgence of the German people during that short period is one of the greatest tributes to the human species known in the annals of written history.

But it was neither the fact of the extent and quality of this resurgence, nor that it had taken place in the presence of so many difficulties both at home and abroad, which most forcibly struck the observer of the German scene in 1930. It was, rather, that underneath all this one sensed a certain lurking fear, a certain indefinable and not-to-be-forgotten dread. Deeply rooted as were the traditions out of which the resurgence came, the tone and mood seemed nervous and somehow unreal. Much of it had a note of artificiality and make-believe about it; much of it seemed sickeningly combative; all of it seemed to be conducted in a mood compounded of a desire to forget and a haste to enjoy before some new and nameless horror should sweep away what little there was left.

What had the war been fought about ? Nobody knew. Nobody knew what caused it, why it began, nor why Germany lost. Everybody knew that it had brought untold suffering, that millions of the flower of the country's manhood had been killed and crippled, that for seemingly endless black years there was little food and that always ready to disappear, that babies died and the bodies of children had been warped by rickets—everybody knew that the country had suffered, and that the war had covered with its scourge the last village and hamlet, and the least and most peaceful of its citizens. All this everybody knew. It had been beaten into their lives by daily experience through a seemingly endless toll of years.

But nobody knew why the war had been fought, nor why Germany should have lost. All the patriotic slogans they had listened to had lost what little power to command attention they may have had when, at the close of the war, the revolution came along. The revolution said, in effect, that the Kaiser and the Imperial system had been at fault. Now all of that was gone, and with it the issues on which they had been duped into such an appalling waste of life. All this seemed clearer, too, since the allied powers which had won the war announced their goals accomplished with the collapse of the Empire and the flight of the Kaiser to Doorn. The terms of the Armistice and of the fourteen points of President Wilson, on the basis of which arms had first been laid down, had served to bring this picture of things into still sharper relief.

Then why the Treaty of Versailles ? If the German people had been duped into fighting a fratricidal war by a ruler now fled and a caste of reactionary power now broken, on what basis could the allied powers not only condemn the German people as a whole, but also lay upon their shoulders a burden which everybody knew they could not possibly bear—a burden which was not only intended to *punish* an admittedly innocent *people*, but which was also intended to beat them into a condition of servitude, generation after generation.

The load of Versailles was, indeed, heavy. The bitter old men gathered together in the famous Hall of Mirrors had no intention to live up to the terms of the Armistice, the fourteen points, or any other promise. Their ethics were no different than those of the acquisitive and completely a-moral forces which had catapulted the world into the long-drawn-out slaughter just past and which it had been their mad fortune to command. Of what price an agreement? Of what worth a pledge scrawled on a " scrap of paper "? With their ears finely attuned to the cheap magic of passing popular approval in coming-home elections—approval of deliberately inflamed and war-propaganda misled electorates, utterly oblivious to the grisly and terrifying implications of their decisions for the future, and dominated by the virulent, world-weary, and cynical old Clemenceau, they moved, not to salvage, but to crush, annihilate, and destroy.[1]

All the world, victor and vanquished alike, knew this to be the case. Neither the ambidextrous word weaselling of Lloyd George, nor the comic-opera invention of Woodrow Wilson, the League of Nations, served to bridge the publicly recognised gulf between the pretence and the actualities. Like the Treaty which sired it, the League of Nations was turned immediately into an instrument for the maintenance of allied power and Anglo-French imperialism, and only the naïve and the sentimental mistook its jaundice for the bloom of youth. As every political realist knew, this blind and crowning impudence could, of itself, have no other effect than to transform the political huckster's shallow phrase, " A war to end war," into a stern " Peace to generate wars." After the open betrayal of Versailles and the thinly disguised magicians' deceit of Geneva, there seemed no other questions to ask for the future of the gods of war than, When? and how? and where?

But the real symbolism of Versailles lay neither in the actual burdens it imposed on the German people, nor its predication of future war. Severe as were the first, and as inevitable the second, what reason could there be for supposing that in the calm of

[1] For this and all other notes *see* page 357 and following pages.

the peace that was to follow the worst injustices could not be righted ? What reason for supposing that returning sanity would not bring with it repudiation of the conditions which, unmitigated and unrenounced, must lead directly to another war ?

Superficially the peace of the interlude promised much along these lines. For one thing, the actual burdens laid on Germany by the Draconian terms of the Treaty, turned out to be, for one reason or another, no ways near as heavy as they seemed at first. In sacrificing her colonies, she parted with an economic liability. Disarmament forced upon the German people abstention from a costly and wasteful drain on the resources and energy of the nation. Inflation wiped out internal indebtedness, leaving in this respect all debtor classes—all low-income groups, and particularly the peasants—in a better relative position than before. The " rationalisation " of German industry, forced by losses of Lorraine and sections of Upper Silesia, soon gave Germany a pronounced competitive advantage over her European rivals. Scientific inventiveness and commercial aggressiveness soon began to regain lost markets abroad. The new German merchant marine was the best in the world. In economic terms it makes no difference whether ore is bought at home or abroad, and the new supplies coming from Sweden, Spain, and Brazil, if somewhat more expensive than those from Lorraine, were of correspondingly greater worth.

Prodigious as were the burdens of reparations on paper, aside from the initial deliveries in kind (locomotives, waggons, steamships, coal, etc.), it is highly significant to notice that in economic terms Germany never paid any reparations at all. The total of German borrowings abroad for purposes of reconstruction and improvement of her industrial apparatus, exceeded reparations payments by somewhere in excess of one billion dollars. At the end of the pre-depression period the product of this rebuilding was the finest, most well-balanced, and efficient industrial system in the world, and one fully capable of repaying interest and amortisation charges incurred as soon as it could operate anywhere near full capacity.

Furthermore, it soon became apparent to business men and politicians in both Germany and the allied countries, that no one really desired reparations to be paid at all. The Dawes

Plan regularised total annual payments; the Young Plan reduced the annual amounts and fixed the total; a subsequent Geneva convention cut these to a fraction of the previous figures. There was every reason to expect that as soon as a satisfactory arrangement could be made between the allied countries and the United States on the payment of war debts, reparations would be eliminated entirely, or rendered so nominal as to be economically unimportant.

The reason for this change of attitude on the part of the allied countries was found in the realisation that practically every conceivable type of reparations must inevitably compete with domestic production. If Germany paid reparations to England in the form of machines and textiles, these undermined domestic markets for her own manufactures. If England received payment in money (foreign exchange) it could only be from earnings made by German shipping and other services competing with British concerns, or by selling abroad in South America or other places where English exporters had previously sold their surpluses. The same situation held for France and the other allied countries, including the United States. The United States, while refusing to forego either reparations or inter-allied debt payments, refused likewise to be paid in goods by her debtors, and in so doing underwrote the common doctrine that international obligations ought to be paid in full while simultaneously promoting a condition under which they could not, in reality, be paid at all.

As the material burdens on Germany were lightened, so did the war dangers seem to fade during the " Indian Summer " of the interlude. The first few disarmament conferences produced a most intriguing display of lofty peace sentiment; the assemblies of the League of Nations called forth dazzling oratorical arpeggios; great statesmen vied with one another in drawing from their lingual depths tributes to the dove of peace more mysteriously uplifting than the charms from a witch's cauldron.

Nor was it all mere display. Behind these verbal pyrotechnics, pacts, conventions, and assemblies dedicated to peace was arrayed the solid popular sentiment of the people of all the participating countries. The people of England, France, Germany,

Italy, and of all other nations wanted peace. There could be no possible mistake about the existence of such sentiment, and because this was true, certain of the pacts possessed some degree of genuine substance. One of the conferences—that which met in Washington in 1922—actually called for some reduction in naval expenditures. During the period that followed, there seemed at times some reason for believing that the sentiment for peace was rising, and that popular pressure might slowly undermine the structure of competitive armaments and melt away the animosities which nurtured their towering budgets.

On the surface there seemed no reason why the world might not return to peace and " prosperity," to international division of labour and its growing international interdependencies—no reason, in short, why the " Indian Summer " of the German people might not ripen into a century-long harvest, nor why the unarmed and industrious state of its people during this period might not become the pattern for all other peoples of the world.

Yet, with the exception of the United States, the period from 1924 to 1929 was no blossoming time for either the people of Germany, the new nations of Europe, or any of the allied countries. Instead of ensuring its return, the end of the period witnessed the almost complete breakdown of international trade and international division of labour. Instead of recovery in Germany, there was collapse. Instead of prosperity there was a world-wide depression. Instead of disarmament there were mounting military budgets which dwarfed those with which the belligerent nations began the war. Instead of peace there was war and the prospect of more war. Instead of internal stability there was mounting social unrest.

All of this might have been called temporary, a product of inevitably recurring cycles of prosperity and depression, had there not been unmistakable signs to indicate a vast and portentous breakdown in the very structure of European society itself. The flare of peace and apparent prosperity which accompanied the middle twenties could not gloss over the fact that peace meant, in the terms of the most optimistic, a return to the conditions which obtained in 1914, the year in which the world war broke out, and prosperity meant not increased standards of living for the mass of the population, but a short wave of increased business activity and the reaping of short-run stock-market gains.

During the post-war years German unemployment totals never fell below the two million mark. Wage rates came back to the pre-war figure, but rising cost of living kept real wages low. Furthermore, direct and indirect taxes took increasing percentages of the net money wage, while part-time employment kept a large proportion of the working population practically on the starvation level. German productive capacity as a whole was never employed better than 80 per cent during the most active period of the post-war interval; for protracted periods it ranged around 50 to 60 per cent. Simultaneously agricultural indebtedness steadily increased, averaging around 400 million dollars (1,600,000,000 Rm.) per annum.

By 1922, four years after the close of the most terrible war in the history of the human race, the armament budget of the world was approximately double what it was when the war began. In another eight years the total was approximately threefold the 1914 figure. These colossal increases came after Germany and her *entente* allies had been conquered and completely disarmed. From 1900 on, in fact, the rate of increase in armament expenditure had remained about the same; the war neither changed the direction, nor affected the rate of increase. Had Germany not been disarmed, the only difference might have been a higher rate of increase, but that is all.

Here, then, was the proposition that faced the German, as it did the ordinary citizen of all other countries of the world, in the beginning of the early thirties: the war settled nothing, solved nothing, changed nothing. Nor did the Peace Treaty in its turn. Versailles merely set the stamp of its grotesque and colossal stupidity upon a process of development which had not yet come to an end, and which it did nothing, absolutely nothing, to alter or amend. If war grew out of division of the world into armed camps, was war any less likely when the camps were thrice armed? If peace were the measure of well-being, was there anything to be said for peace which rendered ever more precarious the livelihood of growing numbers of the nation's workers and peasants? Was there anything to be hoped

from a programme of industrial and economic overhauling—
" rationalisation "—which threw more men on the relief rolls,
and which ended with the worst economic depression of modern
times ?

The real significance of Versailles was that it was not followed
by a return to sanity. In the peace that followed, there was no
righting of fundamental injustices. The specific burdens which
the Treaty itself imposed were modified, but the conditions
which followed tended to deepen rather than to modify the
fear of war, to add to rather than subtract from the privation
and insecurity of the lower income classes and to promote
rather than retard the economic breakdown which came so
soon. If peace was no more than an armed truce, and prosperity
merely an illusion, Versailles was the symbol of the futility of
any organised effort at solution which did not strike at the
heart of the system from which it stemmed.

It was precisely this view which won increasing adherents in
Germany throughout the post-war period. The idea that capitalism, imperialism, war, and poverty for the mass of mankind
were inextricably interwoven was not, of course, new. It was
generated with the very birth of modern capitalism itself. It
gave rise to the socialist and anarchist movements leading to
the revolutions of 1848. In the *Communist Manifesto, Capital,*
and other writings of Marx and Engels, it came to dominate
increasing layers of the labouring classes throughout the last
half of the nineteenth century, and the first decades of the
twentieth. Followers of orthodox Marxian doctrines had en-
gineered the Russian Revolution, and brought one-sixth of the
earth's surface under socialist control. Early in the post-war
period, followers of a more modified form of socialist thought
had gained control in Germany after the more extreme left
elements—the Spartacists—had failed because of lack of sufficient mass support.

Throughout the subsequent period the trend to the left
remained unchecked. Nearly ten million Germans belonged to
trade unions of some sort or other in 1924 (world figure, around
$36\frac{1}{2}$ million). With a population of some four million less, the
number of trade-union members in Germany had more than
doubled since the beginning of the war. More than half of

these were members of the Social Democratic " free " trade
unions, with the exception of the Communists the most radical
of the numerous trade-union *blocs* in Germany.

From 1920 to 1924 the number of workers in trade unions
tended to decline; thereafter and until 1932 they steadily increased. And with this increase in membership went a continuous, if slow, growth in the labour vote, and in the drift
towards the left. Within the various trade unions, the leftward
tendency was especially pronounced from 1926 on. The depression accelerated this tendency. Able to poll but 590,000 votes
in a 1920 Reichstag election, the Communists increased their
election totals to 3,230,000 in 1928, 4,500,000 in 1930, and
5,980,000 in 1933.

The significance of the drift towards the left is not confined to
mere numbers. Far more important, it indicated a precipitation,
a clarification, and a focusing of the issues. Up to 1924, the
dominant note had been generalised, but aimless protest. The
rapid transition from the empire to the republic caught the
old-line " revisionist " socialist leaders unprepared. Unclear in
their thinking, confused in their picture of the array of reactionary political forces to which they were in theory opposed, and
emotionally brow-beaten by their endless compromises during
the war, they were unable to take any decisive steps at all.
Everything they did lacked the cement of theory and the force
of direction. They compromised to the right and the left. The
Weimar Constitution which they designed as the foundation-
stone of the New Reich was a tissue of inconsistencies and a
hodge-podge of undirected compromise.

For the time being, the extent and the nature of the compromises which the Social Democratic Party made was not
realised. Its spokesmen were carried along on a wave of mass
protest strong enough to make those who floated at the crest
of the wave appear to be leading those who floated at its base.
But appearances were deceiving; compromising on all fronts,
they united against the left, and consciously or unconsciously
promoted the interests of the right.

Ebert, the first President of the Republic, organised the
military against the Communists and allied left groups at a time
when his support would have cast the balance in favour of a

socialist Germany. Simultaneously he made the tactical mistake of allowing all the elements on the right to go unharmed—the same mistake, incidentally, which was fifteen years later to be made by the Republican government in Spain, and the Blum regime in France. Neither Ebert nor any of his followers did anything at all to destroy or even undermine the political, economic, or social influence of the *Junkers*. Although recognised as the landed aristocracy which had long exercised a dominating influence in all the affairs of state under the Empire, the Social Democrats and their allied parties allowed them to remain intact. In a series of notable cases, such as the election of Hindenburg and the organising of East Help (" relief " for the large *Junker* estates of the Eastern Provinces), they threw the balance of their forces behind the interests of this class. The same attitude was taken towards capitalist leaders in industry, trade, and finance.

By 1924, or at the latest 1926, it was clear that nothing involving a radical reconstruction of government or the economic order was to be expected from the Social Democratic *bloc*. From that point on, the coagulation of the left and right went steadily forward. Separating themselves from the mass of the confused public, to the right were all the vested-interest minority groups which the Social Democrats and their followers might have at one time undermined or destroyed. Like Anteus, the fabled giant who doubled his strength every time he touched Mother Earth, the right minorities multiplied their power with each passing year of business prosperity. Compactly organised, interest conscious, and completely ruthless, the reactionary forces were able steadily to consolidate their power until it may be said that at the end of the period of " prosperity " (1929) their position in Germany was more strategic and relatively stronger than that of their compatriot groups in any other capitalistically organised country.

Equally significant, equally pronounced, and fed from the same source of interest conflict was the drift towards the left, mentioned above. Just as the consolidation from the right was slowly segregating all the active and interest conscious minority forces of conservatism, so the coagulation from the left was making itself felt throughout all liberal and labour circles. The more active the trade union, the more energetic and interest conscious its spokesmen, and the larger its percentage of younger members, the greater the tendency to militant action. In the unions tied up with mining, metallurgy, and heavy manufacturing this tendency was particularly noticeable. Scarcely a field, however, was left untouched.

Militant action of the unions manifested itself in all the usual ways, by strikes, picketing, mass demonstrations, and political action. Most of this aggressive sentiment was technically non-Communist. However, the growth of the Communist vote indicated above may be taken to serve as a convenient watermark to register rise of revolutionary fervour.

In between these two major coagulant, and bitterly opposed, groups[2] lay the great mass of the middle-class population. In the centre were to be found practically all the " white collar " salaried and professional classes, small shopkeepers, tradesmen, and handicraftsmen, the bulk of the peasantry, the government bureaucracies, the bulk of the rank and file of the more conservative trade unions, the Catholic Church and the Protestant Confessions, and the more timorous adherents of the two extreme wings. Without any forces, organisation, or principles to unite it, made up of the hesitant, the confused, and the compromising elements of society, this amorphous mass was being slowly dissolved between the opposing cross fire. More and more recruits left it to go to the right or the left. Uninterrupted, it seems probable that in the course of time the majority of its members would sooner or later have attached themselves to one or the other of the militant wings—a process which should have been simplified by the modification of programmes which would normally occur with the winning of more moderate elements.

Two highly significant factors intervened to accelerate this coagulating tendency, and to offset any such normal modification of programme. The first of these was the advent of the depression, and the second was the announcement and first great successes of the Soviet Five Year Plan. The first provided the quickening fire for the rise of social unrest; the second provided a striking symbol of success for the entire programme of the left—a symbol which was rendered doubly significant by virtue of the fact that the very successes of the Soviet Union occurred simultaneously with the disastrous breakdown of capitalistic economic systems all over the world.

Time was the essence of the story. Whichever wing could win the larger number of recruits from the middle group stood to gain all. Both the right and left moved into action with speed and determination. Superficially, the better cards were held in the hands of the Communists. The trade unions and the Social Democratic Party in general were potential allies, and the steady radicalisation of both urban and rural proletariat gave every reason to believe that a united, left-oriented, front could easily be arranged. Given, as it seemed fair to assume, a continuation of the depression contemporary with further successes of socialist planning in the Soviet Union, success seemed assured. Everything was to be gained by a play for time; the longer they could wait the more certain their chance of winning.

For the right, time was correspondingly short. It had the advantage of being better and more compactly organised, but it did not have a popular following, nor any basis for quickly whipping one up. It was at this juncture that Hitler and the National Socialist power came to their rescue. Always anti-labour and anti-Communist, the Nazi movement had, nevertheless, failed to secure a mass following although it had behind it nearly a decade of demagogery unexampled in the history of modern times for its virulence, confusion, and unscrupulous opportunism. Despite the fact that it received support from old imperial army circles and, at times, financial aid from industrial and financial sources, the Nazi Party was not able as late as 1928 to poll quite a million votes.

It was about this time that the *Junkers*, and the large industrial and financial interests saw the uses to which the Nazi Party could be put. The specific content of its programme did not matter so far as they were concerned; at the very best it was a hodge-podge of inconsistencies and a comedy of errors. The real significance of the Nazi Party lay in the fact that it had a certain following amongst the amorphous and hesitant central mass, and that it reflected in its confused platform the very state of mind in which the bulk of the citizens found themselves. Ideal for the purposes to which it was to be put, there was a plank in the Nazi platform to meet the prejudices of nearly every group to be appealed to, and it conducted its campaigns so as to combine a proper degree of idea-dulling fanaticism with further confusion of the issues. Whenever need called for it, and at the proper time, anything could be made out of the programme one desired. For the right, the set-up was perfect.

The formal fusion of the party of rampant conservatism, the Nationalist Party of Hugenberg, and the National Socialists, did not come until some time later. Long before that, and beginning seriously as early as 1928, a series of conferences were held between Hitler and various industrial, and financial leaders in the Rhineland. With their support came that of the *Junkers* (though more hesitatingly) and the bulk of the manufacturing and shipping interests of the country. Thereafter organised business lent its support to Hitler either openly or surreptitiously. Most important of the central business bodies were the National Federation of German Employers' Associations, which included all employers in Germany; the National Federation of German Industry, which included all manufacturing interests; the National Chamber of Industry and Commerce, the central clearing-house for all Chambers of Commerce in Germany; and the *Herrenklub*, agitational headquarters for *Junker*-military interests.

Possessed of ample funds, backed by such powerful and interest conscious bodies, and amazingly well organised, the Nazis were able to harvest votes for the right far beyond the expectations of their supporters. In successive Reichstag elections their vote moved up from 810,000 in 1928 to 6,406,000 in 1930, and 13,733,000 in 1932. At this point, however, they apparently reached the height of their power. Four months later in another Reichstag election their vote had dropped by almost exactly two million to a figure of 11,737,000. If the Communists and the Social Democrats had held together at the critical moment, their popular vote would have totalled 13,232,000. It was still not too late for the United Front.

But it was at precisely this point that the Social Democratic Party chose to play a lone hand, and to co-operate with the various Centrist or so-called Republican parties. That is to say, the Social Democratic Party chose to co-operate with the very

group being most seriously undermined by the propaganda from
the right, and by the National Socialists, in particular. Still in
control of the formal machinery of the state, they refused to
use any of their duly constituted legal authority to undermine
the strength of a foe openly sworn to destroy them. They did
not, in taking this position, even force the Nazis to comply with
ordinary criminal law. The rankest of libel was not sued, treason
was not prosecuted, criminal assault did not lead to arrest.

The hesitancy of the Social Democrats at the crucial point
sealed the fate of the left and of all labour. By March of the
following year it was already too late. The Nazis were prepared
to seize power, and the right had won in time.

The regime which the Nazis proceeded to establish is fairly
described, by the very nature of the major interest which
sponsored it, as a *dictatorship of monopoly capitalism. Its
" fascism " is that of business enterprise organised on a monopoly
basis, and in full command of all the military, police, legal, and
propaganda power of the state.*

But it is more than a mere formal dictatorship over economic
affairs. No one knew better than the *Junkers* and the magnates
of industrial and finance capitalism, that in the struggle for
power not only capitalism and a profits economy were at stake.
Far more important, in its final analysis, was the fact that the
very essence of capitalist civilisation itself was in the balance.
All the attitudes and points of view, all the supporting social
codes and doctrines, and all the theories and practices of a *class-
ordered* capitalist society had been under attack from the left.

Furthermore, all the popular trends had been against, not
for, the point of view of the business community. As early as
1930 almost any business man one might have talked to in
Germany would frankly have admitted the eventual success of
" Communism " unless recognised trends could be reversed. In
the spring of 1931 an interviewer in the main offices of the great
Steel Trust at Düsseldorf, was told by an official spokesman for
the industry that the alternative to Hitler and National Socialism was " Communism to the Rhine by 1935."

Thus conscious of the issues, the Nazi dictatorship proceeded,
with the same calculating impersonality used in a chess game,
to reverse the trends, break up labour organisation, and

Bf

completely eliminate the whole ideological foundation which had supported the trend leftward. In this programme it was conditioned by two major necessities. First, it could not promote material interests, since to do so would be not only to concede ground to the left argument, but also to write their propaganda in the coin of the enemy. They might use his terms and symbols —and this they did with considerable success—but they could not concede the terms of his programme (material concessions in the form of wages, hours, working conditions). Nor, further, could it be done without undermining the strength of the right. Therefore, it was first necessary to " divert the gaze of the masses " from material to " spiritual things."

In the second place, to allow any expression of a contrary point of view was not only to make known the continued successes of the Soviet Union, but also to provide the agitational foundation for reconstruction of the left position. For the same reason, it was compelled to suspend all democratic machinery, such as elections and representative government (what the Nazis now call " elections " are, in reality, " controlled plebiscites ").

The Nazi system is, accordingly, set up to completely control all activities, and all thoughts, ideas, and values of the entire German nation. It seeks to " co-ordinate spirit," or point of view, and to " co-ordinate structure," or all the economic machinery of the state. To these ends it embodies three principles: " the leader principle," "the authority principle," and " the total principle." The first two mean centralisation of the power to direct from on top, with each " leader " having final and unabridged control over appointment, removal, and all activities of all subordinates under him. Authority is from the top down; responsibility is from the bottom up. This is a complete reversal of democracy in spirit and form. The third, the " total principle," means the extension of such control over all members of the population in all their activities—work, leisure, and recreational—and over all the forms and media for the expression of any point of view whatsoever.

The Nazi system represents, in short, nothing more than an extension to the nation at large of the rules, the behaviour patterns, and the points of view of the ordinary autocratically governed business enterprise. Nothing more, with this exception, that it adds thereto power to enforce complete conformity with its point of view on the parts of all members of the community, regardless of class, station, or interest.

Here then is the " spectre on the Brocken " which cast its shadow over the " Indian Summer " of the interlude following the return to " normalcy " in 1924. It was not, as commonly supposed, Versailles that disturbed the clear mirror of German recovery during the twenties; Versailles, in fact, did not become much of an issue until the early thirties when the programme for " diverting the gaze of the masses " was well under way. The thing that generated the nervous unrest of those years was the deep-seated and growing cleavage of society into two irreconcilable camps. The " spectre on the Brocken " was the fear, unnerving even to a good many of the friends of reaction, that " fascism " might triumph.

The significance of the pages that follow lies solely in the extent to which they make clear just how this " spectre," quickened into life by the terror of reaction, proceeded to fulfil the wishes of those who sponsored its assumption of power. But the importance of an understanding of German fascism does not end here. Far more vital for the future of all the nations and civilisations of the world, is realisation that exactly the same forces which hoisted the Nazis to the helm in Germany are at work in all other countries at the present time and that, for better or for worse, there is no possibility of avoiding the issues which those forces present for decision to every man and woman who votes, or thinks, or acts.

PART I

THE CO-ORDINATION OF SPIRIT

Chapter II

Science, Handmaiden of Inspired Truth

A TRAVELLER along the main southern-highway route from California to the Gulf of Mexico will come across a huge sign marked, " The Great Divide." One arrow points to the east, the other to the west. There is nothing else the eye can fix upon to mark the boundary-line. On every side a vast prairie, relieved only by occasional out-croppings of rock and scattered low-lying hills, stretches away to distant horizons. Yet underneath the sign and out across the apparently flat expanse runs a twisting unseen line which marks the watershed. Rain that falls to the right moves slowly down to the Atlantic; to the left it winds deviously towards the distant Pacific.

Thirty miles on either side the eye can begin to catch the story which only delicate instruments could tell on the spot. The hills begin to drop down towards the valleys, and the waters to gather in streams towards the major river systems and the sea. Here the slope of the land and the direction of flow become unmistakably clear.

A problem similar to that of the traveller at the continental divide is presented to every observer who surveys the Nazi culture programme. Except here at critical points there are no boldly worded sign-posts to tell the direction of flow. Yet without knowledge of the dividing-line, and *the direction, the leading purposes*, being pursued, no evaluation—scientific or otherwise—of any Nazi programme has any meaning.

All " co-ordinated " and " planned " action pursues objectives. Armies are trained to wage wars. Workmen are organised to produce goods. Business is pursued for the making of profit. Police are established to keep the peace; law courts to settle disputes. The more careful the planning, the more definite the objectives must be. The more activities " co-ordinated " in the plan, the more each and every detail of organisation must be understood in terms of its usefulness in promoting the objectives for which activities are co-ordinated and planned.

The Nazis make a fetish of " co-ordinating." Their literature is replete with references to the " totalitarian state," "uniformity of spirit," the "Leader Principle." These terms have a central meaning which might be stated as follows: the "leader" and his lieutenants will " co-ordinate " the " totality " of all persons and activities in Germany, in order that all, with an inner " uniformity of spirit," will work towards the goals set by the " leader " for them. Nothing, in short, is to escape the drag-net. All economic activity, all political, social, cultural life is to be " co-ordinated," canalised, and directed.

But whither ? To what end ? For what purposes ? These questions must be raised with every plan, every programme, every institution, every activity co-ordinated. Unless one keeps an eye constantly focused on the purpose for which all things are co-ordinated, the product of his observations will be endless confusion. Nothing in Germany can any longer be judged on " its own merits." To do so will be to miss the tactic of advance and retreat, to confuse symbols and realities, to mistake a cleverly executed move intended to circumvent opposition for a genuine concession on principle. Confusions of this sort give rise to the habit of making such indiscriminate and fatuous comparisons as: " Roosevelt, Hitler, and Stalin are dictators." Or, again, " Fascism and Communism are despotisms; they regiment everybody."

Without a *sense of direction*, the Nazi system is replete with contradictions. Just as the casual traveller who sees streams running for short distances against the major lines of flow is not justified in assuming that there is no " great divide," so the observer of the Third Reich dare not conclude from surface contradiction that there is no major plan—a plan which in reality makes much of using the fact of contradiction itself for the major ends being pursued. Not that the Nazi plan is without real inconsistencies; far from it. But that there is a general set of goals, a core of doctrine, and an accepted procedure which affects vitally every detailed move there cannot be the slightest doubt.

The objectives are not so difficult to understand if, to employ our analogy once again, one leaves the level plateau and drops down into the fingered valleys that point towards the sea. The policies for agriculture, economic activity, and labour are, at the lower levels, ribbed clear to view. The major conditions underlying the Nazi system involve assumptions which define the point of view and determine the lines of movement—may be summarised as follows:

1. Productive property and natural resources are to be privately owned; freedom of contract is guaranteed (excepting to " aliens " and the peasants under the Inheritance Laws).

2. Individual initiative, the business entrepreneur, conduct of business for profit (" reward for services performed "), and ownership (individual or stockholder) control are basic.

3. Business men are to be free, if " responsible " (" self-government in business "), to fix by agreement prices, production totals and quotas, marketing areas, and the conditions and terms of purchase and sale.

4. Stock and commodity exchanges, commission houses, brokers, and speculative transactions are inevitable and necessary for the conduct of " organic business." (Business as usual.)

5. Heavy industries, particularly those catering to the military and foreign trade, are encouraged; large-scale units, unless " uneconomical " are to be kept intact; co-operatives are to be broken up.

6. The social class structure of society is sanctified, strengthened, made semi-hereditary, and hardened into caste lines (*Ständestaat*, class state); the " Middle Class " are the Myrmidons of the *Élite* (*Führerstaat*, leader state) and, as such, the backbone of the state.

7. Employers have practically complete control over workmen in regard to wages, hours, and working conditions. They must " take care " of their workmen—i.e. see that they are fed and do not grumble.

8. Collective bargaining is completely abolished; strikes are illegal; trade unions are forbidden; requests for wage increases are *lèse majesté*.

9. Control is completely from on top; there is and can be no such thing as control or discussion of policies from below; the " leaders " decide all things as they see fit; each holds appointed office for indefinite periods at the will of his superior.

10. The National Socialist Party and the German State are one and inseparable, as spirit and body. Legislative, executive,

and judicial authorities are fused together. The central government controls all local government and all activities in all their details.

11. Civil and military are fused together; as in the military there can be no freedom of speech, of assembly, of writing, of acting, of " thoughts." " Anyone may grumble or criticise the government who is not afraid to go to a concentration camp " (Goebbels).

12. Germany must be made self-sufficient at all costs (*Autarkie*).

13. Non-Germans cannot be citizens; as a corollary, all Germans residing outside Germany either belong or owe allegiance to the Third Reich.

14. Communism (Bolshevism, Marxism) is the major enemy. There can be no such thing as equality of rights, opportunities, or income for classes, races, or sexes. The " broad masses " are fools and must be duped and led to meet the purposes of the *élite* (*Herrenstaat*). Class war is the major crime; material rewards for the rank and file sheer folly.

15. All sciences and " culture " must be co-ordinated and made to serve the purposes of the " leader," " total," " corporate " " master " (*Herren*) state. Propaganda is the method. Propaganda knows neither right nor wrong, neither truth nor falsehood, but only what it wants.

This programme is recognisable at a glance as capitalism with all its assets (to the capitalist) and none of its liabilities. It is not, to be true, *laissez-faire* capitalism; it is monopoly capitalism become conscious of its powers, the conditions of its survival, and mobilised to crush all opposition. It is capitalism mobilised to crush trade unions, to wipe out radical and liberal criticism, to promote with the sum total of all its internal resources, economic advantage at home and abroad.

Determined to stamp out all opposition, it proposes for all *Gleichschaltung* (co-ordination). " This co-ordination," Goebbels explains, " only outlines what will be the normal condition of Germany. This Germany is to have only one goal, one party, one conviction, and this state organisation is to be identical with the nation itself." In the name of this new Germany, said Sauckel, Nazi Governor of Thuringia at a meeting of his " followers," June 20, 1933, " I command you now to show intolerance against all else. Henceforth there must be one political faith in Thuringia—National Socialism. Discussion of matters affecting our existence and that of the nation must cease altogether. Anyone who dares to question the rightness of the National Socialist world outlook will be branded as a traitor."

Sometimes this new capitalist state employs the mailed fist, oppression, repression, the terror; sometimes it resorts to blandishments, to emotional appeals and argument; always it promotes intolerance. Sometimes it utilises the symbols of " the people " (*Volk*), the " race," the " community " (*Gemeinschaft*); always it promotes the idea of *Kultur*. The sole question in the choice of instruments or symbols to be used is simply this: in the particular circumstances, which is the most effective ? The central idea of *Kultur* is *useful doctrine* for the maintenance of power.

In the new Germany there has been a fusion of interests between the *Junker* (landed aristocrat), the capitalist, and the army. The capitalist supplies the objectives, the *Junker* the idea of structure, and the army the method. *Kultur* is for the mind and the attitude, what the army is for power. In the Prussian army, the attitude and belief in force were fused together. As every man acted, thus was he led to believe. The Nazis have adopted the Prussian tradition, without modification in any significant detail, and applied it to all groups and institutions within the Reich.

They seek, in short, to turn *culture* into *Kultur* by " coordinating " all the sciences and all the arts into instruments for underwriting class power. And, in so doing, it is by no means an accident that they have paid particular attention to the regimentation of science, for science is the intellectual roof and crown of modern civilisation. It plays the same role in the world of modern thought which engineering—its own offspring—does in the fields of industry and commerce. But its importance does not lie alone in the fact that science and scientific methods stand at the very gateways of all discovery and invention in such fields of tangible achievement as industry, commerce, the public health, and the arts of war. Strategic and fundamental as its position in these fields may be, its influence reaches far beyond laboratory and factory walls and out into the world outlook of every man and woman on the street. There is no getting around the fact that while some may assail science out of ignorance or prejudice, it is accepted as the wonder-working Aladdin's lamp, regardless of rank or station, by practically all.

Because of this naïve and credulous popular acceptance of the expert, the scientist, the university, the professor—an acceptance more pronounced amongst the rank and file in Germany than in any other capitalistic country in the world—the propaganda value of " co-ordinated science " to the Nazis can scarcely be overestimated. By co-ordinating it to Nazi ends they could capitalise on the childlike faith with which science was accepted by both the educated and the ignorant. By calling any body of doctrine, however irrational and self-contradictory, " science " they have been able to cast a glow of impartial sanctity around that which they seek to promote. In this sense and to the same basic purposes they have exploited to the full the well-known advertising techniques of *buying* scientific testimonials, using esoteric scientific terms, and generally playing upon the halo and awe-inspiring mysticism with which the popular mind has surrounded the white-frocked knowers and keepers of the secrets of the universe. And by controlling all media for the expression of scientific thought, they have been able to deflect or neutralise scientific investigation from examination of the theses, the assumptions, the interests, and the very foundations of the Nazi programme itself.

1. CO-ORDINATION OF THE SCIENCES

The Nazis have proceeded systematically to do three things to science: (1) reshape the structure and transmute the guiding rules of existing science; (2) to develop a series of " new sciences " discovered by the National Socialists themselves; and (3) to use all sciences and scientists for the purposes of the state.

For these purposes they seek to prove the following things:

There is no such thing as scientific " objectivity ";

There is no such thing as non-national, or " universally

valid " science; all science is nationally determined as to form,
content, and method;

All so-called " universally valid " science is Jewish, " alien,"
rationalistic, intellectualistic, and, hence, meaningless for
Germany or any other people;

Science offers no clue to the riddles of the universe or of
life; it is merely a tool. Hence, each and every people has its
appropriate scientific tool; hence science is emotionally,
spiritually—by *Weltanschauung*—determined.

These are the elements of their programme for " co-ordinating " science which the Nazis strive with all the resources in their
power to " put across " with foreigners. This is not so difficult
as it might seem because so much of their argument falls in with
current trends in naïve scientific thinking that it requires
seemingly little change in emphasis and interpretation to make
their position seem ultra-modern. Consequently, nowhere else
in the entire Nazi propaganda programme is it so necessary to
be wide awake to subtle turns of phrase and underlying intent.
Careful examination will show that while much of what they
have to say about science sounds quite plausible, the net effect
of their programme is to turn modern science into pseudo-Aryan
mysticism and magic. For this reason it is especially important
to examine the premises from which the Nazis reason. These
may be briefly summarised as follows:

(1) *Science depends on man*, the scientist; since it is a product
of his brain, it is subjective, not objective. There can be no
truth aside from the searcher for truth, no explanation without
the explainer. The meaning, the interpretation of science cannot
be given except by and through the *character of the scientist.*
" The researcher himself is part of the object which he investi-
gates, whether that object be physical or spiritual," writes Max
Planck, world-famous German physicist, and present director
of the far-flung laboratories of the Kaiser Wilhelm Society. As
such " the importance of a scientific idea is often due not so
much to its truthfulness as to its inner value."[1] " Inner value "
depends upon character, the point of view, the " *Weltanschauung.*"

This conception runs throughout the entirety of contemporary

German science. It is compounded of elements of indisputable fact, mental laziness, philosophical naïveté, and wilful misrepresentation.

" The indisputable facts " are of two orders. In the first place, science is not as mechanically exact as it was long thought to be. Measurements are never perfect or precise; there are always—and sometimes large and significant—margins of error in the simplest observations. In many of the larger problems of physics present instruments and methods of measurement appear to possess certain well-defined and inherent limitations which inhibit more than theoretical approximation to reality. Shroedinger's equation, the problem of the Fitzgerald contraction, and—most famous of all—von Heisenberg's " principle of indeterminancy " are all of this order.

The second " indisputable fact " is the breakdown of the notion of simple cause and effect. It is sometimes argued—by persons of no less importance than Compton and Millikan in the United States, and Eddington and Jeans in England—that science " does not explain " because it does not tell " why " (i.e. " what causes ") anything happens, but only how it happened.

If this be so, the scientist is no discoverer of " truth," but merely a technician who employs highly developed skills to split the facts of day-to-day experience into their constituent parts. True, he uncovers the fact of *co-relation*, of happenings together or in sequence, but he does not discover cause. This can only be inferred by the scientist, but the basis of inference is common sense, not science. If this be true, the meaning of science depends upon the point of view and the interests of the scientist, not upon his scientific training and his research technique.

Neither of these " indisputable facts " justifies the conclusions indicated above. They amount to no more than a declaration of modest accomplishments (to date), a declaration which flows from the realisation that the range of phenomena now being dealt with is highly complicated, that " science has a lot to learn yet," and that too much should not be expected now. There is not the slightest justification for the theory that science is any the less dependent upon its tools of analysis than before, any less " objective," any less universally verifiable, and checkable than it has always been. There has been no call for relaxation of the attempt to achieve the maximum *impersonality* and independent verifiability in aims, techniques, and methods. That every scientist works with preconceived ideas is as true to-day as it has always been, but it is no less important for that reason that he continue to seek to find out *whether or not his theories, guesses, and hunches are correct*, and not for *proof of what he already firmly believes*.

The curiously naïve mysticism of Eddington and Jeans, based on scientific puzzles such as the " principle of indeterminancy " and the necessity for inference in complicated causal relationships, has been given a further twist by the Nazis to mean that " all great scientific systems have been supported by faith in the meaning of the universe and fate of human beings." This " faith " is the Nazi *Weltanschauung*, which no one dares question lest he be " branded as a traitor." This means, in summary, that every scientist must not only be a " fanatical preacher of National Socialism," but that he must accept Nazi dictation in all details of his work, from the point of framing his problem for investigation, to the " truths " which he must arrive at— " truths " which support the type of state and society which the " inspired Leaders " have determined for them, even as for all others.

(2) This leads to the second tacit Nazi assumption regarding science,[2] i.e. *Science depends on culture*. Anthropologists, historians, and social philosophers have long recognised the intimate interlacing between science *as a part of culture*, with the rest of the culture itself. The Nazis take this to mean that each and every culture—that of the Aztecs, of ancient Mexico, the Greeks of Periclean Athens, the ancient Ethiopians of Axum, the Russia of the Czars, the Maoris of New Zealand, the Germany of to-day—has its own unique science which has " truth " and validity for no other people than that from which it sprung.

To say that *science is a part of culture*, is not to deny that every culture possesses a degree of unity, and that hence the problems and methods of science are vitally affected by the cast, the direction, the peculiarities of the culture. Both the selection of the *problems which are important* and the *rules governing scientific inquiry* show this dependence on culture. It is a matter of common knowledge that plane geometry originated in ancient Egypt, where scientists were concerned with the problem of parcelling land on plane level surfaces after successive floods of the Nile had wiped out property lines. The algebra of Euclid was conditioned by its use in the solution of fractional parts in Greek and Phœnician trading activities. As Borkenau has suggested in his brilliant book on the scientific philosophy of the early manufacturing period, the mathematical-mechanical " world view " of Galileo, Gassendi, Pascal, and Descartes was conditioned by the fact that the interests of the rising bourgeois classes walled off social relations from scientific inquiry, and concentrated effort on the early factory in which mechanical division of labour, and uniform, repetitive (handicraft) mass-production methods were being widely practised.

It is equally well known, to take a few modern examples, that the warlike activities of European nations has led to the concentration of scientific effort on the instruments of war—firearms, explosives, gas, bombing planes, battleships, submarines. The scarcity of raw materials and the consequent necessity for conservation in Germany has laid extraordinary emphasis on chemistry. The plenitude of raw materials in the United States has led, on the contrary, to emphasis upon mass production techniques which do not conserve materials but which produce cheaply.

There are many interesting variations upon this theme. Slow-moving cultures tend to be technically out of date; fast moving to employ all the latest scientific discoveries. A government policy of subsidy may promote scientific research into hitherto entirely neglected fields. Interest in population growth may lead, on the one hand, to suppressing scientific investigation which promotes birth control, and, on the other, to advancing that which lengthens the life cycle. Finally, and perhaps most important of all, each new field of scientific inquiry more or less develops its own methods of research, its own problem emphasis, its own sets of hypotheses, its own ethical criteria, its own mathematics. As a culture emphasises new fields of investigation and analysis, it necessarily promotes sciences which are *at that time and that place unique, to it.*

But this says only that *science changes* with change in the emphasis and interests of the culture, that the *problems of interest* are different and that the application of scientific rules vary with the problems, the tools available, and the ingenuity of the scientist. It is one thing to say, with Planck, that "every science, just as every art and every religion, grows on national soil "—though the word " national " is certainly ambiguous to say the least—and quite another to argue that there is one science for the Germans, one science for the French, one science for the Japanese, and so on. For this argument, borrowed in its purest form from Spengler's monumental *Decline of the West*, there is not the slightest historical or philosophical justification. In common-sense terms the Nazis are asking that the critical faculties of science be not directed to examine any phase of the Nazi programme—a programme which demands of its scientists " first and above all blind faith in its own mission."[3]

(3) A third Nazi assumption, nowhere explicitly stated, is that there is *no clear line between science and non-science*. With this idea they are, again, in apparent agreement with the now well-accepted notion throughout all learned circles that scientific methods of analysis can be applied to all phenomena and all human experiences which can be condensed into record. But the agreement is superficial, not real, as can easily be seen from the nature of the extensive literature which the Nazis put out attempting to explain their position on science.

They introduce two confusions into this argument: in the first place they treat the findings of non-experimental and immature sciences as though they were as definite, as reliable, and as clear-cut as those of the experimental and more mature sciences. In the second place, *they confuse authoritative preconceptions with working hypotheses*. The combination of these two confusions, allied to the idea that science is nationally determined, leads them to a position in which science is indistinguishable from bigotry and canon (Church) law. Out of this come the new Nazi sciences, of " race and people," which completely discard all the well-accepted criteria of evidence, method, and attitude long regarded as the inescapable distinguishing marks of all science.

The " immature " sciences are of two types. First, are those lying in the field of " natural " phenomena where the underlying and basic principles—such as the gravitational constants and the laws of thermodynamics in physics—are either unknown or in doubt. Examples are colloidal chemistry, the general " field " of bio-physics, psychology and the entire range of " mental sciences." These sciences, besides lacking a balanced set of underlying and commonly accepted principles, likewise lack clear statement of field, accepted experimental methods, and a body of acknowledged results. They are, so to speak, fuzzy, inchoate, and " inexact."

The second type are the so-called " social sciences." They show all the weaknesses of the first type of " immature sciences " and, in addition, all those which are connected with the fact that they involve man, as a scientist, examining himself, his fellow creatures, and his past in relationships most vitally affecting his emotional life. That is to say, these sciences deal with institutions, behaviour, and records having to do with pride and prejudice, with conflicts of interests and philosophies, with bigotry, chicane, and deceit, with hopes, loves, faiths, loyalties, and fanaticisms. Their weakness is their subject matter—a subject matter which is not only surcharged with " irrational " factors, but which is almost infinitely complex. Nowhere can the " anti-scientific " mind, the medicine man and the charlatan range so freely at the expense of those dedicated to more careful probing of evidence. Nowhere else is it so easy under the guise of scientific research to pick and choose—as does the lawyer in the court room—from the facts to prove a predetermined case.

In neither of these two types of " immature science " can one speak with any reasonable degree of certainty, with that sense of *sureness* which comes from conviction that the products of one's research will be verified by independent critical investigation unless there has been a serious flaw in experimental set-up or reasoning processes, as is commonly the case in the physical sciences. To do so, and in particular to base policies upon the assumption of absolute infallibility of results of investigation in these fields is to commit the simple error of the child, the scientifically ignorant, the philosophically naïve, or the professional charlatan.

Yet this is exactly what the Nazis do. They speak of their

findings in history, political evolution, economic analysis, biological and racial inheritance, and mental endowment as though their conclusions were beyond dispute. In actuality the bulk of their conclusions on these matters are not only in dispute, but run directly contrary to those commonly accepted as most probably accurate by practically all non-fascist scientists.

The Nazis cannot be excused on the ground that they are ignorant. (There is not, of course, a single person amongst their official spokesmen who could by any stretch of the imagination pose as a scientist outside of Nazi Germany.) On the contrary, they insist that *their assumption that authoritatively laid down preconceptions are the equivalent of working hypotheses* lies outside the competence of all science whatsoever. In fact, nothing can be clearer than that this position is taken not out of ignorance, but out of regard for the realities—*Realpolitik*—of day-by-day propaganda tactics. It was Dr. Bernhard Rust, Minister of Science, Education, and National Culture, who laid down the dicta at the 550th anniversary festival of Heidelberg: " The new science is entirely different from the idea of knowledge that found its value in an unchecked effort to reach the truth.[4] The true freedom of science is to be an organ of a nation's living strength and of its historic fate and to present this in obedience to the law of truth."

What is the meaning of " true freedom " and the " law of truth " ? Let those answer who know the meaning of the biblical injunction, " I am the vine, ye are the branches: he that abideth in Me, and I in him, the same bringeth forth much fruit: for without Me ye can do nothing." The Nazis identify " truth " with what they choose to call their own " inspiration," and by the same token they identify " false " with " heresy." Truth to them is, in short, Nazi dogma and the sceptic is a heretic, a doubter, a destroyer of the truth.

In this meaning the German scientist is now " free " to study only what he is told, to arrive at just those conclusions which support the Nazi system and no other, and to be as dependent throughout on the dogmas of *Nazi truth* as the branches are on the vine. This is the position of the medieval Catholic Church which brought the great scientist Galileo to his knees, and burned John Huss at the stake, of the Order of the Society of Jesus which inspired Torquemada, dean of the Spanish Inquisition, to his ferocious persecutions of all those who doubted *The Truth* as the Jesuits saw fit to interpret it. It is a position, in short, which is the complete negation of the very type of questioning and searching which has underlaid all science from the beginning of time. Carried to its logical conclusions it will, as it has done throughout all history, wither all scientific thought at the very roots, and substitute in its place arid scholasticism and civilisation-destroying persecution mania.

(4) A final major assumption used by the Nazis is that *all science is useful.* Here again is an assumption that will pass pretty much without question in all parts of the scientific and technical world. But as used by the Nazis it means both more and less than the proposition that nearly all scientific investigation can be used for practical ends—engineering, manufacture, etc.—and human happiness. There is no escaping the conclusion that the Nazis mean by *usefulness* of science, that it can be *used* to serve whatever ends they determine. Science, in other words, is no more and no less than a tool of propaganda.

This point is made perfectly clear by Dr. Walter Frank, who, when speaking as President at the opening of the newly founded " National Institute for the History of New Germany," announced the task of the " new guild " to be that of acting as " honest brokers between the great traditions of German Historical science and the great driving powers of the National Socialist Revolution."[5]

But what are the " great traditions of German Historical science " ?

The institute to which Frank spoke was made up jointly of " politicians " and " scientists." Its character as " broker " for German Historical science is clearly indicated by the roster of those " thanked " for its inspiration and its tasks. These, Dr. Frank listed as follows:

" We thank, first and foremost, the Leader, Adolf Hitler.

" If I can say to-day that once again the sea air can stream through the writing of German History, it is because we know that he alone it was who led back our people on to the high seas of great political destiny. And it was he, also, who broke down the doors for the new creations of science and art.

" We thank from this place also the Deputy of the Leader, Rudolf Hess, for his public declaration that the active sympathy of the whole movement [Nazi Party] would stand behind this institute. We thank the Leader's deputy for education in the point of view of the National Socialist People's Labour Party, Alfred Rosenberg, for the decisive part which his understanding and his energy played in the creation of this institute. We thank the National Minister of Education who brought about the creation of the institute, and whose office must bear the responsibility for its conduct. In addition we thank equally all those central bodies of the political organisation, the Army, the Storm Troops, the Defence Guard [S.S.], the students and the Hitler Youth, who through their appearance here have demonstrated the *living bonds between our scientific labours and the warlike powers of our people.*"[6] *

What does Rust mean by saying, " We reject decreed science, but we also refuse to tolerate a political professor " ? Dr. Frick, his colleague, gives the answer in his fifteen-point programme for the guidance of writers and teachers in the teaching of history. These are so typical of Nazi " decreed science " that they are worth repeating in full. They demand that historians teach,[7] the:

1. Role of prehistory in which is emphasised the high civilisation attained by the ancestors of the Germanic race.

2. Role of the primitive race in which are prefigured all the great peoples and personalities of Germanic origin.

3. Role of the racist and national idea as opposed to the internationalist ideal so perilous to the German people, too much inclined to dreams and Utopias.

4. Role of the great German community scattered throughout the world and inseparably linked to the destiny of the Reich.

5. Role of political history which surveys the ensemble of large historic periods and takes account of their laws.

6. Role of the idea of heroism, in its Germanic form, which is inseparable from the idea of chief and leader.

7. Role of the heroic ideal, peculiar to the German race, always compelled to assert itself against an encirclement of enemies.

* Throughout the book where italics in quoted matter are not stated to be the author's, they are to be taken as mine.—R. A. B.

8. Role of the great migrations of peoples since the glacial epoch, which have determined the history of the Germanic race and assured the preponderance of Indo-Germanic languages.

9. Role of the great Germanic migrations into Asia and Africa which explains the pre-excellence of the Egyptian and Sumerian civilisations.

10. Role of the mixtures of races, with disastrous consequences—to be extensively developed and explained.

11. Role of the ancient Greeks, closest brothers of the Germanic race, with explanation of how they succumbed when the population declined and they were outnumbered by inferior and democratic races.

12. Role of the conquest of territory east of the Elbe.

13. Role of the great Germanic migrations into Italy, France, Spain, and England, which explain the preponderance of these countries over Russia and the Balkans, which have not been fertilised by new blood.

14. Role of modern history which shows how Germany was too easily receptive to alien influences, and then lost consciousness of her own qualities, through lack of knowledge of the laws of blood.

15. Role, in particular, of the last twenty years in the course of which Germany, having struggled against the coalition of her enemies, was betrayed by forces hostile to the nation and led to the verge of ruin by liberal and Marxian idealogues, carried down to the day when, in a heroic resurgence, she gave herself to National Socialism.

What is important here is not only the content, but the mood. What the guiding rules reveal is not only unquestioning acceptance of the assumption—totally devoid of any real scientific justification whatsoever—that " race " determines both ability of a people and the form and content of their culture, but also the deliberate intention to compel scientific investigation to find proof for what the " inspired " Nazis assert to be irrevocably true. *Nazi science*, in other words, *is " expert " special pleading.* Even the word " expert " has its special meaning, i.e. " convinced." The expert who is not " convinced " of the infallibility of Nazi doctrines is repudiated as a " pseudo-scientist," and his findings vilified as " alien " and non-Germanic, and, hence, without form, content, or meaning for the true Aryan.

It is highly important at this point that the reader understand clearly that there is no fundamental difference between the Nazi *attitude* towards the " natural " and the " social " sciences. Let him consider the solutions to the following propositions :

I wish to travel to X, a distance of sixty miles, in half an hour.

I wish to shoot John Doe.

I wish to prove I did not shoot John Doe [having just shot him].

I wish to know that my maid is inferior to myself.

I want to be told that there is no unemployment.

Let the reader then assemble the " expert counsel " required for supply of the answers which I wish given, let each expert be called a " scientist," and he has the full meaning of the Nazi position on both the physical and social sciences. The scientist, in short, is to proceed just exactly as does the conventional lawyer in the court room. He is to find out whatever the Nazis wish to know, and he is to prove whatever they wish to demonstrate.

For example, if the Nazis wish to learn how to manufacture deadly gases out of domestic raw materials, it is up to the physicists and chemists to turn the trick. So far, they may apparently proceed without any other circumscription of their activities than is involved in stating that they must work on this problem, and not on some other. But if the scientist, pursuing his allotted task, should develop a theorem which supports Einstein's theory of relativity, he would be compelled in Germany not to affirm, but to denounce Einstein's theory because the Nazis have decided that Einstein, being a Jew, can only produce non-Aryan and hence " alien " scientific theories. If the physicist should turn, in his quandary, to a biologist friend for advice, he would discover that the latter in his field must now prove that character is determined by heredity and not environment, and that the mixture of German and alien germ plasma would be racial suicide for both. And if he should then turn to his economist or historian friends, he might find them allotted the task of assembling material to prove that there was no unemployment—whether there was unemployment or not would be regarded by the Nazis as irrevelant—or reconstructing European history to prove that all the great discoveries and inventions were made by Germans. In each case the Nazis would decide what should be investigated, and foreordain what should be discovered to be true.

2. THE NEW NAZI SCIENCES

At this point we run into two new types of " Nazi science." The first is commonly known to scholars as " exegesis," or "the science of interpretation." The second are the new " racial-biological " sciences.

The Nazis propose to rewrite all history, all philosophy, and all natural and social sciences for the purpose of " purifying " them from non-Germanic interpretations. It is not that new elements have been discovered, but that old " falsities " must be deleted. The " falsities " are whatever do not support the idea of German biological and cultural superiority, and the roles these play in support of the Nazi *Weltanschauung*. *Exegesis, which to the careful scientist means selection of facts for their relevance in proof or disproof of working hypotheses*, and *a science for discovery and criticism of biased argument*, means *to the Nazis, selection of facts to support fixed convictions and for defence of biased argument*.

A special example of this procedure is found in their second type of new science—the " science of race." To go very far into the prolix, turgid, and confused literature centred around this subject is the most painful task any researcher can set before himself. Fortunately it is not necessary to examine very far, for the simple reason that the underlying propositions are so patently preposterous as to leave no doubt in the most sceptical mind but that the Nazis are not the least bit interested in the " truth " of what they say. Such arguments are only used to serve larger ends. As a further guide to clarity the reader will soon discover that the simplest pamphlet will give all their arguments; the balance of the literature is mere window-dressing and repetition.

The general argument is not without apparent scholarly tradition. As will be pointed out more fully in a following chapter dealing with Nazi agriculture, its first articulate spokesman was, oddly enough, the Frenchman de Gobineau. The Frenchman's ideas were taken over and elaborated with a great show of scholarly erudition in the immense work of the German historian —a hyphenate Englishman—Houston Stewart Chamberlain. The doctrine expounded in his monumental *Foundations of the Nineteenth Century* has found many and enthusiastic followers. Americans will recognise his followers in *The Passing of the Great Race*, by Madison Grant, *The Rising Tide of Colour* and other books by Lothrop Stoddard, and various of the writings of Edward Albert Wiggin.

One can tread through the trackless waste of Nazi race literature without finding a single theory or idea which is not to be found set forth in all candour by Madison Grant—a fact which demonstrates clearly that the Nazi argument is in nowise new. They have done no more than slightly reshape and refurbish an old-fashioned and now thoroughly discredited pseudo-scientific theory which they can turn, like reclaimed scrap iron, to their own good account. By the same token, Madison Grant may be used to show how resonantly preposterous, but likewise how eminently useful these doctrines are for Nazi purposes. Consider the following, taken more or less at random from the first few pages of *The Passing of the Great Race*: " The great lesson of the science of race is the *immutability of somatological or bodily characters*, with which is closely associated the *immutability of psychical predispositions and impulses*. . . . It will be *necessary for the reader to divest his mind of all preconceptions* as to race, since modern anthropology, when applied to history, involves an entire change of definition. We must, first of all, realise that *race pure and simple, the physical and psychical structure of man*, is something entirely distinct from either nationality or language. . . . Race *lies at the base of all the manifestations of modern society, just as it has done throughout the unrecorded eons of the past* and the laws of nature operate with the same relentless and unchanging force in human affairs as in the phenomena of inanimate nature."

" We now know, since the elaboration of the Mendelian Laws of Inheritance, that certain bodily characters, such as skull shape, stature, eye colour, hair colour and nose form, some of which are so called *unit character*, are transmitted in accordance with *fixed laws*, and, further, that various characters which are normally correlated or linked together in *pure races*, may, after a prolonged admixture of races, pass down separately and form what is known as disharmonic combinations. Such disharmonic combinations are, for example, a tall brunette or a short blond; blue eyes associated with brunette hair or brown eyes with blond hair."

" *These physical characters are* to all intents and purposes *immutable* and they do not change during the lifetime of a language or an empire. . . . *Nature cares not for the individual nor how he may be modified by environment . . . heredity alone* is the medium through which she acts . . . these characters are *fixed and rigid* and the only benefit to be derived from a changed environment and better food conditions is the opportunity afforded a race which has lived under adverse conditions to achieve its maximum development but the *limits of* that *development are fixed for it by heredity and not by environment.*"

What is meant by the statement that " race lies at the base of all the manifestations of modern society " ? Madison Grant, following closely the argument of Houston Stewart Chamberlain, forerunner and acknowledged prophet of the Nazis, makes this perfectly clear: " Racial lines . . . correspond closely with the divisions of social cleavage . . . continuity of inheritance has a most important bearing on the theory of democracy and still more upon that of socialism, for it *naturally tends to reduce the relative importance of environment.* Those engaged in *social uplift and in revolutionary movements* are therefore usually very intolerant of the limitations imposed by heredity. Discussion of these limitations is also most offensive to the advocates of the obliteration, under the guise of internationalism, of all existing distinctions based on *nationality*, language, race, religion or *class*. Those individuals who have neither *country*, nor flag, nor language, nor *class*, nor even surnames of their own and who can only acquire them by gift of assumption, very naturally decry and sneer at the value of these *attributes of the higher types.*"[8]

There is not a line in those quotations the Nazis would take exception to. The core of their argument runs about as follows: physical and psychical (mental, emotional, attitude) characteristics are interrelated, inseparable, and fixed for all time by heredity. In the shaping of character, the development of ideas, and the range of achievement, heredity is decisive; environment relatively unimportant. There are pure and impure races. The pure races are divided into superior and inferior. Both are superior to mixed or bastard races. Of the superior and pure races, the greatest of all is the Germanic (Nordic, or Aryan). As the superior race, the Germanic is by heredity destined to be the ruling race over all the world and all civilisations, and over all inferior peoples and social classes.

Within each people, there are degrees of purity and impurity. The pure are the superiors, the impure the inferiors. The ruling classes belong to the pure; the inferior to the impure. The only exceptions to this rule are to be made with respect to those inferiors who have elbowed into the inner ruling circles through low cunning and the lack of vigilance of the superior people. All these persons must be eliminated, ruthlessly. Within each pure race there are different degrees and different combinations of inherited and racially determined abilities. The rulers are the most richly endowed; the followers, the least well endowed. Class structure is determined by these facts, and all revolt against " nature determined " class structure constitutes flying in the face of immutable natural laws.

The following quotations, taken at random from Nazi literature, will illustrate the degree of congruence between their ideas and those of Madison Grant:

" In the centre of the National Socialist world view stands the race problem. It is, according to the word of The Leader, the key problem of world history. It was race instinct which dominated the N.S.D.A.P. [Nazi Party] before it achieved the conquest of power. It was essentially an intuitively grounded sureness of judgment which conditioned the radical position taken by the Party in these things."[9]

" The biological-medicinal sciences of the past 30 years have taught us that man is conditioned in both his bodily and spiritual qualities much more by hereditary endowment than by all environmental factors, whether these be food, or sport, or education. All these outer influences have as a first condition to their effectiveness the existence of corresponding hereditary qualities, and man has no possibility of creating any new hereditary endowments, or of denying those which he now possesses."[10]

" There can be no question about the fact that the human species is in its historical development, as also in many expressions of its life, a unity. But human being first acquires its deeper meaning when these superficial characteristics are deepened and given their peculiar imprint by the spiritual and character-forming properties which have their only sure expression in race and people. *No thinking and feeling can*, if it is genuine and profound, *overstep its racial boundaries*."[11]

" Miscegenation and the sinking racial level resulting from it are the *sole cause* of the extinction of ancient civilisations; for peoples do not perish because they have lost wars, but from the loss of that power of resistance which resides only in pure blood. All in the world that is not good race is so much trash. And all history is only the manifestation of the self-preservation drives of different races."[12]

" Blood and soil, as fundamental forces of life, are, however, the symbols of the national-political point of view and of the heroic style of life. By them the ground is prepared for a new form of education. . . . What does blood mean to us ? We cannot rest satisfied with the teachings of physics, chemistry or medicine. From the earliest dawn of the race, this blood, this shadowy stream of life, has had a symbolic significance and leads us into the realms of metaphysics. Blood is the builder of the body, and also the source of the spirit of the race. In blood lurks our ancestral inheritance, in blood is embodied the race, from blood arise the character and destiny of man; blood is to man the hidden undercurrent, the symbol of the current of life from which man can arise and ascend to the regions of light, of spirit and of knowledge."[13]

" National Socialism is characterised by an heroic attitude towards all problems of existence. This heroic attitude derives from one single but all-decisive profession of faith, namely, blood and character. Race and soul are merely different designations for one and the same thing. This is paralleled by the rise of a new science, a new scientific discovery which we call race science. From a high enough perspective this new science is discerned to be no more than a far-reaching attempt to attain German self-consciousness."[14]

3. USES MADE OF CO-ORDINATED SCIENCE:
THE CASE OF THE JEWS

Statements of the above order could be multiplied to fill volumes. The argument has serious implications for three groups in particular—the Jews, the Slavs, and the working classes of Germany. Most bizarre is the application to the Jews. It is safe to say that there are no recognised limits to the scurrility with which Jews may be safely characterised by Nazi officials in Germany. Nothing indicates, likewise, so clearly the purposes for which this campaign of repression and vilification is carried out. It is interesting to see what lies behind such bizarre statements made by no less a person than Darré, Reich Minister of Agriculture, as the following: " The Semites reject everything that pertains to the pig. The Nordic peoples, on the contrary, accord the pig the highest possible honour . . . in the cult of the Germans the pig occupies the first place and is the first among the domestic animals. . . . This predominance of the pig, the sacred animal destined to sacrifices among the Nordic peoples, has drawn its originality from the great trees of the German forest. . . . Thus out of the darkness of earliest history arise two human races whose attitude in respect of pigs presents an absolute contrast. . . . The Semites and the pig are faunal and thus physiological opposites. It is not unthinkable that the eating of pig flesh by the Semite sets up physiological disharmonies in his body. . . . The Semites do not understand the pig, they do not accept the pig, they reject the pig, whereas this animal occupies the first place in the cult of the Nordic peoples."[15]

Dr. George Norlin, President of the University of Colorado

and visiting Theodore Roosevelt Professor of American History and Institutions at the University of Berlin in 1932–33, tells of an episode in which the Rector of the University of Berlin was forced out of office because he refused to allow the Nazi student federation, the *Studentenschaft,* to post certain theses on the walls of the university. One of them read: " No person of Jewish blood can think German. Therefore, when a Jew writes German, he lies. Therefore, whenever henceforth a Jewish professor or student publishes a book or a piece of research, he must write on the title page: ' I am a Jew, and this is a translation from the Hebrew into the Germanic language.' "[16] *

Equally puzzling seems the purpose of the following, cited by Thurston: " Alien albumen is not only harmful animal serum injected into the blood in the name of therapy, but also is the semen of a man of any alien race. Such male semen is absorbed immediately and completely into the blood of the female in intercourse. Therefore a single contact between a Jew and a woman of another race is sufficient to corrupt her blood for ever. With this alien albumen she also acquires his alien soul. She can never again, even if she marries an Aryan man, bear pure Aryan children—only bastards in whose breasts two souls dwell and in whose very bodies degeneration is clearly visible. . . . Now we understand why the Jew concentrates with all arts of seduction upon violating German girls as early in life as possible; why the Jewish physician ravishes his women patients while under anæsthetics; why Jewish wives even permit their husbands to have union with non-Jewish women. German women and girls, don't let Jewish physicians hypnotise you and drug you —for never again can you bear German children."[17]

At the National Party Assembly in Nuremberg, September 15, 1935, a law was passed in extraordinary session for the Protection of German Blood and German Honour, which

1. forbids marriages between Jews and nationals (*Staatsangehörige*) of German or kindred blood, under penalty of nullity of the marriage and imprisonment with hard labour;

2. forbids sexual relations between Jews and nationals as in the above. Punishment consists of imprisonment with hard labour;

3. forbids the employment in Jewish households as domestic servants of women of German or kindred blood under forty-five years of age;

4. forbids Jews from displaying the national flag or the colours of the Reich, though it permits them to display " Jewish colours " and promises them the protection of the state in exercise of this privilege.

All such laws, statements, and allegations as the above might be, as they most commonly are by foreign critics, set down as the irresponsible utterances of ignorant and deluded fanatics. But to fail to go beyond such characterisation would be to miss the entire strategy which the Nazis have so cleverly and successfully employed in this whole race squabble in Germany.

Since the position taken against the Jews involves all those issues bound up with their anti-alien and anti-labour campaigns, it is worth examining somewhat more closely. The Nazis contend that the Jewish question is not a matter of opinion, but of science. They are not, they will most stoutly affirm, dealing with this issue capriciously, but according to the dictates of scientific law. If one is able to keep carefully in mind that there is or can be in Germany no " science " which does not serve the ends of the Nazi state, it is possible to find here the real meaning of current schemes for co-ordination of German science.

Stripped of all circumlocution and verbiage, the uses which Nazi " race science " has served, with particular reference to the Jews, can be summarised as follows:

1. By outlawing Jews it provides a partial solution for the *job hunger* of loyal Nazi Party adherents. The bulk of these active rank and file adherents fall into the middle strata of professional and trades people on the one hand, and politically active youth in search for jobs in these fields on the other. It is in precisely these fields that the Jews, comprising less than one half of one per cent of the total population, were the most active. A Nazi publication submits the following figures as typical of the degree of Jewish control before the coming of the Nazis:

Year for which figures are given	Industry, Trade, or Profession	Percentage or Number Jewish
1930	Metal trades firms	57·3
	Iron trades	43·9
	Textile industry	31·2
	Grain trade	18·9
	Grain wholesale trade	22·7
	Flour trade	14·2
	Trade in hops	9·4
	Trade in hay and straw	9·8
	Vetch wholesale trade	33·9
	Wholesale trade in women's clothes	60·9
1931	Medical faculty, Univ. of Breslau	45·0
1932	(the same situation)	
	Faculties of Jurisprudence, in "other universities"	47·0
1928	Practising lawyers:	
	Vienna	80·0
	Frankfort on Main	64·0
	Beuthen	60·0
	Karlsruhe	40·0
	Düsseldorf	33·0
	Dortmund	29·0
	Physicians: Vienna	80·0
	Berlin	52·0
	Mainz	30·0
	Cologne	27·0
	Hospitals: Moabit in Berlin:	
	Head surgeons	3 out of 6
	Assistant surgeons	10 out of 16
	Helper surgeons	6 out of 12
	Friederichshain:	
	Assistant surgeons	12 out of 20
	Helper surgeons	8 out of 12
	Neukölln:	
	Head surgeons	2 out of 4
	Assistant surgeons	10 out of 14
1928	Bank director posts	15 Jews had 718 posts
1931	Theatrical producers	118 out of 234
	Berlin theatres in Jewish hands	80·0

It does not matter whether these figures are accurate or not. The Nazis make every effort to identify as Jewish the largest number possible—one-fourth Jewish blood in one grandparent being sufficient to mark a person as "Jewish." The larger the number so identified, the more places that can be made open to Nazi adherents through arousing hatred against these "non-Aryan aliens." As one of the leading industrialists expressed it, in personal conversation during the summer of 1935, the Jews were the only indigenous racial group which could be easily exploited to the advantage of the Nazis. Any other physical criterion would have been just as satisfactory—flat feet, fat bellies, side whiskers—to the Nazis were the peculiarities of such an order that they might be dramatised to the same useful end.

2. The "menace" of the Jews was an *invented terror*. The ancient Greek philosopher, Aristotle, offers this advice to the sovereign who is faced with unrest and the threat of revolution from his subjects: if all other means have failed to settle the trouble, divert attention by "inventing terrors." Find some insidious plot against the state; whisper that the wells are being poisoned, the food destroyed, the daughters secretly ravished, high officials about to be assassinated, the banks subtly undermined, the farmers gouged, military secrets being given away. Find anything that will arouse the people to a pitch of excitement against some common malefactor; then invent a terror against this destroyer of the common weal.

The Jews served very well as "bogeyman" for the Nazi strategists. The German peasant is led to believe that the Jew stole all his hard-won earnings away from him by some devil's magic on the commodity exchanges. The petit-bourgeois classes were told that the Jew aspired to control all professional jobs, ruin small tradesmen (note the campaigns against Wertheims and other large department stores), and dominate for "racial purposes" all big industry and the financial machinery of the country. Labour is asked to believe that cynical and self-seeking Jews, under the guise of Marxism, stirred up labour discontent which they could exploit to their own cruel advantage and in which they did, as a matter of course, continuously betray the interests they affected to represent. Young girls and women are taught that physical contact with the Jew will corrupt them

Cf

biologically, and that every Jew seeks intercourse with the
maximum number of good Aryan girls for the sake of degenerating the German race. All are told that the Jews were responsible
for the greatest national disgraces in the history of the German
peoples, the defeat in the war, the subsequent treaty of Versailles, and the servile Weimar Republic which was built on the
ruins therefrom. In the two most widely circulated anti-Jewish
newspapers, the *Stürmer* and *Judenkenner*—newspapers to be
found prominently displayed on every news-stand in the
country—these points are gone over and over again, with lurid
descriptions of alleged discoveries of scandalous Jewish sex
behaviour, shameless plots against the Fatherland, and so forth.

By these means the " attention of the masses was diverted "
to see the Jew as the cause of low farm prices, high retail prices,
adulteration of goods, onerous tax burdens for reparations
payments, low wages, unsatisfactory labour conditions, and
many other crimes against the Aryan people. But in addition to
serving his useful Nazi propaganda purpose, the new race
science helped to promote the role of the Jew as

3. *Scapegoat for the popularly recognised abuses of capitalism.*
For the popular American symbol of " Wall Street " the Nazis
employ the picture of the greedy Jewish capitalist. It has been
pointed out in previous chapters how such things as " interest
slavery," high agricultural indebtedness, and both commodity
and stock market speculation were branded as Jewish and hence
made occasion for subjecting the Jews to the most bitter
repressive measures. Needless to say, not only did the Jews not
" control " or set interest rates, agricultural indebtedness, or
speculative activity, but also the Nazis did not abolish these
activities. What they attempted to do was to lead the populace
to believe that in suppressing the Jews, they had corrected the
abuses of which so many had with such justice so long and bitterly
complained.

But the service of the Jews to the Nazis was greater than this.
By identifying the Jews not only with the serious evils which
accompanied it, but *with capitalism itself*, they were able to
" abolish " the word " capitalism " while leaving its substance
intact. By identifying Jews with " international finance " when
Germany was losing in this game, with *laissez faire* when

Germany was rapidly advancing towards effective monopoly, with " liberalism " when it was desired to destroy all democratic institutions, and with the *idea* of the wage-dispensing employer when labour troubles were multiplying at a geometric ratio, and then by identifying these factors as the indispensable earmarks of " capitalism " the Nazis were able to say, in destroying the economic status of the Jews, that they had destroyed " capitalism." They did nothing of the sort, of course. What they had accomplished was to blame their evils on a devil, name the devil, and then destroy him. With his destruction they proceeded to rename all the evils for which they invented the devil, thinking thereby to convince the people that the evils had been done away with.

4. An even greater role was assigned *the Jews* in Nazi propaganda by proving them to be *the creators of Communism, Marxism, Bolshevism, Class War, Trade Unions, and Internationalism*, in short, the creators of all the organised groups allied against the idea of the People's Community—the Nazi name for German capitalism. By one of the most curious bits of reasoning to be found anywhere in modern propagandist literature, the Jews are held to be not only responsible for the creation of (Jewish type) Christianity, Capitalism and Bolshevism, but these also are held to be merely different phases of the same thing.

This is historical nonsense, but it is not stupid propaganda. For the common notion said to underlie all three is the idea, uniquely advantageous to the Jews, of *equality*. Christianity is said to have been poisoned by the Jewish concept of " equality of all before God." Private property and individual initiative were transmuted into capitalism by the idea of " equal rights of all persons on the market." This type of system required *laissez faire*, liberal or democratic institutions, and parliamentarianism (representative government). Bolshevism, they conclude, means the " equality of all incomes," i.e. the forced degradation of all persons to the levels of the masses, the rabble, the lowest in abilities and intelligence.

In an 192-page book entitled *Jews and Labour*, carefully " documented " page by page and flanked by an extensive bibliography, the author, F. O. H. Schulz, writing on behalf of the Institute for the Study of Jewish Questions, presents a detailed and picturesquely distorted picture of how the Jews invented the class struggle and, by dividing employer and employee into warring camps, promoted the " tragedy of the German People." The book was published in collaboration with the Anti-Comintern (Central League of German Anti-Communistic Associations). A foreword by a spokesman for the Anti-Comintern, after relating how an earlier book by another author has established " the responsibility of the Jews for the leadership of the bolshevist revolution in Russia," compliments the " no less exact and objective F. O. H. Schulz " for his present book, which shows out of " great fullness of materials that the Marxist social democratic and communistic influence in Germany was produced, nurtured, and made great by the Jews." By the same reasoning process he finds both the second and the third Internationals were " created by Jews, and led to-day by Jews."

The full propaganda use of " racial science " is clearly set forth in this textbook for the Nazi novitiate. " Marxism is uncovered to be a political ideology of *racially determined elements* in their struggles for the acquisition of power. Not only does Marxism stand closely related ideologically to Liberalism, Capitalism, and Free-Masonry, but politically and in substance. All international ideologists are arrayed in close dependence and understanding. The political aims and the objective results are always the same: supernational domination and exploitation."

The chapter headings give a good index of the book's contents: The Jewish Invasion of the German Working Classes, Karl Marx, Ferdinand Lassalle, The Jew in the Socialist Daily Press and Periodical Literature up to the World War, the Political Mass-Strike, the Jewish Power in the Socialist Labour Organisations, the World War, Revolution and World Revolution, Versailles, Jew and Worker in the Parliamentary Democracy. All the radical, left-wing, and labour protest movements in Germany are attributed to the Jews, and from Karl Marx, author of the *Communist Manifesto*, to Rudolf Hilferding, Social Democratic Leader in the late Reichstag, these Jews were said to be distinguished by their hatred of Germany, their contempt for the family, their irreverence for all religion.

The route via which this racial mythology and ruthless

anti-Jewry is brought to its significant form is, then, as follows: to discredit labour demands, first discredit organised labour; to discredit organised labour, first discredit the democratic and equalitarian philosophy; to discredit democracy, first discredit collectivism; to discredit collectivism, first discredit socialism and " Marxism "; to discredit socialism, discredit the Jews; to discredit the Jews, invent a " science " which will prove that they are (a) different from the Germans, and (b) inferior because of this difference. The anti-Jewish campaign, then, serves the dual Nazi purpose of supporting and further entrenching the realities of capitalism, while striking at the very ideological foundations of organised labour.

5. A final value of the anti-Jewish campaign is found in the ease with which " *racial* " *differences* can be established as a fact of everyday experience. The Jews, in the main, do show certain common physical characteristics. These serve as simple, direct, visual proof of the fact of " race " variation. By identifying *difference* with *inferiority*, the Nazis attempt to get across to the ignorant, two ideas: first, the right of the Germans to rule over *inferior* peoples, and, second, the nature-given necessity for a caste, or " nature-determined " class state.

If, as the Nazis assert, it is a law of nature that the superior should rule over the inferior, then the superior peoples should be banded together for better promotion of their mutual interests. On the one hand, this leads to Pan-German Imperialism, which lies at the basis of Nazi Aryan chauvinism. On the other, it promotes the idea of the right and the necessity of conquest. The inferior peoples lie all around Germany. Most important are the Slavic races. The largest collection of these peoples is in the U.S.S.R. Furthermore, the Nazis say, the U.S.S.R. is commanded by a band of cut-throats, culturally degenerates, and haters of the " superior " Germans. Therefore, from all over the world Germans should unite under the Nazi banner and lead a holy crusade against the greatest of all threats to modern civilisation—all portions of which worth saving have come out of the labours of Germans, the superior people—the Soviet Union.

The common tie which unites all Germans into a confraternity of the *élite* is said to be their Aryan blood. But the identification of blood difference with superiority, makes the idea of *ability-differences* stand out in sharp relief. What better way can there be to prove to each that he should be satisfied with that role in society determined by his complement of " racial purity " and the degree to which he is endowed with the peculiar physico-psychological capacities of his race ? The Nazis can borrow the slogan, " From each according to his ability," and make it prove that each should produce the most at that job for which his innate abilities fit him. And they can add, " To each according to his needs," and mean that each should have just that amount which is necessary to maintain his maximum efficiency at the work-bench to which he is destined by nature. Is it not clear that " the superior " need more; the " inferior " less ?

To recapitulate, the facts shown above make perfectly clear that the Nazis are no more interested in the " truth " or " falsity " of their accusations against the Jews than they are in the truth or falsity of science. Their sole interest is in the extent to which situations and facts can be made to serve their stated purposes. They will not hesitate not only to tell scientists what they should prove, but also to destroy any part of science which militates in any wise against their programme. In terms of the generally accepted criteria of scientific methods and scientific proof, they have already completely destroyed the entirety of the social sciences. Any other science that does not " help " the new Germany may likewise be destroyed.

Their scruples will not prevent them from going to the wildest extremes. For example, on behalf of patent medicine quacks, bathing and health resorts, and the local tourist trade, they have attempted to discredit the use of serums and other medicinal preventatives commonly used against ordinary diseases such as tuberculosis and smallpox. On behalf of domestic trade, certain ardent Nazis offer a curious proof that tobaccos, which must be imported, are bad. It is solemnly announced that " one drop of nicotine can kill twenty men," and that its use " gives rise to over one hundred diseases."

4. THE AGENCIES OF CONTROL OVER SCIENCE

The inevitable question arises: How were the Nazis able to put across such ideas with the scientists themselves ? The answer is twofold: first, because they found organisations and institutions for central control over scientific activity ready at hand, and because they applied to these selfsame structures all the highly developed techniques for influencing opinion which they had found so successful elsewhere. And, second, because of the mental attitude and the intellectual outlook of the scientists themselves.

On the first point the Nazis played in luck, for in the general field of science they found the same type of centralisation, the same sort of compact organisation so general throughout the entire German economic world. Each of the scientific, engineering, and professional fields was organised so as to include all practising members throughout Germany in a single association. These, in turn, were recombined into central policy co-ordinating bodies which included the entire range of the related professions. A couple of examples will suffice.

In Germany engineers were organised by their respective professions as civil engineers, electrical engineers, railway engineers, etc. But all these engineers likewise belonged to the Federation of German Engineers—a federation including at the time of the advent of the Nazis nearly 60,000 members, and making up quite the largest scientific organisation of its kind in the world. It possessed a large and spacious general headquarters in Berlin, published a whole series of technical magazines, divided its work amongst a host of special and general purpose committees, and participated in the founding of institutes of scientific research, general scientific congresses, and the activities of closely allied professional societies.

On the more practical and managerial side, the Federation of German Engineers participated in the founding and subsequent conduct of the National Board for Economy and Efficiency, a body which centralised in a single organisation all the various types of associations, technical committees, and research having to do with management, industrial engineering, the promotion of technical and labour standards, mechanisation, scientific agriculture, vocational training, and so forth. There is nowhere else in the world a body even remotely approaching the National Board either in the range of activities it includes, or the comprehensiveness of its supervision over the minutiæ of each separate

committee and member association. Its most important committees are the following: the German Standards Committee; the
Committee for Conditions and Terms of Delivery; the Committee
for Efficient Management; the Society of Organisation; the
Research Bureau for Commerce; the Institute for Business
Cycle Research; the Committee for Efficiency in Management
of Public Activities; the German Committee for Technical
Schooling; Committee for Efficient Production. In addition to
these, it has special technical committees dealing with such
things as materials testing, heat economy, building construction,
paints and painting, welding, time studies, handicraft techniques,
and household equipment and installations.

On the more purely scientific and research side, the Society
of German Engineers is flanked by the chain-laboratory system
of the Kaiser Wilhelm Society. Originally founded in 1911, it
had developed by the time of the coming of the Nazis into an
enormous organisation comprising 33 separate research institutes. Of these 13 fell into the field of chemical, physical, and
technological research, 13 into the biological, anthropological,
and zoological fields, and 7 into the social science fields. In the
first group fell laboratory-equipped research institutes dealing
with such fields as chemistry, physics, electro-chemistry, iron
research, metallography, textile fibre chemistry, silicate research,
air currents, and hydraulics. The second dealt with such fields as
biology, micro-biology, brain research, psychiatric research, and
eugenics. The third included research dealing with German
history, foreign and international private law, and management
of the famous Harnack House.

. The Harnack House was a sort of combined scholars' club
and visiting scientists' international house. Scientists and
scholars from all over the world stopped or registered here, and
through its elaborate machinery were placed in contact with any
scholar or institute whom they desired to visit anywhere in the
entire Reich.

In addition to the comprehensiveness of these organisations
with respect to both organisations and members, three other
facts stand out of marked importance for the ease with which
scientists submitted themselves to " co-ordination " by the
Nazis. The first of these is the fact of extremely close co-operation

between the several specific sciences, as, for example, between physics and chemistry, coal and chemistry, metallurgy and iron, on the one hand, and between the social, biological-psychological, and " natural " sciences on the other. So close was the problem material, so interlaced the structure of research, and so relatively free the flow of information, that barriers between the several fields of science and scholarship tended either to break down completely, or to stand as no more than mere watermarks of tradition and research emphasis.

In the second place the working alliance between research and practice was extremely close, and in many important respects had been almost entirely effaced. This is shown not only by the close working alliances between the several engineering and professional societies—technical research, social research, engineering and management—but also by the multitude of personal and institutional contacts between these different societies and the universities, the government, industry, and trade. Professors from the universities mixed freely with research workers from industrial plants and the various institutes of the Kaiser Wilhelm Society; engineers mixed freely with scientists working in laboratories and with scientific theoreticians, and these with researchers and practitioners in commerce and social science research. But the significance of this tie-up between science and industry lies not only in the fact that the bonds uniting them were growing steadily more numerous and rigid, but also in the even more important fact that, throughout, the business men, not the scientists, held the whip hand. It was the business man who determined programmes for research, who gave the necessary money, and made use of the results. Science and engineering were subservient throughout. When business men changed their titles from employers to " Leaders " under the Nazi system—when the business men were given a chance under Nazism to dictate in all things—they found no need for changing their working relationships with scientists in any single fundamental respect. Nor did the scientists who served them before. Only the previously " unco-ordinated " had to be brought into line, and this required next to no effort on the part of either party to the bargain.

Thirdly, there was a great and growing tendency for all

scientific information to be nationally pooled. In the main, research conducted locally and by individual enterprises and manufacturing establishments—such as by the two big electrical concerns, Siemens & Halske and the German General Electric, and by the Dye Trust—was made available to all German scientists, with the exception of specific applications which led to patent rights and secret processes of manufacture. The theoretical problem matter, however, was pooled almost without exception, and made available, through original publications and a highly refined system of condensation and summarisation, to all research workers in the same and in allied fields of investigation.

Such in general was the situation in German science which the Nazis found when they assumed control of the political apparatus of Germany. Into their programme for co-ordinating all ideas, organisations, and activities in all fields, the research and scientific posture of affairs in 1933 fitted perfectly. Hence, nothing fundamental has been changed as to scope and method. They have merely capitalised on the trends in force by insisting upon even closer working alliances between the separate fields of research and practice, and co-ordinated all activities to fit the purposes of the Nazi state.

But if the " co-ordination " is of the sort described—a co-ordination which seems to run so directly counter to the techniques, the criteria, and the moods of science itself—why have not the scientists revolted *en masse* ? The answer is to be found in the fact that the typical scientist is not, either by virtue of his training or vocation, much more inclined to uphold scientific laws and methods of analysis, *so far as social applications are concerned*, and outside his *own narrow field*, than is the most ignorant layman on the street. Furthermore, the number of scientists and scholars in any capitalistic country who can be found ready to identify their interests with the " common man," and with organised labour, can be counted in extremely small numbers. One of the most naïve ideas ever expressed by a reputable economist was Veblen's notion that the interests of engineers and scientists in workmanship and efficiency would lead them naturally, if not inevitably, to ally themselves with labour's interest in maximising output and improving standards of living. There is not the slightest ground for believing that any so-called " soviet of engineers " in capitalistic countries would be any more progressive than the most conservative club of business men.

It would unduly prolong this discussion to go into the reasons here why this is so unfortunately true. But it may be worth pointing out that the very nature and purpose of the Nazi drive was such as to take full advantage of the rigorousness in scientific criteria commonly accepted as basic in the various fields. As one proceeds from the more mature natural sciences of physics and chemistry, on through biology, psychology, and finally to the so-called " social sciences," the number of variables increases, the range of relative facts grows more numerous, the key problems become more and more complex, and the element of *biased motive and preconceived opinion* grows steadily more influential. It is in the natural sciences that the Nazis have the least interest in changing science and scientists—here applications are to the heavy industries, the techniques and equipment of war and militarisation, utilisation of natural resources, etc. On the other hand, it is in the subject matter of psychology and the social sciences where they have the greater interest in restricting, cutting, hewing, shaping, and interpreting research results according to preconceived plan. Could the reverse have been true, the situation would have been entirely different so far as the conflict with accepted scientific routine and habits of mind are concerned.

But there lurks even here a general misconception regarding the scientist. He is, after all, a human being and not a superman. He cannot be expected under the best of circumstances to be a clear-eyed, matter-of-fact searcher for " objective truth " and an expert in dispassionate analysis beyond the fringes of his own special field. There seems to be relatively little of the so-called " transfer of intelligence," and not any too much of scientific habits of mind, as he passes beyond the boundaries of his own specific knowledge. Nowhere in all recent philosophical literature is there to be found more simple-minded and naïve acceptance of the myths of popular folklore than in the writings of Eddington, Jeans, Millikan, Planck, and other famous scientists. This was as true of German scientists even before the coming of

Hitler as of all other scientists to-day. Scientists, in short, simply let themselves in for the charge that they have abandoned science when they become so careless as to assume that the *attempt to think rigorously in one field* automatically implies thinking rigorously whenever one thinks about anything at all. Here the scientist is no different from any man on the street. If he gives way to the temptation to generalise where he does not *know* he is merely allowing himself to abandon *rational criteria* in favour of *uncritical belief.* Uncritical belief is never science; it is always first cousin to bigotry itself.

The more narrow his field of research—a tendency to narrowing is more common with modern science than heretofore—the more apt he is to approach the bigot outside his own field. It is exactly in the natural sciences, which the Nazis leave the least disturbed, that this narrowing on intensive research is most pronounced. Hence arises the paradox that the physical scientist who would seem by training and disposition the least subject to emotional appeals is, perhaps, most susceptible of all his brethren to the blandishments of the fanatic and the bigot—most bigoted because he accepts uncritically what he can be made to believe is rigorously true.

Nor do their ethics restrain them from being co-ordinated. Physicists, chemists, biologists, economists, etc., can be found in great numbers willing to staff any programme and endorse any idea or product. The scientist only provides that the price paid is for services rendered on either a narrow and seemingly related phase which he knows a lot about, or a general idea which he knows nothing about. And he can be " honest " in both, for in both he can say what he believes to be true even though in so doing he speaks to the advantage of the " co-ordinator " who frames the programme and pleads the case.

The scientist, *per se*, is, hence, perhaps the most easily used and " co-ordinated " of all the especially trained people in modern society. The Nazis, to be true, fired a good many university professors, and dismissed a good many scientists from research laboratories. But the professors fired were primarily amongst the social sciences where there was a more common awareness and a more persistent criticism of the implications of Nazi programmes, and not amongst the natural sciences where thinking is supposed to be most rigorous. Those dismissed in this latter field were primarily Jewish or exceptions to the generalisation made above—because of equally uncritical acceptance of beliefs running contrary to the Nazi philosophy.

Consequently the Nazis were able to " co-ordinate " scholars and scientists with relative ease, and hence to throw behind their elaborate propaganda the seeming weight of the bulk of German learned opinion and support. They have not even had much difficulty in filling the ranks of their " race science " institutes from regular university and similar circles—a success which they have registered by virtue of careful selection from amongst National Socialist university youth, and by forced transmutation of the relevant scientific criteria to meet their own specific ends. Rust expressed the entire situation neatly at the festival for the world famous Heidelberg University when he said: ". . . a change has taken place in the institutions of higher education since the Nazi Party came to power. This change has resulted from the fertile influence of the new *Weltanschauung* [Nazism] and racial realities." He speaks of the " efforts of science to enrich itself from the stream of the new *Weltanschauung*," and commends it for its progress and achievements.

" Progress and achievement " in what ? The opening meeting of the festival at which he spoke gives the clue. Uniformed troops, marching men, draped party flags, and military manœuvres dominated the scene. Dr. Goebbels, Nazi Minister of Propaganda and People's Enlightenment, welcomed the scanty and disappointing roster of visiting scholars. Academic robes were absent. Science had been co-ordinated. The scientists who attended listened; those who did not cheer there, and the wide-world over, sat—to the eternal sorrow of science—uncomplaining and for ever mute.

CHAPTER III

The Arts and Education as Tools of Propaganda

ACCORDING to the Nazis the mass of the people are dumb. They are unintelligent, childlike, and inarticulate. They will accept without serious question whatever they hear or are told. They believe everything they read. They do not bother to think; they feel. Their lives are not pivoted on logic, but on emotion. They have no real initiative, no true creative powers, and they are incapable of any sort of self-discipline. They desire to be fed, to be entertained with exotic and melodramatic fancies, and they yearn to follow.

Like the child they are unstable, irresponsible, and capricious, turning easily from one brightly coloured fancy to another. They will be attracted by whatever is simple and naïve, whatever is dark, dangerous, and thrilling, whatever is extreme in size, or distance, or accomplishment, whatever is heroic and unheard of, whatever brings the gasp of wonder or the hush of awe.

They are likewise essentially and naïvely pleasure-loving. But, though lovers of ease, they are so thoroughly irrational that they do not count the cost of achieving their pleasures. Like the child who works assiduously for hours in the garden, or the soldier wallowing in the mud of the front-line trenches, they will be satisfied for their labour and sacrifices by a cheap bauble, a bit of praise from some furtively admired hero, a medal, a badge, or a bit of palely reflected but resonantly heralded glory.

Nor, the Nazis assume, are the rank and file able to tell the difference between symbols and realities. Thus they may be given symbols instead of realities. They can be made to fight for " God and Fatherland," for " German Kultur," for " Blood and Honour." They can be made to endure poverty and die in rags and filth for " Mother and Home," the " Leader," the " People." They can be brought to sacrifice everything for " the good of the community," and to escape " Jewish Marxism." If necessary they can be conditioned to people the forests with demons, be fearful of black cats, and vomit at the sight of a Jew.

The " leaders," in other words, are free to choose not only the causes for which they wish to rally the support of the people, but also the symbols which sway their emotions. Properly conditioned, these symbols need have no necessary relationship to the real interests of the run of mankind. Indeed, not uncommonly, popular support of the symbols chosen works directly against the individual and group interests of those who follow them, as is typically the case with mystical and patriotic issues.

This is the point of view of the *Junker*, the aristocrat, and the military war lord. It is also the point of view of the *nouveaux riche*, who believe the " able " always " succeed," citing themselves as examples, of the successful business man who identifies his economic power with possession of cultural qualities of which he may not have the slightest comprehension, and of the upstart political hack who has traded his demagogic powers for an overstuffed mansion or the hand of a daughter of the blue-bloods. These self-styled *élite* are always contemptuous of the " man on the street." They speak of labour, of the " broad masses " with condescension and scorn. They have no use for " democracy," for " individual freedom," for " representative government," except as these may be employed as slogans for the purchase and sale of popular support. If these slogans at any time get in the way of the " main chance," they will be done away with on the same principle which a knowing débutante employs when she strikes an unlikely prospect off her social list.

As business men have come more and more to dominate not only the economic but all other phases of modern life, they have come more and more to think of themselves as the *élite*. In the literature of even pre-Nazi Germany, and in that of contemporary America, England, and France, this theme runs strong. A graduate from Oxford, and at present general manager of a thriving London ice-cream business, was positive that " liberty had meaning and value for the able 10 per cent, but feudal status was all the masses were fit for." Lawrence Dennis's book, *The Coming American Fascism*, reflecting the opinions of the Union League Club and the National Association of Manufacturers, identifies the *élite* throughout with the successful business man. In this view the balance of the population cannot possibly be " free and equal," since they are without talent, without capacity for self-sacrifice, without " honesty and devotion " to their tasks.

The following quotation, taken from a speech delivered to

the Illinois Manufacturers' Association (May 12, 1936) by
Bruce Barton, American exponent of practical uplift, and
publicity director of the Republican Party, is typical of the
voluminous and rapidly growing literature in America expressing
this point of view. He takes as an example of the problem faced
by the advertiser, who must sell and civilise " folk whose
ancestors battled for the mere necessities, but . . . themselves
accept . . . as a matter of course that every luxury shall be
theirs," the handicap committee of a golf club:

"Any man in this room who has served on the handicap committee of a golf club has learned something of the curious
involutions of the human heart. *The handicap system is an
instrument of social justice.* It recognises the hollowness of that
ancient lie that all men are created free and equal. A golf club
knows that all men are not created free and equal. It knows that
there are a few men out of every generation who, *by native talent,*
are able to play in the seventies. That there are a few more who,
because of youthful opportunity or *self-sacrificing practice,* can
score in the eighties, that a somewhat larger number, by virtue
of *honest lives and undying hope,* manage to get into the nineties.
But beyond these favoured groups lies the great mass of strugglers
who, however virtuous their private lives, however noble their
devotion to their task, pound around from trap to trap and never
crack a hundred. If the handicaps can be reasonably fair and
honest, a spirit of wholesome endeavour and mutual good feeling
results. If the poor players are unfairly handicapped they will
protest and throw out the officers. If, on the other hand, the
good players are too much burdened they will not compete.
The management of the club passes into the hands of the dubs; the
club is likely to lose tone and eventually break up."[1]

With threat to their rapidly growing economic power by either
the government or labour, generalisations of this sort quickly
lose their benevolent tone. In any crisis which challenges their
position the assertions become more positive, the mood more
uncompromising, the repression of opposition more savage. If
the crisis be grave enough to strike at the heart of the " system,"
this general point of view is apt to crystallise quickly into a
nation-wide programme of action. It is just this which has
happened during the past few years in Italy, in Germany, in

Portugal, Austria, Hungary, Brazil, and Japan. In the United States, as in practically all other capitalistically organised countries of to-day, we are witnessing a similar coalescence of business forces, directed to a similar end.

The end and aim is to make of business men the *élite* in power which they are so firmly convinced they are in fact. This *élite* possesses a peculiar flavour—a flavour which has over the past quarter century, and to an increasing extent as we come down to modern times, done so much to identify the interests of business with the military in fact as well as in the popular mind. The military has always been the strong right arm of the state, and as the state has fallen more and more under the direct control of business interests, the military has been gradually transformed into an instrument on behalf of business. It is not only that " trade follows the flag " in modern imperialism, but also that the flag goes wherever business interests are at stake. If this be abroad, the result is intimidation of weaker nations, the use of the threat of military power in the bargaining process with stronger nations, and at the most, conquest and war. If it be internally, the business men will ask for and expect to get the full mobilisation of the police and military ranks on behalf of any enterprise threatened with strikes or labour reprisals of any sort whatsoever.

Even more important is the mood which dominates both the military and the conduct of business-as-usual. Fusion of the two is particularly significant because the drive, the attitude, and the point of view of both are fundamentally the same. Both believe in the propriety and ultimate necessity of power, brute force, and domineering authority. Neither believes in the principle of freedom of expression, thought, or belief. Whenever either acquires the perquisites of liberty, they proceed, if occasion seems to call for such action, immediately to its destruction. The frictionless ease with which business men have proceeded, under cover of the naïve idea of " self-government in business," to destroy all freedom of action in economic affairs is something perfectly understandable to the military mind.

The entire history of trusts, combinations, monopolies, cartels, and trade associations, of the struggles of employers with labour unions, and of business control over the media for disseminating news and information, demonstrates how fully the business men understand the uses of the symbols of freedom and tolerance for underwriting autocratic control. It is perfectly axiomatic that business men do not believe in freedom of thought or expression in any of the arts if the results are such as will challenge the business system in any significant fashion. In this mood it seems perfectly natural to them to think of the arts and the sciences as they think of a trade agreement, or a device for concealing profits from the tax collector. They do not, as a matter of course, mind mixing a clever advertising talk with a Brahms lullaby or a promotion story with a symphony if they can, thereby, make a few slick sales. In the same mood—" it pays "—they will plaster the country-side with sprawling signboards, exploit the sex fears of the innocent, the innocence and spontaneity of children, and the concern of the mother with a child.

As in the army the weapons of warfare are force, secrecy, repression, and the judicious deployment of the manikins of deceit behind a dress parade (barrage) of cleverly simulated virtues. It is not important, as any candid business man will tell you, that one be virtuous, but it is important that he appear virtuous—a fact which Andrew Carnegie, though most careful to explain in his revealing Autobiography, was not the first to recognise. Likewise there is no place for tenderness and mercy (called " sentimentality " by business men) in business, but it can use sentimentality (called " putting it across ") galore. There is no value in any " truth " but that which can be sold; no merit in any " honesty " unless it can be made to pay. " War is war " they say in the army; " business is business " they echo on the bourse.

It is highly important that one think through the meaning of the union of the contemptuous attitude towards the " great unwashed multitude " with the ethic—or, rather, lack of ethics —which sees nothing wrong in the least with wholesale commercialisation of the arts and sciences. For only then is one in a position to comprehend the real meaning of the Nazi programme for the arts—a programme which sees the arts as tools for putting across the interests of " business-as-usual " in the same matter-of-fact way as any routine advertiser will employ an artist to paint pictures of beautiful ladies in order to sell a patent medicine.

Whenever and wherever the business community is seriously challenged it has been prepared to expand its programme so as to utilise more fully the repressive powers of the military and the demagogic following of the party hack. In any crisis which seriously challenges its general authority such ruthlessness as it has exercised on the persons of its opponents is no more than a simple outgrowth and single expression of the attitude which it demands be effective in control of the arts. For in the arts ruthless suppression of all opposition means no more than expansion of tried and true methods of " business-as-usual." And, quite naturally, it never occurs to any of the active agents in such programmes that they are being either ruthless or dogmatic. They are merely promoting what they see, via the profit and loss account, to be " sound thought " and " sound art." If this means that it will pay to do so, they will keep the symbols of " liberty," of " democracy," of " freedom," and of representative government, however much these may be emasculated in fact. If not they will not hesitate to abolish such symbols and substitute for them others which will be more effective in persuading the masses to follow where the *élite* choose to lead.

In Germany the business-military *élite* chose to destroy these symbols, but with this destruction there is nothing in the vast outpouring of the Propaganda Ministry and all its various subsidiary organisations which calls for serious modification of the foregoing sketch at any point. They name, in fact, what they condemn with bland candour. Speaking of the " liberal " society which the Nazi state has destroyed, they find this hateful past to have as its " highest principles . . . freedom of the spirit, freedom of differences of opinion, of art, of science, and of conviction. . . ."[2]

In " liberal " times, they argue, the state was formally separated from business, science, religion, and the arts. So far as the state was concerned, these were legally free. The state asked nothing more than that it have the right to exercise the police function with respect to these activities. Its attitude was essentially negative, or, more properly, *neutral*. Liberalism regarded all attempts to control the arts and sciences to predetermined ends as acts of barbarism and police regimentation.

But in the new German state—in which the government and business are fused together—there must, according to the Nazis, be a " strong internal unity between state and culture." This condition finds its outer expression in the fact that the spiritual life of the people, as it reveals itself in cults, myths, and art, must in a certain definite way receive as its highest guiding laws directive ideas, the right of formulation of which has been transferred to political bodies and the Leaders.[3] The state, that is to say, must control all attitude-shaping influences completely, finally, and irrevocably. It can have no truck with ideas of freedom. " The sharp, unbridgeable, and absolute opposition of National Socialism to Liberalism lies in the fact that it sets against the idea of a constitutionally guaranteed freedom of ideas, and a state without ideas itself, the notion of an *all-inclusive and decreed idea subjection and idea fixity.*"[4]

There is no mistaking the intent. " For the National Socialist state, culture is an affair of the nation," it is a means for spiritual leadership, and requires, therefore, to be positively manipulated in order that all may be educated to a sense of responsibility which promotes the shaping of the nation."[5] In this state culture will no longer be under the influence of " changing, opalescent voting majorities and coalitions, but under a fixed, definite, absolute law. . . ."[6]

This " absolute law " represents a transformation into " will and act " of the " viewpoint of the state." This viewpoint is, of course, that of the Nazis, and it sees " the state as a natural community—a natural community made up of a people fused together through ties of blood, speech, customs, and common experiences, and which in its most fully developed form we characterise by the term nation."[7] The nation is " fixed and eternal," and stands " at the centre of all historical and political experience."[8]

The culture of this state comes out of a " wholly simple, wholly primitive perception " of the people, and in obedience to their will and law. Since it " grows out of the people " it " cannot be commanded from above . . . it is not a state function," since it is " no less than the spiritual side of the people's life and being."[9]

As actualisation of the feeling and " will of the people," the principles which underlie it " can in nowise be clarified and formulated."

How, the sceptical reader may well ask, can the Nazis assert at one and the same time that culture " is an affair of the nation " and that " it is not a state function " and " cannot be commanded from above " ? How reconcile the statement that " culture is as free now as before " with the announcement that under National Socialism culture must be brought under a rule of law whose guiding principle is " all-inclusive and decreed idea subjection and idea fixity " ? The answer is to be found in Nazi contempt for that type of logic which is based on " reason " and not on " feeling "—in short, on that type of logic which insists that contradictory statements are necessarily inconsistent.

The argument which they advance to circumvent the charge of inconsistency is completely without subtlety or finesse. Speaking of the difference between the pre-liberal and the Nazi cultural authoritarianism, they offer this contrast: " Authority for National Socialism comes out of the people itself, not out of a power which rules superior over it; the will of the state comes out of the folkways, is free, sovereign, and of a new type."[10] The will of the state is the " will of the people," and this is not to be found " on the surface of daily life and in day by day interests," but only where " the final and partially unconscious longing is formed." That is to say, out of the " national soul."

But this " authority " cannot be determined by vote, by popular election, by representation of the people, nor by allowing them any voice in the determination of policy. The Nazis have done away with all these things. The so-called elections still used are not elections but plebiscites, where negative voting is next to impossible, and where the casting of the ballot involves an act no different in spirit and mood than the shouting of amens in a Free Methodist camp-meeting—if one can imagine adding to the hysteria thereof a liberal admixture of fully implemented terror. How, then, is this authority determined ? The answer is worth quoting in full:

" Out of the national soul emerges the law from which the National Socialist leader derives his legitimation and his policies. He is not thus an organ of will superior to the people, but *instrument of the will of the people which exists in him.* Who rules the people of its own will, and who expresses the character of the National Socialist state in two syllables, we know as THE LEADER.

" Leader is the opposite of magistrate. Who leads does not determine the objectives arbitrarily and by himself; that is done by the led. The led are the people. *But the Leader knows the goal and knows the direction. . . . Who carries this spirit in him, who knows the direction, that person is the Leader.*"[11]

Not only does the " leader " know the direction and the goals, but he need not take counsel from the people at any point. He need not ask any of them what they think or believe, because, as the Nazis most emphatically insist, they do not know. And if they think they do, they probably think wrongly, and it is up to the leader to set them straight by cultivating their souls to a " correct " understanding. Hitler's argument on this point is perfectly explicit:

" What we designate as ' public opinion ' has nothing whatsoever to do with self-won experiences or the knowledge of individuals. . . . Just as the confessional attitude is the product of education, and only the religious feeling slumbers in the inner man, so the political attitude of the masses is only the end result of what is frequently an almost unbelievably *tenacious and fundamental re-working of the soul and the understanding.*"[12]

This is, of course, not one whit different from the famous and oft-quoted remark of the Kaiser: " Regarding myself as an instrument of the Lord, I go my way, whose goal is the welfare and peaceable development of our Fatherland, and in so doing I am indifferent to the views and opinions of the day."[13] No different, with the small exception that Hitler does not acknowledge the Lord !

But it is likewise no different from that of the conventional business man, or his paid publicity agents, advertising men, and public relations counsellors. These people speak frequently and sanctimoniously of " service to the public " to whom they sell and from whom they make money. The people are sometimes called " the owners," while the business men are merely " men whom . . . owners have employed to build them more automobiles, to make them some clothes, to furnish them electric light, to bake them some bread."[14] They cannot, the business men will tell you, sell anything the people do not want. Hence, the people, the buyers, control, and they only cater to the " needs," the " positive aspirations " of the real masters of the nation's affairs.

But they likewise assume that " the people don't know what they want," and that they can be made to buy almost anything if properly advertised. Furthermore, they believe that people can by appropriate propaganda be made to accept the business system, to believe that big business is an ideal expression of the will and genius of the nation, that labour unions violate " liberty " and run counter to the principles that underlie the social system, and that all opponents of the accepted business point of view are " reds " or " Marxians " or " Communists " and hence represent the blighting hand of a civilisation-destroying Pluto from the underworld. Like Hitler and the Nazis, they are contemptuous of the people whose interests they pretend to cater for, and they carry this contempt to the point where they see nothing inconsistent between speaking of the people as owners, guiders, and controllers and the position that the populace can be extolled, persuaded, propagandised, and bent to accept any point of view whatsoever. Nor do they see any contradiction in their assumptions when they proclaim the end result to be merely an expression of the " will " or the " soul " or the fulfilment of the " desires " of the people.

The only difference to be found between the Nazi propaganda machine, to which all the arts and sciences are subjected in Germany, and the spirit of advertising and American " Public Relations Counsellors " is in the ease with which the German system is able to function because of its formal capture of the coercive powers of the state. But for this difference, both see in the arts and sciences instruments for " selling " a bill of goods to the public. When this has to do with small matters, relating to such things as the sale of specific commodities or services, it is known in both countries as " advertising." When it relates to larger matters—the " business system," " capitalism," " big business," or " National Socialism," it is called " propaganda " or " public relations." The type of propaganda which in the United States is now being so actively promoted under the

euphonious title of " public relations " is centralised in Germany
under the control of the " Ministry for Propaganda and People's
Enlightenment."

The conduct and spirit of the " Ministry for Propaganda and
People's Enlightenment " is in thorough keeping with the spirit
of advertising, the spirit of " public relations," the spirit of
" business propaganda." Nowhere are these propagandists
concerned in any wise with the " truth," since truth is simply
irrelevant. They are concerned with sale of a bill of goods. The
agency through which culture is co-ordinated for putting across
the Nazi " public relations " bill of goods is called the National
Chamber of Culture. It is worth examining in some detail.

1. THE NATIONAL CHAMBER OF CULTURE
(" REICHSKULTURKAMMER ")

The law which established the National Chamber of Culture
(September 22, 1933) was the first of three giving " expression to
the world view of the National Socialist leader-state." The other
two were the " Law for Author Leaders " (October 4, 1933) and
the " Theatre Law " (May 15, 1934). Of these three laws, Dr.
Karl-Friedrich Schreiber, Counsel for the National Chamber of
Culture, says: " The law for the National Chamber of Culture,
including its enabling clauses, is a law without formal content;
an organisation law without material standards. The Law for
Leaders of Authors and the Theatre Law, on the other hand, go
far beyond form and, with definite rules, reach immediately into
the activities of the affected groups.

" The basic idea underlying the three laws can be brought into
a simple formula: within the unity of creative function, primacy
of the spiritual, suppression of the economic, subjection to the
law of the people's community through filling the cultural professions with a definite sense of responsibility to the nation,
assembly of a class of spiritual leaders dedicated to the task of
overcoming a falsely understood freedom in the exercise of their
professions, and thereby of eliminating the police principle of
negative control."[15] This means, that " it is necessary to merge
together the creative elements from all fields for carrying out,
under the leadership of the state, a single will. . . ."

The National Chamber of Culture is given a large commission. " Its main task is, and will be for a long time, to operate within the cultural professions *separating the tares from the wheat*, and to decide *between the fit and the unfit*. But fitness will not be determined by affiliation with this or that artistic trend, over whose ultimate value perhaps only coming generations can decide; but through *inner conformity with the will and being of the people*. To decide between the sound and the transitory, and *to divide by blood and spirit German from alien*, that is the ' direction ' of National Socialist cultural leadership, since that is also only the direction of national socialist will. [Italics by Schreiber.] What within the new forms will be created is a tremendous leader corps, made up out of all who participate in any wise in the process of forming the national will, from the greatest spiritual creations to the most insignificant helper, from the man who does the creative work to the last retailer who hawks literature and journals on the streets and at the railway stations."[16]

The Chamber is, in short, to include everybody who practises in any of the arts and in any capacity for the sake of making a living. Membership in the chamber is compulsory upon all persons and all associations, whether citizen or foreign, engaged in the production, reproduction, promotion, management, direction, or participation in any other capacity whatsoever in the transmission of written, visual, or audible instruction or entertainment to the German people. Control over membership, associations, and activities is complete in every respect with exception of wages and certain specified price scales—these latter functions coming, respectively, under the control of Labour Trustees and various Price Commissioners.

The organisation of the National Chamber of Culture is extremely interesting, since it illustrates once again the full meaning of the combination of the Nazi " total " and " authority " principles. The application of these principles to the arts means that the Ministry of Propaganda and People's Enlightenment, operating through the Chamber, assumes complete " authority " over the " totality " of all phases of cultural life.

The skeleton of its structure is comparatively simple, as can readily be seen from Chart I on p. 91. It is made up of seven constituent member chambers:

The National Music Chamber.
The National Arts Chamber.
The National Theatre Chamber.
The National Literature Chamber.
The National Press Chamber.
The National Radio Chamber.
The National Film (Cinema) Chamber.

Each national chamber includes all activities falling under its control for the entire Reich. The first four and the Film Chamber are regionally divided, having each 31 regional and local representative bodies. A similar arrangement is planned for the Press and Radio Chambers. The local offices of the Radio and Film Chambers are at present under the direct control of representatives of the National Socialist Party.

As usual, the " Leader " principle obtains throughout. The President, Vice-President, and Secretary of the National Chamber of Culture, and, through him, the officers of each of the member chambers, are appointed by and directly responsible to Dr. Goebbels, Minister of Propaganda and People's Enlightenment. They are personally responsible to him for the conduct of their offices, all the business and professional affairs over which each office has charge, and can be removed or overruled by him for any cause and at any time as he may see fit. The same powers are conferred on each officer under him, so far as the authority of this delegated " Leader " may extend as defined by decree.

Since each of the separate chambers is organised along the same general plan, it may be interesting to follow through structure and methods in some one case to show whereby the Propaganda Ministry is enabled to keep a close grip on every detail of cultural activity for the entire Reich. The National Press Chamber will serve as a good example.

The inclusiveness of its control over all journalism is shown by its division into 14 national groups, and the subdivision of these into an extensive system of local and regional groups, as follows[17]:

CHART I

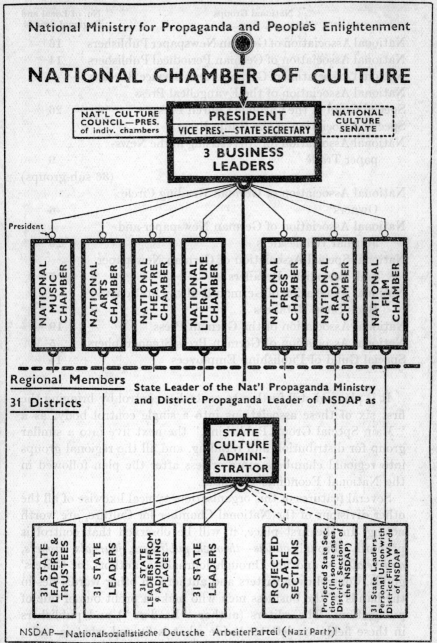

National Ministry for Propaganda and People's Enlightenment

NATIONAL CHAMBER OF CULTURE

NAT'L CULTURE COUNCIL — PRES. of indiv. chambers	PRESIDENT VICE PRES. — STATE SECRETARY	NATIONAL CULTURE SENATE
	3 BUSINESS LEADERS	

President

NATIONAL MUSIC CHAMBER

NATIONAL ARTS CHAMBER

NATIONAL THEATRE CHAMBER

NATIONAL LITERATURE CHAMBER

NATIONAL PRESS CHAMBER

NATIONAL RADIO CHAMBER

NATIONAL FILM CHAMBER

Regional Members

31 Districts

State Leader of the Nat'l Propaganda Ministry and District Propaganda Leader of NSDAP as

STATE CULTURE ADMINI-STRATOR

31 STATE LEADERS & TRUSTEES

31 STATE LEADERS

31 STATE LEADERS FROM 9 ADJOINING PLACES

31 STATE LEADERS

PROJECTED STATE SECTIONS

Projected State Sections (in some cases, District Sections of the NSDAP)

31 State Leaders—Personal Union with District Film Wards of NSDAP

NSDAP—Nationalsozialistische Deutsche ArbeiterPartei (Nazi Party)

From— Organisation von Arbeit und Wirtschaft (erste Auflage.) by Dr. A. B. Krause. (Otto Elsner Verlag, Berlin)

National Groups	No. of Local and Regional groups
National Association of German Newspaper Publishers	16
National Association of German Periodical Publishers	14
National Association of German News Service Bureaux	
National Association of the Evangelical Press	
Special Guild of the Catholic Church Press	26
Special Association of the Radio Press	
National Association for Advertising in the Newspaper Trade	9
	(36 sub-groups)
National Association of German Reading Circle Owners	6
National Association of German Newspaper and Journal Wholesalers	20
National Special Association of German Newspaper and Periodical Retailers	5
National Association of German Railway Station and Book Shop Retailers	
National Association of the German Press	19
National Association of German Press Stenographers	5
Special Guild of Publishing Employees	14

It is planned still further to centralise control by bringing the first six of these associations into a single control body, as a " Main Special Group Publishing," the next five into a similar group for distribution and retailing, and all the regional groups into regional chambers more or less after the plan followed in the National Economic Chamber.

Several features of this organisation, typical likewise of all the other divisions of the National Chamber for Culture, are worth noting. In the first place, it will be observed that control is primarily through *outlets—through publishers, journals, brokers, and retailers*—and not through journalists, authors, or writers' guilds. Control over writers and authors, in other words, lies in the hands of the business men who make a profit out of sale of publications. The editors (author " Leaders ") and publishers in these fields are left to decide what is fit and what is unfit; as business men they sift the " tares from the wheat," interpret the " soul of the people," and make writers " responsible to the community."

In the second place, the National Press Chamber is known as a " self-managing " or " self-governing " body. That is to say, the Chamber has, similarly to the Code Authorities in the defunct American N.R.A. (though without benefit of the latter's befogging publicity), the right to manage its own affairs within the limits of its charter grant. Although the powers actually bestowed are somewhat broader than those given to the code authorities, the basic ideas are typically the same. Three examples may be cited: the maintenance of the principle of " private initiative " and of " competition "; the right to control the conditions of membership; and the right to exclude new businesses.

The " Leader " himself has guaranteed the principle of private initiative and competition. ". . . the Leader, in his speech to the German newspaper publishers on the 28th of June, 1933, expressly emphasised that he would not create a state press but wished to maintain the essential conditions for private initiative in the press field."[18] Likewise for competition. " The fulfilment of journalistic tasks calls for competition between the various press organs. The efficiency principles of the National Socialist world point of view are not consistent with an elimination of competition." Without competition there can be no " assured economic foundation " for the press.[19]

But this is a competition to assure good business—competition of firms for space, advertising, and circulation. It is not a competition based on differences in point of view. It appeals to different sections and interests of the reading public but with the same point of view. ". . . the press can only be an effective instrument when the fulfilment of its multitude of special tasks is carried out under the leadership of a single will."[20] As Goebbels, Minister of Propaganda, expressed it, " The press shall be uniform in will and multiform in the carrying out of that will." This means, of course, that the " Leaders " of the press shall have the right to control membership in all the separate branches and divisions of the Press Chamber. Speaking of the " responsibility " of the " author leaders," a commentator writes that " only those persons can be admitted who are suitable and whose reliability has been definitely shown by specific criteria. In similar ways are the circles of persons for other professions limited by interpretation of paragraph 10 of the first decree for carrying through the Law for the National Chamber of Culture. If facts can be presented that persons in question do not possess the suitability and reliability necessary for the conduct of their activities, the *National Press Chamber can decline to admit or can expel members at will. Therewith such persons lose all rights for further activities in the press field.*"[21]

The Chamber may set up its own rules for testing members, and its own general procedure for accepting or expelling those whom it examines. They must, however, exclude in all cases Jews and antagonists of National Socialism. In some cases the rules are quite explicit. It is provided by decree, for example, that all persons must be excluded from newspaper activity who fall into any of the following classes[22]:

1. Those who mix up individual with community purposes in a way confusing to the public.

2. Whoever is inclined to weaken the power of the German nation at home or abroad, the community will of the German people, the German Military, Culture, or Economy, or who injures the religious sensitivities of others.

3. Who offends against the Honour and Values of Germans.

4. Who illegally injures the Honour or the Prosperity of any other person, harms his calling, and makes him laughable or base.

5. Who opposes the customs on any other ground.

The principle is: rules to writers; powers to business. The business men running publishing enterprises, it is obvious, may employ the above rules to exclude any person at will from giving expression to ideas which run contrary to their community of interests. The rules apply not to the conduct of *newspapers as businesses, but to the opinions that may be expressed.* There is no regulation of business as such—this is left to the business men themselves under the principle of " self-government "—but there is thoroughgoing " co-ordination " of opinion to propaganda ends.

A person excluded from the newspaper field owes his position as outsider entirely to the " leader " of his branch of the industry. The " leader principle " prevails throughout, and the Leader may interpret and decide as he sees fit. As " leader " he is not allowed to hear the accused. Here as elsewhere throughout all the machinery of Nazi Germany the " leader principle " means that the techniques of the military court martial have been substituted for normal civil procedure. The general rule promulgated for all constituent members of the National Chamber of Culture is explicit: " *It is inadmissible that the ' accused ' be heard.* The universally valid rule of legal obedience dare not be infringed."[23]

To the Draconian power it is not surprising to find added authority to prevent the establishment of new business in the press field. A decree of May 2, 1934, forbade, for example, the founding of any new Correspondence and News Service Bureaux. Similar decrees have been issued dealing with the founding of concerns for wholesale trade in newspapers and periodicals (September 19, 1934), advertising journals (October 24, 1934). On January 31, 1935, a decree was issued circumscribing the founding of newspapers themselves.

A third feature worth noting in the functioning of the National Press Chamber is that its rules are publicised as rules which do not eliminate but rather underwrite freedom. This means, however, not freedom as ordinarily expressed, but the new German freedom. The law makes it perfectly clear that there is unlimited freedom to conduct business so as to make money, provided no money is made out of expression of viewpoints contrary to those of National Socialism—or, in short, business-as-usual. This is made clear by the propaganda " duties " laid upon those who publish the news. The Press Law lays down the three broad principles[24]: " The press law must

1. develop the leading idea of the press, and show the press the tasks it must perform in the National Socialist state. The leading idea is that the press is, as a means for people's education, a leadership tool in the service of the state and the nation;

2. make certain the methods of press labour. The leading method is that there shall be no state press established, but that there shall be, under definite conditions, free and voluntary co-operation which will assure the fulfilment of its tasks in the sense of the leading idea of the press, and which will assure it of plenty of room for play;

3. find new forms of management which will transform the press into fighting media and give over leadership into the hands of the state, thus educating those active in the press to become members of fighting troops, and thus to activate them into a goal-conscious closed troop in disciplined subservience to the leadership will."

What does this mean for " freedom of the press " ? Hitler himself answers " It is in the interest of the people and the state to prevent " the " great mass of the people . . . [who believe everything that they read] . . . from falling into the hands of bad, ignorant, or evil-willing educators. Accordingly the state has the duty of overseeing all education and preventing all misdemeanours. It must pay . . . *especial attention to the press*, since its influence over this class of mankind is especially strong and effective. . . . In the uniformity and eternal repetition of this instruction lies an unheard-of significance. . . . The state dare not forget, that all media have a duty to serve which . . . flunkies of a *so-called* ' press freedom ' dare not be allowed to confuse. . . ."[25]

The word " so-called " is significant, for it implies that there is no restriction of genuine or " sound " press freedom. And such is exactly the case, since only those persons are defined as " sound " who are National Socialist. When, for example, the Leader of the National Association of the German Press, Wilhelm Weiss, could say before a national gathering of the German Press (Cologne, November 30, 1935) that all association offices " are filled to-day exclusively with National Socialists," he meant that all journalists were " free " to write and be National Socialists, and no more. That this is true is indicated by his following comments, in which he stated, " Even a year ago I was able to inform you that, following the National Socialist revolution, the *German press had been freed of at least* 1,300

Jewish and Marxian journalists."[26] To the " freedom " of journalists to be ". . . men with soldierly discipline, fighting natures, and at all times responsible to the new Reich and The Leader, Adolf Hitler," was added " freedom " from Jews, Marxians, and, in short, all enemies of the state ! A twice-blessed freedom !

It is for precisely these reasons that that section of the American press—the Hearst publications for example—most vocal in their demands for " freedom of the press " in the United States, is likewise the section which is uniformly and insistently most laudatory of Mussolini, Hitler, and " fascism " in general. What these papers demand is freedom to exterminate opposition, and in particular organised labour, " liberals," and " reds." Were this section ever to be granted its desires, it would be for ever after " free " to promote its own ends, just as was the case in Germany. The " co-ordination " of the press in Germany met with next to no opposition aside from the left press and a small number of the great metropolitan papers of a more or less " liberal " point of view.

As indicated above, much the same picture holds for each and every one of the seven member chambers of the National Chamber of Culture. Throughout all organisations the " leader principle " obtains, and " leaders," in addition to being always appointed from above, are typically drawn from business ranks. All the separate chambers and their member bodies are known as " self-managing " groups, and function on the basis of " private initiative " and competition, all conduct their activities so as to exclude new competition as far as possible and so to regulate prices and output as to be able to make satisfactory returns on capital invested for member enterprises. All are " co-ordinated " to the " will " of the National Socialist state that they may promote the goals which their inspired Leader, Adolf Hitler— and those subordinates to whom he may delegate the duty of being inspired—discover for them.

The goals, here as always, appear on the surface to present a serious paradox. If the purpose is to promote the joint economic advantage of the business community and their strong right arm, the army, how account for the rule cited above—that all member bodies of the National Chamber of Culture shall

Df

promote " primacy of the spiritual " and " suppression of the
economic " ? The Nazi literature allows no equivocation in
reply; the answer lies readily at hand: All employees in all
capacities should have their " eyes diverted from the material
to the spiritual values of the nation," and no business man
should make money out of any of the arts and sciences by
promotion of any point of view which militates against the
ingeniously cultivated fancies of the disinherited. It is not that
the people should not buy goods—far from it—but that they
should not want to buy more goods than they can pay for out
of the wages and salaries allowed them by their " leaders "—
" leaders " perpetually engaged in plumbing the " longing of
the people " and so fulfilling their " spiritual duties to the
National Socialist people's community " !

Special plumber for people's " longing," and sole mentor for
instruction in the proper use of the arts is:

2. THE NATIONAL SOCIALIST COMMUNITY OF CULTURE

Alfred Rosénberg, given charge by the " Leader " of the
" entire programme for the education of the Party in spiritual
and *Weltanschauung* matters," organised the National Socialist
Community of Culture immediately upon accession of the Party
to power. According to Dr. Ramlow, an official spokesman, the
Community of Culture immediately took over the membership
of the theatrical-goers' union, some 300,000 in number, and
from that nucleus expanded rapidly until it came to include,
by the end of 1935, better than a million and a half members.
According to another version, the bulk of the members now
claimed came not from expansion but from absorption in 1934
of two other organisations, the " Fighting League for German
Culture," and the " National Association of German Theatres,"
the latter of which counted over 500,000 members on its roster
nearly a year before joining the National Socialist Community
of Culture.[27]

The Community of Culture, as spiritual mentor of the National
Chamber of Culture, concentrates on the organisation of clubs
or circles through which the stimulation of the approved art is
fostered. Thus the Community of Culture has organised an art

ring, a theatre ring, a book ring, and a lecture ring. To these rings any true German may belong, whether or not a member of the Nazi Party. The membership fee is one mark (about 25c.) per annum per ring.

By buying in blocks, thereby ensuring a reliable market, the Community of Culture can obviously secure greatly reduced rates on many things for its membership. Whatever it is that the members are interested in buying, they can, according to Dr. Ramlow, generally obtain at one-half the market price or less.

As possessor of the sole legal authority " to set up an organisation of audiences, the National Socialist Community of Culture considered a strong structure of organisation its foremost problem. Being at the same time a *community of ideals* purporting to make vital contributions to the cultural reconstruction of the people, it *rigorously sees to it that admission to membership means a declaration of allegiance.*" Thus " strong " and " centralised . . . it feels united with its millions of adherents in the idea that a genuine reformation of Germany's cultural life can be achieved only through *unconditional devotion and perfect consistency.*"[28] To this end it has not only sponsored, but undertaken active management of, theatrical productions, exhibits, prize competitions, etc., but it has also organised its membership into some 2,000 local groups, each of which is in the care of a " culture guardian."

How it functions can be seen from brief examination of two of its main lines of functions: (1) those dealing directly with the theatre, and (2) those involved in agreements for co-operation worked out with other Nazi " corporate formations." These latter " agreements " have been made with a considerable number of organisations; notably, with the Army, the Police, the National Association of Jurists, the National Socialist Students' League, the Labour Service, the General Inspector of the National Highways, the National Socialist Strength through Joy, and the Hitler Youth.

Up to the present the Community of Culture has concentrated upon co-ordination of the theatres to the National Socialist *Weltanschauung*. In performance of this function it sponsors plays, gives advice to Party officials who wish to take their " followers " to the theatre *en masse*, sponsors the plays of

" unknown " writers who advocate Nazi viewpoints, arranges block sales of tickets, etc. More recently it has gone directly into the field of theatrical production.

The latter are of two sorts—those given in large metropolitan theatres, and those given in rural areas by small travelling theatres. Productions which prove successful in Berlin, Munich, and other large cities are sent out to travel through all the large cities of Germany. For this purpose the Berlin Theater am Nollendorfplatz has been used as a sort of " culture laboratory " for the development of model plays, model theatrical leadership, model players, and model audiences. Here the Community of Culture has worked out a " Play Plan " including historic drama, folk plays, and other types of productions which comply with the " new German style."

A number of *News in Brief* propaganda leaflets, for the " information " of foreign journalists, gives examples of the types of plays reproduced. A cantata called *A Man Builds a Cathedral* represented " the first attempt on a large scale to cast into a mould of art the great experience of the last twenty years and the sentiment and faith of the new ' myths ' " and " demonstrated the possibility . . . of giving . . . a religious meaning to our national resurrection." An opera, *The Return of Joerg Tilman*, by " leaning on Greek drama " and employing " interlocking music " gave " heroic " effects " both as to talent and intention " to battle scenes. Of this opera a commentator writes: " The battlefield an opera ! The trench a scene ! Does this not imply a danger ? " If the excited Nazi can survive the thrills of such " great music drama expressing the soul of our age " he can then go to a moving picture called *Culture and Everyday* which demonstrates that " in the last analysis every film ought to be a cultural film."[29]

Whether this same mixture of pomposity and the *opera bouffe* obtains in the travelling theatres is difficult to say. Apparently, somewhat the same type of production is shown, though there appears to be greater stress on folk plays and subject matter than is the case with the metropolitan theatres. Some 24 of these " wandering theatres " were active in Germany by the middle of 1935, carrying the gospel of National Socialism into villages and outlying hamlets all over the Reich.

The influence of the Community of Culture does not stop with mere sponsoring and management of theatrical productions. According to Künkler, its " theatre division has taken over the sifting of the entire dramatic production of the present time." How extensive its labours have been can be seen from the fact that " in a single year the censor of the Theatre Division tested over 3,000 manuscripts."[30]

The criteria by which manuscripts are judged is indicated clearly by Goebbels. Speaking at a meeting of the heads of the various member chambers of the National Chamber of Culture he said: " The National Socialist state must, on principle, uphold the point of view that *art is free* and that attempts should never be made toward replacing intuition with organisation. *Art as such can only flourish when given the greatest possible freedom of development.* Those who think that they can confine art or civilisation in general within fixed limits are sinning against art and civilisation. When I say ' art is free,' I wish to steer clear of the opinion, on the other hand, as though absolutely anarchical tendencies in art should be given free vent. However free art must and can be within its own laws of evolution, *it must feel itself closely connected with the elemental laws of national life. Art and civilisation are implanted in the mother soil of the nation. They are, consequently, for ever dependent upon the moral, social, and national principles of the state.*"[31]

Art and artists have, in other words, " the spiritual duty " to place themselves " into a *correct angle* with regard to themselves and the people," and to receive " inspiration only from the national character in its totality." That is to say, it must be controlled, root and branch, by the National Socialist *Weltanschauung*, which, as Alfred Rosenberg is very careful to state, expresses " a definite view of the world." Preliminary to adoption of this point of view, he says, it is necessary to " *break the philosophy of democratic levelling. . . .*" Only then will it be possible to " attach once more a direct value to our unbiased eye and therewith to our unspoiled instincts as against the speculative theorems of hollow fancies."[32]

With this same idea of co-ordinating " free art " to obey such National Socialist doctrinal pronouncements, the Community of Culture has established a special youth division known as the

" Culture Community of the Youth." Its duty is ". . . to unify all efforts directed towards the cultural education of the youth. Accordingly it endeavours to harmonise all efforts of school officials, the National Socialist Teachers' Federation, the Labour Service, the Hitler Youth, and other service bureaux in order to achieve the cultural objectives of the youth."[33]

The objective is that " culture shall become an iron strength in the personal life " of the youth, who, with " hearts beating in unison " will be " welded into a voluntary service community which will cut across all formations, occupational groups, and layers of the population." Culture, in short, will become a weapon for co-ordinating the youth to National Socialism through creating " receptivity of the ear, the eye, and the heart for the great master of works of German art." With this receptivity will go, they expect, a willingness to give " voluntary service because of an inner personal sense of duty. . . ." The youth will thereby be " assembled and bound into a cultural works community."

To this end they select those cultural activities for special stress which play most effectively upon youthful love of play, delight in novelty, and sense of humour. Activities promoted include youth theatres and films, puppet theatres, lay and folk plays, holiday celebrations, folk music, and writing competitions. The number of puppet theatres included in this programme is especially extensive, and apparently pretty well attended.

The prize competitions for works written by children indicate somewhat less success. This may be because the competitions are restricted to those with an " unconditionally reliable *Weltanschauung*," must promote National Socialist doctrines in all respects, and are judged solely by officials from the Nazi Party. At any rate, an announcement of such a prize competition in the *Völkischer Beobachter*, official party medium, gave as the reason for the competition being opened that, " despite the large number of new publications there is scarcely an inexpensive manuscript in which *Weltanschauung* questions and the necessities of National Socialist instruction in the schools and in the educational work of the youth associations is handled."[34]

In one other respect the work of the Community of Culture is particularly significant, and that is in connection with the

National Socialist Community Strength through Joy. As will be explained in more detail in subsequent chapters, this organisation has control of all recreational activities of the central control body over labour, the Labour Front. Inasmuch as the purpose of the Labour Front is to " neutralise " anti-employer and pro-trade union sentiment on the one hand, and to " abolish " the class war on the other through " diverting the gaze of the masses from material things and towards the spiritual values of the nation," collaboration here with the central Nazi Party organisation to which is delegated responsibility for all " point-of-view " affairs is of great importance.

A good deal of this work, however, seems to be shrouded in mystery. The Strength through Joy organisation works openly with the Community of Culture in the theatrical field, the latter making a general rule of sponsoring plays being put on in theatres owned by the former. There are a number of such theatres scattered around throughout the larger cities of the Reich. Outside of the theatrical field, little can be told about the exact nature of the co-operation, though it seems clear that the Community of Culture is in close and active contact with the Strength through Joy organisation in all phases of the latter's work with the exception of its excursion and travel programme.

As a final step in explanation of the Nazi programme for the co-ordination of the arts and sciences, mention should be made of the nature of formal governmental control through the Ministries in charge of religious affairs, education, and propaganda.

3. THE THREE PROPAGANDA MINISTRIES

Three Ministries divide the work of regimenting the mental, emotional, and cultural life of all good Germans. Reichsminister Kerrl has charge in the Ministry for Ecclesiastical Affairs of all religious matters. Rust rules all-powerful over the Ministry for Science, Education, and National Culture. And Goebbels has supreme command of the third and central propaganda co-ordinating body, the Ministry for Propaganda and People's Enlightenment.

Either an outline of the functioning of these agencies, or a sketch of the history of controversy leading to present structures and programmes would require a volume in itself. It suffices that the reader clearly understand that the Nazis allow no escape from the conclusion that each agency is to act in its sphere as a policy-centralising and policy-co-ordinating—or *propaganda*—body, and that to this end the power vested by Hitler in them is complete, all-inclusive, and ruthlessly final. A few leading facts will show how unequivocal the power granted is.

In setting up the Ministry for Ecclesiastical Affairs, July 16, 1935, it was emphasised that " Adolf Hitler's Government does not fight against Churches or religious denominations. It rather *gathers them under its wings for protection, whenever they have mental tasks to perform. It rejects materialism and atheist free-thinkers; it did away with secular schools of Marxist character,* thereby declaring unmistakably that it leaves intact an ideological attitude. . . ."[35]

" Protection " here has the same meaning as in " protective " custody, or as in ordinary gangster terminology. It means, be protected or arrested; be protected or dissolved.

Similar statements that the Churches must serve National Socialist ideologies, rejecting materialism and Marxism, are to be found running all through the subsequent literature. And here again the Nazis do not hesitate to brand this control " religious freedom." The argument advanced in the " Law for the Preservation of the German Evangelical Church " is disingenuous to say the least. The " German Government " observed with " profound anxiety " how " *dissensions of Church groups* among and against one another gradually brought about a situation disrupting the unity of the believers, *infringing upon the freedom of faith and conscience of the individual,* hurting the national community, and exposing the very existence of the Evangelical Church to grave dangers."

In order, therefore, to enable the " Church to regulate itself its problems of creed and confession, *in perfect liberty and peace,*" Hitler authorised Kerrl to " *issue legally binding ordinances.*" The first ordinance issued by Kerrl required that he himself establish a " Reich Church Committee consisting of clergymen " all the members of which he would appoint, and which would have power to " issue regulations for *internal* Church affairs " and to " appoint or dismiss the officials of the German Evangelical Church."[36]

A month earlier, in an exchange of greetings with the new Catholic Bishop of Berlin, Konrad Graf von Preysing, Kerrl made clear the basis upon which the Catholic Church was to be tolerated. " If you, Sir, in an unbiased appreciation of the requirements of the present, *cultivate among your clergy and diocesans loyalty to the new State and its Führer* and respect for its authorities, you may rest assured that the German and Prussian Governments will assume full guarantee for freedom of religious exercises and will show complete understanding for the necessities of the Church."[37]

The Church, in short, must support National Socialist principles in all things. It is not to discuss political matters, nor to harbour dissidents. Its activities for young and old must, " in things of the spirit," promote " conviction and fellowship." It is to fight secular and material ideas, Marxism, and all non-German patterns. As will be shown in later chapters, this means fight against " trade unions," " class-war," " liberalism," " representative government," and it means readiness at all times to submit to military service and to work uncomplainingly as ordered by " born "—employer—" leaders " at whatever jobs leaders in communion with " the longing of the people " may determine.

A resolution passed at the pro-Nazi National Conference of German Christians, April 1933, states the case: " God has created me a German. To be a German is a gift from God. God wants me to fight for Germany. War service is never a violation of the Christian conscience; it is obedience to God. The faithful have the right to revolt against a State which promotes the powers of darkness. They have the same right against a Church authority which does not endorse without reservation the National Rising. The State of Adolf Hitler calls for the Church. The Church must heed the call."

As the Church, so must all education fall in line. It is to be no longer " intellectual," but training in " character." " Education," says Alfred Rosenberg, " in the last half-century became a magic means of trickery, unbiological and contrary to all inner laws of race and people. . . . German education will not be formal and æsthetic, it will not strive for an abstract training of reason, but it will be in the first instance an education of character. . . . This cleansing of spirit and instinct, the recovery of the emancipation of the blood, is perhaps the greatest task which the National Socialist movement now has before it."[38]

Presided over by Dr. Rust, the powers of the Ministry for Science, Education, and National Culture are inclusive and absolute. A decree by Hitler of May 11, 1934,[39] gave the Ministry control over the following items:

1. *Sciences:* General affairs in the sciences including relations to foreign countries, physico-technical institute, chemico-technical institute, institute of seismography, nationally important scientific institutions at home and abroad, library science, folk-lore, archæological institute.

2. *Education:* University affairs, student aid, federal leaders of student groups at the *Hochschulen* (colleges and universities) and vocational schools, general school affairs, public schools, technical schools, German schools abroad, foreign schools.

3. *Youth organisations.*

4. *Education of adults.*

How wide the scope of its authority actually is can be seen from its first departmental set-up[40]:

1. Central Office (administration, legislation, foreign countries).

2. Bureau of the Ministry.

3. Department of Science (including *Hochschulen* and research).

4. Department of Education (schools; vocational, agricultural, and social training).

5. Department of Public Education (Academy of Arts; public *Hochschulen*; public libraries; museums and palaces; monuments; conservation of natural scenery, etc.; colleges of music; fine arts; literature and the theatre; cinema and radio).

6. Department of Physical Education (including sections for physical exercise and young people's training).

7. Department of Rural Service.

8. Department of Ecclesiastical Affairs (subsequently made the Ministry for Ecclesiastical Affairs under Kerrl).

All the activities pursued under the ægis of the Ministry are in conformity with Hitler's dicta that " intellect " and " scientific training " are at best of secondary order of importance. In his autobiography he wrote: " The racial state must build up its entire educational work in the first instance not on the pumping in of empty knowledge, but on the development of healthy bodies. Only in the second place comes the training of mental faculties. Here, however, comes first again the development of character, especially the promotion of Will and Decisiveness, united with education toward joy and responsibility, and only last, scientific schooling."[41]

In pursuance of this goal, plans call for reduction of the usual technical subject-matter of the elementary schools by about one-third, new emphasis on purely *national* subjects, establishment of Nazi " character " requirements for admission to the technical schools and universities, and detailed control over faculties and of students of all ages and grades by officially recognised Nazi agencies. The Report of the German Delegation at the Fourth International Education Conference, held in Geneva, August 1935, sets forth the leading ideas of the whole programme. It is worth quoting at some length[42]:

" In the Guiding Principles for School Organisation of December 18, 1933, is a clear explanation of the new plan. The *Leitgedanken,* or " guiding principles," state the question clearly by naming three forces which must work together in the reform of German education. These are the Schools, the Hitler Youth League and the Family. These three institutions are recognised as the natural and indispensable agencies in the education of boys and girls. It will be the endeavour of school reform to guarantee the efficacious working of these three forces.

" The scheme had its first formal expression in the establishment, by decree of October 24, 1934, of the ' School Councils,' to replace the former ' Parents' Councils.' To quote from the decree : ' When Home, School, and Hitler Youth League, each in its own sphere, assume their proper share of responsibility, they will not only be able to co-operate in making a success of the education of the young, but will also be able to watch the progress which is being made by this threefold arrangement.' In order to fix this joint and common responsibility, the School Councils will be composed of parents, teachers, and leaders of the Hitler Youth League. It will be the duty of the Council to act as adviser to the director of the school in all important educational questions.

" The new element in this plan is the part which will be played by the *State through the youth organisations* which have developed out of the ' youth movement ' of former years, but *freed from Marxist influence and religious sectarianism.* The idea is personi- fied in the Hitler Youth,[43] whose basic principle is self-education and self-discipline. . . . By decree of June 7, 1934, Saturday of each week is devoted exclusively to the educational work of the Hitler Youth in all German schools. All boys and girls between ten and fourteen years of age are included in its jurisdiction.

" So far as the schools themselves are concerned, a series of regulations have been put into effect which are distinctly revolutionary in the history of common school education. It is well known that the German Government considers as its fore- most task in the realm of the education of the young to bring the youth of the nation into a proper conception of the relation- ship between the nation and the home, and to cultivate the healthy instincts of mind and body along the most rational lines. To reach this goal it was necessary to make fundamental changes in school routine. It was not enough to do away with the un- natural limiting of the education of the young to theoretical instruction within the four walls of a class-room. Far more important was to *break down the dangerous social barriers between city-bred and country-bred children.*"

The means taken to effectuate this latter programme are twofold. First, to send the elementary boys and girls to the country for a " rural year " in which the " idea is to bring these city children into personal contact with the life and work of the peasants. The method is that of self-management under strict discipline according to the rules of the Land Year Leader."[44] The second plan is that of " sending the boy and girl students of the two upper classes of the high schools for a three weeks' ' national Political ' course of instruction on the farms."

Prominent in the new curriculum are to be biology, race doctrine, and Nazi propaganda: " . . . courses of instruction in biology shall deal primarily with questions of heredity, Mendel's law, the theory of the *survival of the fittest, family history, the heritability of physical and mental traits,* and, in general, ethnology and ethnological hygiene. As subdivisions of this subject, the *distinction between race and nation* and the ethnology of German and other European racial groups are given special attention. The importance of physical exercise and gymnastics, for the development of *will-power and healthy thinking* are recognised in the form of three compulsory gymnastic classes each week. . . . Stress is not so much to be laid on *mere instruction or occupying the mind* of the student, but upon *positive character-building.* In other words, the schools should teach not only how to think but also how to act."

To the same purpose, that of regimenting the " character " to unquestioning acceptance of Nazi political principles, a special decree of March 27, 1935, has established criteria for " Selection of Students for the Higher Institutions of Learning." The decree reads, in part: " The task of these institutions is to train the bodies, the characters, and minds of the young Germans selected, so that they will be fitted later in life to *fill commanding positions* in our political, cultural, and economic national life. It is therefore the duty of such institutions to *separate the unsuitable and unworthy from those more fitted and capable* of advancement and promotion. Constant tests must be made as to physical, moral, mental, and general qualifications."

In these qualifications " character and personality " are the earmarks of " suitability "; " intellect and intellectual capacity " are to play a secondary role. Those denied admission are all who suffer " from an incurable physical ailment, *students who violate the demands of propriety, comradeship, discipline, or integrity*; students whose mental development continues to remain below a certain standard."

The sceptical reader may well ask, " But how choose? " What are the criteria for " character " and " personality," of " propriety " and " integrity " ? The Nazi answer is simple—

" Those of National Socialism as interpreted by the Leaders."
And the answer, of course, is " pure caprice." Since there are no
reliable criteria, no " units of measurement," the Nazis can
select whomsoever they choose and for any reason they may
elect. There is nothing to prevent them from selecting only the
sons of *Junkers* or successful business men. Or, nothing again to
prevent them from selecting boys from peasant households or
working-class families—nothing, that is to say, except the whole
array of *Junker,* business, and military forces which stand
behind, and which guide, control, shape, and use the *movement* !

Programmes similar to these are being put in force for all
vocational, technical, agricultural, and teachers' training
schools. In all cases " training in character building " is to be the
most important single emphasis. That is to say, in all cases the
schools are to be made media for the disseminating of Nazi ideas
on state, race, and people. All else is to be subordinated to
putting across propaganda for the " authoritarian," " totalitarian," " leader " state.

To render still more complete the throttle-hold of the Nazi
Party on the educational system of Germany, students and
faculty are organised into special guilds possessed of extraordinary powers over the conduct of educational affairs.

All pre-existing teachers' organisations have been dissolved to
make way for the National Socialist Teachers' League. As in all
other cases, this body is organised on the Leader Principle in
which all power is vested in the Leader's right to appoint and
dismiss officers at will—a power which lies, in this case, in the
hands of the Minister of Education. The same Minister has withdrawn the right of all universities to appoint their own faculties,
and centred this power in his own office. " Candidates for
professorships no longer have the right to give courses after
passing the *Habilitationsprüfung* (teachers' examinations) and
obtaining the right to teach, but are selected and appointed by
the Minister if they prove to have a clean political record, to
have been active in Nazi political organisations, and to have gone
through the requisite periods of labour service, and, finally, after
being politically quarantined in the newly created *Dozenten-
akademien* (Academies for University Lecturers) for political
training."[45]

An example of what this makes possible is offered by the outline given on p. 112 for a model course in modern history, recommended by the *National Socialist Educator*, the official pedagogical journal of the Third Reich.[46]

The student organisation is possessed of similar powers over student and educational affairs. " To-day the *Deutsche Studentenschaft*—the German Students' Union—comprises all German students of Aryan descent. This . . . organisation is backed by the State. In addition there only exists a special party organisation among the students, the *Nationalsozialistischer Deutscher Studentenbund* (National Socialist Students' League). To it the leadership in matters of a general view of life and of politics is entrusted within the scope of the *Deutsche Studentenschaft*.

Membership in the students' organisation is compulsory. Management of the organisation lies, not in the hands of the membership, but in the hands of the National Socialist Students' League, and control in this League is, of course, directly in the hands of the Nazi Party.[47] It is expected that all members of the League, and the bulk of the members of the Union, will be simultaneously members of the Storm Troops, the Special Guard (S.S., or Special Guard to Hitler), or the Hitler Youth.

The Students' Union is organised into a number of special departments. The office of " science " organises the students professionally according to their main line of interest—theology, law, medicine, history, natural science, etc. Amongst other activities designed to prevent the rise of " any wrong and conceited specialists' spirit," this office arranges vacation " group camps . . . where the students are made acquainted with the requirements of life on the basis of a disciplined camp fellowship. . . ."

A Foreign Department " . . . helps the students to widen their outlook by looking across the frontiers of their own nation and to glance at the national life and national properties of other nations. At the same time it shall draw attention to German nationality on the borders or beyond the borders. For this reason it is subdivided into the Foreign Department, the Borderland Office, and an Eastern Department."

Other offices perform analogous functions. The " Office for Comradeship Training " comprises the younger students and is carried on in " comradeship houses," a new form of common

Weeks	Subject	Relations to the Jews	Reading Material
1.—4.	Pre-war Germany, the Class-War, Profits, Strikes.	The Jew at large !	Hauptmann's *The Weavers.*
5.—8.	From Agrarian to Industrial State. Colonies.	The peasant in the claws of the Jews !	Descriptions of the colonies from Hermann Löns.
9.—12.	Conspiracy against Germany, encirclement, barrage around Germany.	The Jew reigns ! War plots.	Beumelburg: *Barrage ... Life of Hindenburg, Wartime Letters.*
13.—16.	German struggle—German want. Blockade ! Starvation !	The Jew becomes prosperous ! Profit from German want.	Manke: *Espionage at the Front.* War reports.
17.—20.	The Stab in the Back. Collapse.	Jews as leaders of the November insurrection.	Pierre des Granges: *On Secret Service in Enemy Country.* Bruno Brehm: *That was the End.*
21.—24.	Germany's Golgotha. Erzberger's Crimes ! Versailles.	Jews enter Germany from the East. Judah's triumph.	Volkmann: *Revolution over Germany.* Feder: *The Jews.* The *Stürmer* newspaper.
25.—28.	Adolf Hitler. National Socialism.	Judah's foe !	*Mein Kampf.* Dietrich Eckart.
29.—32.	The bleeding frontiers. Enslavement of Germany. The Volunteer Corps. Schlageter.	The Jew profits by Germany's misfortunes. Loans (Dawes, Young).	Beumelburg: *Germany in Chains.* Wehner: *Pilgrimage to Paris.* Schlageter—a German hero.
33.—36.	National Socialism at grips with crime and the underworld.	Jewish instigators of murder. The Jewish press.	Horst Wessel.
37.—40.	Germany's Youth at the Helm ! The Victory of Faith.	The last fight against Judah.	Herbert Norkus. The Reich Party Congress.

student life. The " Labour Service Office " is active in propagandising the Labour Service and the Land Service.[48] " The Press and Propaganda Office shall help the students to find opportunities of working for the German press and as broadcasters."[49]

Serving as a keystone over all these new rigid controls in the educational system designed to regiment the schools on behalf of National Socialist doctrine is the system of " Leader Schools." These are to be found associated with practically every basic line of propaganda activity in the entire Reich. Thus, there are " Leader Schools " for Leaders of the youth, for the Labour Service, for Peasant Girls, for General Political Education, etc. In these schools all pretences at education, as the term is commonly understood, are dropped; they become out-and-out seminaries for indoctrination of Nazi theology—*relevant to the Nazi programme for the particular class of the population for which Leaders are being trained.* The extent of the specialisation carried through in different " Leader Schools " is adjusted entirely to the degree to which it is intended to implement Nazi doctrine for particular sectors of the population. For labour and the peasantry, or for women and other submerged groups, these schools teach Leaders how to keep their followers uncomplainingly to the last. For the *élite* the appropriate schools train Leaders in the tactics of maintaining power over the masses.

A couple of examples will suffice to show how these different " schools " are adjusted to perform their proper functions:

The National Food Estate, central Nazi control body for all agricultural officers, has established six " Leader Schools " for peasant girls. Each school accommodates about 50 students at a time. Here are assembled outstanding peasant girls from ages of fourteen to eighteen, selected from all over the Reich on the basis of general intelligence, purity of race, and political reliability. They are expected to stay for from six months to three years before they return to their home districts, where they are to become supervisors of school activities for peasant women. A typical school, regarded as model by the leaders of the Food Estate and by Adolf Hitler himself—who has visited it in person—is " Trilke-Gut," located at Hildesheim. It has the following curriculum:

Household Economy: Under this heading come all the womanly arts such as: cooking, sewing, spinning, weaving, laundry work. To avoid training the girls away from their environment care is taken that the teaching shall be in accord with the past life and the future expectations of the girls, e.g. in cooking the girls are taught not only on coal-burning stoves, but also to cook with gas and electricity.

Womanly Duties: To be a good wife, mother, and helpmate. Great stress is laid and classes are taught in child-bearing and child-rearing. Along with this goes, of course, teaching in the principles of racial purity and racial degeneration, health, and hygiene.

Practical Farm Management: The girls under the supervision of their teachers run and operate a farm. They tend chickens, turkeys, sheep, cattle, horses, and pigs. They delouse the chickens, slaughter pigs, shear sheep, milk cows, and curry horses. This training is much more detailed and practical than that given to the girls in the Women's Labour Service Camps. Likewise the girls are taught the best ways of keeping milk and eggs fresh, how to make butter and cheese, how to make thread from the wool, etc. Further, they are taught the best ways of handling rudimentary farm tools, such as scythes, hammers, etc.

Social Activities: The girls are taught old folk-songs, peasant costume dances, and are expected upon returning to their villages to become active in formation of all manner of social circles devoted to the life and the good of the community.

The girls are instructed, in short, how to teach the rudiments required in order to become good hard-working peasant women. It is good Nazi doctrine, as will be pointed out in somewhat greater detail in a subsequent chapter devoted to the Nazi programme for women, that women's duties consist of bearing children, waiting upon husband and child, and indoctrinating the child from cradle on with Nazi ideas of " blood and soil," " plough and sword." Woman has no other functions; she cannot possibly be equal with man; she must recognise her station, her duty, her role, and remain contented with that which " nature " has allotted to her. And, as peasant woman, she must orient her eyes to performance of the detailed round of exacting duties on the small petty holding of which she is predestined mistress.

Most of the " Leader Schools " have curricula of a more rarefied character, though always adapted to meet the specific peculiarities of the group addressed. Most important of all are the three new " Leader Schools " for training the future rulers of Germany. In three " castles of the National Socialist order " will be enrolled some 3,000 picked men between the ages of twenty-five and thirty whose training will constitute a sort of Nazified adaptation of Plato's ruler " guardians." " Their training . . . is to be based on an adaptation of the educational principles of the Prussian officers' corps and the Catholic Church. Their mental training will be supervised by the best available teachers in racial research, history, the history of art, philosophy, economics, and sociology, whose soundness in National Socialist dogma has been tested by Alfred Rosenberg, Supervisor-General for Ideological Training of the National Socialist Movement."

They are to listen to lectures on these subjects, hold discussions on the problem of " comradeship " and receive special " training in character, manhood, courage, quickness of decision, and boldness of action." This will be accomplished by sports, dangerous stunts such as parachute jumping and difficult Alpine climbs. In order to better " steel their will and self-control they will be required to abstain for a certain period from alcohol, tobacco, and all other " indulgences " !

It is reported by *Der Angriff* that all those selected will be saved from material worries for the rest of their lives. " They will not be able to gather wealth, but neither will they have to worry about money matters."[50]

These are the chosen youth who, in the words of Hitler, " must be slim and strong, as fast as a greyhound, as tough as leather and as hard as Krupp steel." They will be the perfect product of the Nazi educational system, for their minds will be as fixed and rigid as their bodies are hard. They, and they alone, even as The Leader to-day, will know the difference between right and wrong; only they will know the goal and the paths. " Right," said Rosenberg to the Academy of German Law assembled at Weimar, " is that which Aryan people find right; wrong is that which they reject." "Science," Ley, Nazi Leader of the Labour Front, has added, "is only that which is useful to the people." And to this edifice of doctrine Goebbels adds that propaganda is art.

Speaking on the subject " Art and Propaganda," Dr. Goebbels said: " We have been criticised frequently for degrading German art to the level of mere propaganda. ' Degrade '—how so ? Is propaganda a matter to which anything else can be degraded ? Is not propaganda as we understand it a kind of art ? . . . Would it mean degradation for art, if it were placed side by side with that noble art of mass psychology which was instrumental in saving the Reich from destruction ?"

And it is in the hands of Goebbels that all propaganda activity —through newspapers, periodicals, publishing, the radio, the church, the school, the public forum, and all other media for influencing the mass of the people—is centralised. He is at once National Propaganda Leader for the Nazi Party, Minister of Propaganda and People's Enlightenment on behalf of the Government, and President of the National Chamber of Culture in the name of the arts themselves. In each capacity he wields, subject only to check from Hitler himself, all-inclusive, absolute, and final authority. He has the right to suspend any publication, forbid the performance of any play, deny the privilege of utterance over the radio or through any medium to any person, close down any school, institute, or museum, and punish any person for any real or imaginary offence if and when he pleases. He appoints all officials under him, and delegates to them the type of authority he wields over all.

He can issue decrees at will, and rescind those previously issued at his pleasure. He need not in any wise or at any time observe any " due process of law " except as he may please. And nothing in Germany has any chance of escaping his drag-net. The Ministry is divided into nine main departments—Administration and Law, Propaganda, Radio, Press, Film, Theatre, Defence, Writing, Music and the Plastic Arts. Each department has complete and final control over all activities falling into its bailiwick. And each of them is represented in the 31 regional offices of the Ministry.

Likewise under his immediate direction comes publication of the official Nazi newspaper, the *Völkischer Beobachter* (Alfred

Rosenberg as editor), and 310 other newspapers scattered throughout all sections of the country and reaching into every nook and cranny of the Reich. Through the Advertising Council of German Economy he has control over all advertising and public relations activities. Through the German University for Politics he controls the present central " leader " training school. And finally, as indicated above, through the National Chamber of Culture, and its allied associations, leagues, and guilds, he has complete authority over all the audible, vocal, and visual arts.

As supreme co-ordinator of all attitude-shaping and opinion-forming activities, this immense, complicated, and meticulously organised machinery serves Goebbels in two capacities. In the first place, it is an elaborate and apparently very effective intelligence service, whereby he is enabled to keep in close and constant touch with all expressions of opinion and all changes in popular moods, whether these centre around large national problems, or whether they are focused on minutiæ of administrative routine in the most out-of-way corner of the Reich. " We wish," he said on one occasion, " to put our ears to the soul of the people." And now he has at his beck and call means for catching every modulation of tone, every murmur of dissent.

But scanning the popular mood is only preliminary to constant readjustment of the propaganda for conquest. The second function of the machinery at the call of the Ministry for Propaganda and People's Enlightenment is to put over the Nazi ideology —to put it over with every class, every group, every interest. As the group varies, and the class interests change, so must the propaganda be modulated, fitted, and adjusted. If possible, it must be made palatable to all. But—and on this point Goebbels, as with all other Nazi leaders, is perfectly candid—it must be accepted by each and every man, woman, and child, whether the means be force or guile.

Just what is Goebbels, chief propaganda and public relations director of a capitalist-militarist state, attempting to put across with the German people ? What is his principal concern ? Wherein lies the heart of his doctrine and the core of his attack ? Who most needs to be convinced, and for what purposes ? What does his " ear," as he places it to hear the responses emanating from " the soul of the people," tell him it is important to do ?

A veritable mountain of Nazi literature on ideology prevents all possible equivocation in reply. The new state stresses " the folk," the " community," " comradeship," " communal labour," " unity." As pointed out above, and as will be detailed at some length in subsequent chapters, these are slogans designed to give a pleasant front to the drive against " class war," " Marxists," " trade unions," " internationalism." As Ley, Leader of the Labour Front, expressed it on one occasion, the chief concern of the National Socialist Party was " the struggle for the worker's soul." Organised labour, and all groups or interests antagonistic to business capital, are to be crushed completely, finally, ruthlessly, and at all costs.

Goebbels's activities constitute the German answer to the current drive of business men all over the world—to prevent the drift towards the left by neutralising or crushing all organised dissident opinion and all organised opposition activity. The labour programme of the National Association of Manufacturers (U.S.A.) and the " spirit " of such as the New Deal, of the Oxford Movement, of the Nazi *Weltanschauung*, the novel *Eyeless in Gaza* (Aldous Huxley) and the *A New Nobility out of Blood and Soil* (Darré—in German), spring from the same basic set of drives, and are actuated by the same common goals. To deny division of interest; to circumvent or crush those who believe or act upon such assumptions; to argue, wheedle, entice, and cajole if these methods are effective, but if necessary to use unrestrained force—these are the defensive manœuvres set in motion throughout the capitalistic world to-day by the ever-widening forces of social unrest.

The crux of the Nazi programme for the sciences and the arts —as, indeed, of all Nazi programmes, civil and military, domestic and foreign—is to be found in their " struggle for the worker's soul."

CHAPTER IV

Labour Must Follow Where Capital Leads[1]

IN the National Socialist State, " the German Labourer will be the mainstay because he is *susceptible to that feeling of faith and confidence* which does not always think that it should use the probe of personal opinion, but *which consecrates itself to an idea in blind faith and obedience.*"[2] This " idea " is the National Socialist *Weltanschauung*, in which the " leader principle " dominates all forms of social organisation according to the rule, borrowed from the experience of the Prussian Army, " *authority of every leader downwards and responsibility upwards.*"[3] " Decisions are made by one Man," the Leader. The Leader in industry is the employer, and is responsible for making decisions " in all matters affecting the establishment,"[4] which he owns and operates as " an administrator of public property."[5] In this capacity, " this is the foremost and fundamental requirement for the employer: always use your capital in such a way as to *make it yield profits corresponding to the necessities of national business.*"[6]

In order to make profits without interference from labour, it was necessary to " co-ordinate spirit " to the Nazi *Weltanschauung*. This required a double-edged programme. First destroy the trade unions, eliminate class war, and " neutralise " all opposition to the employers—destroy, in short, " Marxism " and " Communism." Second, see that the " gaze of the masses was diverted from the material to the ideal values of the nation." The first was designed to prevent sabotage of the employers' interests, the second to take advantage of one of the most interesting scientific discoveries of the modern age—that noncommercial incentives promote labour efficiency more effectively than do commercial.

1. DESTROY MARXISM

" Marxism " is used by German employers and the Nazis in exactly the same fashion as " red " in the United States. By it are meant trade unions, the principle of collective bargaining, class warfare, strikes and lock-outs, all enemy political parties, the old co-operative societies, and any other group or idea in any wise opposed to the Nazi point of view. " Owing to economic and political developments, the idea of class warfare had become a firmly established dogma in Germany. Not only did the workers believe in this Marxist doctrine, but even the bourgeoisie adopted the idea of class warfare as a guiding principle in their doings and thoughts. The division into classes was considered to be a divine institution, and it was therefore considered perfectly right to form alliances of people with common interests and to organise them in order to render their interests effective."[7]

" The old pre-revolutionary " (before Marx !) trade unions served a useful historical purpose in protecting labour rights from " the blind arbitrariness of certain individuals."[8] But this useful aim was perverted, according to the Nazis, by Jewish and alien influences. Speaking of the old Social Democratic Party, for example, an official commentator writes, " That the party dogmas, in the main, were represented by Jewish intellectuals, as against the Trade Union Leaders who had emanated from the ranks of the German Workers—at least, as far as the older generation was concerned—and that, with the increasing influence of the Jewish Academics in the Trade Union Movement, whose best men sometimes—unfortunately without telling success—attempted to resist the foreign influences, the Marxist and political destruction progressed, is a fact which should not be forgotten in a retro-active consideration of the social history of Germany, and which contributes essentially towards an understanding of the fundamental conflict between National Socialism and the social system hitherto prevailing in Germany." The trade unions " had been betrayed by Marxian principles and alien Social Democratic leaders." Since " it was impossible to fit infected organs into the new social body " it was necessary, say the Nazis, to " declare war against the Marxist Trade Union, not only as an organisation, but, above all, as an idea."[9]

To destroy Marxism as an " idea " the Labour Front was established under the wing of the Nazi Party, not with the functions of deciding " the material questions of daily labour life," but with the " high aim " of " educating all Germans active in labour life to the National Socialist State and to the

National Socialist Doctrines."[10] That is to say, upon the ruins
of the former trade unions, the Communist and Social Democratic parties (and following the formal liquidation of the
Employers' Associations),[11] a " positive " programme ideally
adapted to the needs of German business enterprise was to be
erected. This programme, identical in detail and at large with
American " Welfare Capitalism,"[12] seeks the maximum :

2. EXPLOITATION OF NON-COMMERCIAL INCENTIVES

Social philosophers, anthropologists, and reformers have long
held that " man does not work for bread alone." But only
recently has industry learned that significant as hours, wages,
and other conditions of employment may be, they do not of
themselves call out the highest levels of labour productivity.
Given the minimum on these grounds, non-commercial are far
more potent than commercial incentives. All those factors that
combine to give the " sense of workmanship," of group participation, of unfolding creative power, fall into the non-commercial
class. Interest and emotional drives lead to higher and better
sustained levels of output than can be provided by mere wage
and hour considerations. With non-commercial incentives
fatigue is lowered, improvements in processes and methods are
more easily introduced, and friction between management and
men is reduced to a minimum.

The Nazis were not the first to make this " discovery "—
more accurately, " rediscovery." Dawning realisation of the
possibilities inherent in non-commercial incentives lies behind
the elaborate and varied programmes of " welfare capitalism "
found in all the western industrial countries. It provides the
principal drive behind the rapidly proliferating psycho-technical
research institutes, personnel selection and training systems,
occupational conferences, bureaux and committees, industrial
and public relations counsellors. Pioneering work in this field
has been done by the world famous British Institute of Industrial
Psychology, Moede's laboratory at the Technische Hochschule
at Charlottenburg, the German Institute for Technical Education and Training (D.I.N.T.A.), and many others. In America the
Industrial Relations Counsellors, the National Occupational

Conference, and the Personnel Research Federation are merely the leading organisations in this field.

Many of the largest corporations in the world have been applying these techniques on a large scale for many years. Outstanding examples are the National Railways and the Dye Trust in Germany, and the Western Electric and the Goodyear Tire & Rubber Company in America. The " Hawthorne Experiments," carried out in one of the largest plants of the Western Electric, for example, provide both the experimental results and the argument for a position with respect to organised labour identical with that held by the leader of the German Labour Front. Labour, if interested and made to feel important, would work harder without demanding more pay.

A publication of the British Institute of Industrial Psychology, *The Problem of Incentives in Industry*, lists, among the exploitable non-commercial incentives, the following: Interest and Pride in the Work, the Incentive of Appreciation, the Incentive of Knowledge, the Incentive of Loyalty, the Incentive of Welfare Schemes, Interest in the Firm, Encouragement of Suggestions, Co-operation in Time Study, and the Incentive of Efficiency.[13] Experimentation with and study of the working effects of such incentives has shown, step by step, the preponderating importance on the worker's whole attitude towards life. It is an American, not a Nazi, author, who penned the following lines in one of the most significant books of the past decade dealing with social-economic problems: " To study a subject merely as the doer of a particular piece of work is of little value; the work to the worker is part of a whole, made up of his numerous reactions to situations, real and ideal, over and above his work. Sometimes it is the phantasy life that is of more importance to the individual than the apparent real life. It is clearly impossible to obtain a thorough knowledge of anyone, but *it has proved possible to get the point of view of a subject with sufficient clearness to yield an insight into the relation of the work he does to his general attitude to life.*"[14] (Italics in original.)

The author of the above lines was thinking of the Hawthorne Experiments as he wrote. At Hawthorne and other places it has been demonstrated that cleverly introduced non-commercial incentive schemes will bring increases in labour productivity of 50 per cent and more per worker without appreciable increase in fatigue—and, of course, without corresponding increase in pay.[15] Uniformly these schemes are tied up with the worker's " attitude towards life," his willingness and interest in work for larger ends, his social and cultural values. Intelligent investigators have come quickly to see that these factors are interwoven with the whole economic and social systems of our times, and that, hence, capitalism, socialism, and communism are up for review not only in their larger bearing on problems of equality and human rights, but also with respect to their direct bearing on the homely problems of high man-hour productivity.[16]

Here as elsewhere it is realised that productivity is connected by a thousand intimate bonds with the problem of the " attitude to life," the *Weltanschauung*, the social philosophy of the individual workman. Doctrine, purpose, and policies are intertwined as the efficiency fundamentals of the human factor just as rigidly as power, connecting belts, and organisation are key to the efficient functioning of machines. As Mooney and Reiley have put it, where " spirit is co-ordinated . . . the man who is permeated with . . . doctrine invariably sees everything, the hard causes as well as the small matters, in their relation to the whole . . . "[17] and, because he sees, agrees, and supports, he will work harder and produce more.

Control over the inner life of the worker leads by slow degrees to control over the entire culture—the worker's entire intellectual and emotional environment, the sciences and the arts. Once begun there is no turning back. Since philosophy of life is at stake, the underlying tenets of the economic system are being weighed in the balance. The Communists teach that only those who produce should govern, and, since none except the weak and the disabled should live from the labour of others, the ideal is a classless society of producer-users. The Nazis seek to prove that the existence of separate and distinct social classes is not only indispensable but the necessary law of life and social organisation. To prove their point they resort to arguments not unlike those advanced by the ancient Greek philosopher Plato. And like Plato they propose a socially stratified society, governed from on top, in which each belongs to that class allotted to him by virtue of his " natural " gifts and capacities, and in which complete harmony obtains so long as the point of view of each and every man in each and every class is controlled through appropriate education and propaganda.

The Nazi position boils down to this: How far can the " co-ordination of spirit " be used for the fullest possible exploitation of the working capacities of the German population on behalf of the business enterprise—the " works community " ? How far can this exploitation be carried without giving rise to revolt, without causing labour to resort to strikes and sabotage ? How far can labour opposition, labour class interests—and of the existence of these interests there is not the slightest question in any of the literature—be " neutralised " on behalf of " service to the public " by " self-governed " business ?

The Labour Front is the Nazi answer.

3. ORGANISATION OF THE LABOUR FRONT

In order to see that all officials, major and minor, of the Labour Front should be " permanent, fanatical, idealistic preachers of National Socialism,"[18] the Labour Front was placed under the direct supervision of the National Socialist Party, and its organisation patterned very closely after that of its spiritual parent. The identification between the two is practically complete. As Ley, Leader of the Labour Front, stated in an address to the foreign newspaper reporters following the Leipzig Agreement,[19] " . . . the management of the Labour Front is in the hands of the National Socialist German Labour Party . . . as regards its structure and its regional divisions " and " as regards organisation and personnel, but especially as regards policy."[20]

Ley himself is simultaneously Organisation Leader of the Nazi Party and National Leader of the Labour Front. The thirty-three regional offices, as well as the district, local, and cell offices of the two organisations are in the same places, and in each the leader of the Party office is *ex officio* Leader in the Labour Front office. Groups one to sixteen of the National Business Community (see Chart II at end of book) are " entrusted " to the National Socialist Business Cell Organisation (N.S.B.O.), which is Main Office 5 of the Nazi Party. Groups 17 and 18 correspondingly belong to Main Office 6, known as the National Socialist Commerce, Handicraft, and Trades Organisation (N.S.-Hago). The various national offices of the Labour Front dealing with the youth, vocational education, women, legal advice, and so on, are under the direct control and administration of the corresponding offices in the Nazi Party.

Party members and Party organisation, then, dominate the Labour Front. As Party members they are organised in Business Cells, Local Groups, and Districts. The Business or Works Cell is " built up on the principle that the most reliable and keen party men in each firm employing over 20 hands shall be formed into a cell which will primarily do political proselytising and educational work among the men, but will also see that the whole concern is run in a true National Socialist Spirit."[21] The national organisations (N.S.B.O. and N.S.-Hago) are set up along industrial lines and serve to co-ordinate Party work within each and amongst the several main branches of economic activity. They are built up on the usual " group principle." " A given number of cells in firms form a local group under a leader (Ortsgruppenbetriebswart) with a fairly elaborate staff consisting of propaganda, personnel, organisation, training and legal sections and a technical section to advise on the provision of work. The local group leader reports to a district leader (Kreisbetriebszellenobmann), and he in turn to the provincial leader (Gaubetriebszellenobmann); above them are the leaders of the areas corresponding more or less to the States (Landesobmänner) who are in direct touch with the N.S.B.O. chief office at Party headquarters. Each of the leaders has a staff similar to that of the local leader."[22]

While all the offices and all the functions of the Labour Front are under the direct control of the Nazi Party, the membership of the Front itself is represented to include practically all economically active persons and organisations. It includes on the " basis of equal rank the members of all the previous trade unions, the previous salaried workers' associations, and the previous employers' associations."[23] As " corporative members " it includes the National Economic Chamber, the National Food Estate, the National Transport Industry, and the National Chamber of Culture.

Formally individual membership is voluntary, in reality it is practically compulsory. Membership for employers is made " a matter of honour," and for the workers a solemn " duty." Employers are encouraged, though not compelled, to employ only members of the Labour Front—a provision which seems somewhat superfluous in view of the fact that all workmen are regarded as automatically members of the " works communities " in which they are employed, and that these are the units of organisation in the Labour Front !

The Front is organised along' three different lines, regional, along trade and industrial lines (or vertically), and by professional affiliation. The regional organisation is similar throughout to that described above for the Nazi Party. The sole difference lies in the units of organisation. While the Party Cell is made up solely of trusted Party members, the " works unit " includes the employer and all employees.

This regional division, on the works unit, " is paralleled by a vertical division—trade and industrial—into works communities. In accordance with their economic structure there have been organised eighteen Reich works communities." They are (see Chart II at end of book):

Food and luxuries (tobacco, beverages, etc.)
Textiles
Clothing
Construction
Timber
Metals
Printing
Paper
Chemistry

Traffic and public utilities
Mining
Banks and insurance
Free vocations (physicians, lawyers, etc.)
Agriculture
Leather
Masonry and excavation
Commerce
Handicrafts

Finally it is possible for the members of the Labour Front to organise along professional or occupational lines on any of the different regional levels from the national groups down to the local units.

As indicated by the chart, each of the National Business Communities is divided into 17 offices, presided over by a Leader appointed on the direct instance of the Leader of the

Organisation Office. Each of these offices is to be found again for each of 18 works communities in each of the 33 provincial offices. In the main the title of the separate offices is self-explanatory. Thus the Press Office has control over all Labour Front publications, the Propaganda Office over all propaganda and demonstrations, the Youth Office over all relations between the Labour Front and Youth organisations, the Women's Office over all female labour, etc.

Parallel to the Organisation Office are the Personnel Office, the Treasury Office, and the National Socialist Community, Strength through Joy. The first handles matters pertaining to the selection of all officials of the Labour Front, the second all financial details and the third " co-ordinates " all leisure time, vacation, and after-work activities of worker members.

Several special features of this complex organisation require some elaboration in order to properly understand where the line can be drawn between the inconsequential and the significant. Of more than usual interest are the Council of Trusted Men, the Trustees of Labour, the Honour Courts, the Leipzig Agreement, and Strength through Joy.

4. THE COUNCIL OF TRUSTED MEN (" VERTRAUENSRAT ") OF THE
WORKS COMMUNITY

" The lowest, but also the *most important rung* of the social political structure is the individual enterprise and the individual management. The labour constitution proceeds directly from the nature-given, destiny-determined community in the enterprise, the works community, in which the entrepreneur as the *born leader of the enterprise* is bound together with his workers and employees, the followers, in a community of work ' for the promotion of business purposes and the common service of people and state.' "24

The " works community " is made up of Leader (employer) and Followers (workers). The Leader has absolute authority in the conduct of all affairs in his enterprise so far as these do not contravene law. " *The Leader of the enterprise makes decisions over against the Followers in all affairs relating to the business, in particular over the fixing of all labour conditions.*" It is difficult to conceive how far-reaching these powers handed over to the employers are. Krause goes on to say, " Out of the entrepreneur's sole right of making decisions it follows that he alone must determine the general labour conditions and the wages to be paid in his business. He is called upon in the first instance, in full view of the economic and social conditions of his business, to *determine the just wage,* and in this connection to decide what individual efforts, corresponding to efficiency principles, must be especially rewarded. In individual cases the establishment of working conditions follows immediately upon conclusion of the labour contract. For larger businesses and managements, employing as a rule 20 (or more) workers and salaried people, the Leader of the enterprise must, following consultation with the Council of Trusted Men, issue *Works Ordinances* in which the wage level and miscellaneous working conditions are regulated. Compliance with these are legally binding as minimum conditions upon all members of the enterprise."

The Council of Trusted Men referred to is the Nazi substitute for the old trade union Factory Committee. It is regarded as one of the most significant of the Nazi inventions, and the one which perhaps best expresses their idea of how to give voice " to the will of the people." In effect it is an employer-designated committee of especially trusted workmen whose duty it is to explain and interpret to the workers the will of the " Leader," and to convey to the Leader, for his consideration, complaints made by the Followers.

It is set up in this fashion: from a list of trusted workmen who are members in good standing of the Nazi Party, and in consultation with the Leader of the Nazi Works Cell, the employer selects a panel of names which he submits to the workers for ratification. The panel is accepted or rejected as a whole. If rejected a new list may be drawn up, but by the same method. The panel ratified becomes the Council of Trusted Men, holding office at the pleasure of the business Leader, and responsible directly to him. Every member of the Council has an alternate who is authorised to act in event of his absence or temporary incapacity.

As indicated above, " the Council of Trusted Men is the Trust Intermediary between the Leader of the Business and his followers.[25] Its foremost task is the deepening of mutual ' trust ' within the works community." Employer " trusts " labour to work hard and not complain; labour " trusts " the employer to " care for the welfare of his Followers."[26]

Their functions are, however, purely advisory. " As in every community so also in the business there can be only one Leader; only he can make decisions and he alone is responsible for economic and social affairs. . . . The *Leader of the enterprise alone makes the decisions.* Only for advice on his decisions does he call to his aid the Trusted Men, but these cannot, however, take away from him the sole responsibility for his decisions. The Trusted Men are not to proceed from any special interest, but are duty-bound to place the common interests in the foreground. They dedicate themselves, consequently, to serve in their offices only the good of the business and the community while holding back individual interests. *The interests of the followers must be placed behind the interests of the business community, and be brought into conformity with the economic requirements of the business.*

" Every member of the Council of Trusted Men has the duty to *mitigate the sharpness of the natural conflict of interests within the enterprise, set aside every mistrust, and arouse appreciation for the decisions of* the business leader amongst the followers."[27]

As the above official pronouncement makes clear, division of interest is not denied. Ley, in fact, goes so far as to say " that we cannot get rid of the divergence of interests, nor do we wish to do so." The Labour Front is nothing more than the " honest broker between the contending parties." The worker has the right to demand recompense for his accomplishments, " and in the same way *the employer who cannot sanction these demands ought to have enough backbone to reject them.*"[28] But if the Council of Trusted Men performs properly, the business leader will be able to make his decisions " only after gaining exact knowledge of the atmosphere of his business and the sentiments of his followers." Thus will the " partnership of capital and labour " be assured, industrial harmony be made to prevail, and the employer allowed to " serve the public " in compliance with the doctrines of the Labour Front, " advocate of the people."[29]

In this felicitous state, Ley proudly announced: " Leader and followers shall be enclosed in a band of mutual loyalty and

Ef

comradeship. *The leader need not be lenient to his followers as regards unjustified or impracticable wishes,* and *the followers do not by any means exhaust their loyal duties in a renunciation of their claims* and of the representation of their particular social requirements. If conditions in the establishment, or higher economic considerations should demand it, then the leader should also be firm and the followers must then acquiesce to a just refusal of their wishes."[30]

Should disputes arise, however, general principles and machinery exist for their solution. Factory Ordinances must comply with general principles laid down by the Trustees of Labour for the District (see pp. 131–32 following). These relate primarily to hiring and firing. For example, before discharging workers who have been in service a year or more the employer must give notice. Failure to do so may result in fines being levied by the Trustees of Labour (see p. 134 following) up to one year's wages.[31] Other rules relate to " mass discharge " of workers, it being provided that where the plant is over a certain size more than a certain percentage of total staff cannot be discharged without giving notice to the Labour Trustees in writing.

Here as elsewhere the whole machinery redounds primarily to the advantage of the employer. Every effort is made to cut down labour turnover. In later chapters various methods for achieving this effect will be discussed. But the Labour Front has not been content with programmes for attaching workers to a given plot of ground, and hence to a particular employer, nor with an absolute prohibition against strikes of all kinds. These it heartily endorses, but it goes even further.

It goes so far, for example, as to declare workers who leave agricultural employment during the crop season *saboteurs* and unworthy of German citizenship. It warns all that " to gather well and surely the harvest is your foremost and weightiest task. Whoever neglects this duty and leaves his position with the farmer without due warning in order to go into industry is a *saboteur*, and must be excluded from the community of the German people. . . ."[32] There are other and more direct punitive measures: " A labourer who gives up his work place without important or justified grounds or who has lost his position through a situation which justified his immediate discharge can

receive as a rule no unemployment subsidy for six weeks. . . ."
Simultaneously, he may be "locked out" from his place of
last, and all other, employment until such time as he can submit
proof of the reasons for losing the first job.[33]

Disputes which arise are taken care of by arbitration machinery set up under the Trustees of Labour and by judicial process
in the so-called "Social Honour Courts."

5. THE TRUSTEES OF LABOUR

According to the Act for the Organisation of Labour, arbitration officials known as "Labour Trustees (*Treuhänder der
Arbeit*) shall be appointed for large economic areas, the boundaries of which shall be fixed by the Federal Minister of Labour
in agreement with the Federal Minister of Economic Affairs and
the Federal Minister of the Interior. They shall be Federal
Officials and shall be under the service supervision of the
Federal Minister of Labour. The Federal Minister of Labour in
agreement with the Federal Minister of Economic Affairs shall
fix their headquarters." Accordingly 14 such Labour Trustee
Districts have been established as follows (headquarters in
parentheses):

East Prussia (Königsberg in Prussia)
Silesia (Breslau); branch office in Gleiwitz
Brandenburg (Berlin)
Pomerania (Stettin)
North Mark (Hamburg)
Lower Saxony (Hanover); branch office: Bremen West-
phalia (Essen)
Rhineland (Cologne)
Hessia (Frankfurt on the Main); branch office: Kassel
Middle Germany (Magdeburg); branch office: Weimar
Saxony (Dresden)
Bavaria (Munich); branch office: Nuremberg
South-West Germany (Karlsruhe); branch office: Stuttgart
Saar-Palatinate (Saarbrucken); branch office: Neustadt

Each Labour Trustee may appoint as many Deputy Trustees
as circumstances may seem to require—when the amount of

work to be disposed of and the size of the area are too great to be handled from a single office. Deputies may also be appointed for special areas, special districts, separate branches of industry, and for the performance of a special piece of work. At his discretion the Labour Minister may appoint Special Trustees of Labour when a " tariff ordinance affects more than the given Labour Trustee District," i.e. when the wage agreement affects the Reich. Similarly he may appoint Special Trustees for cases falling out of the usual business line. Such appointments have been made for domestic labour and for employees in the public service.

The Labour Trustee, usually a trusted Party member, is, according to the Leader Principle, complete master of all affairs coming under his jurisdiction. He has, however, two advisory bodies at his disposal.³⁴ (1) " Every Trustee of Labour must call together a Council of Experts to give him advice on general and fundamental questions concerning the conduct of his duties. The Council is made up of sworn-in experts drawn from the various economic branches of the Trustee District. Three-fourths of the Experts must be taken from a list submitted by the German Labour Front, and must be, in the first instance, members of Council of Trusted Men in individual enterprises in the Trustee District." (2)³⁵ For special questions he may call together a Committee of Experts. This action is compulsory whenever the Labour Trustee must issue an ordinance concerning wage scales. Experts are not supposed to represent any particular group and " are bound by oath to exercise their office as non-partisan experts, renounce their own special interests, and serve only the good of the community."

The law provides that " the labour trustees shall ensure the maintenance of industrial peace. In order to achieve this task, they shall take the following action:

" 1. They shall supervise the formation and operation of the confidential councils (Councils of Trusted Men) and give decisions where disputes occur.

" 2. They shall appoint confidential men for establishments and remove them from office in accordance with subsection (2) of Sec. 9, subsection (2) of Sec. 14, and Sec. 15. (Sec. 9,

Followers fail to approve list; Sec. 14, Labour Trustee thinks the Confidential Council Man unsuitable ' in circumstance or person '; Sec. 15, the Labour Trustee appoints new confidential men when no more substitutes are available).

" 3. They shall decide respecting appeals from confidential councils in accordance with Sec. 16. (Sec. 16 reads: ' A majority of the confidential council of an establishment may lodge an appeal in writing with the labour trustee without delay against any decision of the leader of the establishment respecting the formulation of the general conditions of employment, and in particular respecting the establishment rules, if the said decision appears incompatible with the economic or social situation of the establishment '); they may quash the decision of the leader of the establishment and themselves issue the necessary ruling.

" 4. They shall decide respecting proposed dismissals (in accordance with provisions regarding ' mass dismissals ').

" 5. They shall supervise the observance of the provisions respecting the establishment rules.   .

" 6. They shall lay down principles and collective rules under the conditions specified in Sec. 32 (relating to general guiding rules for fixing wage schedules), and supervise their observance.

" 7. They shall co-operate in the exercise of jurisdiction by the social honour courts.

" 8. They shall keep the Federal Government supplied with information respecting social progress, in accordance with detailed instructions issued by the Federal Minister of Labour and the Federal Minister of Economic Affairs."[36]

In reality these powers, elaborate as they appear thus summarised, are three in character. In the first place, the Trustee is supposed to co-operate with the employer in all labour troubles in the factory. He is not supposed in any wise to interfere with the conduct of business as usual. All this is left entirely to the discretion of the employer. The employer signs an individual wage contract with each employee. Only under unusual circumstances is this wage contract subject to review. The same holds for methods of wage payments such as piece-rate systems. While

Ley was excoriating " the piece-work system of the present
day " as " the most shameful that mankind has ever invented "[37]
he was upholding a law in which the employer is given full
legal authority to lay down " establishment rules " which
determine:

" 1. The beginning and ending of the normal daily hours of
work and of the breaks;

" 2. The times for the payment of remuneration and the
nature thereof;

" 3. The principles for the calculation of jobbing or bargain
work, if work is done on a job or bargain basis in the establishment;

" 4. Regulations for the nature, amount and collection of
fines if provision is made for them;

" 5. The grounds on which an employment can be termin-
ated without notice, in cases where this does not rest upon
statutory grounds;

" 6. The utilisation of remuneration forfeited by the un-
lawful termination of an employment, in cases where the said
forfeiture is prescribed in the establishment rules or contract
of employment or statutory provisions."[38]

Never, in all the bitter annals of labour conflict—including
that period of hitherto unparalleled and ruthless brutality known
as the beginning of the English Factory System—never could
the most cynical and inhuman employer have asked more from
the state than this. He is by law here granted complete control
" respecting the discipline of the establishment and the conduct
of employees "—provisions which go so far as to confer on the
employer the right to assess fines and punishments for violation
of " discipline " up to the point of confiscation of wages of
employees discharged for violations in the judgment of which he
sits alone.

Even in laying down the general guiding principles for the
issuance of " establishment rules " by the employer, the Labour
Trustees do not circumvent his real power. The employer is
allowed to ignore these whenever in his judgment " carrying
through of these principles is not possible, considering the

economic and social conditions of his business " and if it is his opinion that compliance therewith would " damage the followers."[39] While the Labour Trustees possess formal legal authority to investigate these conditions, in actuality nothing of the sort occurs except where abuses are so flagrant as to border on public scandal.

The second power or function of the Labour Trustees is to supply current data to the Nazi Party and its spiritual double, the Labour Front, with information concerning the state of labour unrest. This intelligence and spy function it apparently performs in close collaboration with the secret police and the Party " Cell " Organisations. For example, the Nazi factory cells in the Rhine area have each month to fill out a *questionnaire* which asks, amongst others, the following questions:

" (3) How many (among employees) are convinced believers in our philosophy ? "

" (5) What is the attitude of former opponents ?

" (6) How many workers in your factory understand the steps taken by the State ?

" (7) How many workers agree to the measures taken by the State ?

" (8) What are the main arguments against these steps ?

" (9) Who criticises ? Marxists ? Centre Party ? Others ? "

" (11) What does not suit the workers in your factory ?

" (12) What theme should be especially handled (without discussion) at factory meetings ? "

" (15) Can you show successes in political and instructional training ? "

" (19) What are the relations between Factory Leader and followers ? "

" (22) What steps are being taken to establish ' Beauty of Labour ' ? "

As Braun remarks in his book, *Fascism: Make or Break ?*, " Not one question concerning wages, hours or other working conditions appears in this comprehensive *questionnaire*." These matters are presumed to lie entirely within the proper authority of the employer.

Finally, the Labour Trustee acts as a prosecuting attorney in cases where labour disputes are carried to the Labour or Social Honour Courts. The procedure is roughly as follows: Either an employer or an employee complains of violation of agreements which require legal action or which constitute a breach of Labour Honour. Complaints from employers are apparently made directly to the Labour Trustee. Complaints from workers go first to the Council of Trusted Men. In the latter case, the Council acts as an intermediary between the individual workman and the employer. If disputes cannot be settled directly, they are then remanded to the consideration of the Labour Trustee and by him to the appropriate court.

These disputes may centre around any issue involving conditions of payment and employment. The Labour Trustees are bound by certain general principles. In the first place they are not supposed to interfere with the employer's decisions except in cases apt to involve an issue of Labour Law. The employer is, despite Nazi protestations to the contrary, in all affairs significant for the conduct of normal profit-seeking business, *Herr im Hause* (Lord of the House). However, he is not supposed to cut pre-existing wage *rates* without show of cause to the Labour Trustees. In practice it has been done, though advance in the cost of living has made this dangerous procedure. By the same token, he is not supposed to raise wage rates so long as there is a supply of unemployed labour.[40]

Certain special powers exercised by the Labour Trustees are particularly interesting. Amongst these is the authority to decrease the higher wage rates of older employees in order to prevent " discrimination " against them in favour of younger workers because of such rates. A somewhat similar rule holds with respect to female labour. The number of women in all employments is falling rapidly under pressure to exclude them from all business and industrial employments and to compel them to return to take up their natural " household duties " as wives, mothers, and servants to the men.

However, women are typically paid less for doing the same work. The Nazi solution is not to pay the women the same amount for the same work, but to substitute male for female labour only where wage conditions allow. However, for

" determinate periods of working time a lower wage can be paid," hence the substitution is going forward rapidly !

Finally, the Labour Trustee can *set upper limits* to the amount which can be paid relief labour. " He can, for example, determine that wage payments shall not exceed a given percentage of the relevant basic wage rate; he can also decide what wage scales shall be regarded as basic." If he so decides, " he may announce that another than the wage schedule customary in the given locality be employed " for this purpose.[41]

6. THE SOCIAL HONOUR COURTS

" For every District and at the headquarters of each Trustee of Labour an Honour Court has been set up, made up of a member of the judiciary as chairman, and a Leader of a business, a Trusted Man, and an assistant judge. The assistant judge is named to office by the German Labour Front." Appeals from the decision of district courts can be made to the highest Court of Honour, instance the National Honour Court in Berlin, made up of five persons.[42] The function of these courts is to deal with offences against " social honour." " Such offences shall be deemed to have been committed in the following cases:

" 1. When the owner of an undertaking, the leader of an establishment or any other person in a position of supervision abuses his authority in the establishment by maliciously exploiting the labour of any of his followers or wounding their sense of honour;

" 2. When a follower endangers industrial peace in the establishment by maliciously provoking other followers, and in particular when a confidential man wittingly interferes unduly in the conduct of the establishment or continually and maliciously disturbs the community spirit within the works community;

" 3. When a member of the works community repeatedly makes frivolous and unjustifiable complaints or applications to the labour trustee or obstinately disobeys instructions given by him in writing;

" 4. When a member of the confidential council reveals

without authority any confidential information or technical
or business secrets which have become known to him in the
performance of his duties and have been specified as confidential matters."[43]

These provisions show clearly that while both employer and
workers come under the jurisdiction of the Honour Courts,
primary emphasis is placed on offences of labour against the
Leader and the establishment. Only the first rule applies to
offences committed by employers. Even in cases covered by
this provision, it seems clear that the employers proceeded
against are primarily—perhaps solely—owners of small shops
and establishments who have not been particularly favourable
to the Nazi regime. In a Charlottenburg court, visited by an
assistant to the author, all employer cases were entirely of this
sort.

Primary emphasis is placed on crushing labour opposition.
The second and third provisions are designed to scotch all
agitation, organised and unorganised, for improvement in
working conditions. The fourth provision effectively puts a ban
on disclosure of business secrets in the determination of disputes
over working conditions and wages. Since the Trusted Men are
hand-picked by the employer in co-operation with the Nazi
Party, dedicated to " self-government in business," little more
need be said than that these provisions supply means for completely sterilising labour protest. A few examples will suffice
to show how the courts function:

Case No. 17291/35, Arb. II. 10.35: Landlord of an inn was
accused by a maidservant of " desiring " her and making
advances, though no overt act was committed. The defendant
was acquitted; costs borne by the Reich.

Arb. II. 17.35: Peasant accused of violating the decree of
National Labour. The defendant owns a Farm Estate, and
employed the plaintiff. The plaintiff's son fell ill with case
diagnosed as diphtheria. The peasant would not permit plaintiff
to use his horses to drive the sick child to the hospital. Child
subsequently died. On another occasion the defendant had
accused plaintiff, who had seriously injured his foot, of malinger-
ing. Court decided that one who treated his employees in so

heartless and unsympathetic a fashion was " unworthy " of being permitted to continue as Leader of his enterprise. Costs met by defendant.

Arb. II. 21.35: Defendants, a butcher-shop owner and his brother, employed a nervous, neurotic, half-orphan as apprentice. There was constant dissatisfaction with his work. The boy was accused of being lazy and " worse than a communist," and several times beaten by the butcher's brother, his foreman, until the blood ran. The boy wrote home that he could bear the treatment no longer, and finally committed suicide. The court decided that the defendants had made the lad " sorely ill in his honour " and that they were totally unfit to handle such apprentices. Defendants must pay 2,000 and 1,000 Rm. respectively and meet half the costs of trial.

Arb. III. 19601/35, Eg. 20/35: Defendant, an extra worker employed intermittently since 1929, at one time member of the Trusting Council and later Chairman of the Industrial Cell, was accused by the Trustee of Labour of having " with evil intent stirred up feelings in the industry, disturbed the unity of spirit and undermined the authority of the overseers." Court reprimanded him, and ordered that he pay one-half the costs.

Case No. 14611/35, 7/35: Defendant, a mine foreman and member of the Nazi Party since 1931, was accused of manhandling one of the workers and, by kicking him, of having " made him sick in his honour." Court ruled that no actual kick had been witnessed, that there is a certain roughness in the line of duty in the mines, that the act had not been committed with evil intent nor was the defendant found to have wounded the plaintiff's honour. Defendant not guilty, costs by Reich.

All decisions by the Honour Courts are to be carried out by the Labour Trustees. Government officials, officials of the National Food Estate and the Labour Front, and soldiers do not come under the jurisdiction of the Honour Courts. For government officials all such matters are handled by the National Federation of German Officials, which is an organisation affiliated directly with the National Socialist Party.

It is clear in the handling of all these cases, and in the activities of the Trustees of Labour, that the line between a " labour " and an " economic " issue, and, hence, between the jurisdiction of

the Labour Front and the Economic Chamber, the National
Food Estate and other corporate bodies seems so vague as to be
almost indistinguishable. But to the business men all labour
issues are business problems. Prior to the coming of the Nazis,
however, they had found it necessary to organise a fighting body
to handle this sector of business activity. Thanks to the Nazis
this was no longer necessary since the new regime was bent
upon destruction of the trade unions, their natural enemies.
Hence the fighting organisation—The National Committee of
German Employers' Associations—could be disbanded, its
" economic functions " transferred to the National Economic
Chamber and its subsidiary bodies, and special machinery
established to handle problems of discipline, labour morale, and
systematic diversion of the " view of the masses " away from
material to spiritual things.

Jurisdictional disputes, however, were constantly coming to
the fore. Despite the fact that the function of the Labour Front
is to neutralise and sterilise all militant labour, it was mistaken
by many for an all-inclusive labour union—under Nazi control,
to be true, but a labour union nevertheless. Many of the workers
shared this view themselves. There was a tendency, accordingly,
for the Labour Front and its Leader, Ley, to be regarded as
" radical." Such was not and is not the case, but so far as general
labour discontent was able to make itself felt, the Labour Front
and the National Economic Minister were compelled to take
steps to further clarify jurisdiction, control, and functions. Thus
arose the famous Schacht-Ley-Seldte Agreement.

7. LEIPZIG AGREEMENT

" Organisation, within the German peoples community,"
said Hitler, in giving his official blessing to the Agreement in
March 1935, is necessary, " but they must not work against but
with one another." To this end the " Agreement between the
Reich Minister of Economic Affairs, the Reich Minister of
Labour, and the Leader of the German Labour Front " entered
the National Economic Chamber into the Labour Front
as a corporate body, made the Chamber and its subsidiary
bodies the " business representatives of the Labour Front,"

and confined the activities of the latter to inculcation of
the " spirit of National Socialism " and the suppression of
" materialism." In short, it arrogated to the National Economic
Chamber and the business men control over practically all
" material " things, including the foundations of labour contract
and working conditions, and left the Labour Front with practically no other function than that of " promoting fanaticism " and
the movement, Strength through Joy.

The Agreement did, however, provide some more elaborate
new machinery. Parallel with National Economic Chamber
and its Regional Economic Chambers it set up a National
Labour Chamber and 18 Regional Labour Chambers. The
National Labour Chamber has 80 members, " called " by
the National Leader of the Labour Front, and constituted as
follows:

Leaders of the National Business Communities	18
Leaders of the Districts of the Labour Front	33
Leaders of the central bureaux of the Labour Front	20
Individual persons	9 [44]

Following the Agreement of October 6, 1935, the various Organs
of the National Food Estate were added to this membership.

The membership of the Regional Labour Chambers is made
up of the District Managers of the Nazi Party, the District
Leaders of the various divisions of the N.S.B.O. and the N.S.-
Hago, Local Leaders of the Nazi Party, and individuals selected
at the discretion of the Leader of the Regional Labour Chamber.
In addition to these are the representatives of the National Food
Estate, and the National Socialist Society of German Jurists.
All members must take the following oath: " I swear loyalty to
Adolf Hitler, I promise to aid and promote the Community, I
promise to be an honest helper to all my Labour comrades in
all their troubles, I promise at all times to place the interests of
the nation above all others."[45]

As stated above the National and Regional Labour Chambers
exactly parallel the National and Regional Economic Chambers.
Under the Leipzig Agreement, the paired bodies join in the
formation of parallel National and Regional Labour and

Economic Councils (see Chart II at end of book), in which Leaders of the related bodies meet to discuss matters of common interest dealing with " social and political problems," and to carry out policies decided upon by the Labour Front and the National Economic Chamber.

Midway between the Regional Councils and the individual establishment are to be found Labour Committees, to which all enterprises within a radius of 50 kilometres must belong. The entire country is split up into these Labour Committee districts, the administration in all cases lying more or less directly in the hands of the Nazi Party industrial organisation—the N.S.B.O. and the N.S.-Hago. Employers and employees are supposed to be equally represented, all must be members in good standing of the Labour Front, and at least half of them must be simultaneously members of the Experts' Committees of the Labour Trustees.

The Councils, though all members are appointed from above, are labelled " organs of pure self-management." As such their *functions are determined in detail* by the Labour Front acting through the Trustees of Labour. They are not authorised to deal with wages or wage policies, nor are they in any wise competent to act as arbitrators in labour disputes. Their sole duty is to act as organs for discussion of super-enterprise problems in order to avoid as many cases as possible from coming to the stage where active interference of the Labour Trustee is required. Should these discussions call for learning more about the operations of any particular business, visits may be made to the premises by the Committees, provided approval from high officials of the state and the Labour Front can be obtained, and the Leader of the business to be visited consents.

At the bottom of this " *self-managed* " *pyramid, autocratically controlled in detail from above,* is the Council of Trusted Men of the individual enterprise. In connection with the above-mentioned Economic and Labour Committees their functions are, no different than in other capacities, to " advise " the employer and employees, to consider their demands, and to " clarify to the followers the necessities of the business." All this is to the end that, " within every community everyone shall have his place." But, " it does not satisfy us that every German should

have a work place, but our objective is that every German shall
have *his* work place . . ."[46] that is to say, each and every person
shall have *his* particular allotted role, *his* allotted function, *his*
allotted work place in that level of the hierarchy into which he
was born, which by assumption approximates his innate abilities
and capacities, for the due performance in which he is responsible, singly and solely, to such persons as those who have set
themselves above him may be, and in service to whatever ends
they may, in their unlimited right to exercise discretion, determine !

8. STRENGTH THROUGH JOY

What are the " ends " which National Socialism serves ? To
what goals are the masses to be led ? " The working masses,"
replied Hitler, in answer to the plea of the Strasser brothers for
a more radical social programme, " want only bread and circuses,
they have no understanding for any kind of ideal and we cannot
count upon winning the workers in large numbers."[47] But Ley,
Goebbels, Seldte, and others thought better. The trick was to
reduce the German worker to little more than a steady supply of
bread, and to make ideals out of circuses—or, perhaps better,
circuses out of ideals. This is now paraded as an original idea of
Hitler's and, under the guise of a " revelation of National
Socialist will,"[48] the National Socialist Community Strength
through Joy—or, as *News in Brief* translates the original, Be
Strong and Happy—was given life to carry out the " second
phase of the National Socialist Revolution[49] . . . the cultural
renewing of [the] people."

What " cultural renewing " means Ley makes perfectly clear.
Speaking in March 1935, he announced: " We could not offer
the working masses any material benefits, for Germany was poor
and in a state of confusion and misery. New rates or wages and
similar things were out of the question." Hence it was necessary
to " *suppress the materialism* " which gave rise to demands for
improved standards of living, and " *instead divert the gaze of
the workers to the ideal values of the nation.*"[50] When it became
more obvious that standards of living were not even being
maintained, but instead steadily lowered through shorter hours
of work, higher prices, and the cutting of the quality of consumer

goods through the *Ersatz* programme (a programme for substituting German artificial products for imported raw materials) —without corresponding increases in wages—this programme received new emphasis. Following the Leipzig Agreement, Strength through Joy has become the primary concern of the entire Labour Front.

But it will not do to conclude from Ley's statement that he has in mind only a short-run programme, worked out merely to meet the needs of a temporary crisis. The plan is not only to " divert the gaze of the masses " from " material values," but also to educate and accustom them from early youth onwards to find in " ideals " the substitute for more bread. Freeing German labour from the " shackles of capitalistic exploitation and human enslavement "[51] is regarded as consistent with the rule that " it would simply be a crime to disturb business " so long as business does not " act contrary to the interests of the nation,"[52] because the German " soul " transforms the employer-employee relation into a Leader-Follower relation. This stands, the Nazis say, in sharp contrast likewise with the materialism of the Marxists. " All those who in their degradation see the highest expression of life in class hate or in darkness are Marxists. All those who believe that life is beautiful, and who believe that in life there is a holy mission to be fulfilled, are National Socialists,"[53] said Ley on a memorable occasion. To persuade all Germans that they have a " holy mission " in life to perform, the " inner man " must be conquered, must be won for the Nazi *Weltanschauung*.

Therefore the emphasis on the youth, on leisure hours, on control over all the ways and means of shaping, hewing, and moulding opinions to an attitude satisfactory to the social and political philosophy of the employers. Way back in 1926 the Dinta organisation was set up to promote these ends. Formed in the offices of the Steel Trust, and presided over by the Chairman of the Trust, the Dinta system was expanded rapidly until its vocational training cells reached into the bulk of the largest plants in nearly every industrial field in Germany. Its numerous house organs, set up on a factory or enterprise basis, required relatively slight transformation to become the factory media of the Strength through Joy movement. Its ideology, when fused

to the traditions of the German Youth Movement, required no
more than systematic organisation and state backing in order
to be painlessly transformed into the new structure of the Labour
Front.

The house organ, *Strength through Joy*, of the Works Community of the German Dye Trust, quotes Hitler on the real
meaning of the Strength through Joy movement: " We believe
in our people and its strength, and we know exactly that every
element of strength is born out of true and honourable joy."
To which the editor of the organ adds, speaking of the importance of vacation trips to workers, " the Strength through Joy
trips have a large task to perform. They will help the labouring
man of brain and hand to make of the vacation day an untroubled source of strength." " When one has a positive
attitude towards life, and takes pleasure in community activity,"
Renteln adds significantly, " his energies will be [multiplied]
an hundredfold."[54] And since Germany is poor in materials and
rich in men, here is the source of productivity which can be
exploited by the Leaders—by law in economic affairs, the
business 'men—to the greater glory of the Fatherland. In
economic terms, this means " sound and profitable business."

The results desired are clear and to the point. " Yes, truly,"
Ley exclaims, " we may be poor, we may have no money, we may
lack foreign exchange and everything else. But we have a
glorious people, and that is our return and our capital." This
capital must be duly nurtured and cared for. Upon Ley the
Leader, Adolf Hitler, laid the injunction: " Take care that the
people holds its nerve. Take care for me that the German worker
following his heavy labour and his long day is able to recuperate.
Take care that these men can for once learn to forget the day's
burdens."[55]

The machinery for " diverting the gaze of the masses," for
supplying " holy missions " to be " blindly and fanatically
followed," for manufacturing the proper soporifics for whatever
occasion may arise along the line of " bread and circus " covers
the entire Reich, and performs a wide variety of functions. The
Strength through Joy Community is divided into 32 Regional,
771 District, and 15,061 Local groups. The Leaders of these
separate divisions, combined with the Chairmen of the factory

cells, some 57,000 in number, gives a total official staff of
approximately 75,000. Membership, which is supposed to be
entirely voluntary, is claimed to approximate about 30 million
persons, including wage earners, salaried workers, and employers. The organisation is divided into 11 departments:

1. Organisation
2. Finances
3. Propaganda and Publicity
4. Travel, Hiking, Vacations
5. Folkways, Traditions of the Home District
6. Education and Training
7. Sports
8. Beauty of Labour
9. Housing and Settlements
10. Culture and Arts
11. Youth

It is extremely difficult to learn anything accurate concerning
the functioning of these different departments. Elaboráte claims
are made for every division, but the facts presented vary so
much from tale to tale, the literature is so prolix and filled with
hyperbole, and it is so impossible to check any claims made that
a true picture of accomplishments is out of the question. The
whole set-up is designed so clearly to serve propaganda purposes
that distortion of the truth on its own functioning is regarded
as a virtue, not as a fault.

But the programme is shrewdly and ingeniously contrived to
serve many purposes. Thus special consideration is given to
distressed areas which might benefit from tourist traffic when
selecting routes for tours. Others who benefit in a material way
from these tours are the railroad, passenger shipping and
omnibus companies, keepers of local inns and hotels, the official
tourist agencies, professional musicians, artists, dance instructors,
etc. During 1935 seven oceanic steamships were kept constantly
occupied with Strength through Joy tours to Norway, Lisbon,
Madeira, the Azores, and other places. Tours are worked out in
co-operation with official tourist agencies by shop stewards who
belong to the firms contracting for the tours.

Participants in the tours, sports, and other activities are carefully selected, with particular emphasis upon " political reliability " and the youth. In contrast with the Social Honour Courts, whose real purpose is apparently to search out and punish persons recalcitrant or indifferent to Nazi principles, the Strength through Joy movement is designed to provide inexpensive rewards for the Nazi faithfuls gifted with proper Germanic " fanaticism." The rewards may include the entire family, since the programme is designed to encompass all ages and all sexes.

The tour programme was borrowed directly from Soviet experience, the objective being given as that of providing a trip for every workman in Germany once per year. For the year 1934–35 it was claimed that 5 million Citizen Comrades (*Volksgenossen*) went on such tours. The most of these trips were short, from one to three days in length, though it is claimed that approximately one-third of them were for periods of 7 to 14 days.

Even more emphasis is placed on sports, since the ideal pattern for the " fanatical preachers of National Socialism " is one in which there is a perfect " harmony of body, spirit, and soul."[56] The Sports Office, which has complete dictatorial control over all sport activities in the entire Reich, seeks to provide " the foundation for an inner soulful and spiritually sound development " of all members of Be Strong and Happy (the official translation of *Kraft durch Freude*—Strength through Joy). Courses are given, athletic programmes and facilities are provided, equipment is purchased, and programmes are widened so as to include all who will come. It is claimed that the number of athletic courses given in 1934–35 increased over the previous year from 8,500 to 48,500. Simultaneously, the exercise evenings increased from 55,000 to 190,000 and the persons attending from 450,000 to 3,034,687. Similar figures are quoted for attendance to the various sports activities, such as swimming, pleasure gymnastics and games, general calisthenics schools, and for receivers of the National Sports Badges. Special courses are given for small children, and for older persons. Amongst the latter are bicycling, pistol shooting, folk dancing, and golf. By the end of 1934 there were 48 Regional Sports Departments scattered throughout the country. Several more have been set up since.

Folk customs and traditions likewise play a role in the Strength through Joy attempts to promote " joy in merry doings with one's fellows." Courses, partly intended for women, partly for men, and sometimes for mixed groups are given. In the " culture field "—" culture " is defined as " the sum of the labour performed by German men in the course of hundreds and thousands of years "[57]—courses are given in

1. The philosophy of life, the political and practical schooling of the Officials of the National Socialist Community Strength through Joy.

2. Public speaking, inclusive of speeches in connection with stereopticon slides.

3. Writing of books and composition.

4. Planning and conduct of business community evenings.

5. Promoting of sight-seeing and leading of every sort.

6. Planning and conduct of village community evenings.

7. Testing the programmes of all institutions within the National Socialist Community Strength through Joy with respect to the content of their philosophies of life.

Several features of this programme are adapted from Soviet experience. Thus it is planned to construct in every large city buildings called *Haus der deutschen Arbeit* (House of German Labour), more or less along the line of the Russian workers' clubs. In some cases such club quarters are actually provided in Germany in connection with factories. Exhibitions of factory products and of art—paintings and plastic arts—are held from time to time in factory quarters. According to the official literature some 144 such exhibitions were given for the plastic arts from May 15 to November 1, 1935. Numerous sales to workmen have been reported.

Other borrowings from the Soviet Union[58] are the travelling theatre and the travelling cinema. Similarly, special productions are provided in the form of concerts, folk music, theatres, variety and cabaret entertainment, and films. The Business Community Evenings are organised by the separate divisions of

the Nazi industrial and trade formations (N.S.B.O.), and take
up primarily problems of " spiritual co-ordination." The Village
Community Evenings are supposed to take place once a month
on the initiative of the " Educational Officer of the Party."

One of the main purposes of these local gatherings is to promote
the activities of the department Beauty of Labour. The effort
here is to sentimentalise industrial work. A folder, discussing
the joys of toil in " beautiful surroundings," has a cover design
with a spider spinning symmetrically his gossamer web in the
silvery morning light above dew-laden grass. Two hundred
million Rm. were spent by the business Leaders of Germany
during 1934–35 to make labour for German men as beautiful as
the craftsmanship of the spider. According to the propaganda,
170,000 enterprises made some improvements by way of cleaning
up litter, putting in small gardens and lawns, brightening up
waiting-rooms, washing-rooms, toilets, and making " happy,
beautiful work places."

Nor do the Business Leaders neglect the " spirits " and
" souls " of their workmen. In the factory schools workmen can
attend courses which minister to his deeper cultural needs. One
commentator cites the following as typical of the courses
offered:

Programmes of the National Socialist Party
History of National Socialism
German History
The Leader's Principles
Adolf Hitler
The Leaders of the Movement
History of the Labour Movement
National Socialism and Economics
The Right to Work
National Socialism and the Race Problem
The Jews and the History of the Peoples of the World.

To put across its general programme the Strength through
Joy cells have an elaborate press and news system, appropriately
brought under the supreme control of the department of Propaganda and Publicity. These are put out on a District basis, and

operate through individual Business Establishments. Uniformly
they extol the " beauty of labour," the " duty of labour," the
public-spirited and unselfish aims of the Business Leader,
" work for the community," how " success " comes singly and
solely through honest, diligent toil, how those who are at the
top got there because of superior endowments of honesty, thrift,
hard work, fidelity to commands, and the possession of all the
superior arts of the superior German race.[59]

9. RULE OF THE MASSES BY THE SUPERIOR RACE

The German worker who wants a job must secure it through
the National Institute for Labour Placement and Unemployment Insurance. When he loses his job he comes back under the
same jurisdiction. But in most cases he must be of " Aryan
stock," " politically satisfactory," and, typically, male. That
is to say, non-Jewish, Polish, or Czech or " alien," " non-
Marxian " (i.e. non-social democratic, non-communist, non-
trade unionist), and willing to work on the terms at which labour
is offered.

The National Institute is divided into 13 Provincial Offices,
and these, in turn, into 362 local Labour Offices. In all problems
coming under their jurisdiction, its officers must show, within
the limits indicated above, special attention to age groupings.
Amongst the older people, special consideration is given to
" children-rich " families, members of the Nazi Party, and those
who give heavily to its various funds.

Unemployment services fall under several heads: (1) Pre-
ventative measures include occupational advice, admission to
apprentice schools, the " Household Year " (for girls, see pp. 191,
199 following), research into capacities and aptitudes, and supply
of information regarding occupational fields. (2) Regulation of
labour supply includes control over labour immigration and
emigration, division of labour between different areas, occupations and types of jobs, payment of family premiums, payment
of productivity deficits to older labourers, promotion of labour
creation programmes, financing and advice to female labour,
etc. (3) Direct unemployment aid includes unemployment insurance, crisis relief, aid for short-time workers, sickness insurance,

and special support for released soldiers, police, and provincial gendarmes.

The National Institute for Labour Placement and Unemployment Insurance is presided over by a Leader, appointed by the National Minister of Labour, and " co-ordinated " to meet the dictates of the Leader of the Labour Front. As such, it is co-ordinated with the programmes of the National Food Estate, Rural and Urban Settlements, and the National Economic Chamber, on the one hand, and the military, youth, female, and " culture " administration on the other.

It is likewise co-ordinated with the Winter Help campaigns. Some 362 million Rm. were spent in this wise during 1934-35 for those whose destitution had reached the acute stage. Money for these purposes came partly from government coffers, partly by crisis relief funds split off from sums gathered by levies on labour, and partly by tag-days, lotteries, etc.: " 76 million pins and badges, amounting to a total price of production of almost 4 million Rm., were produced in Germany's suffering territories for the benefit of poor home-workers."[60] Amongst these activities are the " meatless days," and such things as " godmother work." For the first, all persons are supposed to go without meat, giving the proceeds to Winter Help. Under the latter, women take over a destitute child as a " godchild " and provide it with " Christmas gifts, with clothes, shoes, etc., and invite them to dinner as often as possible."[61]

.   .   .   .

Thus, in summary, all must work who can find it, on terms dictated by the employer. The employer seeks to attach labour to him, by controlling wages, hours, and attitudes. He attempts to " fix and bind " them to the soil (see Chapter VII, pp. 213, 215), to make them marry and have children that he may have a plentiful labour supply in the future, and to make them " loyal " through a sense of participation in matters not affecting the life of the enterprise. Those who cannot find work are divided into the helpless and—those who may properly be called—the " damned." The helpless are taken care of through charity such as Winter Help, decreased unemployment benefits, and compulsory labour. The " damned," branded as " Marxian,"

" Communists," " Jews," and " traitors," likewise helpless, are sometimes incarcerated in concentration-camps, always neglected when destitute, for ever socially ostracised, and permanently excluded from all preferred occupations.

On all, old and young, preferred and damned, judgment is passed by the self-appointed guardians and interpreters of the " people's state " (Volkstaat). It is the business of the Leaders to allocate to each and every person that place allotted to him by nature as determined, typically, by social station at birth. In the Nazi view, the bulk of these people are capable only of hard work, sacrifice, and amusement. To them an intelligent man, born to his higher station, despises the stupid masses he exploits, but since the rank and file have the minds of children, they must be flattered, cajoled, amused, and occasionally threatened.

For the conduct of a state so ordered, " what we want," said Hitler to Strasser in May 1930, " is a picked number from the new ruling classes, who . . . are not troubled with humanitarian feelings, but who are convinced that they have the right to rule as being a superior race, and who will secure and maintain their rule ruthlessly over the broad masses."[62]

CHAPTER V

Training the Youth to Become Soldiers of Labour

IT was evident to Nazi Leaders " untroubled with humanitarian feeling " that to secure their right to rule " as being a superior race " was not enough. They must hold it. They must so shape the attitudes of " the broad masses " that the right they assumed would remain unquestioned.

But how ? The answer lay ready made before them—ready made out of the experience of all great organised religions, and out of the countless experiments of scattered sects, cults, and faiths throughout the world and all history: Control the child ! Manipulate its environment. Determine its values. Shape its mind. Mould its character.

And to what end ? This the Nazis make unmistakably clear; at the centre of all their propaganda " for the broad masses " is the concept of the " soldier of labour." •

1. THE SOLDIER OF LABOUR: VOCATIONAL EDUCATION

This conception is a straight line development from the programme of the German Institute for Technical Education and Training, known as Dinta (*Deutsches Institut für Arbeitsschulung*), and organised by the heavy industries in 1926 under the direct sponsorship of Vögler, Chairman of the Board of Directors of the Steel Trust (*Vereinigte Stahlwerke*). Arnhold, originator, organiser, and chief propagator of Dinta from its inception, is now in complete charge of the entire vocational education, training, and advisory services of the National Socialist Party and the Labour Front. Practically every important programme of the Labour Front, including the underlying ideas of that organisation itself, the concept of the division Strength through Joy, the programme of the sub-division Beauty of Labour, and the idea of the complete control of the entire thinking and working environment of every factory employee by the business man above—first called by Arnhold the " Leader "—were outlined by him in detail before 1930. Furthermore, and of still greater importance, Arnhold was the first person in Germany to lay out a detailed programme for achieving these ends via schooling of the youth. His whole approach, then, becomes of considerable importance to an understanding of the role played by this programme for the youth of Nazi Germany.

In a long interview given to the author in 1931, subsequently checked from his writings and an examination of the extensive Dinta literature, Arnhold explained the origin of Dinta, without any circumlocution whatsoever, about as follows: In the postwar period the profits of German business and industry stayed low, despite reorganisation, rationalisation, and improvement of internal and external market. Why? Because the growing power of the trade unions, aided and abetted by a socialistically inclined government, siphoned off all possible margins by successfully enforcing demands for shorter hours, higher wages, costly improvements in working conditions, various forms of social insurance, and so forth.

Why, asked Arnhold, did labour see fit to make and organise to achieve these demands ? Because German labour had become materialistic. Because it found the only worth-while things in life to be material matters of hours, of wages, of standards of living. It looked upon wages as income with which to buy material goods. In so doing, work became a means to an end, not a pleasure and a joy in itself. The new values—material values—were being substituted for the old values, which were of a handicraft, intimate, personal character.

The employers were equally culpable with the men, not because they were interested in profits as such, but because they had become so preoccupied with mechanising processes, reducing costs, maintaining market prices, and rationalising the minutiæ of factory and office procedure that they had lost the *art of leadership*. They lost this art precisely at the time when it was most important that they develop it to the maximum—i.e. when Germany was poorest in materials, in land and natural resources, and richest in men. Proof for all this was to be found in the enormous burden on the natural economy of raw materials and capital imports, while the army of unemployed was growing steadily. Why not substitute men as creative economic power for more mechanisation, rationalisation, and indebtedness? If the *art of leadership* could be revived, these men could be drawn into productive labour, and given a new, or rather an old, set of incentives.

These incentives, which were designed to lead to unquestioning acceptance of certain specific values, are of non-commercial character. They have been elaborately set forth in numerous reports and brochures. Typically they relate to such things as a sense of duty, response to discipline, pride in craftsmanship, sense of group solidarity, joy in effort, and struggle to overcome odds. The values they lead to are those long associated with the German home—children, church, and kitchen—belief in after-life, fear of God, and patriotic loyalty to the Fatherland and all its culture.

The listing of values worth preserving indicate the institutions worth reviving, namely, the German concept of the home, the German concept of the army and its service to the Fatherland, and the German concept of religion. To have Hans, Fritz, and Gretel in the mind's eye while sitting at the lathe is better than a grudge against the boss. To think of the evening at home, the violin with good old German music (Arnhold opposed jazz, saxophones, and other sexy, sensual, and " secular " musical ephemera), the dappled cow which would soon calve, the picnic on the edge of the lake—to think of all these was to warm the cockles of the workman's heart, to cause him to glow with good feeling, to be warm and friendly to all those he met.

To this the army added military discipline, sense of loyalty to rules of action and superiors, unquestioning obedience to orders given, rigid authority from above and sense of duties to be solemnly fulfilled from below. Religion added belief in mystic values, faith in higher laws, sense of security in righteous conduct, and belief in rewards to be found in the after-life for walking humbly in the paths of God. The things that count, in short, are intangibles not tangibles, non-commercial not commercial incentives, immaterial not material rewards.

A Dinta fairy-tale for factory children illustrates the point. After a visit to the factory at noon, where he saw his father at work amongst the blazing furnaces and thunderous machines, Manni told his mother with great enthusiasm just how thrilled he was with the work-day church: " Aha ! Oma ! On Sunday you go to the church of dear God. But father goes to dear God's work-day church, which is much larger and more beautiful. There are no bright windows there, but organs ! Organs ! The dear God blows them Himself. One never sees dear God there, but one feels in every bone that He is there. I was never before so reverent as then ! Never before ! "[1]

" The problem," said Arnhold in 1927, " is to take in hand leadership of all from earliest childhood to the oldest man in order, not—and I must emphasise this once more—for social purposes but from the point of view of productivity. I consider men the most important factor which industry must nourish and lead."[2]

Concretely, this meant three things: (1) to develop a staff of highly trained and especially skilled workmen; (2) to give " schooling to a German labouring class " which " will be prepared to see things as the Leader intends them in the smallest details "; (3) to " reawaken joy in labour."[3] The procedure was to select from the families of especially trusted employees recruits for special technical schools, organised on a factory basis, and subject directly to management control. The families of the children were subject to regular visit and inspection; the boys were controlled in all work and leisure time for all but one day in the week. Roughly half the time in the plant was spent in actual work, and the other half in the factory school. Vocational subjects were taught in the one place and practised in the other. Both were supplemented with propaganda on the good work of the management, the devotion to high ideals of its leading figures, and so on.

Special recreational facilities were maintained for the boys, where they could go at noon and in the evenings. The facilities provided included, with variation as to detail, athletic halls and equipment, little theatres, music-halls for practice and concerts to be given by the boys, etc. In many plants outdoor facilities were provided, including playgrounds, swimming-pools, and the like. On week-ends the boys frequently went on conducted hikes through the near-by woods and hills, or visited museums and historic spots. On their annual vacations they took long trips into the south mountains, went on boating trips on the Baltic, or made pilgrimages to some famous city or wonder spot.

All routine and leisure was handled in a strict military way. All trips and tours were conducted in military fashion, and accompanied, quite commonly, by religious leaders. The boys were kept insulated as far as possible from the rest of the men, and an eye was kept constantly alert for the slightest heresy in act or utterance. As a matter of policy, unions were not openly opposed, but such restraint did not apply to socialism, communism, and " materialism." It was expected by management that these boys would become the economic janissaries of the employer in the future, and that, once installed as the effective managerial " leaders," their influence would gradually undermine sentiment for trade unionism and " materialism."

As indicated in a previous chapter, units of the Dinta organisation were established in the bulk of the largest industrial establishments in Germany—by 1933 in excess of 350. Many other establishments had similar schemes. Most of these were either influenced directly by Dinta, or were worked out in close co-operation therewith.

The larger programme of Dinta was centred around a definite plan of action, and was designed to include the entire labour active population. That programme had five principal phases. First, every employee was to be examined by a " psycho-technical qualifications testing " method, designed to indicate, segregate, and qualitatively evaluate specific traits, aptitudes, and capacities. By this process workers would be classified into types such as " fast " or " exact " type, " intelligent " or " monotony-irritable " type, and so on. " Men," wrote Arnhold, much later, " are unlike, unlike in knowledge, unlike in will, and unlike, therewith, in their labour.[4] Again, " we know to-day that men are not equal, and that neither their rank nor returns can be equal." Each and every man, each and every child, therefore, must be first tested to see for what occupation he is ideally adapted and in what line of activity his particular qualifications will, considering the state of the national economy, promote the maximum productivity.

Second, each type must receive its appropriate training for its nature-allotted tasks. This training should be simultaneously designed to promote maximum type-job adaptation and the highest productivity in each job. It is a major Dinta assumption

158 THE CO-ORDINATION OF SPIRIT

that while most, if not all, persons may be by nature capable of more than one of many jobs, each is better adapted for some particular job or type of job than any other. To this particular job or type of job he should be directed, and for it he should be especially trained.

Third, he must be made happy in his job. Arnhold has never wearied of pointing out that much, if not the most, of physical, nervous, and mental activity is never paid for at all—activities such as playing music, sports, joining in celebrations, and the whole round of tasks and painstaking work women perform freely out of love for their families. In these activities, he points out, the individual " applies his strength with joy, without expectation of material reward, and accomplishes thereby— reckoned in terms of kilograms per second—frequently and without effort much more work than by the drudgery of daily work in the factory." And then he adds significantly, " The problem of modern human efficiency is to render this tremendous spiritual and emotional energy available for production of goods."[5] He must, in short, acquire strength through joy, and that strength can be harvested without " material " cost by the factory-owner. Foremost problem of the employer, then, is to make his workmen happy and satisfied.

Fourth, every workman must be relieved of all those hindrances and cares, streaming from his family or outside factory life, which militate against his industrial efficiency. The workman, for example, may have a spendthrift, uneconomical, or ignorant wife. Or the wife may be going to have a baby, with its attendant monetary and medical problems. For these purposes Arnhold recommends factory-conducted schools for wives and mothers of employees in which they will be taught how to buy intelligently, the elements of household science, and allied matters. In addition, special bureaux were to be set up to give advice to expectant mothers on the care of nursing children and so forth. Such schooling and advice was to be extended to daughters of employees likewise. The women, in other words, were to be taught how best to do " women's work " so as to lessen the worries of the men, and make them happy and productive on the job.

Finally, special facilities were to be provided for the invalids and the aged. Jobs to be provided included such things as making cushions, chairs, baskets, splitting wood, making and repairing files. The supply by factories of facilities for such jobs for the invalid and the aged would tend to free them from the irritation of becoming the acceptors of alms and of becoming burdens on their relatives, reduce certain social insurance charges on the enterprise and the employees, and free the latter from the direct burdens of support.

To put all these ideas across, Dinta concentrated primarily on the boys in the training schools under its direct control. Special literature, however, was put out to appeal to both old and young. The factory papers apparently enjoyed long before the advent of the Nazis a very large and rapidly growing circulation. Especially interesting was the journal *Youth Land* (*Jugendland*), designed to appeal to youngsters from three to fourteen years of age. Got up in an attractive format, well and in some cases beautifully illustrated, and filled with a wide variety of stories adapted to the adolescent reader, they apparently enjoyed a considerable popularity. The May issue previously referred to is a good example of the set-up. The cover design is a brown and grey woodcut of children playing underneath some trees growing alongside two tall coal tips, flanked by smoke-stacks. On the cover page is another well-executed woodcut of a sparkling industrial scene at night. Underneath is a poem to the creative power of industry. There follows a story, " Fritz Klaffke Writes to his Teacher," on how miners go down to mines, play accordions, and produce tons of coal which the wonders of chemistry break up into tar, ammonia, naphtha, benzol, creosote, lubrication oils, and many other remarkable things. Following that comes a quotation from Goethe, and " The Miners' Song." On page 5 there is a story of how by song, sorrow, hard work, frugality, and unselfish devotion Alfred Krupp rose to captain the gigantic works named after him. Then come quotations from Tolstoy, Goethe, Spruch, Ruskin, and Carlyle, flanked by an initialled poem on jumping the rope and playing football. On page 8 appears the article referred to, " The Work-day Church "; facing it is another story called " Crane and I." Both are well illustrated with woodcuts romantically limning the excitement of factory life. Follow more poems, an album corner, a drawing and poem on " The Festival of German Labour," and recommendations on books, poems, etc., to be read in leisure hours.

None of this emphasis has been changed with the advent of the Nazis. On the contrary, what they did was to accept the programme without alteration in any significant detail, as a basis for the " co-ordination " of all labour via " co-ordination " of the youth. The old Dinta plan lacked the power and the force, the prestige, the apparent separation from " narrow selfish interests," required to command general popular support. This National Socialism supplied, and, so doing, it transmuted the precepts of Dinta into the law of the land and made them legally valid and binding on every employee, old or young, working in every factory and workshop from one end of the land to the other.

" Dinta," wrote Arnhold in 1934, " was unable to put its programme across without the backing of National Socialism; without National Socialism and without its high labour idea, realisation of its plans would never have been possible for Dinta."[6]

Writing a year later, about the time he was given his new position as co-ordinator of all vocational education in Germany, he announced that of the ordinary kind, Germany has " many, too many schools because these schools do not train labour properly. The natural location of the labour school is the factory, the workshop, and the office. The school must be built up in the factory."[7]

These schools are to establish a stern regime. Vocational education is for us no labour play, but labour battle. But it is to be a battle against the elements, not against the employer. The German workman, in contrast to the American " serving man," is a " fighting man " who has " set before him work goals, as incentives for the fighting man " to fight, struggle with, achieve, and overcome. This " fighting " instinct is his peculiar German, Nordic endowment, and is the source of that aggressive energy which, in combination with the unique German " reflective and meditative endowments," is responsible for the fact that " all the great discoveries have been made by German men."[8]

But each individual fights to provide what Germany needs—productivity. To this end, the Fatherland's ends, all must co-operate without friction, without internal dissension. With will to labour, labour energy, and diligence equipped with " manual dexterity, practical intelligence, constructive capacities and organisational gifts " above all other races of men, all, regardless of rank or station, task or authority, must march shoulder to shoulder to the glory of the " Common Good."

This posture of affairs, so uniquely satisfactory to German employers, has become the pattern of law on which the whole of the German youth is built for the vocational training of young Germany. All the trends represented by Dinta before the Nazis have been strengthened throughout Germany under the present regime. All those militating against have been ruthlessly suppressed. The number of such vocational in-the-factory schools and occupational advisory bodies has increased markedly under the Nazi regime. Ultimately it is planned to submit all youth to the ministrations of such agencies.

Special emphasis is laid throughout on the development of skilled labour. Employers in Germany, despite the high levels of unemployment, have long been wont to complain of the shortage of skilled labour, especially in such fields as mining, metallurgy, and machine-building. The Nazis have sought to fill this need, while " combating " unemployment by increasing the number of young apprentices, by dramatising vocational skills through " National Trades Competitions." The first of these was held in 1934. Gärtner describes them as follows:

" This competition is a professional contest of efficiency held for the whole German youth, and is carried out every spring. A million young entrants reported for the first contest, which was divided into 14 trade groups. These groups are sub-divided into smaller units, called *Fachschaften*. The National Trades Competition was held in 2,000 different localities in Germany, 18,000 competition centres, and 100,000 co-workers carrying out the necessary functions. The winner in the local contest competed against the best in the district until there were only 20 left in Germany. These, the " Reich victors," 14 boys and 6 girls, were received on May 1st, the national labour day, by the Führer himself, whereby their efficiency received the highest

FF

recognition possible. Each competitor is required to solve the following problems: (1) brief questions regarding *Weltanschauung*, (2) a practical task belonging to the competitor's particular trade, which must be constructed in the workshop or place of work, (3) elementary written exercises in arithmetic, German composition, practical questions in the trade."[9]

The competitions are carried out under joint auspices of the Labour Front and the Hitler Youth. The following competitors (in 1935) were eligible: (a) all male young workers between 15 and 18; (b) all male commercial office and technical apprentices between 15 and 21; (c) all girls between 15 and 21; (d) all male and female students of trade or professional schools. Further requirements were membership of the National Socialist Movement (Party), Storm Troop, Special Guard, Labour Front, or the State Youth, Hitler Youth, Federation of German Girls. In 1935 the competition was held within the following trade groups: hotels, restaurants, etc.; transport and traffic; shipping and aviation; wood and timber, metal workers, individual groups.

By these methods, proudly announces the author of an attractively designed little pamphlet, *Youth at the Work Place*, the Hitler Youth and the Labour Front fulfil one another, they grow in Trades Competitions to a unity. " The harmony of technical knowledge, skilled will to construct, and youthful idealism is stamped on the face of the young National Socialist worker."[10]

In industries and areas where the younger generation is numerically inadquate to satisfy the needs of the future, special " apprentice homes " are being built. Youths may be transferred from surplus areas to deficit areas by this means, a movement which may be particularly significant as plans proceed for regional decentralisation of industry. The first two apprentice homes are located in Sauerland and Gummersbach (Middle Rhine).

Similar training is provided for the agricultural youth. In an agreement made between the National Food Estate and the Hitler Youth in July 1935, the independent rural youth organisations were finally dissolved, and all such functions " co-ordinated " with the work of the Hitler Youth. In the compact, the tasks of the Youth Guardian of the National Food Estate,

who must be " a fundamentally satisfactory Hitler Youth
Leader or Party Comrade," were carefully delineated. " The
task of the Youth Guardian (Division I.D.) of the National
Food Estate is to promote additional agricultural education
and training of the rural youth—in particular along vocational
lines, schooling of the young village community in the objectives
of agricultural policy and the Odal (entailed hereditary estate),
instruction of the future farmers in problems of the National
Law of Entail, the exchange of agricultural youth within the
national borders, exchange of agricultural youth amongst the
folk groups, selection of the agricultural youth for economic,
cultural, political, or bodily special training."

A final programme in the plank for turning youth into soldiers
of labour is preparatory to the fusion, discussed in subsequent
chapters, planned between country and city, and the psychology
of rural and urban workers. The goal set is to bring about a rigid
binding of the younger generation to the soil for the rural youth
and " to order the life rhythm of the urban youth after the
prototype of the peasant life,"[11] a life praised as one of hard,
exhausting toil performed every long day of his narrow, care-
ridden life without complaint, protest, or yearn for change.
Aside from formal liaison work between the National Food
Estate and the Hitler Youth, two other activities are relied
upon to promote among the youth the fixed attitude of the
peasant to the globe to which he is hereditarily bound. These
are the Land Year and the Labour Service.

The Land Year of eight months is a year of compulsory rural
labour service for graduates of lower schools. These children,
falling typically in the 14 to 16 age group, are " lodged in Rural
Homes," each of which accommodates from 60 to 150, placed
under the management of carefully selected leaders and assist-
ants and trained to work on farms and be indoctrinated with the
Nazi ideas. Though compulsory, the Land Year has so far
apparently not been uniformly enforced, some 31,000 children
only being taken care of in this way during 1935. The typical
programme calls for spending the forenoons in actual work on
" farms where the farmer and his wife serve as instructors. The
afternoons are devoted to community training and sports. On
Sundays extended excursions are carried out."[12]

The specific purposes announced are: (1) to familiarise boys and girls with " the ideas of blood and soil," (2) to assist the farmer as helpers, (3) to teach each how to serve for his bread, (4) to accustom them to a regimen where " military discipline and simplicity determine life." The real purpose of this regime is made clear in the principles of selection. " In selecting rural year pupils, those districts are preferred which constitute a danger for the young generation in regard to political opinions and to health. This means, above all, the big cities and industrial regions."[13] More specifically it means areas which tend to be radical, and where such " political unreliability," coupled with threat of unemployment, provides the most receptive soil for the destructive propaganda of class struggle.

Here again we find uncovered the central thread of all Nazi argument and the doctrinal core of all Nazi programmes: to fit the disciplined, regimented, uniform pattern of the soldier on to Labour, to make labour willing to work hard and live frugally in the sweat of its brow all the long days of life without murmur or complaint, because each and every member has been accustomed to this scheme of living through the most formative years of life. For the Nazi " born leaders of labour," the employers, there can be, then, no trouble from Marxism and materialism, no demands to be satisfied from antagonistic unions, no threat of class war to disturb the even course of " organic business."

The crowning achievement of Nazi inventive genius along this line is to be found in

2. COMPULSORY LABOUR SERVICE (" ARBEITSDIENST ")

By the " Law for National Labour Service," passed on June 26, 1935, labour service was made " obligatory for all young Germans." The phrase " young Germans " is to include all males and females of " Aryan " descent in good standing between the ages of eighteen and twenty-five. The compulsory feature now applies generally; the Women's Labour Service was made compulsory at the end of 1936. The service period runs from six months to a year, and normally begins with the completion of the nineteenth year of age. It is possible to volunteer for an earlier age, and under certain cases enrolment can be postponed for one or more years. But every young German is required to be possessed of a Labour Service discharge card, indicating completion of his labour service before the end of the twenty-ninth year (he must enrol before the end of the twenty-fifth year). The men then become automatically subject to conscription for the regular compulsory military training.

As membership in the Hitler Youth is gradually made all-inclusive, it is expected that all recruits for the Labour Service will have behind them the military training and the labour discipline which the various activities of that organisation are designed to inculcate. At any rate, all Nazi writers are insistent on the proposition that the Labour Service is the necessary and logical fulfilment of the programme and training of the Hitler Youth. Since service in the Labour Service is compulsory prior to entrance into the regular military training period, likewise compulsory, the organisation and functions of the Labour Service give a pretty good picture of the real purpose of the entire programme for co-ordinating the youth.

The origin of the Labour Service is partly economic and partly military. In 1922 the Bund Artem was organised for the purpose of sending German Youth out into the harvest fields to provide free labour in order to displace foreign (primarily Polish) seasonal labour which was taking millions of marks out of the country annually in the form of wages. In 1925, a somewhat similar organisation was established, the " Landwork " of Professor Schöpke, to re-educate the city unemployed and put them to work at agricultural tasks.

The Artem movement was subsequently taken up enthusiastically by the National Socialists. In 1928 Goebbels, Kretzschmann, and Eizenbeck carried through the first Labour Service Congress. In the years to follow, various work camps were established by students and the Youth Movement. The first direct predecessor of the Labour Service was established on a voluntary basis by Chancellor Brüning in 1931 for the purpose of taking young people off the streets and to relieve the financial burdens of relief. In 1932, still on a voluntary basis, Labour Service was extended to include all Germans under twenty-five years of age. With the coming of the Nazis, Hierl took over the co-ordination of all the various types of camps and works then existing. Two years later, Labour Service was made compulsory by law.

The Labour Service is under the Ministry of the Interior, and in charge of a National Labour Leader. The Reich is divided into 30 Labour Regions, each under the charge of a Regional Labour Leader. Each Labour Region is divided into 8 Labour Service Groups, and each Group into from 8 to 10 sections. Each section has about 215 workers. The Women's Labour Service is similarly organised, though, due to the lack of adequate facilities and the absence of the compulsory feature, enrolment is much smaller than in the regular Labour Service. While from 200,000 to 250,000 are regularly enrolled in the Labour Service, but 60,000 girls had gone through Women's Labour Service from the entire period from April 1, 1933, to March 31, 1936.

Hierl, leader of the Labour Service, is simultaneously in charge of the Labour Service Division of the National Socialist Party. He is, thus, jointly responsible to the formal state machinery and to the Party for the proper performance of allotted functions. For carrying out the details of management, the Labour Service has the following divisions: (1) Service Bureau, (2) Bureau of Administration and Management, (3) Planning Bureau, (4) Personnel Bureau, (5) Legal Division, (6) Health Service Bureau, and (7) Bureau of Press and Propaganda. In addition, there is an Inspector of Education and Instruction, under whom are an Inspector of the Teaching Division, an Inspector for Physical Education, and a Leader for Instruction.

In connection with the Labour Service, but separate as an organisation, is the Labour Thanks (*Arbeitsdank*), set up as the tradition-preserving custodian of the Labour Service and to work in the closest co-operation with the Regional Leaders of the National Socialist Party. " Tradition preserving " means to see that " the values awakened and won in the Labour Service not be lost again, but their full unfolding and working out brought into the service of the Party."[14] It is more concerned with the framing of further legislation relating to the Labour Service and acting as a welfare agency to help those discharged from the Labour Service and who may now be in need. Among its miscellaneous services is provision of a savings and credit system, seeing that ex-leaders are given special vocational schooling and leading all discharged members into the Labour Front, the Storm Troops, the Party, and other subdivisions thereof.

The Labour Service is looked upon as a political training-ground with three major duties: (1) to supply universal vocational training, (2) to promote universal defence duty, and (3) to teach all the duty of work. Its economic functions are three-fold. In the first place, it is designed to promote "bread freedom" (*Brotfreiheit*). The boys are put to work draining swamps, building irrigation ditches, constructing roads, and working in the forest in order to cultivate and make more fruitful the land, that Germany may be increasingly independent of foreign food markets.[15]

In the second place, the Labour Service is promoted because it offers direct aid to various branches of business through demands for materials and supplies with which to carry out its activities. Its very existence " alone means the placing of orders in the sum of many million Reichsmarks for clothing, provisions, housing, medical care, etc., for the 200,000 service men, as well as for motor-cars, motor-trucks, etc. During the last six months of the last budgetary year (1935), orders in the sum of 12 million Reichsmarks were placed with the timber industry; in the sum of about 8 million Reichsmarks with the industries engaged in the manufacturing of wooden and iron furniture; 64 million Reichsmarks were spent for provisions ... while for underwear and repairs 5 million and for educational appliances 4 million Reichsmarks were expended."[16] While some of this money might otherwise be spent in order to keep body and soul together, most of the expenditure is additional, and hence welcomed as a fillip to unemployment elsewhere. " 16·67 million working hours," our source goes on to add, " were involved in trade and industries for the execution of orders involving the furnishing of textiles, cloth, fabrics, ticking, etc., which meant work and bread for 7,000 workers engaged in the free trades."

In the third place, Labour Service offers relief from unemployment. It is believed that the land and its various projects could actually absorb one and a half million men, while the settlement programme could absorb a similar number. At any rate, by so much as it keeps young men off the regular labour markets, it tends to lighten the burden of unemployment on the industry and the state.

It is a well-established principle that all " work undertaken by the Labour Service may only be supplementary, i.e. work which would not be undertaken in the ordinary way by private enterprise. And in planning the work of the Labour Service great care is taken not to prejudice such interests."[17] This is quite similar to the policy followed by the American government in all Works Progress Administration programmes, and in the work of the Civilian Conservation Corps.

Not only is there no competition with business, but " the men engaged in Labour Service realise that they do not work for wages or pocket-money (the Labour Service man receives 25 pfennigs, the supervisor 75 pfennigs, the troop leader 1 Reichsmark pocket-money per day), but that his service is an honourable service rendered for the purpose of improving the German soil, and to the German nation." This " service rendered to the German nation " is carried out in labour camps which are organised to function as military camps. A typical day's programme is offered by Krüger[18]:

6 a.m.	Rising (5 a.m. in summer).
6.05–6.20	Early exercises.
6.20–6.40	Washing, bed-making, room-cleaning.
6.40–6.55	Breakfast.
7 a.m.	Falling in line, flag parade, the day's task and speech, march to the place of work.
	Six hours of agricultural labour, average of 45 minutes spent on the marching route, ½ hour for late breakfast.
14.00	Return from work.
14.30–15.00	Midday meal.
15.00–16.00	Rest period in bed.
16.00–17.00	Sport or cleaning up.
17.00–18.00	Political instruction.
18.00–19.00	Issuing of tasks, instruction period, polishing and mending, roll-call.
19.00	Supper.
20.00–21.00	Festivities (singing, oratory, games).

| 21.45 | Locking up. |
| 22.00 | Retiring. |

The entire routine is patterned after that of a military camp from reveille to taps. Upon waking up, exercise is conducted by military procedure. After falling in line, regular military drill with squad and company manœuvres is practised. All the men wear uniforms, march in military formation with spades over the right shoulder to and from work, and are subject to military supervision in the entire day's work routine. The evening instruction includes lectures on military matters and the general Nazi *Weltanschauung*.

Both these require that all compulsory labour be oriented towards promoting national self-sufficiency on the one hand, and the military programme on the other. National self-sufficiency is thought of primarily as a necessary condition to the waging of a successful war. Admittedly most of the land reclamation projects are without any sort of economic justification, the labour and money input being in all recorded cases in excess, and in some cases many times the possible crop output. But to an increasing degree such forced labour is devoted to direct military purposes, as, for example, the construction of the new unified Reich networks of military roads.

The concept of military—the Nazis prefer to use the word " soldierly "—identifies labour and the soldier pattern throughout. " Labour ennobles man even as the sword," writes a Nazi enthusiast, but only so long as the two are identified in service to the Fatherland. " As the soldiers in the World War, so we live in a front shelter. We transfer the firing-trench unity into the trench *camaraderie* of swamp and moor, but likewise the inner attitude of German soldiery: the will to sacrifice, to renunciation, to service, and to devotion to the totality which we show daily through acts."[19] Labour Service will then promote, Krüger argues, the new society in which gold, possessions, and material things are not the highest values, but rather character, performance, and labour.[20]

Specifically, this means " that it is the mission of the National Socialist Labour Service to lift men out of economic interest, out of acquisitiveness, to free them from materialism, from egoism, from the spirit of liberal interest-thoughts and Marxian internationalism."[21] The solution of the world's difficulties is not economic but moral, and the moral victory must be simultaneously over capitalism and Marxism. Capitalism is understood to mean the domination of gold and the Jews. When the Leader —in industry the employer—is not Jewish he will not make profits to promote the interests of gold-lust, but to promote the interests of the Fatherland. Thereby is capitalism abolished, and labour enthroned as the greatest economic force. " Liberalism (capitalism)," said Goebbels, " means, I believe in Mammon. Socialism, National Socialism, means, I believe in labour."

What does it mean to " believe in labour " ? All the literature is agreed on this point. " National Socialist organisation means . . . to arrange and articulate the masses so that each, according to the measure of his capacity, will place himself at the service of the totality, the community, means that Leader and Followers will be brought into the proper relation to each other."[22] That proper relationship is the one discussed above in the chapter on the settlements programme. The Guild State (*Ständestaat*) is one hierarchically arranged from generation to generation according to an assumed gradation of capacities and " honour," where each and every person will perform his duties, assigned to him from above, with expedition and without complaint, and where the entirety of the hierarchy will be governed in all details involving initiation of policy, execution of decisions, and adjudication of disputes, according to the rules of conduct forged out of the hard school of war from times immemorial.

All loyalties and duties are performed as initiated from above; the giving and taking of command is entirely personal. The allegiance, hence, rests not on rules of law but on personal caprice. Loyalty is to the individual, not to the state. Since the leader hierarchy is identified throughout with the party, and the party with the state, the oath of loyalty is to the Leader who decides for both party and state. To Hitler, as both party and state, every member of the Labour Service takes the following oath: " I swear that I will dedicate myself in unbreakable allegiance to the Leader of the German Kingdom and the German People, that I will unconditionally obey him and all the Leaders designated by him, that I will resolutely fulfil all my duties of service and that I will be a good comrade to all members of the National Labour Service."[23]

3. THE SOLDIER PATTERN

The " soldier of labour " is to be an exact replica of the " soldier of war."

" The soldier of war," regardless of rank or station, is supposed to recognise in all things and at all times the superior judgment of the officers above him. In the rules of warfare, nothing he can say or think can at any time justify any expression of opinion, or any action to the contrary of that ordered. A properly drilled soldier will, in fact, accept at its face value the superiority of all judgments and commands issued by those in control. The longer the soldier has been drilled, and the more thoroughly his mind has been set in the mould, the more automatic, undisturbed, and satisfactory his responses will be. When " soldiers of labour " are first cast in the mould of " soldiers of war," they will naturally carry into fields, factories, and workshops the same blind and fanatical loyalties to the employer which they have learned as the unbreakable law of action from the drill-master.

The will of the superior officer is imperious, his commands final, and his powers to enforce ruthless. As such, he can brook no control from below. He is not responsible for the health and livelihood of those beneath him, but only to those above him. The autocratic power of the top-sergeant grovels before the autocratic authority of the captain, the captain before that of the major, the major before the general. Appointment and control are from on top down, responsibility is from the bottom up. This law of military life, as old as organised warfare itself, has been carried to its highest stage of perfection in the conduct of the German military machine. In adopting this pattern for all phases of economic, political, and social life in Germany, the Nazis are imposing on its people the most rigid, uncompromising, and autocratically controlled straitjacket ever devised by the human mind.

But the more rigid the straitjacket, the more necessary to be sure of the complete lack of the spirit of opposition from the " inner man." On this point the Nazis are clear: hence their emphasis on the youth. From the earliest days the youth must be taken in hand, their actions controlled, their thoughts regimented, their ideas fixed, their habits determined, the ebb and flow of their character development manipulated to the ends laid down by the Nazi " soldier state " hierarchy. This emphasis on the youth is designed with rare subtlety and cunning. To the unregimented mind, coal-pits and factory walls have little romance. Not so the life of the soldier. However onerous the duties he must perform, and however rigid and arbitrary the commands he must obey, he has long been made a creature of fiction and fable, of richly coloured and emotionally charged history, of music, myth, and song, of strange and wild adventure.

In life the juvenile mind finds the soldier for ever on the march to new places, through crowds of weeping women and excited throngs of children. The soldier is always doing battle with strange and deadly foes. There are movements at night, with stealthy creeping over unknown ground to surprise and overtake the enemy. There are pitched and deadly battles in the daytime with some brave soldier always capturing fifty of the enemy alive and earning the plaudits and medals of a grateful Fatherland. There are triumphal returns, and again the beat, the drum, the roar of bands, barked orders, marching feet, and excited crowds. Even in death the soldier moves to his grave with romance—a draped flag, a garland of roses, a silence broken only by muffled weeping, a mournful bugle, and a salvo from the guns of lost comrades. In life romance, imagery, excitement; in death heroism and a place in the story-books.

Here is the necessary sugar-coating for the purpose in mind. To regiment the " soldiers of labour " properly, first regiment the soldier. To make the soldier attractive, surround him with all the myth, the romance, the exciting experience possible. That is, take full advantage of the juvenile love of romance and strange adventure; focus and co-ordinate the many-coloured and exotic imagery of the child.

Effective co-ordination of this sort requires control over all agencies—school, sport field, camp—and media for shaping and influencing the juvenile mind. Furthermore, it calls for cen-tralised organisation, the complete elimination of all competing or disillusioning activities, and unquestioning power to enforce all commands. The German programme along these lines is not yet complete, but in the Hitler Youth the whole plan is laid bare.

The Hitler Youth is described as " an organisation that arose spontaneously from the members of the young generation who wished to place themselves at the service of the National Socialist Party."[24] " Spontaneously " is to be understood as meaning organised from above to meet the spontaneous need of the National Socialist Party. So organised, it is characterised by the Nazis as the only " self-led " youth organisation in the world. " Self-led " likewise requires interpretation. " Youth must be led by youth," said Hitler in one of his inspired moments. " Therefore their leaders are *chosen* by a system of *promotion* from the leadership of one group to another within the organisation."[25]

Membership in the Hitler Youth is said to be entirely voluntary. " Voluntary " has its special Nordic meaning, which is that any youth desiring to belong to any organisation must belong to the Hitler Youth. Since the Hitler Youth is now the sole route of entry into the National Socialist Party, and since Party membership is the only Open Sesame to any position above that of day labourer in any economic, political, social, or military office in the entire Reich, the " voluntary " membership feature loses some of its distilled democratic beauty.

The history of the Hitler Youth goes back to the foundation of the National Socialist Youth League (*N.S.-Jugendbund*) by Adolf Hitler in March 1922. The League disappeared with the dissolution by the police of the National Socialist Party in 1923. Following the Party reorganisation by Hitler in 1925, two new youth organisations were established, the Schill-Youth and the Great German Youth Movement. The name Hitler Youth was first applied by Julius Streicher, later to become notorious for his virulent attacks on the Jews, to the members of the Great German Youth Movement in 1926. The various Hitler Youth clubs were brought under the control of the Youth Committee of the National Socialist Party. In 1928 the first attempt was made to form a nation-wide youth organisation involving regional divisions and subdivisions on the one hand, and separation of the sexes on the other. It was at this time that the Young Men's Bands, predecessors of the Young Folks League, and the Sister Bands, predecessors of the Federation of German Girls, were formed.

The formal history of the Hitler Youth is commonly dated from the appearance of 2,000 Hitler Youth in the ranks of the paraders at the 1929 National Socialist Party convention. Shortly thereafter the National Socialist Pupils and the National Socialist Students League were formed to propagate Nazi doctrines among *gymnasium* and university students respectively. In 1931 Baldur von Schirach was named National Youth Leader in charge of all three organisations under the immediate control of the Storm Troop administration. Somewhat later these organisations were fused together and placed directly under Party control. In 1932 the Hitler Youth organised the National Socialist Youth Factory Cells for co-ordinating factory juvenile labour to the Nazi *Weltanschauung*.

Subsequent to acquisition of power by the Party, all Socialist and Communist youth organisations were liquidated, and their membership brought under Schirach's control. The same fate befell the various religious youth organisations of the several Protestant confessions. At the present time only the Catholic youth organisations remain outside. These are allowed to function solely with respect to religious matters. All educational, leisure, and occupational activities of the Catholic Youth Leagues have been co-ordinated with the Hitler Youth.

On June 17, 1933, Hitler named von Schirach " Youth Leader of the German Nation," and entrusted to him control over all youth activity in the German Reich. Schirach is responsible directly to Hitler, and holds office at his pleasure. His first job was to complete " co-ordination of all youth organisations." " I shall unify the youth," he told an Associated Press reporter somewhat later. Already " I have merged with the Hitler Youth the youth groups of all organisations and associations."[26] Detailed control he maintains through his unrestricted power of appointment and removal of all " leaders " in all offices and for all divisions of the Reich.

The hierarchy of " leaders " via which he controls all youth activity is similar to that employed by all other Nazi organisations. " The first rung of the ladder is the leadership of the small

Comrade Band (*Kameradschaftsführer*), which comprises only
ten members. Next comes the Troop leader (*Scharführer*),
following that we have promotion to the respective grades of the
Sub-district leader (*Unterbannführer*), District leader (*Bann-
führer*), and Regional and Chief Regional leaders (*Gebietsführer*
and *Obergebietsführer*)."[27] The girls are similarly organised into
the Federation of German Girls.

A further division of duties and privileges is in the process of
being worked out. Under the new scheme, all the German youth
will be included in the Reich Youth League. Out of the League
will be selected those regarded as most promising and trustworthy from the Nazi point of view. These will become the
leaders of the League, and simultaneously will constitute the
corps of the Hitler Youth and the League of German Girls. The
size of these two organisations will be adjusted to the membership requirements of the National Socialist Party. According
to von Schirach, the " Hitler Youth and the League of German
Girls are not to be larger than absolutely necessary to assure the
National Socialist Party of the necessary recruits of young
National Socialists who are adequate both in character and
accomplishment."[28] Members of these two allied organisations
are, thus, to become a sort of *élite* amongst the youth, and their
activities are to train them to become good Party members, the
élite of the adult world.

Here we have the "picked number" who are to learn at an
early age to " rule as being a superior race," through thorough-
going indoctrination with National Socialist principles. In training to become National Socialists they are believed to be obeying
the " command of God " that they dedicate their lives to
" service " to the " community " in whatever capacity their
" nature-given capacities " may determine. That is to say, if
each will learn to walk humbly but proudly in the path of his
nature-determined calling he will serve Germany, and " fulfilment of service to Germany is service to God." True leaders will
see to it that the led shall not only follow, but learn to love the
leaders selected and appointed over them by the Leader (Adolf
Hitler) himself. And " who loves Adolf Hitler loves Germany;
who loves Germany loves God."[29]

" Man is a unity," writes Arnhold, " he does not exist as a

single factor which can be one-sidedly developed." Body, mind, and soul must be promoted simultaneously and towards the same end. The proper education must include work and play in all its phases and facets, and its underlying co-ordinative principles must be so completely woven into the conscious and subconscious life that it must appear that education of every man has " gone into his flesh and blood."[30]

This education must be authoritative. " History has shown that it is always dangerous to permit the young masses the education of their leader group from below upwards and without the correcting influence of strong, authoritative lead."[31] Authoritative, complete, and uniform is, hence, the organisation of the Hitler Youth. Its functions are patterned after that of the Nazi Party. Schirach's staff consists of thirteen divisions: Organisation, Personnel, Management, Culture, German Youth Abroad, Social, Press and Propaganda, Radio, Physical Education, Spiritual Development, Youth Hostels, National Guardians of the Union of German Girls.

The same division of functions holds for each of the four major subdivisions: the Hitler Youth, the German Young Folk, the Young Girls, and the Union of German Girls. The pattern for each central organisation permeates down through the regional hierarchies. Every unit is supposed to hold weekly meetings throughout the year. Every Wednesday evening the members gather in their local headquarters to hear an address or study lectures broadcast by radio from the Berlin central office, following which discussion takes place. Parades, demonstrations, and festivals play an important part in the training. These latter generally take place on Saturday, the children being given the alternative of attending school classes or marching (and thus joining) with the respective group.

The Youth organisations also have " agreements " with other Party organs or governmental bureaux. An agreement has been reached with the Labour Front whereby the youth in factories, etc., are organised into the National Socialist Youth Business Cells (N.S. Jugend B.O.); with the Labour Ministry, whereby the formulation of, and penalty-infliction of, the juvenile laws is carried through jointly by these two bodies; with the Department of Education, under which the Youth organisations will in time be given full and complete control of all athletic courses in schools, and will likewise administer government appropriations in support thereof; with the Ministry of Aviation, whereby youths are given instruction in aviation training; and with the Union of German Students for a division of labour in propaganda between this and the parent organisation.

The programme for training "the picked number . . . to secure and maintain their rule ruthlessly over the broad masses," and to make the younger generation of the broad masses obey their leaders as though commands given were of the stuff of their own flesh and blood, has three functional lines of emphasis: sports, military training, and occupational or vocational training. The latter has been dealt with above; the first two can be considered as two phases of the same thing—training in acquisition of " soldierly qualities."

4. TRAINING THE YOUTH TO BECOME SOLDIERS

Under the banner of " Sword and Plough for Freedom and Honour," Hitler's own personal journal, the *Nationalsozial-istische Monatshefte*, sounds the tocsin of duty for the young: " The National Socialist people's youth affirms battle, and submits to the carrying of arms as the obvious foundations of all people's labour. They hope for the day in which the weapons will be placed in their hands which are associated with the full consciousness of manhood."[32]

The National Youth Administration has prepared a manual, *Hitler Youth in Service*, for guidance of instructors and leaders throughout all divisions of the Hitler Youth. The first half of the book is taken up with physical exercises, games, and calisthenics. These are outlined in great detail, illustrated with charts and drawings, and full instructions for proper performance, including standard performance for different age groupings. The second half of the book is devoted entirely to military activities.

Transition from the first to the second half is provided by conclusion of sports activities in competition. The German word is *Wettkampf*. *Kampf* means struggle, fight, battle, combat. All sport ends up in *Wettkampf*; the military training division begins with the first instruments of *Kampf*, or guns and shooting. The bodily development and discipline of ordinary sport is, thus, the necessary background for the more strenuous demands of war-like activity. " Shooting sport," the manual asserts, " demands the greatest concentration and control of all physical and spiritual powers."

Such shooting promotes virtues commendable to the Nazis. " It develops inner and outer calm and cold-bloodedness (*Kaltblütigkeit*), awakens and promotes decision and self-confidence in the shooters. Through the necessary arrangement and subordination at the shooting stand, shooting sport promotes discipline and the spirit of comradeship."[33] Arms supplied to promote amongst the Hitler Youth " joy in shooting service " consist of air rifles for boys under sixteen and small calibre rifles for boys over sixteen years of age. Manual instruction is given in assembly and cleaning of all rifle parts, arranging sights and finding range, and various postures and techniques of firing.

The following section of the manual gives full instruction for squad and company formation, the rudiments of military drill, and the execution of the principal troop movements in drill, drill review, and marching. This work is supposed to promote " education of the Hitler Youth to adult discipline, obedience, and subordination." The next section gives instruction in the elements of field movements: knowledge of terrain, how to estimate heights of hills and distances, how to proceed over the ground unnoticed by taking advantage of humps and depression in the ground, how to use flora and woods to the maximum advantage in advance and retreat. " In walking through a forest," the manual instructs, "the Hitler Youth must always pay attention to the following principal fundamentals: one always uses the shadows and avoids sunshiny places; one always seeks the dark undergrowth."

Section E gives full data on the elements of the march, journey, and encampment. It includes preparations for the march, breaking ranks, and setting up camp, pitching tents, making fires for cooking, and methods of hanging pots, etc., over fires, securing pure water, and making provision for proper sanitation, division of labour between the various service divisions, etc. A final section gives instruction in first-aid methods.

Titles of children's books widely sold throughout Germany express a similar spirit: *The Battle of Tannenberg, Two Lads in the Navy, Horst Wants to be a Soldier.* Thurston quotes from a review of one such booklet bearing the title *A Child goes to War,* in which it is proudly announced that the novel " provides a thrilling insight into the youthful soul, with its capacity for enthusiasm and thirst for adventure, and shows how that soul, in the school of war, swiftly develops to maturity and manhood. The chance, as volunteer, to get away from school, and to be able to rush into battle and adventure, works like an intoxicant upon the soul of the fifteen-year-old hero of the book."

Plans are now being formulated for systems of crèches and kindergarten schools which will be thoroughly co-ordinated to achieve the same ends. Provision has already been made for the child when he or she reaches the age of ten. Beginning with that year, they become, more or less automatically, members of the German Young Folks League (*Deutsches Jungvolk*). Originally entirely voluntary, it is being gradually transformed into a compulsory organisation in which all Aryan children are obliged to join. In early January of 1936, Baldur von Schirach, Reich Youth Leader, proclaimed a " German Young Folk Year " for the purpose of carrying into practice, as reported in the *New York Times,*[34] the programme outlined by Hitler in 1933, for " taking children from those parents who can no longer learn new ways and educate them into what the National Socialist State needs."

A vast propaganda literature is being written for these children. Typical are the series known as " Youth Leaflets for Home Evening Activities for the German Young Folk," published by the Division of the National Youth Leadership. These lay out the details for the evening gatherings. Number 10 of the series, *Expeditions and Camping*, will serve as an example of the series. The cover design shows tents surrounded by flags, standing on the edge of a forest. Inside the cover a flap holds thirteen sheets of loose-leaf literature, consisting of short articles and abstracts, with the following titles: " On a Long Trip to East Prussia," " How the Good Thorkel Became a Hero,"

" Words for the Flag," " Old German Peasant Wisdom." The stories, interspersed with heroic songs, all have to do with brave deeds involving fighting, combat, overcoming the enemy, saving the Fatherland, being strong, brave, and bold. A bibliography of recommended reading at the end is about evenly divided between books on sports and on military heroics. A final two pages are devoted to outlining a model programme for the " State Youth Day " (Saturday by decree) beginning at 8.30 in the morning and going to 4.30 in the afternoon. All exercises begin with military line-ups, roll-calls, songs, and marching.

There is nothing in all the Hitler Youth literature to mitigate this picture of the proper activity of young Germany. All the children are in uniform who belong to the divisions of the central organisation. All those over fourteen years of age carry guns, are schooled before the age of eighteen in the entire range of the rudiments of military training and warfare, and are taught to believe that there is no manliness, no true virtue, no real citizenship, no honourable German, when the rules of military life are relaxed. The vast literature put out by the Youth Press is uniformly chauvinistic, truculent, and bristling with all the favourite theses of the Nazis regarding inferior races, circles of unscrupulous enemies, the dangers of Communism, and so forth.

All activities are made subordinate in the first instance to this military feature. Even some of the more apparently innocuous features, such as the Comradeship Evening At Home literature, dealing with old German cities and local history, is oriented to promote patriotic Germanism. And it is the official view that " In German customs [ways] lies the original strength of soldierdom firmly anchored."[35] What the pamphlets, newspapers, and periodicals are supposed to supply in the way of reading matter, the almost innumerable trips and tours, and the whole system of German Youth Hostels supply in the form of living experience. There are reputed to be some 2,500 of these Youth Hostels scattered around the country, and equipped to give at extraordinarily low rates overnight lodging to travelling bands of children.

A Nazi author quotes with approval a statement made by

Joseph von Eichendorf, written in 1812, containing the promise of life to the youth of his day: " For our youth there is no ease of carefree play, no blithe immunity; the quest of life engages it early. We come to birth in the midst of struggle, and in the midst of struggle, vanquished or victorious, we decline."[36] In the Youth Hostels and many of the camps, serious efforts are made to make life amenable to youthful spontaneity and love of play. But it is all to the end that the child shall be hardened for the grim and arduous life of which von Eichendorf spoke by first becoming a soldier—by having the soldier pattern completely dominate his entire life.

5. SOLDIER OF THE CRADLE

As the youth, so the man; as the little child, so the youth. If the man is to be a soldier of labour, then the youth must be trained to become soldiers, and the babies taught to imitate and admire the soldier with their first gasps of air and first faltering steps. Stern Aryan logic demands that the bubble and vivid flow of child life shall be co-ordinated in the pattern of the goose-stepping legionnaire of war. For what should the good German mother pray ? " Every German mother should pray," said a Nazi orator to a gigantic gathering in the Sportpalast of Berlin in 1930, " to see the glint of fight when first she looks into her new-born baby's bright blue eyes." She will then know in her proud mother's heart that she has given birth to a true German man. " The warlike endowment is the first [characteristic] of the German man," wrote Arnhold in a circular issued from Hamburg in 1935. " Struggle is the life expression of the German People," and, this being so, true Nordic parents will surround the infant cradle with the toughening mood and atmosphere, the stern discipline, the music and the song which is best adapted to fit the child for the grim and arduous road that lies ahead.

This holds with considerable rigidity for all those parents belonging to the Nazi Party. It holds for all subject to " guidance " at the hands of the " leaders " under whose jurisdiction they come. As indicated above, the right of Nazi Party officials to enter any home or any premises to see whether occupants are politically unreliable or not is paralleled by the right of other recognised " leaders," industrialists, business men, etc., to do the same thing.

In the co-ordinated home, all the music, the literature, the care and conduct of the house, the methods of handling, and the conduct of, the children are subject to review. The business men may do this directly only under special circumstances, where loans and mortgages are held on land and in similar cases, but they may at all times do so indirectly through the Nazi Party. This prerogative is important, for the " second basic value of the German People, which is bound with the closest ties to the warlike, is [our] creative handicraft endowment," as Arnhold puts it. This " uniquely German creative power " of making things is the foundation for the workmanlike performance of the labourers-to-be. Hence, the " leaders " of labourers-to-be are " responsible to the state " for nurturing this form of national wealth from the tenderest age on.

As will be seen in a later chapter, mothers are " responsible " for the care and maintenance of their children according to good Nazi principles. Child rearing and child training are the objects of the most detailed instructions in schools over which the Nazi Party maintains the most rigid control. As the mother is trained, so the child. The child is the mother's contribution to the state. That state demands of all citizens soldierly qualities, hence the mother must begin to train her boy to be a soldier from his first gasp of breath. There must be rigid discipline, performance of duties, training for labour, and acceptance with the nipple of the divine mission of the Leaders of the National Socialist state.

In accepting the Nazi state he must learn to hold German achievements superior to all other things—its arts and sciences, its history and terrain, its museums and industries. He must be led to believe that all the world emulates, or is envious, or seeks to destroy, these finest flowers of human genius which have all been achieved through struggle, involving Germany against the world. Hence every child must be made to love the idea of war, must be made to cherish and value uniform, knowledge of guns, and the arts and history of combat. A Nazi *Military Mother Goose*, best seller in Berlin during the Christmas season of 1935, is filled with nursery rhymes which the true Nazi child may repeat with his porridge, such as the following[37]:

> *What puffs and patters ?*
> *What clicks and clatters ?*
>
> *I know what, O what fun !*
> *It's a lovely Gatling-gun !*

Or again:

> *In perfect step the Reichswehr comes*
> *Along the avenue,*
> *With merry fife and rolling drums.*
> *Come, we'll go marching too !*

In the toy-shops of Wertheim, Tietz, and Karstadt, or any other large department store, can be seen hundreds of thousands of toy soldiers in grey, green, blue, and brown. All the paraphernalia of war, including tin hats, toy guns, sabres, miniature canteens, tanks, gas masks, and the like were to be had for children from the ages of three to fourteen in the greatest profusion. Most popular were the tin hats—" trench helmets for boys and girls "—and the tanks. The latter were to be had " in a dozen ingenious forms, all painstakingly realistic," ranging from tiny replicas four inches long, wound up with a key, which race about the playroom spitting electric fire through miniature machine-guns, to " one-child " tanks on the model of the American go-carts and baby autos, inside which the playful Nazi child may himself sit and manipulate the steering-wheel and gun to his heart's content.[38]

As he steers his baby tank around the floor, and arranges his many-coloured toy soldiers in battle formation, the spirit of the Leader floats over the nursery floor. Out of the excitement and laughter the heart of the child shall murmur a prayer to this spirit brooding over the toys: Baldur von Schirach offers this prayer to the " Leader ": " Adolf Hitler, we believe in Thee. Without Thee we would be alone. Through Thee we are a People. Thou hast given us the great experience of our Youth, Comradeship. Thou hast laid upon us the Task, the Duty, and the Responsibility. Thou hast given us Thy Name, the most beloved Name that Germany has ever possessed. We speak it with Reverence, we bear it with Faith and Loyalty. Thou canst depend upon us, Adolf Hitler, Leader and Standard-Bearer. The Youth is Thy Name. Thy Name is the Youth. Thou and the young millions can never be sundered."

And what does the Leader and Standard-Bearer ask of this toddle-gaited suppliant playing on the nursery floor? He asks that he shall so live, play, dream, and hope that when his summons comes to join the first organised ranks of the Hitler Youth pointing towards his soldier destiny he shall find nothing else worth doing at all. Then he shall be able to write from out the womb, the cradle, and the nursery, such testimonials on the tug of his Aryan heart as this:

" I had spent weeks in the library among books. I had spent days in wandering about museums. I felt the urge but could not stop it. Then I wandered through the country again, over the meadows and wide plains of North Germany. There I saw soldiers on the march. I knew not whence they came nor whither they were going nor who they were. Soldiers. I followed them for hours, tried to make the same steps, to halt when they did and to look like them. And, while my marching seemed long, there arose between us a silent debate. Again and again I tried to look in their eyes—they appeared cold and steely, and then deep down there trembled something like frenzy or a glowing fervour. They spoke of the most mysterious, greatest, and deepest passion of life—of battle. I had known all this before. First through the group and then through the individual it all became living and real.

" Then their faces, their gait, their bearing, all began to speak to me. We are the greatest philosophers, they said, because always and above all we assert our contention that the Idea is higher than the Material through action. And isn't that the only manly philosophy? Art? Aren't we the greatest artists, because we are where life is lived at its strongest and is fashioned out of flesh and blood?

" Isn't being a soldier the only thing that makes us genuinely immortal? Because it envelops us as travelling companions in the beating waves of the eternal sea from whose foam we have sprung. How do you know that? I asked. How do you know all that I have for years been seeking? They only stared, these scorners of words."

What " Idea," what vision of the shape of things to come, did these " scorners of words " see as they stared at their youthful questioner? Baldur von Schirach gives the significant answer: the nation in the death-grip of war.

" That once there stood a people in arms, Catholic, Protestant, beggar and millionaire, peasants and writers, merchants and workers, and that all of them heeded but one will, were only German, nothing but German, that is what set us marching. Then neither title nor station in life, neither money nor difference in any class, meant anything. That is what we desire. . . . The black years of the war are over; the spirit of the warriors remains."

This is " to-day's spring " in the new Germany. Not war, but the warrior in field, factory, and workshop, in trench and bivouac.

And at the fountain-head of " to-day's spring " stands the new German ideal of woman, woman as mother at the germinal source of life, attitude, and mood; as the first creator and maker of the obedient, self-sacrificing, and fantasy-led warrior.

CHAPTER VI

Women, the Cradle, and the Plough

THE Nazi " philosophy " lays upon the woman two duties which she must perform " for the state." She must generate and nourish the bodies of its children, and she must shape the infantile mind to accept Nazi ideas and attitudes in all things. She is " mother " for the Third Reich, and, as mothers, women in Nazi lands have an affinity of function with the soil. From the women flows the stream of men who people the Reich; the soil feeds all. On the " fertilities " of these two rests the greatness of the new Reich. Both must be cultivated on behalf of productivity. As the soil must be cleared, drained, seeded, and harvested, so the women must be reared, made strong and healthy, married and bred. As output per hectare must be increased at whatever cost, to free Germany from dependence on imported foodstuffs, so output per woman must be advanced, that the Fatherland may have bounteous supplies of her " richest resources," men—men to fill the ranks as warlike " soldiers of the state " and men to serve as docile " soldiers of labour."

The Nazis are proud that they regard the woman as the peasant regards his cow. Both supply services to those in a position to command them. To the peasant his cow supplies calves and milk; to the true Nordic male his woman supplies him with children and service to bed and board. As the subservient, hard-working, and pious peasant is the ideal of German manhood, so the obedient, hard-working, and fruitful peasant woman is the ideal of German womanhood. The core of Nazi theory on woman runs about as follows: woman serves the man, man serves the state; the state must become great; great states —especially Germany—rest on labour; women create the supply and can render subservient the attitude of labour; hence women must be co-ordinated in service to the state, i.e. to perform the " duty of motherhood," which means to increase child output for the state.

Hitler himself has laid down this doctrine in no uncertain terms. " Liberalism has a large number of points for women's equality. The Nazi programme for women has but one: this is the child. While man makes his supreme sacrifice on the field of battle, woman fights her supreme battle for her nation when she gives life to a child."[1] The Nazi " equality " for women, the German " new freedom " of which they are so fulsomely proud, involves, thus, a double but related set of loyalties and a three-fold set of duties. The loyalties are to men and the state, the duties are those of housewife, mother, and propagandist. In all phases of these activities her functioning is exactly determined by her femininity. Since, according to Nazi theory, physiology determines all psychological attitudes and rates all capacities, the femininity of women determines all duties, loyalties, capacities, and roles in society.

When she fulfils her nature-allotted roles properly, she will gain the respect which is due her as an embodiment of German womanhood. " The German woman who is bred in a true National-Socialist sense to be a German mother will secure from German youth the respect which is due her."[2] She will not be the " Gretchen type," but rather a " . . . woman intellectually capable to stand by her husband in his interests and his struggle with life and make his life richer and fuller. . . ."[3] To be " intellectually capable " of standing by her husband, she must fulfil certain definite specifications. " Every Aryan hero should marry only a blonde Aryan woman with blue, wide-open eyes, a long oval face, a pink and white skin, a narrow nose, a small mouth, and under all circumstances virginal. A blond blue-eyed man must marry no brunette, no Mediterranean-type woman with short legs, black hair, hooked nose, full lips, a large mouth, and an inclination to plumpness. A blond blue-eyed Aryan hero must marry no Negroid type of woman with the well-known Negroid head and thinnish body. The Aryan hero must marry only his equal Aryan woman, but not one who goes out too much or likes theatres, entertainment, or sport, or who cares to be seen outside her house."[4]

Feminine means to lack creative power, according to Alfred Rosenberg, one of the chief Nazi theoreticians. But " creative power " with respect to work, the sciences, and the arts. However this is not all. " The creative will of man relates to work, running machines, doing business, organising and conducting research, while the creative will of women applies to men. . . .

To be true, women can do things of this order, but they must . . . not. But the woman must form men, develop men, rear, shape, and love them or she will perish." She is not only the creator of men, but she is the earliest hewer, shaper, and moulder of the infantile mind to fit the pattern of the state for which she first bore him. " And," asks Hitler, " is it something inferior to form the soul of a child than to write a book or to accomplish some piece of work ? "⁵

In giving life to the child and moulding its infantile mind, the women become " warriors for the common life." What this means the Nazis are always sure to make clear. " The slogan, *emancipation of women, has its roots only in Jewish intellectualism.* The German woman in the truly palmy days of German life *has no need for emancipation* any more than in those same good days need the man fear that he may be wrenched out of his place by woman. Only when there was a lack of absolute certainty in the knowledge of her task did the eternal instinct of self and race preservation begin to revolt in woman, then there grew from this revolt a state of affairs that was unnatural and which lasted until both sexes returned to the respective spheres which an eternally wise Providence has pre-ordained for them."⁶

There can be no antagonism between the sexes " so long as each fulfils the part designed for him by Nature." Man's place is in the larger outside world, woman's in the smaller but equally important world of the home. " When one says that the man's world is the State, his struggle, his preparation for solidarity, then one may perhaps say that the woman's world is a smaller one—*her world is her husband, her family, her children and her home* . . . what would become of the greater world, if there were no one to tend to and care for the smaller one ? The greater world is built upon the very foundation of this smaller world. The two worlds are not antagonistic—they complement one another, they belong together just as husband and wife belong together."⁷

She must in this " world " of hers exercise the virtues of hard work and self-sacrifice to husband, children, and the state. " The woman of the future shall be at home in her kingdom, will not torment herself with fruitless worry about equality, will learn to find happiness in the accomplishments of her man,

and will not disdain to support him by her bravery, her willingness to sacrifice, and her diligence in the field of life allotted to
her."⁸ So, living for her man, she serves the nation. " The
German woman, as we see her, must, when the exigencies of the
Race require it, give up luxury and pleasure, she must be
physically and spiritually able to work and she must be able,
out of the harsh, severe existence that we are to-day forced to
live, to make a good, sweet life. She must be innately aware of
the need and dangers that beset her Race and *she must gladly
do all that is expected of her.* She must, in a word, be able to think
politically . . . so that she feels with, sacrifices with, the entire
people in self-assured and proud support."⁹

The German woman has within her " the best guarantee of the
nordification of our people, and she will give birth to Nordic
children only and thus for generations to come she will ensure
German kind and German greatness. Being of Nordic race, she
is mentally different and superior to the women of other races.
. . . This must be considered as sublime and equal in value to
the profession of warrior and hero."¹⁰

That she may generate as many as possible future candidates
for " the profession of warrior and hero," or future mothers of
the same, the state promotes marriage and births. Both are
duties. " Marriage, and that in the National Socialist state must
be strictly adhered to, is stipulated by fate."¹¹ To help fate
along the Nazis subsidise marriages with loans for long periods,
make it difficult for women to attend higher schools of education,
or to find jobs. For neither party is it important that love enter
as a factor. " What matters is not that the husband finds
satisfaction [in his marriage] but that his children are of pure
race."¹² In none of the literature is there more than mere intimation that love is or can be a factor of any importance at all
for the woman. At the best it is a negligible factor.

To help births along the sale of contraceptive information or
devices is prohibited, operations for abortion are illegal, and a
premium is laid on child production. In February of 1936, the
Reich Finance Ministry announced that a family allowance of
Rm. 10 ($4·00) per month will be granted for every child born
after the fourth, if the parents' income does not exceed Rm.
1,800 ($720·00) per annum.¹³

The question remains, how is it possible to make such a programme palatable to the women ? How is it possible to persuade women to give up their recently found liberties, their freedom to go into the professions, to take jobs, make money, and lead a more or less personally independent life of their own choosing ? How can they be made to acquiesce in the doctrine that they are necessarily inferior to the men in everything that lies outside the strict confines of the home ? How can each be made to feel that her highest duty is to bear children, serve her husband, and sacrifice her life to the welfare of these on behalf of the state ? On what basis can she be convinced even if she regards any or all of these as first in order of importance, that she should forego the ballot, the office, the job ?

How convince mothers that they should bear children not for themselves, but for the state; that they should train their boys to be soldiers and their girls to become the mothers of soldiers, dedicating, in their turn, their lives in sacrifice to children, husbands, and the state ? How can she be led to accept Hitler's blood-curdling dictum: " Everything, from the baby's first story-book to the last newspaper, theatre, cinema . . . will be put to this end . . . until the brain of the tiniest child is penetrated by the glowing prayer: Almighty God, bless our weapons again . . . bless our battle ? "

By what methods can wives be persuaded that love does not count in marriage, that they should have nothing to say about the number of children they should bear, that neither male children nor husband can regard them as one amongst equals ? By what pressures can she be compelled to teach her children that all aliens are inferior, that all Jews are depraved, that the warrior is the highest product of human evolution, that it is virtuous to do and die without murmur when commanded from above and regardless of the object for which orders are given, that (if she be not upper middle class) one is born to station with its round of bitter and inescapable toil at long hours and for meagre rewards ?

All this and more must she accept as the governing laws of her special ministry—her " kingdom of the home." The Nazi solution, as with labour and all other groups, is to control education from the earliest age possible, and to co-ordinate all phases of the growing girl's life from young girlhood on through to maturity, the subsequent inescapable induction into her " pre-ordained " feminine duties.

Five agencies have been established for this full co-ordination of the women: The League of German Girls (*Bund Deutscher Mädel*), Women's Labour Service (*Frauenarbeitsdienst*), the Women's Office of the German Labour Front (*Frauenamt der D.A.F.*), Women's Work (*Frauenwerk*), and Women's Activities division of the National Socialist Party (*Frauenschaften der N.S.D.A.P.*). In addition to these are three highly important activities for women in the services of Rural Aid (*Landhilfe*), Rural Year (*Landjahr*), and the Household Year (*Haushaltsjahr*).

1. THE LEAGUE OF GERMAN GIRLS

As pointed out in the preceding chapter, the League of German Girls is exactly parallel, in membership and organisation, to the Hitler Youth, with the exception that the age coverage is from fourteen to twenty-one instead of fourteen to eighteen. The junior division, the Young Girls in the Hitler Youth, is likewise parallel to the junior division of the Hitler Youth, the German Young Folks of the Hitler Youth, and includes all girls' organis-ations and activities from ten to fourteen.

Not much was said in the preceding chapter about the girls' division of the Hitler Youth. The reason for this was partly because of the attitude shown throughout all the literature dealing with youth organisations. For every book written on the boys' division, there is but a brief article on the girls'; for every chapter on the one, a hasty and almost forgotten line on the other. The whole Nazi attitude towards women could not be shown more clearly than by the tone and emphasis of this literature. A whole booklet will be devoted to the Hitler Youth, and will possess a single short paragraph on the girls. For every ten " candid camera " cuts showing boys' activities there will be one on the female side. Everywhere comment on the latter is tucked away in the obscure corner, and their activities be-littled by the fact of omission or half-apologetic comment. In a manual on the Hitler Youth, covering some 352 pages, not more than two are devoted to the activities of the girls.

From what can be learned by inspection of the scanty literature available, all the generalisations applied to the boys'
divisions can be used to characterise the girls' activities with the
exception of the specific objectives. (The former girl scout
movements of one sort or another apparently never amounted
to very much, and the new organisation has apparently had less
success than the Hitler Youth proper.) The girls are not trained
to be soldiers, but to take care of soldiers. But taking care of
soldiers means learning early the duties of housewife, wife, and
mother. The girls' camps follow this pattern through with
apparently the same rigour and persistence as in the boys'
camps. Here likewise they learn to become soldierlike, and to do
quickly, well, and uncomplainingly what officers command.

2. THE WOMEN'S LABOUR SERVICE

Much the same picture holds for the Women's Labour Service,
though here the literature is somewhat more copious. The
Service is compulsory for only those women who expect to go
into professional work; for the remainder it will be made compulsory at the end of 1936. The number of women enrolling is
very small (between 10,000 and 15,000) each six months. A
propaganda bulletin summarises their activities as follows:

" From the organisatory [sic] aspect, there are three different
types of labour-camps for women.

" The first type is the *rural camp*, which is situated in the
country and forms a small economic unit by itself. Here the
girls are taught settlement work and are trained in all matters
relating to agricultural settlements, in work on the farms, fields,
gardens and barns. After a few weeks the girls come to the
camp for settlement work this [sic] is the second type. These
camps are located in districts of new settlements and in needy
districts with poor peasants. Its aim is to assist the settlers and
peasants in their work. The young girls live in communal camps
and go to the peasants and settlers in the neighbourhood for
six hours a day lending a helping hand to the peasant's wife in
the house or in the field. The rest of the day the girls spend in
the camps hearing lectures on different subjects, playing
theatricals, singing and dancing folk-dances. The third type is

the *camp for social welfare work*, which is usually situated near the industrial cities and towns. Here the girls are trained in household work and social work and are sent for six hours a day to do social work in the homes of indigent families requiring such help.

" The girls who volunteer for service are usually housed in groups of 35–50 in vacant houses in farming districts. Each camp has a responsible and specially trained girl as leader. Besides the girl-leader there are often trained women-teachers, who instruct the girls in a life of service and co-operative living. The work, as I already told you, is limited to six hours a day, the rest of the time being given to political instruction, sports, and physical education. The discipline in the camp is a very rigid one, the girls are not allowed to leave the camp except on one Sunday in the month, on the other Sundays they undertake joint excursions."[14]

The food is very simple, consisting of grain-" coffee " or tea with black bread and marmalade for breakfast, and meat and potatoes for the other two meals. In a camp visited at Fürstenwalde the diet included no vegetables and no fruit. Rooms were quite plain. Mattresses were of straw laid on wooden boards. The daily routine began at 4.30. After setting-up exercises, making beds and cleaning-up rooms, and taking breakfast the girls went to work. The work consisted of doing the washing and ironing in peasant households, taking care of cows and hogs, and doing other miscellaneous farm work. In many places they hoe the peasant's fields, dig his potatoes, and harvest his crops. Every girl spends a minimum of six weeks in a peasant home, where she takes over a considerable portion of the routine work. The same holds good for the urban aid proffered. Aside from lodging and food, the girls receive 20 pfennigs (8 cents) per day spending money.

The work and propaganda is shaped up to fulfil a twofold purpose. On the one hand it is designed to develop in the girls the entire range of petit bourgeois economic virtues, and on the other to provide free subsidised labour for the indigent rural and urban poor.

The bourgeois virtues are those of property, industriousness, and thrift. These lower-class German burgher virtues become
GF

positive necessities in the life of the peasant woman who, as Frau Scholtz-Klink, Leader of the Women's Work activities, proudly declares, must normally work sixteen hours per day. In addition, everything in the hard narrow life of the peasant is dependent upon the phenomenon of fertility. His fields and the seed he sows must be as fertile as possible. His chickens must lay, his cows calve, his hogs litter. Since his labour force is made up of his sons and daughters, his wife must bear as often as possible. All these are property—property which he must keep as productive, as " fertile," as income-bringing as possible lest he starve. Nowhere else are the concepts of holy property and sacred fertility so closely intertwined, so inextricably interwoven, and so necessarily complementary to each other as in the poor peasant's life.

It is highly significant that most of the Women's Labour Service camps cater to the rural indigent. The peasant woman not only accepts the " duties " of property and fertility, but she most fully embodies their practical union. The Nazis believe that the very nature of woman is as property conscious as it is fertility oriented. In the Women's Labour Service they see the most perfect fulfilment of the idea of " Blood and the Soil," where each is rooted to property which he fertilises with his body and his labour. " This idea of property," a Nazi author explains, " finds much stronger roots in the hearts of the female youth than with the young men. In the case of male Labour Service it is a matter of provision of sustenance, work place, field of sport, but the girl says, My camp, my home ! "[15]

Of the arduousness of the labour performed there can be no question. The girls are taught to combine hard work with " rigid discipline," suppression of the " ego," and " joy." A German-American girl who enrolled at one of the camps tells how this was done. After a week involving " a daily six hours of digging and pounding turf . . . I helped to wash, iron and mend the camp linen in the ' laundry service,' where a day of dipping and wringing out of heavy quilt-covers over the bath-tub—an article of double utility in camp—proved more strenuous than shovelling out the light, loamy soil of fields and gardens. As an extra feature of this special week there arrived a load of amazingly dirty and torn bed linen, shirts and socks from a near-by boys' camp. . . . " In common with the whole Nazi programme, that machines must not be used except where indispensable auxiliaries to labour, this hard work is extolled as virtuous and made palatable by being mixed with music and song. Into this dirty laundry, our writer adds, " our whole force pitched full tilt to the tune of merry songs and witticisms. For music always accompanied the rhythm of our work: the pounding of the spade, the clicking of the needle and the swish-swash of the scrubbing brush. . . ."[16]

The purpose of this labour, " joyfully performed," is to prepare the good German peasant-like woman to sacrifice all personal considerations for her heavy round of duties. " Whoever has lived in one of these Labour Service Homes [camps] has experienced that the work, the duties, the tasks are so varied and so many that no room remains for the ego—there is so much work to be done for others that there are no claims to or demands on a personal individual existence."[17]

But if she gives of herself freely, she must be economical of all other things. To be always industrious, and waste nothing is the holy economy of the Nazi *Hausfrau*. " Every unnecessary waste in the household, just exactly as every idleness in economic life, as every unemployed who can be used, constitutes a loss to the community of German values and property."[18] Since the most of Germany is poor, the proper system " will have to see to it . . . that our household training of women always stresses a standard of living adapted to the modest conditions prevailing."[19]

Of this much, furthermore, the Nazis can always be relatively certain, the city girl, almost regardless of whatever level of " modest conditions " she may subsequently experience, is pretty apt to find herself above the level of those desperately poor and toil-driven peasant women she came to know during her " service " year. She can always remember herself as better off than some, can be thankful for her superior " station," and can be ever so frugal and still consider herself relatively fortunate in a land where such depths of poverty can not only be found in many places, but apparently endured without murmur to the end of life.

This " idea of being frugal " of all means, adapted as a

permanent policy " in time of need," has national implications
as well. First, the women now purchase a large percentage of all
goods used for ultimate consumption purposes. If the women can
be persuaded to exercise this purchasing power on behalf of
domestic production, Germany can be made more self-sufficient.
A great deal of stress is laid on this point. Hence it is necessary
to train women " politically " to accept without question the
nationalist chauvinism of the Nazi Party. Every day the girls
must be given " political instruction " by teachers especially
indoctrinated in a National Socialist Women Leaders' School.
What these teachers are prepared to transplant is indicated by
the political programme of the school, in the foreground of
which " stand the History and Programme of the N.S.D.A.P.,
Problems of Population Policy, Geo-political Problems, Settlement Problems, The East Problem, Tasks of Women in the
Third Reich."[20]

Furthermore, what and when women purchase is of considerable importance in the expansion or contraction of particular
industries, and in the regularisation of production. " The
housewives as the largest consumer layer of the population have
a high responsibility to the economy, the people, and the state.
In whatever channels they direct their expenditure for goods
will originate the future German economic life."[21] As this will
determine the amount of employment, the division of economic
energies between heavy and light industries, between necessities
and luxuries, so the women must be co-ordinated in the main-
springs of their wants and their spending habits.

The other side of the background of the Labour Service
programme is much simpler and more direct. Every girl taken
into Labour Service, every girl married, and every girl persuaded to abandon callings which " are apt to incite forces out
of harmony with the nature and soul of woman," relieves by so
much the pressure of unemployment. The Nazis are quite proud
of their achievements along this line. They have relieved some
300,000 women of their jobs by such methods. By so much they
have " relieved " unemployment, and by so much increased
the ranks of the potential mothers.

There is another and perhaps more important result flowing
from these activities. In both cities and the country there are

large numbers of indigent poor—poor whose insufferable economic burdens were gradually reducing them to the worst straits of poverty, dispossessing them of what little property they might possess, and driving them steadily to the left. Into these disaffected areas the Labour Service ranks have been poured. A double saving to the state has been effected. The unemployed and potentially unemployed are forced to help the indigent in lieu of receipt of unemployment benefits while the state is thereby relieved of the necessity of subsidising the large and growing rural poverty fringe. So far as the men's Labour Service is concerned, there is no escape from such forced labour. Many of the women have no better alternative than to join the Women's Labour Service, and if they do they have absolutely no choice whatsoever over the work they shall accomplish. The net result is that the Nazis are able, under the protection of an elaborate, pretentious, and superficially iridescent barrage of mysticism, to make the poor peasants believe much is being done for them, while the girls are being led to believe that they are obtaining practically free instruction for their life's highest calling.

The same sort of services are provided for the owners of big bankrupt estates. Thousands of young men and women are supplied to the *Junker* estates, particularly in the Eastern provinces, practically free of charge. It appears that the estates must pay at least a portion of the customary social insurance charges; otherwise the labour is supplied to them by the state absolutely without cost to themselves. Never, in all the past chronicles of slave history, has a cleverer and more cynical system of forced labour been discovered than this.

All the various subsidiary programmes for training young girls serve the same complicated purposes. In both the women's division of Rural Year and Land Service, work is performed analogous to that of the Women's Labour Service. The girls help the overworked peasant women perform their multitude of tasks in their miserable huts, take care of children while the peasant women work in the field, or go to the fields to do this labour themselves. There has been some talk of providing every German woman with a short vacation each year. In this event it is planned to provide the husband and family left behind with a girl who will care for the household during the mother's absence even as she would have done.

The Land Year is closely patterned after the Labour Service. During 1935 some 7,000 young girls were affected by the Prussian Law " which binds young people from the cities and the industrial centres to a ' land year.' " As with all the other literature dealing with such programmes for the women, the emphasis is jointly upon transfer from city to country, and upon all phases of the natural phenomena of fertility. A propaganda sheet explains that " our youth is growing up in narrow lanes and streets in the cities. They do not know when the grain, which supplies us with our daily bread, is ripe. They do not know how the potatoes, which they eat every day, grow, they have no idea of what storm and hail, drought and floods mean to the farmer, nor do they know the starry sky above us and have never experienced the changing of spring, summer, autumn and winter in nature."

" Their world was the lane, the street, the glare of the lights of the cinemas, rushing motor-cars, dressed-up women, strange and indifferent people who run, hurry and rush past them and who never find time to sit down next to a crying child, to stroke its hair gently and to comfort it in its sorrow." All this is in sharp contrast to the happy bucolic life of the peasant's daughter who is not anæmic, not *blasé*, and who has learned to experience " the earth with all its great secrets and beauties and the work which it also demands of human beings." They work with the peasant's wife " at her work in the house, farm, and garden ; they become attached to their new home, to the soil they cultivate, to the fields and to the woods, to their neighbours and their comrades. Their pale cheeks become pink, their walk becomes free and proud. They now become real human beings, get to know themselves and the secrets of nature and life. They once more learn how to fold their hands, and know that there are things in life that are holy."[22]

If numbers mean anything, the amount of cost-free and forced feminine child labour mobilised by this crude and awkward sentimentality to neutralise the mounting complaints of the lower poverty-stricken peasantry has not been anything to boast about. It is doubtful, in fact, whether the amount of peasant protest neutralised is equal to the persistent and likewise apparently growing complaints of mothers that the effect of this rural work is disastrous for the morals and futures of their daughters. There is a bawdy limerick current about the Strength through Joy co-educational tours which is commonly applied to the rural experiences of the youth:

> *Auf dem Feld and auf der Heide,*
> *Verlier' ich Kraft durch Freude.*
>
> (*In the fields and on the heath,*
> *I lose strength through joy.*)

That the complaints made along this line are not without foundation is proved by a recent request made to the Relief Administration for special aid to 2,000 *Landhilfe* girls, mostly under twenty years of age, who had become pregnant in the " service." The following letter from Germany is typical[23]:

" DEAR E.: Some days ago three girls, two of them sisters, came back from the *Landhilfe*—all three of them pregnant—all three from the house next door. You can't imagine what a rebellion there is against the *Landhilfe* in our street. Those most excited are the mothers whose daughters are still in it, because they fear that the same thing will happen to their daughters. Just think—the girls lived on a big farm, and the manager of the farm, a married Nazi official, raped them. . . ."

What the Rural Year does for the peasantry, the Domestic Year is supposed to perform for the city housewife. " For the ' Household Year for Girls ' any healthy German girl can apply that left school at Easter 1934 [in 1935 there were 600,000 of them—R. A. B.] and can find no situation as apprentice. The girls can apply at the nearest Vocational Advisory Office or Employment Office. By one of the same she will be directed to a suitable family. While the girl remains with the family she will be looked after by the Federation of German Girls, take part in their outings and homely evenings."[24]

The girls are known as " young companions " to the housewife and are singly and solely responsible to her. The housewife gives her bed and board, makes contributions for the girl to the Sick Fund, but pays no wages. She is supposed to look after the girl, " act with kindness in introducing her to her daily duties, and lead and teach her in a conscientious way." It is hoped by the Propaganda Ministry that housewives and girls alike will " come to grasp this fine idea," and that " in the end " it " will become a blessed experience both for housewife and household help."[25]

The duties prescribed by " this fine idea " cover the entire range of ordinary domestic labour, such as cooking, washing, cleaning the house, purchasing groceries, and taking care of the children. If there is a school for domestic labour in the vicinity, she must attend it regularly. In all activities the girl is learning " what every German woman must know." " It will," this propaganda circular goes on to say to the girls, " be useful to yourself, to your man and your children." For the housewife the advantages are clear, she will get cheap labour which at the regular rates for domestic labour she could not afford (regular servant girls are not supposed to be laid off through the Domestic Year Service), while at the same time " fulfilling a national task."[26]

3. THE BOARD FOR WOMEN WITHIN THE GERMAN LABOUR FRONT

This Board has charge of all activities of every working woman which have to do with her role as female in the job she occupies. It includes about 4 million women, and is charged with four sets of duties: (1) It must " see that every working woman's health is cared for and supervised by women, with a special view to motherhood. No woman in Germany is to suffer from the effects of her work to such an extent that in the event of her marrying, she has been robbed of the best and finest quality." (2) It must take care that hygienic conditions are satisfactory, that " light, air, and lighting facilities are adequate and are maintained." (3) It " . . . has undertaken the care of the working woman from the economic and social point of view. This Board carries weight in regard to questions dealing with wages and salary, in the fixing of tariffs and in legal decisions." (4) Special efforts are made to " see that every working woman is given the practical foundation necessary to conduct a household and necessary for a family and a home. The opportunity is given to the women workers and to the employees to attend courses in cooking, sewing, and mother-craft free of charge. Sometimes the courses are given in the factories during the afternoons and evenings."[27]

The Leaders, here as elsewhere, are appointed entirely from on top, are responsible solely to those above them, and are especially chosen for their loyalty to Nazi doctrine. Especially important are their labours in succour of those who are mentally and spiritually " ill." The leaders " . . . must help and advise the fellow-workers in their troubles. They must possess the strength to awake that feeling of consciousness and responsibility in those women who had succumbed to Marxist influence and are still opposed to the new state and its aims, that they must not only work for their own means of subsistence, but teach them to realise that each of them is a link in the big community of the German nation."[28]

It is by and through this organisation that plans are being effectuated for the large-scale supplanting of female by male labour. It will be noted that here as elsewhere all stress is laid on the mother-wife role of the woman, on her " service " to husband, children, and state, on her eventual displacement by virtue of her peculiar sex " ability and her nature." Some careers are provided for, but if women become doctors, lawyers, or Leaders, it is always with respect to women's organisations and activities. She can have no career outside these, and she is never encouraged to believe that she can under any circumstances combine outside (non-home) activities with her manifold duties in the home.

4. WOMEN'S WORK (" FRAUENWERK ")

The central co-ordinating agency for all the varied women's activities of Germany is called Women's Work. All women's organisations in every field, irrespective of their religious, professional, social, or other functions, must belong to it, accept its dictation on policy and in all details, and be " led " by appointees from the head " Leader," Frau Scholtz-Klink. " The idea of the unification of all these diverse women's

societies in the *Frauenwerk* . . . is this: the different societies do
not only exist individually for their own sake, but they are also
supposed to take an active part in the life of the nation." That
is to say, they must be co-ordinated so that every detail of
policy and action shall promote the programme of the National
Socialist state with respect to women, so that all women may be
co-ordinated with the policies of the Third Reich.

To fulfil this role it controls the activities of all the organisations previously discussed in this chapter. Each line of activity
is organised as a separate department. In addition to those
previously discussed, the *Frauenwerk* has the following departments:

(1) National Mothers' Service
(2) National Economy—Household Economy
(3) Film
(4) Press
(5) Foreign
(6) German Female Academicians
(7) Red Cross

(1) A propaganda bulletin which gives some idea of the
completeness with which all women's activities are co-ordinated
describes the National Mothers' Service as follows: It " . . . is
a working community for the instruction of mothers, in which
the National Socialist Women's Groups, the Evangelical Service
for Mothers, the department National Economy and Household
Economy, the German Union for the Safeguarding of Babies
and Infants, the Red Cross and the German Froebel Society, all
work hand in hand. The idea and the object of the training of
mothers is laid down in paragraph 1 of the *Reichsmütterdienst*
and is to this effect: ' The motive underlying the training of
mothers comes from the idea of the national community and
from the consciousness of the importance of the mother for both
the nation and the state. The task of the *Reichsmütterdienst* is:
to train mothers who are healthy both in body and mind, convinced of the high duties of motherhood, experienced in nursing
and educating their children, and who are capable of fulfilling
their household duties.' The working communities establish

schools for mothers with courses in cooking, sewing, book-keeping, hygiene, and nursing. A special interest is taken in the instruction of the expectant mothers with reference to the time before and after child-birth. The care of babies, their feeding, and their clothing, is demonstrated by means of baby-dolls in the natural size and weight, on which every woman has to practise these simple manipulations."[29]

There are 80 of these permanent schools located in towns and cities, while the country is provided with an ambulatory service. " For demonstrating purposes the ambulatory teachers are provided with a case containing a baby-doll, a bathing-tub and all articles necessary for a baby. The courses, which every girl or woman over eighteen years of age may attend, are arranged once or twice a week for several hours. The courses in the country run for a fortnight or three weeks daily. The money for the maternity schools is obtained by the sale of badges on mothers' day all over Germany, the contributions from municipalities and village boards, where the courses take place, and by taking a small fee from the woman."[30]

(2) The department National Economy–Household Economy deals with the women " in their capacity as consumers of a large part of the people's income. By these lectures and this instruction, the housewife's demand is directed in the right way to meet the supply."[31] The National Committee for People's Enlightenment has collaborated with the German Women's Work in a special " buy German " propaganda bulletin. In it is reproduced a table giving the distribution of supply of various garden products over the months of the year. The housewife is told that she " must buy that which is plentiful on the market. She must adjust her eating-schedule according to German harvest times." She must consume fresh eggs when fresh eggs are on the market; she must use domestic butter and animal fats (in compliance with the National Fats Plan) instead of imported oils.

The same holds for all other products. She should buy only those handicraft and industrial products which use German materials and employ German workmen. She must buy *Vistra* and *Wollstra* instead of imported woollens, linen, half-linen, and rayon instead of cotton and silk. Kitchen utensils should be of aluminium (90 per cent German) instead of copper and zinc (imported from abroad).

" Where and how do I buy ? " the bulletin asks, and then answers significantly: " A broad, independent middle class is the guarantee for stable social relations; it provides workers and employees opportunities to rise, and it is in addition the bearer of a sound culture resting on private property. Through the creation and growth of giant enterprises (department stores) independent handicraft and merchant classes have during the past decade been severely injured. National Socialism fights for a revival of the middle class. Closing of the department stores is not possible for the time being on account of the numerous employees who would thereby go hungry. But the housewife can strengthen the middle class and thereby support the organic break-up of the department stores by purchasing wherever possible from handicraftsmen and independent retailers.

" It is likewise important that there be a certain regularity in purchase and continuous reliance on dependable local merchants. This will bring about a steadiness of the market and certainty in keeping accounts; it makes it possible for the merchant to run his business according to plan, and thus better serve the wants of his customers. Between housewife and merchant honest co-operation . . ."[32]

Simultaneously she can beautify her home with good German culture objects and give work to " hard-fighting German men " by purchasing as many objects for house adornment and children's play as possible.

It is not hard to see the cunning hand of the hard-pressed little merchant and small work shop-keeper in the framing of this programme. If the good, sacrificing Aryan mother of Aryan heroes will only buy to these specifications, the wolf will be kept away from the door, and his business will pick up. And at the same time her new " moral values " and her noble patriotism will destroy his chief enemies, the large and hitherto rapidly growing enterprises of mass production and mass distribution.

But it will " destroy " without damaging. A careful survey of the field will show that the programme for expansion of the " middle class " does not at any point seriously impinge upon large-scale enterprises in either the manufacturing or distributive fields. Rather it favours the domestic against the foreign producer on the one hand, and the individual merchant against the *co-operatives* and *foreign-owned* chain and variety stores. Behind the cunning hand of the " little man " is the even more cunning brain of the " big boys."

The (3) Film, (4) Press, (5) Foreign, and (6) German Female Academician Departments are all supplementary to the general propaganda " services " of *Frauenwerk*. The Film Department produces and collects small films " for training purposes, i.e. the schools for mothers and for all sorts of demonstration purposes in the different courses." The Press Department keeps extensive archives on " women's work at home and abroad." The Foreign Department " keeps German women in touch with the women in foreign countries, and informs German women at home about foreign countries and their civilisation." The German Female Academician Department controls all activities of German University women, doctors, lawyers, teachers, etc.

It is claimed that the number of women in the various professions has actually increased, though the figures cited are sufficiently scattered to make any conclusion to this effect pretty risky. The Department works in close co-operation with the General National Socialist Women's Student Federation, helping " the girl-students in reference to scholarships, students' homes for girls, etc." Until recently the enrolment of the women in the universities was limited to 10 per cent. While this restriction has been formally removed, indications from newspaper comment and the testimony of eye-witnesses are that actual practice keeps the percentage down to some such figure.

(7) The activities of the Red Cross Department are similar to those common abroad.

5. WOMEN'S ACTIVITIES (" FRAUENSCHAFTEN ")

Frauenschaften makes all the decisions for Women's Work and hence for all organised women's activities in the entire Reich. It is presided over by Frau Scholtz-Klink, likewise " Leader " of Women's Work, and is one of those constituent members of the National Socialist Party which are responsible directly to Rudolf Hess, personal representative of Adolf Hitler.

A propaganda bulletin summarises its functions: " The *Deutsche Frauenschaft* is the political organisation of the National Socialist women and was organised long ago as the auxiliary of the National Socialist Party. To-day every German woman can join in the *Deutsche Frauenschaft*, irrespective of whether she is a party-member or not. In a similar manner to the National Socialist Party the *Frauenschaft* is built up on a system of local units, i.e. *Gaue* (districts), *Kreise* (divisions), and *Ortsgruppen* (subdivisions). There are 32 districts in the Reich, each is divided into divisions. The divisions again into subdivisions. A subdivision comprises 30 to 200 women according to the density of the population in the district. The subdivision is divided into cells and these again into blocks about 4 houses each. Every one of these units has a woman as leader.

" The main task of the *Frauenschaft* is to train the women in what we call *Weltanschauung*, i.e. the National Socialist outlook on life (an organic national culture, an accepted way of looking at life—as James Murphy calls it in his book *Adolf Hitler*). Each local group of the *Frauenschaft* holds regular monthly meetings for lectures on many different political, social, and other subjects, on racial problems, the interpretation of law, music, and literature, as well as on foreign countries and their civilisation. . . . The members of the *Frauenschaft* join in organising all the special spheres of activity, i.e. maternity courses, the cooking, sewing and household courses, the courses and lectures of the department National Economy–Household Economy. For each of the different above-mentioned departments special women-advisers are to be found at every local unit."[33]

It is clearly a straight propaganda agency, vested with enormous powers of coercion through its identification with the state and the party on the one hand, and its complete control over all policies through its Siamese-twin organisation, the *Frauenwerk*, on the other. As with all the other Nazi " corporate " organisations, the network of control penetrates to every nook and cranny of the Reich, and the interlacing of spheres of influence with other party, government, and semi-public agencies is exceedingly close and intricate. Nowhere is this better illustrated than in the public welfare service, " Mother and Child "

—a service, incidentally, which likewise illustrates in detail and with unusual clarity the aims and objectives of the Reich programme for women.

The service is intended as a sort of " Community Chest " charity programme for indigent " expectant mothers, mothers with many children, widowed and divorced mothers, the unmarried mother, and the children of these mothers." It has three groups of functions:

I. General Aid for the family
    1. Economic support
    2. Employment aid
    3. Housing assistance

II. Welfare of the mother
    1. Aid for expectant mothers, women in lying-in hospitals, and care of nursing children
    2. Health of the mother
    3. Care for non-married mothers

III. Care of the Children
    1. Health of babies and children
    2. Children's day institutions (kindergartens and shelters)
    3. Feeding of children
    4. Occupational guidance for gifted children graduated from schools

This whole programme is tied up with the " education of mothers " in social welfare and national propaganda via the Reich Mothers' Service of Women's Work, discussed on p. 202 above. All activities come under the control of a national committee whose membership illustrates beautifully the thoroughness with which all Nazi propaganda activities are interlaced. The committee is made up of the following member groups:

I. Governmental:
    Ministry of the Interior
    Ministry of Labour
    Ministry for Propaganda and People's Enlightenment

Ministry for Science, Education, and National Culture

National Bureau for Employment and Unemployment
Insurance

German Communal Guild (central co-ordinating body
for all local and municipal governments and their
functions)

National Public Health Office

National Insurance Office for Salaried Workers

National Insurance Office

II. Branches and Associated Federations of the National
Socialist Labour Party:

Chief Office for Public Health

National Socialist Women's Activities (*N.S. Frauenschaft*)

National Mother Service of German Women's Work
(*Frauenwerk*)

German Womens' Labour Service

National Youth Leadership

National Socialist Teachers' League

German Labour Front, in particular the Women's and
Youth's offices

National Food Estate

III. Independent Public Welfare and Miscellaneous Organisations:

Central Committee for Internal Missions

German Caritas Association

German Red Cross

National Works Community for " Mother and Child "

Works Community of the Central Sick Relief Associations

National League of Many-Child Families

National (special) Association of Midwives

National (special) Association of Women Social
Workers

National (special) Association of German Sisters

The work of this committee promotes the programme of " Mother and Child " through a national office to which are attached provincial offices covering the entire Reich. These are broken down into Regional Offices, and these, in turn, into Local Group Offices. Similarly the provincial regional, and local offices of each of the above-mentioned organisations participate in the various subdivisions of the work of this far-flung programme.

The programme covers all phases of the life of " Mother and Child," caters to all problems and all needs. Formally it includes all the women in Germany, but in practice its sole care and emphasis is upon the lower income groups, the indigent and the poor. It ministers to the " sick, the lame, the halt," the broken down and the hopeless, the care-ridden, the despairing, the bitter and resentful. All the vast and complicated machinery of the party and state, and every interested pressure agency, is hereby focused on the mother with child. Nowhere else is there such elaborate and prolix praise of function. To no other group of the population do the Nazis address phrases of such soft and ingenious subtlety; imagery of such richness and luring power. They are playing here on one of the richest and deepest of all human emotions, and their literature for Mothers and Children is lush with sugary sentiment, fanciful tales, and emotion-charged song.

Why ? Not alone, nor even principally, on account of the women in and of themselves. The underlying attitude towards women is unmistakably condescending and contemptuous. It was one of their favourite heroes, Nietzsche, who made the famous remark, " Thou goest to see a woman ? Forget not to take thy whip." Though the Nazis are very careful not to quote such indiscreet utterances, the attitude of Nietzsche—the attitude of the *Junker*, the soldier in his free hours, of *Herr im Hause*—is typical of a party and set of Leaders which deliberately and purposefully sets out to exclude women from all the arts and sciences, on the roster of whose officers not a single woman is to be found, and which plans to force them back to the place where they are to be found in only the least enlightened and most primitive tribes.

The Nazis give the answer themselves. In an almost syllogistic form, a spokesman for the party viewpoint states the case: " We live in a Leader State. It will stand or fall with the selection of Leaders. The Leader nature is determined through character. In every German man—also in the woman—it is imperative for the future to recognise and develop qualities of leadership. *The mother shall be, according to the will of Adolf Hitler, the builder and shaper of the soul of her child in the most decisive years of its life —between the 4th and 7th years of age.*"[34]

As the mother believes, so the child. As the mother accepts, advocates, and inculcates National Socialism, so will the child begin with the " idea in his blood." In the ripening of each woman's body she shall, according to Nazi plans, plant the seeds of the National Socialist *Weltanschauung* (world philosophy). She is propaganda-agent Number 1. By controlling the mother, mistress, and preceptress of the children's room, they control the germinal ideas. It is by no accident that the Nazis have written large across their banners the old adage, " From out the children's room the world is ruled."

PART II

THE CO-ORDINATION OF STRUCTURE

CHAPTER VII

Agriculture: Rigid Status of " Blood and Soil "

IN the second month of the new regime Hitler stated the Nazi interpretation of the crisis in German agriculture: " My Party comrades, make yourselves clear about one thing in all its consequences: There is only one last, one final, last chance for the German peasantry ! Following this administration logically only one other can come, Bolshevism ! . . . But if this regime can carry through the objectives which I have laid before you, then the peasantry will become the supporting foundation for a new Kingdom of Blood and Soil."[1] To this end Germany must become a " peasant state ": " The Germany of the future can only be a peasant state, or it will disappear as the empires of the Hohenstaufens and the Hohenzollerns, because they forgot to seek for their popular and economic centre of gravity within themselves. All the blows of fate, all crises, can be overcome if a healthy and strong peasantry forms the living foundation of the people ! Nations which sacrificed their peasantry to a mammonism not rooted in the people vanished for ever from the stage of history."[2]

To the creation of a peasant state of " Blood and Soil " as a bulwark against what they term the social disintegration which spells " Bolshevism," the Nazi government has contrived a programme resting on four basic assumptions, stated approximately as follows: (1) The peasantry must be given back a body of law inherently suited to its social station and which is adapted to its " earth-bound " economic forms; (2) The position of this " earth-bound " economy within the framework of the total economic system must be fixed and made fast, i.e. upon agricultural production must be laid the duty of nourishing the people; the marketing of agricultural produce should, with the aid of commerce, be systematised to serve " the people "; (3) Previous agricultural indebtedness must be wiped out by contriving a new form of credit backing for that which has already broken down; (4) The peasantry must be led, corresponding to its significance in the life of the people, out of a condition in which its existence is merely tolerated into one under which the young peasant in a new estate will freely procreate, become " rich in children," and thus promote a " growing peasantry through being rooted to the soil."[3]

In simpler terms, the programme is designed to achieve three effects: *Fixity of occupation* will be the product of binding the peasant to the soil in a rigid and permanent relationship. *Fixity of status* is to be brought about by fitting the peasantry into a rigid social-economic class hierarchy, unalterable, except at the discretion of the state, from generation to generation. *Fixity of residence* will ensue from the fixity of occupation and status so far as the inheritors of agricultural estates are concerned. The same result will follow for the remainder of the peasant population through absolute prohibition of immigration and emigration across national borders and through rigid control over movements to and from cities and between agricultural localities.

With these elements under rigid control, it will be possible, the Nazi leaders argue, to " co-ordinate " German agriculture to achieve its two major functions: nourishing the race with men, and supplying the people with food. *Blut und Boden*—Blood and Soil—are to become the alpha and omega of German agriculture. The blood of the peasantry is the principal life-spring from which flows the ever-renewing supply of men to the expanding glory of the Fatherland. The soil which the peasants till nourishes all in the tasks which the " divinely inspired Leader " lays before them.

To implement the programme laid before them, the Nazis have resorted to three major devices. The first is the new National Law of Inheritance or Entail[4] (*Reichserbhofgesetz*), under which the bloodstream of the peasantry is " purified," their bounden duties clarified and duly laid upon them, and their attachment to the soil rendered fixed and immutable to the end of time. The second is the National Food Corporation (*Reichsnährstand*) which centralises and controls administration of all phases of agricultural production, distribution, and social relationships. The third is the Settlement (*Siedlungen*) programme by way of which the expanding agricultural population is to be turned back from the cities and fixed on the land, industrial concentration in the large cities is to be decentralised, and militant labour " neutralised." The first two provide the foundation for the new social order amongst the peasantry, and together furnish a prototype for the widely advertised " Corporative State " of the future. For this reason they can best be handled together. The third will be dealt with in the following chapter.

1. THE CONDITIONS OF THE GERMAN PEASANTS WHEN THE NAZIS CAME INTO POWER

As indicated in the first chapter, the conditions of the German peasantry by 1933 were critical in the extreme. An author in the *Frankfurter Zeitung* characterised the situation as the worst since the disastrous Peasants' War of 1524–25. This may be an exaggeration, but it does seem perfectly clear that the condition of German agriculture in that year had become so critical that even in this typically conservative sphere of the national system, further hardships would have inevitably led to revolutionary uprisings.

Agricultural income in 1932–33 had fallen to the lowest point since 1913, being, at the total figure of 6,463 million Reichsmarks, better than one thousand millions below the worst post-war year, 1924–25. Meanwhile, agricultural indebtedness had increased with startling rapidity. Professor Sering[5] is authority for the statement that nearly the entirety of the 12 thousand million Rm. owed by German agriculture in 1932 had been accumulated during the eight years since the stabilisation of 1924–25. The interest burden on this huge sum mounted steadily as a total and as a percentage of the value of all crops sold. Two years after the first measures were taken to reduce agricultural interest rates, an annual interest burden in excess of one thousand million marks took nearly fourteen per cent of all agricultural income. Simultaneously the tax and social services loads steadily increased. In the most favourable post-war year, 1928–29, to an annual interest burden of 920 million Rm. had to be added taxes of 780 million Rm. and social services of 330 million Rm. With the coming of the depression these latter obligations became unbearable.

Nearly all layers of the agricultural population suffered from the incidence of these trends. The large estates of 247 acres (100 hectares) or over were hopelessly in debt. This was particularly true of the *Junker* estates of the eastern provinces, where

thin soil, extensive farming, reckless living, and hopelessly inefficient management had brought a large percentage of them to
ruin. Powerful in the counsels of state, the *Junkers* became increasingly insistent that the government take drastic measures
to relieve them of their growing burdens.

Beneath the *Junker* class was a large layer of at one time
moderately well-to-do peasants, owning land varying in size
from 12 to 247 acres. It was on this class of agriculture that the
forces mentioned above weighed the heaviest, and it was the
slow destruction of the economic foundation of these peasants
which alarmed all classes who saw in the naïve, hard-working,
frugal, and property-minded peasantry the centre of gravity of
social stability. In this layer were to be found the oldest peasant
families, and the leaders in the economic and social activities of
rural life in all sections of the country. They were the most sen-
sitive to any threat to established rural customs, property and
inheritance rights, and the most resistant to demands of the
steadily growing rural proletariat. From them were recruited the
peasants who were willing to participate in any movement to
eliminate " debt slavery," remove foreign competition, re-align
prices of agricultural produce, or check any threat of communal-
ising the land.

Beneath the middle peasants was a still larger class owning
small parcels of land varying from a fraction to about 12 acres
each. With their families this group made up slightly over half
of the entire agricultural population in 1925 (7,974,939 out of
15,416,953). Considerably less than half of them were engaged
entirely on the land; the remainder spending a portion or the
most of their time working for the wealthier peasants or in local
(usually seasonal) industries. While not so heavily indebted as the
larger farmers and the estate owners, nor obliged to contribute
much by way of taxes or social services, the margin of living of
this class of the rural population was typically so extremely
narrow that any misfortune to jobs, crops, or prices was apt to
bring them speedily to a condition of acute need. Many, if not
most, of these people lived under poverty-stricken conditions
reminiscent, even in good times, of those which prevailed
throughout the rural areas of medieval Europe.

At the bottom of the scale were the lowest class of day

labourers and servants—numbering in 1925 better than one-fifth of the total rural population—they were recruited largely from the ranks of those whose ancestors had lost most or all of their land holdings through foreclosure or through operation of earlier inheritance laws which provided that the estate must be handed down intact from generation to generation. In ancient times they made up the bulk of those available for forays and wars. Prior to the war they constituted a large and growing percentage of those emigrating, or moving into the large industrial centres as day labourers.

The war killed off a large number of the poorer peasants and the rural proletariat. During the period of rebuilding from 1924 to 1928 many of them were able to find jobs in the larger cities. But with the slowing off of reconstruction they were left without any alternative except, poverty-stricken and without resources, to drift back to the land. A first measure to relieving the pressure on rural unemployment thus created was to exclude Polish and Slavic migratory labour brought in for the short crop seasons. Foreign labour, which used to be imported in 1913 in numbers around 400,000 annually, was cut down year by year in the post-war period. In 1930 only 87,000 were allowed to enter Germany. Subsequently all such labour was denied admittance to the country. Simultaneously the operation of the relief laws, supplemented by direct prohibition, began an emergency movement from the land to the city. In fact, acute distress in the cities had a tendency to reverse the directional flow whenever there was any movement at all.

Meanwhile, a number of factors combined to cut down on the supply of labour required on the land. Most important, perhaps, were programmes which called for eliminating the time-consuming strip system (holdings scattered in strips sandwiched in amongst holdings of other persons) and for improving agricultural technique. In certain sections of the country, the former was very bad. Sering cites a case in which a peasant owning a total area of 49·4 acres, divided into 67 individual parcels, would be compelled to travel 131 kilometres in a single trip to and from his house if he were to include every strip in his tour. While this is an unusual case, experiments carried out by various government agencies showed that a programme which combined pooling and common cultivation of the land with employment of modern machinery and equipment could in many cases cut the time and labour required to but a fraction of the former figures. The same holds for rationalisation of the middle-sized and large estates. Grievances on this score were aggravated by the absorption of farm lands by the big estates, since such concentration of land ownership meant not only the transformation of independent farmers into a rural proletariat but also substitution of machine for hand labour. According to Darré,[6] Leader of the National Food Estate, " the total area of farm land that passed into the hands of the big landowners during the nineteenth century . . . is estimated to be 4,320,000 acres. The farm land area absorbed by the big estates in the eastern provinces of post-Versailles Prussia may be figured at approximately 3,200,000 acres." Estimating the average size of farms to be about 60 acres, in excess of 70,000 farms during the nineteenth century, and over 50,000 farms since the war have been eliminated in Prussia alone, the farmers turned into labourers, and growing percentages of these deprived of work through rationalisation of agricultural technique (scientific farming; use of farm machinery, etc.).

Needless to say in a depressed peasant economy where approximately seven-tenths of the land area is owned by " independent farmers," the bulk of the labour will be supplied by members of the family. Out of a total of 8·66 million persons engaged directly in cultivation of the soil in 1925, 6·04 million, or 70 per cent of the total number, fell into this class. To farmers adult sons must be added, normally, most of the women and the children above five to ten years of age. Child labour is not the exception in the German country-side, but the rule. And women are as much a part of the working capital of the peasant's estate as are his limited stock of horses and cattle, adding, as they do, to the cares of bearing a family and housework, long hours in the fields—during the planting, growing and harvesting seasons 16 field hours is regarded as normal—at all kinds of heavy and exhausting labour. The closer the peasant is to the margin of subsistence, the heavier the burden placed on the women and the children.

Mounting indebtedness—which equalled one-third of the estimated value of all agricultural property by 1930—in other words, merely reflected the growing pauperisation of the mass of the rural population. A crushing burden of " debt slavery," and an unbearable load of taxes and social services were associated with growing land and job scarcity, " flight from the land " and cumulative pauperisation of peasants. To stave off mass revolt in the country-side—the " menace of Bolshevism "—the Nazis devised first the Law of Inheritance.

2. THE LAW OF INHERITANCE [7]

" The National Inheritance Law saves German Peasantry " for " Blood and Soil " by " purifying the blood stream of the peasant " and attaching him in a " community of duty " to the land. To the first end it excludes all " non-Germanic " elements from agricultural pursuits, revives and re-adapts the antique German allodial laws of inheritance through entailment (inalienable hereditary estates) and renders the patrimony inalienable and no longer subject to debt. To achieve the second, the peasant is attached by law to his glebe, his specific " duties " to the " common good " (Gemeinwohl) detailed and circumscribed, and his activities properly supervised through an elaborate machinery of special courts and associations brought under the central direction of the National Food Estate.

The theory behind the race side of the new peasant laws is extremely simple and amazingly naïve. It runs about as follows: In the hierarchy of peoples, the Indo-Germanic, or " Nordic," race occupies a place of unusual distinction. Typically fair-haired, fair-skinned, blue-eyed, of tall stature, and with thin facial features (the dolichocephalic type—long narrow heads), they represent the highest order of mankind known to history. Among their spiritual characteristics, which are just as definite and peculiar to the Nordic race as their physical endowments, the following are of especial importance[8]: " great strength of will and power of action, spirit of undertaking, urge to activity, clear understanding, and certainty of judgment. Externally the Nordic man is calm and reserved, although he has great depth of feeling and a rich phantasy. We find in him frequently political, war-like, and artistic talents and a high capacity for leadership." If he goes wrong at any point, he will tend to go arrogantly his own way, little subject to discipline and lacking in appreciation of the communal feeling. But typically " communal feeling " is higher in this race than in any other.

With these endowments, Nordic man has, when undisturbed, developed a particular *Weltanschauung*—" world point of view " —and forms of society peculiar to himself. This form of society is common to practically all early Europe, the great cultures of the Mediterranean and North European peoples alike being largely ascribed to infiltration of energetic and gifted Nordic stock. It is especially peculiar to pre-Romanic Germany. The coming in of the Romans succeeded in a partial destruction of this old Germanic law and social system. With the defeat of Varus by Arminius in the Teutoburg Forest in A.D. 9 came a reversion to the old order in the west. But the advance of Christianity, says Darré, subsequently completed the process of Romanising Germany where force of arms had failed. This Romanisation meant the gradual break-up of the old German society, and the slow degradation of the phases of culture which were most uniquely the product of the peculiar genius of the Nordic peoples. With the new National Socialist regime an attempt will be made to revive the conditions which correspond more closely to the pre-Romanic world.

From this point on the theory becomes even more bizarre. According to Darré the triumph of Roman culture meant the ascendancy of Roman law, paved the way for the rise of Christianity, capitalism, and Bolshevism, and renders the efforts of the Nazi government to recapture Germany for the Germans an heroic struggle of Germany against " oriental " forces on behalf of those elements of western civilisation which are supremely worth saving, i.e. those attributed to the unfettered play of Nordic creative genius. By " oriental " influences are meant those which foisted on the European peoples the " incredibly stupid " doctrine of " equality of all men before God."

The Jews, says Darré, brought this doctrine into the west under the somewhat altered form of Christianity, a doctrine which fitted perfectly with the imperial designs of a rapacious line of rulers who had given up the social and ethical codes of Republican Rome. Early Rome he assumes to have been dominated by farmers whose rule of life approximated closely that of the primitive Germans. The long struggle which ensued between this " fallacious doctrine " and that which was championed by the Germans resulted in a temporary triumph for the former, with deep-seated and disastrous consequences for Europe. Roman law triumphed throughout Europe and thus provided the legal sanctions for the rise of capitalism.

Capitalism, the Nazis find, required " liberalism," under which the " I " or ego side of life was elevated to a position of commanding importance. In its wake this capitalism brought parliamentarianism, materialism, mammonism. It promoted the idea of " each against all," the revolt against nature involved in " equal rights of women," and the simultaneous disintegration of " father rights " and the institution of the family. It crowded people into cities, broke up all sense of community feeling, destroyed the natural hierarchy of duties and responsibilities, reduced all to a socially undifferentiated mass of rootless, senseless, despairing people, and opened wide the gates to the " degrading philosophy of Bolshevism."

And Bolshevism, the Nazis discover, is the logical descendant of Christianity, liberalism, and capitalism. It takes what there is good in the ideas of individualism and socialism and perverts them to the despotic equalitarianism of the Orient. The Jew Ricardo perverted the otherwise sound economics of Adam Smith; the doctrine of the Jew Marx triumphed over those of the German-blooded Robert Owen and Friedrich Engels. The two great enemies then, are capitalism and Bolshevism. Capitalism is the Jewish oriental perversion of the doctrine of individual initiative and the institution of private property. Bolshevism is the lowest common denominator; it is seen as the sum of all the perversions of all the great social values geared to the idea that the lowest elements in society shall force the equality of their inferior talents on all gradations of ability.

Against these doctrines the Nazis, champions of the Aryan, Nordic, Germanic peoples who are true to their natural, cultural, and biological heritage, raise those of National Socialism. In the National Socialist state, there is to be an ordered gradation of abilities which places the " nobility " capable of leadership at the top, and the orders of the inferior below in strict correspondence with their native endowments. Each shall have property, and each shall be granted freedom to exercise the maximum of initiative corresponding to his ability, i.e. his station, i.e. his delegated functions of his delegated occupation. The more intelligent and capable will be those of pure Nordic blood. In the state best adapted to their leadership, they will be first among equals, or the most talented amongst a pure Nordic people. The Nordic peoples will have occupations suited to their peculiar racial endowment, which means that all will engage in some agriculture, all will be part of some agricultural communities, and all will promote the rule, " The common before the individual good."

According to the Inheritance Law,⁹ every peasant must have an estate. " Estate " is defined to be used farming or forest land in sole possession of the peasant and cultivated by the peasant and his family themselves, must have a minimum size large enough to provide a livelihood to the farmer and his entire family, and must not, except under special circumstances, exceed 309 acres in size. Estates larger than this are placed in a special class for the nobility. At the discretion of the National Peasant Leader, the large estates can be broken up into smaller provided the above rules are not violated. While the idea is that there shall be one peasant holder to an estate, for the time being it is possible to both own and inherit more than one such allotment. In the event of inheritance, all buildings, necessary equipment, and family heirlooms are regarded as an integral part of the estate.

The owner of the estate must be " racially pure," since from his loins springs the blood stream of the race. As *Bauer*, or Peasant, he is the bearer of an " honoured title," one that is conferred upon him by the state. As such, he cannot be named *Bauer* unless he is a German citizen and of German or similar blood. Specifically this excludes Jews and all coloured people, though it does not apply to Roumanians and Slavs. Every would-be *Bauer* must prove his racial stock " pure " as of the date of January 1, 1800, and his proof must be passed upon by a special court established for that purpose.

If incapacitated at any time, the peasant may be declared no longer a *Bauer*, and deprived, by decision of officials of the

National Food Estate, of his land to the benefit of the next in line of inheritance. The same holds if the peasant is declared no longer " honourable "; that is, if he has given evidence of inability or unwillingness to abide by the " peasant honour code." Finally, the peasant is obligated to keep his estate in good condition, to cultivate the land to good advantage, and not to contract long-term indebtedness. Failure to do so can lead to investigation by the National Food Estate, and deprivation of the use of the land. This is not to be interpreted to deprive a minor nor an aged person of the inheritance, since the estate can be administered under these circumstances by the nearest of competent kin.

The order of inheritance is fixed by law as follows: " (1) the son of the testator; (2) the father of the testator; (3) the brother of the testator; (4) the daughter of the testator; (5) the sisters of the testator; (6) the female descendants of the farmer and the (male or female) descendants of these, with exception of the daughter and the son and the son's son of the daughter of the farmer as these belong already to the fourth order." Adopted children are never entitled to first inheritance. Illegitimate children are " dishonourable children," and as such cannot inherit unless the landowner is a female. In this case, and where the farmer marries the mother after birth of the child, illegitimacy is no bar.

This testamentary order can be altered within certain bounds at the will of the testator, the rule followed being that the customs which prevail in any given locality shall be determinate in the event of dispute. The same holds for division of the estate and any of the equipment and appurtenances belonging thereto as defined by law. The law, further, makes exceptions for multiple estate owners, problems of transition to the new order, and latitude of court interpretation. But no exceptions are allowed on the citizen, racial, or " honour " status of the individual peasant, nor on the right of all unmarried of first kin to asylum at the home estate in the event of loss of jobs or other need. This right is guaranteed to all children and all elders, as well as the widows of deceased peasants, and can be exercised at any time of felt need.

" The estate is fundamentally inalienable and cannot be

encumbered."[10] That is to say, the peasant can no longer borrow money except on short term (one year or under), nor in excess of his capacity to repay out of current crop receipts. The only exception made is where improvements in the estate are called for, such as land drainage or irrigation, which lead to long-run improvement of the earning capacity of the estate. Permission is required from the National Food Estate for such exceptions. There seems to be some dispute as to the specific purposes for which money can be borrowed. The opinion seems to prevail that if money is wanted for purchase of machinery, equipment, or construction, the obligations should not be larger than the amount which can be repaid from seasonal income. Under no circumstances can the peasant be deprived of his estate merely because of previous indebtedness, nor can he at any time have his property foreclosed upon. Nor can he sell the land at any time to any person outside of the line of inheritance or without the express permission of the National Food Estate. Indebtedness accumulated without permission or beyond the capacity to pay constitutes a violation of " peasant honour," and subjects the perpetrator to loss of property and all property rights. All future borrowing is to be " personal," not property credit.

Administration of the National Inheritance Law is in the hands of Central Administrative Division I of the National Food Estate; all disputes, especially those having to do with rights of inheritance, are handled through the Estate Courts (*Erbhofgerichte*). Court of first instance is the Inheritance Court (*Anerbengerichte*). Cases appealed are remanded to the Regional Estate Courts, and from thence to the National Estate Court (*Reichserbhofgerichte*). These courts are all subject, in the final analysis, to the administrative control of the National Peasant Leader.

A principal task of the Inheritance Courts is the registration of estates in the Estate Roll. Every estate is to be entered on this roll, with its exact status as an " estate-active " enterprise determined, passed upon, and duly registered. Registration entitles the peasant to use a special insignia which is really a " coat of arms." All this requires a special procedure which law details at some length. Every ten years the Estate Roll will be examined and revised, especial attention being paid to the manner in which the estates registered have been administered.

3. ORGANISATION OF THE NATIONAL FOOD ESTATE

The Estate is organised as a corporation of public law with self-administration under authority of an original enabling act of July 15, 1933, which " established the competence of the Reich for the regulation of agriculture as a vocational estate (guild)."[11] The legal basis of the Estate was provided and the scope of its work was laid out in a law of September 13, 1933. The specific functions to be performed were delineated in a series of three ordinances issued subsequently by the National Minister of Nutrition and Agriculture. " The first ordinance deals with the general, fundamental, regulations of the juridical character, scope of work, membership, management, representation, local divisions, fees and funds, government inspection and statutes. The second ordinance regulates in detail the relations of agricultural unions to the National Food Estate. The third ordinance demarcates the relations to the National Food Estate of the rural trade and all those enterprises that have to do with the industrial manufacture of agricultural products."

Membership, which is inclusive of all individuals, associations, and organisations working directly in the agricultural field, is divided into five main classes[12]:

" (a) Persons engaged in agriculture or directly related to it. This group includes all proprietors, persons capable of ownership, beneficiaries, lessors or tenants of agricultural enterprises, relatives, labourers, employees, or officials permanently occupied with agriculture; furthermore, former owners or beneficiaries of farms having claims from contracts for the transfer of real estate or from old-age pensions connected with such contracts, i.e. persons still closely connected with their original land.

" (b) Agricultural unions including their head-organisations, particularly leagues of control, central unions, and other arrangements. (Detailed stipulations are contained in the second ordinance.)

Hf

" (c) All natural and juridical persons who carry on a rural trade (wholesale and retail) or the manufacture of agricultural products. This group of members has been defined by the National Minister of Nutrition and Agriculture and by the National Minister of Industry in the third ordinance. It comprises ten divisions, according to par. 1 of the third ordinance:

(1) Agricultural products
(2) Cattle
(3) Brewing
(4) Sugar refineries
(5) Starch factories and distilleries
(6) Fisheries
(7) Fat refineries and dairies
(8) Victuals
(9) Timber, and garden, forest and other plants
(10) Retail groceries

Each individual group is divided into enterprises of trade and manufacture respectively. The latter require a special treatment because of their intimate connection with the industries and handicrafts.

" (d) Organisations attached to the National Food Estate (societies, unions, leagues). The relations of the National Food Estate to the numerous agricultural organisations existing were regulated in the following manner: for representative vocational organisations of public law the new law provides a total legal membership: Council of German Agriculture; Prussian Central Chamber of Agriculture; Chambers of Agriculture. The Federal Leader of Farmers was authorised to incorporate, dissolve, or co-ordinate the existing agricultural unions, etc., which promoted the economic, vocational, and intellectual interests of agriculture. Total legal successorship and incorporation means fusion with the National Food Estate. Dissolution involves liquidation according to law. Attachment means corporative membership. Attached members are, e.g. the National Bureau for Colonisation, the Working Union of Rural Supply Companies, the National League of Rural Sick Funds, etc.

" (e) Marketing organisations and institutions in the sense of par. 1 of the basic law and par. 2 of the ordinance of the Federal Leader of Farmers of May 4, 1935. These are concerned, in the first place, with economic associations organised on a national basis. As in the case of the co-ordinated bodies, they are corporative members of the National Food Estate. These are, without prejudice to the supervisory and control authority of the National Food Estate, and particularly the National Leader of Farmers, corporations of public law with their own independent legal personalities. The most important of these combinations are:

(1) The Central Association of the German Grain Trade, inclusive of the Economic Association of the Rye and Wheat Mills

(2) The German Milk Association (Central Association), inclusive of the Economic Association of the Condensed Milk Producers and the Economic Association of the Fluid Cheese Producers

(3) The Central Association for Packing House Products

(4) The Central Association for the German Egg Industry

(5) The Central Association of the German Sugar Industry

(6) The Economic Association of the German Fruit and Vegetable Products Industries

(7) The Economic Association of the German Starch Industry

(8) The Economic Association of the German Potato Flake Industry

(9) The Economic Association of the Margarine and Artificial Food Fats Industry

(10) The Economic Association of the German Fisheries Industry

(11) The Economic Association of the Mixed Feed Producers of Germany "

For a series of products where adequate economic associations do not already exist, special marketing commissioners have been set up. It is expected that central association will eventually replace the commissioners, and that the functions delegated to them will be accordingly transferred. The most important of these are the following:

(1) The National Commissioner for the Marketing of Garden Products

(2) The Federal Commissioner for the Marketing of Potatoes

(3) The Federal Commissioner for the Marketing of Legumes

(4) The Commissioner of the National Food Estate for the Marketing of Vineyard Products

(5) The Commissioner of the National Food Estate for the Regulation of the Hop Market

(6) The Commissioner of the National Food Estate for the Production and Marketing of Grünkern (a special German product consisting of dried green grain widely used in soups)

(7) The Trustee for the Raw Cocoa Refining Industry

(8) The Commissioner of the National Food Estate for the Marketing of Wool

Membership in the National Food Estate is compulsory for all individuals and intermediate bodies. No announcement of intention to become a member is required, nor can membership be renounced at any time.

At the head of the National Food Estate (see Charts III and IIIa at end of book) is the National Peasant Leader, appointed directly by the Chancellor of the Reich, and responsible singly and solely to him. The Leader is in complete control of all officers, duties, and functions comprised in the scope of the National Food Estate. He holds his office for no definite period of time, nor do those of any officer appointed by him. All inferior officers are responsible singly and solely to him, and so on throughout the hierarchy to the bottom of the pyramid.

Immediately beneath the Leader is a Federal Administrative Officer, in whose hands are concentrated all administrative routines. The details of administration are divided between two main groups, the Staff Office under the charge of the Staff Office Leader, and the Administrative Office, under the control of the Leader of the Administrative Office. The Staff Office, whose function is that of " general staff " supply of information and the giving of expert council, is divided into seven divisions:

(*a*) Economics; (*b*) Law; (*c*) Interracial Farmer and Economic Problems; (*d*) Newspapers and Publications; (*e*) Advertising; (*f*) Farmers' Traditions and Farm Social Station, and (*g*) Blood Problems of the Farmer Class.

The functions of the Administrative Office are subdivided into three main divisions which consider the problems of agriculture with respect to: Man (Main Div. I); the Estate (Main Div. II), and the Market (Main Div. III). It is worth following this organisation through in some detail for the picture it presents of the nature and drive of the whole Nazi programme.

The Main Division " Man " considers its field of duties to be " [13]. . . custody of the world point of view and the vocational spirit of peasant man, inclusive of the peasant, the landlord, the agricultural labourer, etc., and the regulation of their social relations. To its spiritual-physical trusteeship belongs the world view of blood and the state idea of blood and soil, the nobility of blood, the clan organisation, tasks of the clan, the nobility-estate, spiritual training through old and new usages as well as bodily training, schooling of mothers, care of nursing infants, children's homes, etc. It is the national trustee of all legal matters relating to the land dealing, specifically, with legal counsel and legal policy, peasant and land law, land transportation rights, property and dispossession rights, the national settlement law, legal questions in the reformation of German peasantry, leasehold matters, water, hunting, and fishing rights, debt relief rights, credit matters, foreclosure rights, and matters relating to the status of the agricultural guild: the National Food Estate Law, arbitration, and the vocational guild courts. Main Division I is further entrusted with supervision over all social and occupational (guild) problems, in particular movements of men and labour absorption (flight from the land, labour employment problems, work creation, rural servant and helper problems, etc.), rural labour and farm-dwelling construction, tenant work days, labour-legal relations problems, insurance— in particular social insurance—questions of enterprise and village communities, guild courts, etc. Finally, it is charged with the New Building of German Peasantry (selection and settlement of new peasants, land reclamation, etc.)"

In order to avoid overlapping of functions and dual membership, a special agreement was made on October 6, 1935, between the Leaders of the National Food Estate and the German Labour Front. Previously part of agricultural labour was included in the Food Estate; part in the Labour Front. Inasmuch as the latter is supposed to have complete control over all labour-employer relations within the entire Reich, it was decided to enter the Food Estate as a corporate member of the Labour Front. By this agreement the entire membership of the Food Estate was brought under the jurisdiction of the Labour Front so far as labour problems were concerned.

Main Division II, " The Estate," has charge of all functions and activities having to do with the farm as a productive enterprise, " inclusive of agricultural science, professional education, and agricultural schools, etc."[14] It has complete control over the functions of the former agricultural chambers and societies, and it is charged with the duty of carrying through the " Battle of Production " to make Germany self-sufficient in her food supply. This latter is regarded as a function of special importance, and within limits it constitutes the point of departure for the entire co-ordination of not only all agricultural activities, but also of agriculture with all other governmentally controlled activities of the Reich.

The " Battle of Production " is construed to mean national self-supply of the largest possible percentage of Germany's food requirements so as to reduce to the minimum the drain on foreign exchange required for this purpose. By this means more purchasing power is released for import of basic raw materials—principally metals—required for Germany's rearmament. Rearmament, in turn, is regarded at once as a matter of " national honour " and as the key to the " labour creation " schemes of the Nazi regime. It is the special duty of Main Division II to search out all possible substitutes for imported foodstuffs and agricultural raw materials used in industry, to promote land reclamation and better agricultural methods, and to plan and co-ordinate all crop production so that the supply of each type of crop will be adjusted to the structure of national need.

Main Division II is divided into eight Divisions, each under the control of a staff Leader aided by a Board of Directors, as follows[15]:

Division A, *Management*, with the following Sub-Division: General Management, Treasurer, Personnel Questions, Newspapers and Press, Publicity and Exhibitions, Legal Questions.

Division B, *Fundamentals of Business Leadership*, with the following Sub-Division: Business Relations (Statistics and Accounting), Production Data, General Agricultural Statistics, Freight Tariffs and Transportation, Taxes and Assessments, Agricultural Credit and Finance.

Division C, *Soil and Plants*, with the following Sub-Division: General Plant Culture, General Soil Preparation and Fertilisers, Seeds, Special Plant Culture, Feed Stalls and Silos, Potato Culture, Plant Protection, Soil Culture, Gardening, Vineyards.

Division D, *Animals*, with the following Sub-Division: General Animal Breeding, Breeding of Small Animals, Fisheries, Animal Care and the Dairy Industry, Efficiency Testing and Co-operative Methods of Control, Veterinaries, Agricultural Shows and Exhibitions, Egg Supervision.

Division E, *Occupational Training*, with the following Sub-Division: Agricultural Occupational Schools, Training and Examination in Practice, Economic Counsel and Advice, Professional Schooling of Rural Labour.

Division F, *Forests in Private Ownership, Peasant, and Agricultural Enterprises*, with the following Sub-Division: Forest Culture, Forest Appraisal, Forest Exploitation, Forest Protection, Associated Special Forest Activities.

Division G, *Agricultural Equipment, Machinery, and Construction Service*, with the following Sub-Division: Tools and Equipment, Machinery, Buildings.

Division H, *Household Economy*.

Main Division III, " The Market " occupies a special place in the structure of the National Food Estate, being in charge of all marketing and marketing associations, as well as of all financial and credit matters having to do with the marketing of agricultural produce from the point of production to the point of sale to the ultimate consumer. With the sole exception of the auditing co-operatives, it has consequently complete control over all agricultural co-operative associations and activities.

According to statistics published by Main Division III on May 1, 1934,[16] there were 111 Central Co-operative societies and 41,753 individual co-operatives in existence in Germany, divided as follows:

<blockquote>
19,240 Savings and Loan Banks
4,084 Purchasing and Selling Associations
7,004 Dairy Co-operatives
574 Packing Plant Co-operatives
529 Egg Co-operatives
321 Fruit and Vegetable Co-operatives
417 Wine-growers' Co-operatives
5,639 Electrification Co-operatives
873 Threshing Co-operatives
208 Farm Machine Co-operatives
446 Drainage Co-operatives
747 Animal Breeding Co-operatives
324 Pasturage Co-operatives
1,347 Miscellaneous Co-operatives
</blockquote>

The principal functions of Main Division III are carried out through the intermediation of the co-operatives and the 13 economic central organisations. Parallel to these are two staff divisions, A and B. " Chief Division A " is concerned with general problems of Administration and Management. "Chief Division B" is subdivided into five units: (1) (a) Market Reviews; (b) Co-operative Review; (2) Credit; (3) Insurance; (4) General Co-operative Problems; (5) General Questions of Rural Trade.[17]

In a special service capacity to the Central Administrative Office, is a staff office dealing with general administrative problems, such as personnel, property, statistics, archives, etc. Attached directly to the office of the National Peasant Leader are three advisory bodies, respectively known as the National Peasants' Council, the National Peasants' Assembly (Thing), and the National Peasants Diet. These latter are apparently not taken very seriously, since none of the literature pays any more than passing attention to them. At any rate, it has been next to impossible to learn anything of their duties and functions.

The regional organisation of the National Food Estate is patterned closely after that of the central body, the 19 regional units[18] being each under the control of a " Regional Peasant Leader " and a " Regional Administrative Officer," subdivided into Divisions I, II, and III, and advised by Regional Peasants' Council, Assembly, and Diet. Under each regional office is a " Provincial Peasants' Leader " in charge of an office organised exactly the same as the central and regional offices. There are 514 of these altogether. At the bottom of the pyramid are the " Local Peasant Leaders " responsible to the Provincial Peasant Leader for the conduct of all activities coming under the control of the National Food Estate within the multitude of small separate localities into which the Reich is divided.

It is extremely difficult to find out how this vast and complicated organisation functions in detail. Theoretically the control is complete over all phases of agricultural life, including the social and cultural as well as the technical and economic. But how far changes have been wrought in the actual conduct of agricultural operations is another matter. For one thing, it appears obvious that relatively few changes have been made to date in the actual structure and functioning of the pre-existing co-operatives, associations, federations, and peasants' unions. For the most part they were simply taken over intact, membership made compulsory instead of optional (though apparently not in all cases), and the " Leader Principle " substituted for the elective rule.

Under the Leader Principle, nominations are made from the top down; responsibility is from the bottom up for all offices, duties, and functions. The National Peasants' Leader delegates or " entrusts " " duties " to his inferior designees; these delegate or " entrust " duties to other inferior officers. At the bottom of the scale the peasant is " delegated " or " entrusted " the duties of cultivating the land to the maximum advantage of " the people." In plain language, this means that the National Peasant Leader *tells* his designees what they are to do, these *tell* their inferior officers what to do, and these in turn *tell* the peasant, according to the law, whether and what he may own, may produce, or may sell. Since the Nazi philosophy calls for complete " co-ordination of spirit and ideas," the same " delegating " or

" entrusting," or *commanding* applies to social life, leisure-time activities, and what the peasant, his family, and all rural labour may think, where they may go, and how they may feel about anything which affects Germany, which is everything. This, Nazi writers refer to as the " new German freedom."

The only place where it is easy to follow the implementing of this doctrine is in the administration of the authority of Main Division III, which has complete

4. CONTROL OVER MARKETING

According to Reischle-Saure, Darré, and other leading Nazi writers, the weakest link in the old " capitalistic " " liberal " system for agriculture was to be found in the field of markets. Supply for specific commodities was not adjusted to demand; in any given year there might be a grave shortage of important elements in the national diet while still other products were produced in great excess. This could happen because there was no co-ordination of production to supply what the people wanted, and no knowledge of co-ordination of demand that the farmers might know what to produce. Instead a vast multitude of poorly organised, rapaciously conducted, and wholly planless institutions and organisations were interlarded between farmer and consumer. These were part and parcel of an order dominated by " egocentric capitalism," " interest slavery," " Jewish commercialism," and " world price slavery." A dominant role was played in this system by that arch enemy of all Germans, the alien " Jewish " invention of the commodity markets.

The new organisation of the markets is to have the stamp " not of capitalism nor to serve the purpose of private market control, but of marketing federations which show the socialist character of market supply and have, simultaneously, the people's economic task of promoting production of all economic circles who participate in the production, refinement, and distribution of agricultural goods."[19] Specifically, they are to exercise power to fix production, farm prices, processing, transportation, and distribution margins, and over-the-counter qualities and prices. They are ultimately to be a " strictly Germanic " type of " Marketing Federation." Only a few of these now exist; the balance of the products are marketed under the administration of the Market Commissioners mentioned above. One or two examples will serve to show how each of these works in practice.

A German Hop Trading Company was set up with monopoly powers in 1933 to protect German farmers from the consequences of a spectacular fall in world prices of hops at a time when German breweries—normally dependent to a considerable extent on world prices—were overstocked. In the following year a Hop Commissioner was appointed to organise the industry on a more permament basis. He was authorised to call on interested economic groups, establish at his discretion an advisory council, and work in close co-operation with producers, traders, and users. Similarly, he was given power to fix maximum and minimum prices for standard quality grades, and to take measures for proper inspection to avoid misrepresentation of either. Breweries were allowed to purchase directly from farmers, but only on condition of paying a small " equalisation sum " equal to the margin required by traders who purchased for resale. Actual purchases involved the compulsory keeping of accounts and giving of properly receipted notes. The procedure here is as follows: the purchaser obtains receipted note blanks from the Market Commissioner. As a condition to purchase he must be duly qualified and certified. If the buyer has at any time proved " unreliable " or has " offended against the marketing rules," he may have his certification withdrawn. After that he is no longer allowed to purchase, nor can any farmer sell to him under any conditions. If certified, he is obliged in conducting a transaction to fill out a receipted note blank in triplicate; one is given to the seller, one goes to the Market Commissioner, and the third he keeps. By this means the Commissioner is enabled to keep track of all transactions.

The Commissioner is further empowered to prevent the intermediation of all pressure salesmen, to regulate at will all conditions and terms of delivery, and to determine amounts and places of storage and warehousing. He may, also, assess small amounts against deliveries which will be cumulated into an "equalisation fund." The fund can be used for " export premiums, fighting damage to hops and for special measures which are necessary in the interests of hop production or marketing."[20] Violations of these provisions can be punished by fines to a maximum of 300 Rm. per hundredweight involved. The condemned are allowed recourse to the courts.

Finally, the Commissioner is authorised on behalf of the National Food Estate to limit the amount of land devoted to hop production. " He may determine the area to be cultivated, make the new construction of hop houses dependent upon his permission, and compel the hop producer to supply him with facts and information."[21] To force compliance with these regulations, the Commissioner is authorised to assess fines for violation to the amount of 10,000 Rm. per violation, and to seize stocks of hops.

Regulations similar to these are to be found where other Market Commissioners have been established for wool, potatoes, wine, sugar beets, *Grünkern*, legumes, seed stock, and garden produce.

The Marketing Federations are more elaborate and more finished forms of marketing control. In general they are authorised to exercise complete control over production areas, conditions and terms of deliveries, regulation of specified costs, fixation of prices, establishment of standards of quality and labels of quality identification, advertising allowances, and to compel reorganisation of any and all pre-existing co-operatives, federations, and other types of organisations. They are all-inclusive in that the membership of all affected groups is compulsory, whether in an individual or a corporate capacity. Typically they are known as " corporations of public law " and are said to be " self-administered " though they are subject legally in all phases of their work to the irrevocable decisions of the duly authorised officials of the National Food Estate.

The case of milk is illustrative of the organisation type. Under authority of the " Second Law for Alteration of the Milk Law of July 20, 1933 " the National Peasant Leader was authorised to amalgamate all enterprises and associations in Germany concerned with production, refining, and marketing of milk and milk products. A Commissioner was first established for the Rhine-Maine-Necker area. Shortly thereafter this commissioner was given control over milk problems for the entire Reich. Subsequently the National Commissioner for Milk transferred his power to an all-inclusive " self-administered " body known as the " Central Association of the German Milk Industry." The Commissioner then retired from active direction, giving over his prior functions to the new organisation, " while he, as delegate representative of the National Minister for Food and Agriculture, watched merely to see whether the self-administration of the significant measures allowed were brought into conformity with the relevant laws and decrees and did not endanger the common good."[22]

In reality, the powers of the Commissioner and his staff of supervisory officers does not seem to have been even thus far curtailed. " The Leader Principle " was carried through with the greatest rigour into detailed management of the new " self-administered " body during, at least, the reconstruction period. In the reconstruction the Reich was divided into 15 milk districts. Within each of these districts all organisations of milk producers, milk products' industries, and milk distribution were fused together and brought under the control of a regional director appointed by the National Commissioner. As a first step, a number of enterprises distant from specified markets were excluded from distribution, as were, likewise, most farmers who had previously delivered their own milk. Zones were established, and only especially licensed distributors were allowed to deliver milk within them. Existing contracts were voided wherever necessary. Duplication and overlapping, it is claimed, have been largely eliminated with the result that middleman's costs have been reduced for many areas from 9 to 10 pfennigs per litre to 5 pfennigs and under. Freight rates have been reduced around one pfennig per litre by estimate. It has been likewise claimed that costs to the ultimate consumer have been lowered, though quoted rates on actual markets do not show this to have happened generally.

Relations between the fluid milk and milk industries, and the details of business of the latter have been dealt with in an elaborate series of decrees and ordinances. These provide for assessment of an equalisation fee between the two branches of the industry, co-ordinate milk products with the Reich " Fats Plan," co-ordinate butter and cheese importations with domestic supply, and similar matters.

The organisation pattern for and the functions to be performed by the milk industry do not vary greatly from that common to the other Marketing Federations. In some cases, particularly that of grain, especial measures have been taken to deal with " commodity speculation " and the commodity exchanges. Despite the virulent language used in describing these " Jewish " creations, and the apparent rigour of a number of the regulations issued dealing with the conduct of such businesses, brokers continue to function and the Bourses to transact grain exchanges about as before. In fact, it seems apparent that the intention has not been to eliminate either the " broker function " or the exchanges, but rather to " purify " them of " Jewish " influences and make them " subservient to the common good." Fixed prices are apparently evaded by manipulation of standard grades, varying combinations of different grades, or manipulated quantities of different types of grain. Exact information, however, it is next to impossible to obtain.

In addition to the Market Commissioners for special products, and the National Commissioners for grouped commodities, a third auxiliary activity has been built up to regulate imports, the " National Offices " (*Reichstellen*). These have been established for a number of commodities, and they may function regardless of whether or not domestic control in any particular agricultural line comes under the Commissioner or Market Federation type of organisation. They are commonly regarded as purely temporary devices for equalising imports and domestic supply. Three situations may arise: (1) There may be a great domestic shortage; in this case the appropriate *Reichstelle* will " sluice " the proper amount from abroad into the domestic market either at the prices quoted for the home product or at some given differential. In the latter case, the commodity processors or distributors may be compelled to absorb the home supply in fixed proportions. This was done in the case of wool. (2) The home supply may be adequate, but produced at a cost above the level of the importable commodity. In this case importation can be shut off entirely. (3) The home supply may be in excess of home demand. If so, the *Reichstelle* has control of the marketing of the surplus abroad, with the rule that the surplus itself shall not provide occasion for price cutting at home. Typically this means dumping of all surpluses abroad. First attempts along this line were made before the advent of the Nazis in a law of April 26, 1930, for the regulation of the import of corn. Under the Nazis the office set up was expanded to include all grains and feeds, being entitled, under the Law of May 1933, the " National Office for Grain, Animal Feeds, and Miscellaneous Agricultural Products." A second office was established for oils and fats. To it was subsequently added milk products, the new office being known as " National Office for Milk Products, Oils, and Fats." Others established were for the egg industry and animals and animal products.

Their functions are, as stated above, to regulate the flow of imports and exports with respect to domestic supply and demand. To this end they function not as purchasing or selling syndicates, but as regulatory bodies with final authority so far as their field of competence extends. That is to say, all imports and exports of foodstuffs must receive the official approval of the appropriate *Reichstelle*. Without such approval the importer would find it impossible to purchase the required foreign exchange from the banks, since this exchange is, in turn, pooled and completely controlled through the Reichsbank. Since, on the other hand, all payments to the pool (all foreign payments automatically flow to the pool) come under direct supervision, no drafts can be made against claims unless permission has been given for the sale abroad from which the claim arose.

5. THE RESULTS OF NATIONAL FOOD ESTATE CONTROLS

As in the case of the Agricultural Adjustment Administration in the United States, the peasants have apparently gained considerable price advantages from the regulatory machinery set up. Merkel[23] submits evidence to prove that the wholesale prices of important commodity classifications have generally advanced to the 1931 level. The general wholesale index for agricultural prices increased 19·9 per cent between January 1933 and December 1934. Similar increases for the same period for different classes of produce are given as follows: cattle, 22·3 per cent; milk, eggs, and butter, 22 per cent; animal feeds, 23 per cent; vegetable foodstuffs, 26·2 per cent. The various publications of the National Food Estate for subsequent periods submit the same general picture; steadily advancing prices to the producer (wholesale prices), increase of agricultural income, higher rural standards of living.

No account is taken by Nazi statisticians, in estimating increase in real farm income, of increase in the prices of the industrial products which the peasants must buy. Furthermore, the Food Estate now administers rural indebtedness as a *first claim* on income. Add the fact that the peasant is no longer able to borrow except under the most unusual circumstances, and one gets some intimation of the reason for continued and widespread complaint.

So far as retail prices are concerned, matters stand quite otherwise. The official literature intended for popular domestic consumption[24] is designed to show that prices to the consumer are kept constant, and that the increase of wholesale prices is due solely to rationalising of the distributive apparatus. However, the official indexes of retail prices are notoriously unreliable. It is difficult to find anybody in Germany, even in official circles, willing to defend their accuracy. A personal check made by the author in the summer of 1935 showed that, for a single district examined (one which would classify as " upper middle class ") in Berlin, actual store prices had increased over the preceding year as follows: fresh fruits, from 100 to 300 per cent; legumes and fresh " leafy vegetables," from 40 to 100 per cent; eggs and dairy produce, from 10 to 40 per cent. The director of a large packing plant told that he paid approximately 50 per cent more for cattle " on the hoof " in 1935 than in 1934; for hogs the advance was approximately 40 per cent. The bulk of this increase was " passed on to the consumer." The shortage of edible fats during the latter part of 1935 became so acute as a result of low domestic production and import restrictions that they practically disappeared from the markets. Restriction in the importation of oil-cake led to serious cuts in the production of corn; the slaughtering of livestock, incidental to drought and fodder shortage of the previous year, rendered the situation still worse. While the government hesitated to resort to actual ration cards because of the bad psychological effects, local stores did attempt to introduce " consumers' cards " to regular customers.

In general, attempts made to keep prices down have been unsuccessful where shortages were acute. Occasionally the facts have been officially admitted, as was the case with veal when an increase in retail prices of approximately 100 per cent over a single year led to sufficiently widespread slaughtering of calves to endanger the stock of cattle for some years to come. At the same time the advancing price of pork led the poorer classes to seek a substitute in eggs, resulting in a reduction of hogs slaughtered from 445,000 in the month of September 1934 to 148,000 in September 1935. Simultaneously this increased demand resulted in great scarcity of fresh eggs and the complete exhaustion of the supply of cold-storage eggs by the end of December. Normally the cold storage supply lasted well into February and sometimes to March.

In addition to actual scarcity, the quality of agricultural produce and of commodities manufactured in whole or in part from agricultural raw materials seems to have seriously declined. German deciduous fruits, for example, are of a decidedly inferior quality to those imported from the United States, Holland, and Denmark. German wheat, being typically soft-grained, produces an inferior flour to that imported from overseas. The compulsory addition of large percentages of " acorn meal " in the making of chocolate, of mineral fats in the making of soaps, of inferior vegetable fats in various types of edible fat compounds, of inferior German wool in woollen garments, and of *Vistra,* *Wollstra,* and other rayon mixtures, in woollen, cotton, and silk fabrics—all result in marked lowering of quality. There are dozens of such examples available to inspection. Under these circumstances " stable prices " mean little even when kept " stable," since, rated in terms of quality, real prices have necessarily advanced in proportion with quality debasement.

Furthermore, it is highly doubtful whether the " Battle of Production " can any more than take care of the normal population increase. Of the total land area of Germany when the Nazis came into power, around 63 per cent was cultivated or meadow land; 27 per cent was forest land; 4 per cent was moor and wasteland, and 6 per cent was occupied with cities, buildings, etc. The moor and wasteland can only be recovered, with rare exceptions, at prohibitive costs. If Germany is to be " self-sufficient " in wood, wood pulp, and wood by-products, the percentage of forest land cannot be cut down. There remains the sole significant alternative of more intensive exploitation of land already under cultivation.

In the main, every increase in acreage of any particular crop is bound to be at the expense of acreage needed for other crops. Thus if flax production is increased from 25,000 tons in 1934 to an expected 46,000 tons, some other type of crop must be curtailed. In the case of wool, self-sufficiency would involve increasing the number of sheep from 3·5 to 50 millions, an increase which is obviously out of the question without diverting large areas of land for pasturage which are badly needed for other purposes.

Taking the country as a whole, varying estimates place the lowest percentage dependence of Germany on foreign agricultural supplies prior to the coming of the Nazis at 20 or above. According to the Institute for Business Cycle Research, if coal required for manufacture be left out of consideration, 35 per cent of the entire German food industry, 95 per cent of the entire German textile industry, and 60 per cent of the entire German leather industry depended upon supply of foreign raw materials in the year 1928. " Autarchy " in foodstuffs is, then, obviously impossible, short of marked improvement in agricultural technique.

The reasons for doubting whether total agricultural production can be increased very much are numerous and convincing. The bulk of German farming land is poor in quality. Output per hectare can be increased primarily by intensive means. Most of the land is already farmed on this basis; that which is farmed extensively will be needed—total area considered—mostly for grazing if the stocks of sheep and cattle are to be enlarged. If not used for this purpose, but broken up into small farms for intensive farming, the larger proportion available will be found in areas where rainfall, types of soil, and other factors are distinctly unfavourable for such agricultural methods. Improved cultivation in many cases requires either expensive equipment which the peasants cannot afford, or more artificial fertilisers, or both. While considerable improvement is possible without anything more than hard labour, it is doubtful whether all the means employable which do not add to farming costs can increase production beyond the point indicated above. If not, then the standard of living of the population is being cut more or less in proportion to curtailment of agricultural imports. That something of this sort is happening seems clear from the available evidence on food shortages, expert opinion of un-prejudiced observers, and the numerous speeches of Nazi leaders in which they continue to admonish the population to " make sacrifices for the Fatherland."

In proportion as these appeals are made are the war drums beaten. No more illuminating picture can be had of the acuteness of growing internal strains than is provided by comparison of the tone and quality of the speeches delivered at the second and third meetings of the National Farmers' Assembly (*Reichs-bauerntag*) in Goslar, November 1934 and 1935, respectively. The first are typically descriptive, more or less factual, and relatively restrained. There is relatively little mention of and not a single speech devoted exclusively to, the " menace of Bolshevism " and the " non-Germanic capitalism of the Jews." But those of the 1935 assembly are strewn with hysterical references to Bolshevism, Marxism, and the Jews. According to the 1935 spokesmen, the " menaces " from all these quarters grows apace, the " protective role " of the Nazi system in general and the army in particular are of growing importance, the spectre of hunger in Germany is the product of " Jewish hate boycott " of German goods abroad. Some of the titles are highly significant: " The Battle of Production as an anti-Bolshevist Defensive Means " (Rudolf Hess); " The S.S. troops as an anti-Bolshevist Fighting Organisation " (Himmler); " A People's Regimented Economy in Contrast to Jewish Economic Methods " (Backe); " Property in the Germanic-Peasant Con-ception and in the Jewish-Bolshevist Point of View " (Merkel). To these could be added seemingly endless sweeping and un-restrained generalisations on " Blood and Soil," " The Battle of Production," " Clan Ideas," " Follower Problems," " Women as Blood Carriers of the People," "Sins against Blood and Race," " Blood and Body Education," the " duties " of the peasants, the holy mission of the Nazi Party, the inspired role of " The Leader," and so on.

The specific purpose for which all this elaborate machinery in agriculture has been contrived is brought into much clearer focus when considered in connection with the third angle of the programme, the plans for rural and urban Settlements (*Siedlungen*). In this field there has been little attempt made to disguise the exact character of the model agricultural system proposed for the future Nazi state. For purposes of clarity the Settlements' plans are dealt with separately in the next chapter.

CHAPTER VIII

Settlements: Hierarchy of Fixed Social Classes Rooted to the Soil

THE point of departure in the Nazi settlement programme centres around a fact of common experience to all great industrial nations: the growing preponderance of the city population, and the gradual urbanisation of the country-side. In the course of the last half-century the ratio of German urban to rural population has been exactly reversed; from 30 per cent urban to 70 per cent rural the balance has shifted to a ratio of 70 per cent urban to 30 per cent rural. Herein, according to Ludowici, writing as spokesman for the Nazi programme, is found the kernel of the most serious problem facing the New Germany.

In common with Spengler and all the officially approved Nazi writers, he believes the city to be bad. It is in the city that the mind brightens, the critical faculties are developed, and the sciences flourish. And it is in the city, likewise, that labour congregates, learns the principles of organisation and mass action, and that the smouldering embers of discontent are fanned into the flames of revolutionary protest. Since the stated purpose of Nazi control is to stamp out all semblance of organised opposition to the existing order, their programme drives hard against the urban trend which nurtures values leading to their own undoing.

Like those economists and politicians who blame machines for the evils of industrial civilisation, and not the people who exploit them, so the Nazis condemn the city *as such* for the attitudes which they wish to destroy while at the same time upholding the system which has made of the modern city what it is. Following the principle that the attitudes of which they disapprove—attitudes leading to promotion of labour interests —must be identified with conditions against which protest is organised, they have developed an argument which is bound to hold considerable appeal for the simple and the naïve. In this the Nazis take the very things against which labour has protested as a basis for proving that protest is wrong, not the forces responsible for the conditions which engendered it.

The argument which Nazi spokesmen advance along this line is remarkable for the subtle fashion in which they have played upon the anger, the despair, and the frustrations of the disinherited of the great cities in order to promote one of the most bitterly and ruthlessly anti-labour programmes which has ever been devised. It may be briefly paraphrased as follows:

" The city is bad. Its growth has brought in its train a series of disastrous consequences. ' . . . In the cities families sink down in a few generations from their high levels of efficiency and decline into an ever-widening, degenerating, and directionless mass . . . because they have lost their inner connection with the soil. Not only the plant dies when we tear it out of the soil, but also men when we do not see the roots which bind them to the land.'[1] The order must be reversed. Cumulative ' degeneracy ' must give way to Nazi indoctrination. Men must be placed back on the land and once more ' rooted to the soil.'

" The population ascendancy of the cities has been paralleled by infiltration of urban value systems on widening layers of the population. This urban mode and tone of life involves a particular set of values, a particular habit of thinking, and a particular point of view. These are typically the exact reverse of those cherished and lived by the peasantry. The point of view and the life values of the peasantry are those which the Nazi government finds pre-eminently worth while. Therefore, in proportion as the rural point of view is submerged, the values of the Nazi system are bound to fall on barren soil. In proportion as the city is reconquered by a ' peasant's state ' will the people realise the Nazi promised land.

" The chief characteristics of city man are found in his doctrinal loyalties, or, rather, his loyalty to no doctrine except that of ' greed.' Overshadowing all other emotional drives is the thirst, the lust, the madness of ' materialism.' The upper classes gear their living to ' Jewish invented ' money-gathering and speculative avarice. They are culturally sterile. They stuff their maws with overplus, and slowly their spirit dies. They feed like vultures on the lifeblood of the nation, and give it back nothing but poverty and despair.

" The degenerate values they foster are aped by all who come in contact with it. Labour sheds its rural heritage of communal feeling, its manifold loyalties to the gods of hearth and home, its piety, and its sense of duty as it degenerates into an undifferentiated proletarian mass. This mass is dominated by the same values as those held by the rich: to get, to gain, to hold property; to acquire riches, comforts, and material plenty. The labourer wants higher wages, shorter hours, better working conditions, leisure time, more goods, higher standards of living.

" These values of ' mammonism ' involve the poor in an endless life-destroying hunger after vanities which can never satisfy, which ever and always lead to a demand for more, regardless of how much was had before. Things come to a pass where nobody recognises station, where none are attentive to the limits of natural endowments. Labour does not know its ' duties,' its proper role, its place. Women invade offices and take jobs in factories where they do not belong. In the face of any proper limitation upon their ever-growing demands, these socially and culturally rootless people embrace the ' degrading philosophy of the Jew Marx '—the doctrine of ' mass-man,' of ' equality of all men.'

" Out of this senseless life comes class war, race suicide, and cultural degradation. In the centre of all this aimless madness stands the race suicide of despair. ' Mammonism ' and the city rot the love for children, and hang the sacred ties of the family, tatterdemalion, on the black cross of lust.

" A mordant poster refers to the ' Mass Grave of the Great City.' At the top a peasant and his wife, rugged with life and rich with six children, are leaving the peaceful country-side for the gloomy city. By the second generation the number of children in the family has sunk to three. There is only one child left in the third generation. The fourth generation has no issue to keep the race from tumbling into the darkening graves of the great city. From generation to generation the clothes have become lighter and gayer, but the aimlessness of life is written ever more clearly on the face. At the end, world-weary and dull with nameless terror, there is nothing left but death and the unremembered tomb.

" Deaths are increasing faster than births, and with this balance book of life the greatest race of people in the history of

the world—the Aryans—is slowly dying out. This spells a weakened foundation for the culture destiny of the Germanic peoples,
not to mention acute shortage of labour for fields and mines,
and a dearth of man-power to guard the country from its ever
rapacious foes.

" If the loss of the sense of the worth of children and family
life through selfish chase after the will-o'-the-wisp of material
plenty and sensual ease is a race suicide of lust, the loss of
respect for the values of a nature-ordered hierarchy of talents
and status—a loss which divides society into two major warring
classes—is the culture suicide of mass kleptomaniac madness.

" Since the natural order of society is to be found in the graded
class structure of peasant life, and since the natural life of all
true Germans is found in contact with the soil, the solution for
all internal unrest centred around the emerging class struggle is
to be found in *returning all labour to the land.* ' The New Germany
must rest on two pillars: the peasantry and labour. The pillar of
the peasants is fixed fast by binding the peasant through tradition to the home soil. In order to ground firmly the pillar of
labour and see that it stands equally fast, the labourer must,
exactly as the peasant, be rooted in the soil and in his work.'[2]
Thus all labour will be returned to the land, the giant cities
undermined, and a new nature-ordered caste society rise,
resplendent in its Germanic glory, from the ruins and the ashes
of the old."

The intent of all this argument is perfectly clear: it is the
ideal social state of the pre-war *Junkers* ! All the rest is merely
window-dressing, designed to put a pretty face on the ugly
reality of a rigidly ordered caste system. Specifically, this means
giving every labourer some land, however small, and attaching
him, through his new glebe, simultaneously to his " nature-
chosen " occupation (agricultural or industrial) and to his locale.
These adjustments are to be dovetailed with other programmes
whose net effect will be to regiment every workman according
to his assumed capacities, and then so to " co-ordinate " his
spirit that he will perform duly allotted " duties " with a
minimum of friction and without desire to alter his status.

Settlements are, then, of very great importance in the Nazi
system. They are to be of two types, rural and suburban. Each

type has already a long history behind it. Together they are now being designed by the Nazis to achieve a set of common objectives. These objectives are concerned with problems of population and race, labour unrest, agricultural self-sufficiency, enhancement of domestic markets, and plans for future wars. These acquire meaning only when taken together and centred around plans for the abolition of class-war and the destruction of the one serious threat to Nazi control, organised labour.

The ways and means vary for the different types of settlement. The objectives and the drive are in all cases the same.

1. RURAL SETTLEMENTS

The centre of the present rural settlement programme is in the east, where such programmes go back to the settlement plans of the Teutonic Knights in the twelfth century. Designed at that time as a defence measure against Slavic pressure to the west, policies since have kept this feature to the fore. The bulk of the land in this region, however, has always remained in the hands of large estate owners, collectively known as the *Junkers*.

With few exceptions, former attempts to break up the estates for one reason or another had foundered for want of adequate energy and authority to overcome the political power of this class, and so long as the indebtedness which the estates had accumulated had not combined with other economic misfortunes of the war and post-war period to provide insuperable burdens. But as these grew in importance *Junker* pressure resulted in the establishment of a special East Help (*Osthilfe*) policy for direct financial aid to the big eastern estates and government price-fixing for their principal products. The result of this policy was to save the estates from foreclosure and choke off the supply of land available for rural settlement. In so doing, the rural settlement programme was brought to a complete stalemate.

The coming of the Nazis resulted in a renewed drive for expansion of the old settlement programme, but this time primarily for political rather than economic reasons. The arguments used before, to be true, were refurbished, but only to be " co-ordinated " with Nazi philosophy. Thus it was contended again that the small-size farm was technically superior to the large estates, that the peasantry were inherently more national-minded, and hence more reliable in the event of war, than the other classes, that a peasant system was economically more stable in time of crisis, that a growing peasantry would enlarge the internal market for machinery and other manufactured goods, that intensive cultivation of the soil would make Germany more nearly self-sufficient in her food and agricultural raw materials supplies, that the country must depend for population increase on high rural birth-rates, and so forth. But what counts under the Nazi rural settlement programme is not their use of the old arguments but the slant which these are given and the use to which the settlements are to be put.

The truth of this generalisation becomes apparent when the above arguments are analysed one by one. For example, it is not at all clear that the peasant middle-sized farms are technically superior to the large estates, and for two main classes of reasons. In the first place, the large estates were badly managed, technically under-equipped, and inefficiently farmed. Labour on the estates prior to the war was primarily performed by imported and badly sweated Slavs, principally Poles. As the estates were transformed more completely on a business basis, with concomitant relative increase of seasonal and relative decrease of permanent workers on the one hand, and introduction of money wages and corresponding proletarianisation of labour on the other, reliance on Polish labour tended to become steadily greater. Local labour became seasonal and migratory, and eventually drifted into the factories and large towns.

This " flight from the land " constituted a virtual strike of domestic labour against the new system. Low-class Polish labour was the answer, but the measure of their employment was likewise a measure of the technically backward methods of farming used on the estates. There is no reason to believe that under a system of scientific agronomy and mechanisation of operations the estates would not be in every significant respect superior to the smaller peasant farms. In fact, some of the experiments conducted by the National Bureau for Technique in Agriculture (*Reichskuratorium für Technik in der Landwirtschaft*) before the coming of the Nazi regime would seem to indicate that the peasant system of agriculture was extremely inefficient compared to pooled and communally farmed holdings. So far as technique is concerned, there is no reason why the big estates could not be farmed just as efficiently as could the pooled peasant holdings.

In the second place, it has never been argued that peasant holdings result in increase in man-power efficiency, but simply in more return per unit of land. The latter does not necessarily exclude the former, but a point does arise beyond which the ratio of man-power to the land can only result in decreased output when both land and men are included. That the bulk of the peasant farms will fall beyond this point is implicitly admitted when it is urged as one of the principal advantages of the settlements that they will absorb the energies of otherwise foot-loose peasants—the only class which will be willing to work as hard as is necessary to make a bare subsistence living on plots of the size planned.

Even at that, opinion seems divided on the question of whether or not the peasant holding will return a larger quantity of produce to the market. If the margin of advantage is so small as to be highly questionable, then it is probably true that no more can be claimed for the settlements on this score than that as many more people will be fed as are domiciled on the land. But it seems clear that they are compelled to work on a scientifically bad land-man basis.

Nor can the population argument be taken any too seriously, since rural as well as urban population has been declining for a good many years. In fact, the ratios of decline were such as to lead to the conclusion that they would ultimately approximate each other pretty closely. Rural birth-rates began to decline later than urban, and actual decline was less. The rate of decline, however, has been greater.

True, if birth-rate declines were to be stopped, pressure along this line was apt to be more effective in rural than in urban areas. But this argument bumps into three facts which are difficult if not impossible to explain away. The first is the oft-repeated complaint of the Nazis that Germany is overcrowded, that she needs room in which her surplus population can expand, and that without this release the German people are so bottled up that ultimately they must burst, by main force if necessary, the bonds which restrain them from occupying more territory.

The second fact is that Germany does not face " race suicide " because of falling birth-rates, but that falling birth-rates are a function of such things as decimation of the adult male population in the war, the large army of unmarriageable females because of the male shortage, and general unwillingness to undertake the burdens of raising a family when unemployment stalks the future like a nightmare and when every peasant knows that no child can have any assured future at all.

Furthermore, the supply of land is wholly inadequate even if all the large estates were used for middle-sized peasant settlement purposes to support any considerable part of the population. Loomis cites Professor Lang to the effect that complete utilisation of the several million acres that remain " for new and supplementary settlement purposes should support about one million persons." In a country with close to 67,000,000 inhabitants, relief from population pressure of this order of size cannot be taken very seriously.

Most of the other well-worn arguments merit the same negative judgment. Agricultural self-sufficiency is out of the question. What can be gained along this line is of relative unimportance for other than short-term reasons, and then it comes more from " pulling in the belt "—by reshuffling population, and getting people accustomed to lower standards of living—than by expanding production. Nor, again, are domestic markets apt to be expanded by ruralisation of only 1,000,000 more people working on a bare subsistence margin. What stimulation there may be to certain trades, such as the building trades and rural commerce, is relatively unimportant, and is probably offset by losses elsewhere in the economy incidental to such transfer. Finally, and perhaps most convincing of all, it must be noted that the first move made by the Nazis was actually to give up rural settlement as a means for relieving unemployment, on the grounds that little relief could be expected from this quarter. The most they have ever claimed along this line was that settlements would keep a certain number of surplus peasants from drifting to the towns, and would offset to a certain extent the process of proletarianising agricultural labour.

Though they used the older arguments, it is clear that to the Nazis such arguments were merely window-dressing for a larger programme. This programme faced on three fronts: (1) It was designed to counteract rural proletarianisation and the threat of agricultural revolt; (2) It was intended to provide a loyal peasant counter-weight to the radical urban proletariat; (3) It was hoped that it would promote the military defences of the country.

All three programmes apply equally to both rural and the small suburban and " company town " settlements. Through rural settlements the number of middle-class peasants are to be increased to as large a number as possible. By the small suburban and factory settlements the number of persons partly dependent upon agricultural pursuits will be increased to include a substantial majority of steady, "reliable," full- or part-time factory labour. Both types are designed to promote creation of a peasantry socially and culturally amenable to Nazi doctrine, i.e. possessed of a " middle-class outlook," coupled to a belief in the value of a semi-feudal caste system.

Since agricultural revolt is associated with proletarianisation, the focal points of unrest, associated with gangs of labour on the large estates, are to be liquidated as far as possible. The limit to such liquidation is assumed to be that point where there is a proper relation between land supply for the necessary nobility, and labour supply which can be drawn from the lower ranks of middle-class farmers, peasants, and rural tradespeople.

All the estates, in other words, are not to be broken up. In practice this means only those which are bankrupt and whose owners are willing to sell in order to be cleared of indebtedness and thus enabled to retire with substantial annuities to one of the large cities or local towns. The estates broken up are to be so divided as to create small villages and cross-roads community centres. In the normal-type village there will be a proper gradation of size of estates depending upon the " worth " of the different peasant stock. The stock will be pure German, or of Aryan type. The rule of inalienable hereditary land will, under the Law of Inheritance, hold good in all cases. Every village will have its group of farmer settlers, and its suburban settlers. Both will own property, each group will be largely self-sufficient, all will be possessed with a middle-class or " petit bourgeois " out-look on life. There will be no independent or floating labour of the usual type. The bulk of all labour will be supplied by members of the family—wives, sons, and daughters. The remainder will come from Land Service (*Landdienst*) and the Labour Service (*Arbeitsdienst*).

The latter have been dealt with in chapters discussing Nazi plans for the " co-ordination of labour " and the " co-ordination of youth." Suffice it to say here that Land and Labour Service are utilised to provide free labour for rural reclamation projects and for supplying direct servant help to peasants and peasants' wives (Women's Labour Service). These two forms are known as Land Help (*Landhilfe*). Land Service includes other groups, amongst them youngsters sent out by the Nazi Party after having finished boarding-school, and university students. These " cheerful helpers come from the towns to share life and work with the peasant and the newly settled small-holder," announces a Nazi propaganda circular. The university students, if the propaganda can be believed, flock enthusiastically to the country to offer their help free of charge to the peasants engaged in the most arduous of labour.

The argument presented by the Nazis on this score is particu-larly interesting for its peculiar mixture of God, guile, and gullibility. According to one of their spokesmen, students tend to specialise, and " the natural consequence of studying such special subjects is a certain tendency to a sublime one-sidedness, a condition of mind which is strongly resented by all people who vigorously embrace the universal interests of practical life. . . . In the new Germany the student does not exist for himself alone, but is a link in the chain. . . . But was it merely a question of manual labour as a counterweight against the strain of intellectual pursuits ? Certainly not ! Work in field and orchard which they undertook was intended from the very beginning as the means for cementing a closer union with the whole popula-tion of the village in which they had started this new venture. . . . Such joint labour shows the way to overcome the inner reserve of the taciturn farmer. . . . What else is the student serving on the land attempting to achieve ? He is trying to approach more closely the mind of his own people, and to get nearer the root of strength and efficiency of the German nation."[3]

The students sent out, the circular does not fail to mention, were members of the *Deutsche Studentenschaft* (German Students' Union), the Nazi propaganda agency amongst the university students. In reality the functions which these students are called upon to perform do not relate so much to hard labour as they do to the searching out of rural discontent with an eye to focusing propaganda efforts at the points of "infection," preliminary, if necessary, to the taking of punitive measures.

The usual type of rural and migratory labour, in short, will be eliminated so far as possible. In their stead the state will supply " free " labour in such quantities as the peasants and estate holders may require. Simultaneously, the peasants, large and small, will be " fixed fast " to the soil by possession of inalienable property rights in the land—" rights " which, coupled to the necessity of discharging debt obligations now existing, are more properly interpreted as " chains." They will become, in other words, a geographically immobile, socially stationary, and property-minded petit bourgeois class. As such they are expected to uphold the Nazi " middle-class " *Weltanschauung*. This will put a quietus on rural unrest and supply the Nazi regime with a solid corps of " dependable " people who will align themselves against the radical urban proletariat.

It is plain on the surface that rural settlements are regarded not so much as a solution of the problem of excess population as a means for consolidating control over the peasantry. This control, furthermore, is exercised with an eye to the political fortunes of the Nazis in war and revolution. " Settlements and breeding of men have both been grounded in the fortunes of war. Rooting of the subjects to the soil was taken over from Frederick the Great and systematically pursued in full consciousness of the fact that only in this way can the Fatherland maintain a soldier who will defend it to the last drop of blood." It is, in other words, loyalty to National Socialist Germany which is at stake in the country-side.

The settlers, as becomes their lowly station, are " to lead a hard life on the new land, but will transmit valuable racial qualities to their children and descendants so that a healthy peasant stock will live there in the future." Without exception these " racial qualities " are claimed to be found in adherence to the " warlike virtues " and the " Germanic culture " values which only the Nazis are capable of properly interpreting and bringing to focus.

The rural settlements may be of two types—those which are carved out as fully independent units from land acquired or newly brought into cultivation, and those known as " additional land settlements " (*Anliegersiedlungen*). The latter represent purchase of additional land required to round out holdings to full occupancy size, i.e. the size which will absorb the entire energies of the peasant and his family during the agricultural seasons.

" At present the choice of settlers is the duty of the Reich's Office for the Choice of German Settlers. This office has twenty-two local branch offices, and, although under the National Food Estate Ministry, stands directly under the new official Commissioner for the New Construction of the German Peasantry, which latter office forms a connecting-link between settlement officials of the states and the National Food Estate."[4] The qualities which the settler must possess have been indicated above. In addition he must be at least twenty-five years of age, married or about ready to marry, and willing to have or already possessed of a family.

Since settlers are typically unable to supply all the funds required for their new properties, various financial enterprises, public and private, have been established for the purpose of making the necessary funds available. The three most important types of settlement credit are: (1) Settlement Preliminary Credit, which furnishes capital to settlement companies for procuring land and building materials, (2) Settlement Long-Term Credit, which " helps the settler to buy the property from the settlement company," and (3) Settlement Credit for the Financing of Public and Community Installations to supply credit for public buildings and permanent land improvements. The actual details of acquiring and financing new properties are handled through private promoter or " bearer " institutions, organised as limited liability companies, whose stock is owned by state, provincial, municipal, and other civic units. Credit policies are

co-ordinated under the control of the Leader of the National
Food Estate through the instrumentality of the German Bank for
Settlements (*Deutsche Siedlungsbank*).

2. THE SMALL SUBURBAN SETTLEMENTS

The full settlement programme of the Third Reich becomes
clear only when the suburban settlements are brought into the
picture. When this element is fitted into the story, the final
picture presents a complete cross-section of the Nazi social
programme.

Suburban settlements are of two general types: those scattered more or less at random on the edges of the larger industrial
cities, and those grouped around large industrial plants and
settled primarily by company employees. The latter, more or
less like American " company mill towns," are the more important of the two in the Nazi programme.

The former are of much more recent origin, their present
importance being primarily due to governmental aid during the
depression. Experimentation with this type of settlement led to
a series of rapid changes in policy, the final result being a programme which closely approximates that of the second type.
And the second type represents in microcosm the finished social-
economic nucleus of the future Nazi state.

How this came about may be shown by the changes of emphasis governmental policy went through as experimentation
with suburban settlements progressed. Since 1929 government
policy has passed through four phases. In the first phase prefer-
ence was given to unemployed who had been out of work over a
long period of time, with emphasis on " self-help " as a measure
to lighten the state load of unemployment relief, promote the
government housing policy, and—a factor of dominating importance—overcome the growing unrest of the unemployed. In
the second phase, short-time workers were added to the unemployed as eligible settlers, with the added rule that both must
have had some agricultural experience. It was, likewise, becoming apparent that not much reduction in the relief burden could
be given by this means, since the costs to the state of establish-
ing and financing the settlements were as large, if not larger

I*

than, the decreases by way of self-help. Hence the shift in emphasis to part-time workers.

In the third phase, consequently, emphasis on unemployment was entirely dropped, and the privilege of settlement was extended only to short-time workers, even though not on relief, and full-time workers willing to become short-time workers for the privilege of receiving settlement allotments. In the fourth phase, which represents the present emphasis, three types of persons are made eligible for settlement: (a) those whose incomes do not exceed the average for the local community of middle-class workers and tradesmen, (b) families with small incomes and four minor children, even if the father is employed full time, and (c) short-time workers averaging less than thirty-two hours' work per week.

This fourth phase places an extremely ingenious emphasis on a long-range plan for unemployment. Combined with other elements previously discussed, the Nazi programme for eliminating unemployment runs about as follows: an increasing percentage of the youth coming of employable age will be absorbed into the army, the Nazi Party, and given positions in the various government services. Propaganda, through direct control over the Hitler Youth organisations, and indirectly via newspapers and the general cultural programme, will mould the youth into the Nazi pattern. So long as the bulk of the younger generation can be kept out of the normal channels of employment, the army of unemployed will tend gradually to shrink through decimation of their ranks because of accident and old age.

Of those who remain to be employed, the politically " reliable " portion will be given part-time work in the factories and allowed to supplement their earnings with produce grown on small settlement holdings. The women will be drawn off the market by a special programme combining marriage loans with preferential treatment given to the men in factory and office employment. (A woman will not be regarded as " unemployed " if she can get married, or has a male breadwinner.) The balance will be put to " compulsory labour " in the more normal sense of the term, or scattered so as to no longer constitute a political threat to the ruling regime. The children of labour attached to plants will be, so far as they are not drawn into the military and political services, expected to inherit the jobs of their fathers when the latter are no longer able to maintain factory *tempos*.

The plan, then, will call for a long-range unemployment programme which redistributes the out-of-work so as apparently to abolish unemployment entirely. Of key importance in this plan is its combination in what was described on p. 258 as the fourth phase of the government small settlement programme with the growing emphasis upon factory settlements. So combined, the final plan calls for a programme of industrial decentralisation predicated upon the building up of small factory towns designed to achieve two purposes: completely " neutralise " factory labour and strengthen the military power of the country.

As remarked above, the Germany factory settlements are quite similar to American " mill-towns " such as Gary, Indiana, and Longview, Washington. There were a good many of these towns or suburban villages in Germany prior to the coming of the Nazis. Practically every large enterprise and a good many of the smaller ones have built something along this line, their programmes going all the way from the completely self-contained villages of the Krupp and Siemens plants to merely the supply of the type of supplementary housing commonly seen in the Rhineland coal-fields.

The oldest of the more or less fully developed factory settlements in Germany is that of the Krupp steel works, the first housing supplied to employees by this concern having been constructed in 1861. The original plan, altered from time to time in detail, and subsequently made the basic pattern for most of the industrial towns constructed elsewhere in the country, was based on the following stated principles: (1) Rents for employees must not be too high, since " it is not low wages which makes the labourer dissatisfied, but the small enjoyment he obtains from the amount of money, especially because of high rents and the high cost of living. . . ."[5] (2) It can be done without any additional cost to the company; in fact, projects of this sort can be made to return a fair margin on the money expended. (3) It is imperative that this be done as a measure of allaying social unrest.

The social function these factory settlements were to perform was visualised early. " I am firmly convinced," wrote the elder Krupp in the seventies of the past century, " that everything

I have recommended is necessary, and that the results will more than pay for themselves. We have much to gain thereby. Who knows but that when, after years and days, a general revolt will go through the land, when there will be a general uprising of all labourers against their employers, but that we shall be the only ones passed by if we are able to do what is required in time." To this end he decreed as basic laws for the Krupp plants, " The command of the establishment shall not be lost, the sympathy of the people shall not be forfeited, there shall be no strikes called." (4) This can be most easily accomplished as follows: " Alongside the settlement of full-time workers there stands in the foreground of general objectives, increasing the attachment to the plant, the working place, the profession." [6]

The full implication of this programme for the sweating of labour, as well as for exercising control over its ideas, is seen when we proceed to the details of the plan. The core of the plan is to offer settlements in the neighbourhood of the plant to the regular full-time workers. The full-time workers are to agree to give up from one to two days per week, i.e. to become part-time workers, in order to help in construction and then to cultivate the small plots of ground which will subsequently be theirs. The maximum number of hours allowed in the plant will be thirty-two per week. The labourer will work harder during the shorter hours; the hours released will be used to give employment to other workers.

The settlements will vary in size, with maximums being set for different classes of workers. The ground typically belongs to the plant, the rights of the worker being restricted to *Erbbaurecht*, or, in effect, squatter rights under terms of the contracts drawn up. The land is commonly ground which has been purchased by the companies during depression times for purposes of future expansion; the settlements make it possible to turn the ground into a source of profitable income until such use is desired.

The methods of financing vary. Loans may be advanced either by the company or through some government agency to a given percentage of the total value of the property. The Krupp plan is regarded as ideal. Every prospective settler must take out a life insurance policy to an amount at least equal to the loan advanced; this policy is then made over to the company. The company supplies all the materials, plans, etc., at what are alleged to be " cost to the company." The labourer helps build his own house in most cases. The loans required are secured by the insurance policy. Payment of the premiums on the insurance, and of interest and amortisation on the loans, is guaranteed by deduction of these amounts from the pay-roll of the employees.

Siemens follows the same policy, though commercial companies participate in the loans at standard market rates. Deductions for interest and amortisation are made in the same fashion.

In both cases the company controls the type and construction of the house, the size of the plots of ground allotted (usually a quarter of an acre or less), financing, repayment, and other details involved in establishment of the individual holding. Furthermore, it examines both husband and wife for physical condition and " racial purity," background in farming experience, habits of work, which include diligence, thrift, cleanliness, and such matters, and " fitness " socially and politically. " Fitness " means ability and desire to have children, or, if unable, to adopt at least two (these requirements vary somewhat from plant to plant). Furthermore, and most important, their attitude towards work, their loyalty to the plant, and their subscription to National Socialist ideologies.

" From the children of the settlement families will come a large percentage of the younger generation for the enterprise."[7] It will tend to immobilise labour, give it a property interest, cut down on costly factory turnover, and make possible payment of lower wages in " case of need." The individual labourer will always have a portion of his income coming from the land, the expectation being that the combined income after settlement will be no smaller than that earned before by full employment in the plant. The average settler will be indebted to the plant or to finance and insurance companies, payment on whose claims are guaranteed by the industry founding the community. He will be, hence, loyal and permanently attached to the plant. Should hard times come which " justify " cutting down on his work time or laying him off indefinitely, guarantee of his subsistence will be found in his plot of ground.

After a " test period " of four years he is allowed to assume title to the settlement. If the loans advanced were made at usual market rates and under customary commercial terms calling for complete amortisation within ten to twelve years, the rate will amount to about seven per cent per annum (Siemens plan). If a long-term financing plan calling for amortisation around forty-five years is used, the rate will be about one per cent per annum (Krupp plan). In the former case the price per month per room will be above those normally charged for flats in the cities. In the latter case the rate will be about the same. At the end of the amortisation period monthly costs should be lower—that is, after ten years in one case, and forty-five in the other. Throughout this period the settlements and the settlers are subject to inspection on any grounds chosen and at the discretion of the company.

Amongst additional arguments advanced on behalf of these plans, the companies suggest that it provides business for private loan, insurance, and building supplies companies (which may or may not be subsidiaries of the company promoting the plan), that it places all labour on a short-time basis, thus increasing their dependency on the plant while decreasing unemployment by spreading factory work, that it by so much unburdens the government from relief payments and the consequent necessity for levying usuriously high tax charges, and that it takes the government out of business where it does not belong.

The Nazi government, in turn, finds that this plan not only has all the advantages the companies claim for it, but that it tends to more or less completely " neutralise " labour by giving it something to do during off-work hours, gives it a property interest, prevents migration, and promotes control of worker morale through the instrumentality of the " Leader " control. Under the labour programme dealt with in Chapter IV of this book, it was shown that the factory owner is the governmentally recognised " leader " of the plant, and the labourers are defined as his " followers " (*Gefolgschaft*). When the " Leader " has his own little flock of " loyal followers," i.e. employees, who are attached to his plant from year to year and generation to generation, " misunderstandings " are apt to be totally eliminated, and all will work on the principle, " The common before the individual good." Such is the happy dream the

German employer has for the beatific future of his co-ordinated labour !

Finally, if industry can be decentralised and the great cities gradually broken up, this scheme can be generalised for the entire country. This is advantageous from a military point of view as well as from the social, economic, and political. There will, then, be no single or small number of " vital spots " which an enemy " in an age of aerial war " can strike at in order to paralyse the entire nation. In common with the military, leadership of the new formation will be under the control of a national " planning " group made up jointly of " scientific soldiers " and " economic soldiers." These will constitute a body of responsible " scientific storm troops " who will organise the fight against " Jewish " and " bolshevist " " intellectualism " in word and deed. That is, they will lead the war against dissent and " communism."[8]

Here, then, is a picture of the future " peasants' state ": the Reich will be divided into a series of divisions and subdivisions. Every local community will be made up of a mixture of social strata, for " nature does not like sameness." There will be two pyramids of social station. At the top of the agricultural pyramid will be the landed nobility, who, endowed with superior talents for " leadership," will direct the peasants' strata below them to perform their allotted " duties " in " service to the common good." At the bottom will be the poorer peasants, heavy of foot and less strong of intellect, who will perform services dictated from above. Those above are responsible to those below in the role of " trustee "; they receive their " mandate from the people " so long as they " lead " the people where the people want to go. The people " want to go " where they are " led " so long as the " leaders " know what is best for " the people."

The second pyramid is the industrial, economic, and commercial. At the top are the most able " leaders "; at the bottom the least competent of the " followers." The same " leadership " principles hold here as for agriculture. Every community will be made up, to some degree or other, of both agricultural and industrial elements. The " leaders " of the two social-economic pyramids will be bound in a common fraternity of " service to the Fatherland," and, presumably, by blue-blood intermixture.

But the " followers " at the bottom will be united by common
tie to the soil. Every worker will be so " bound," so " fixed "
to job, locale, and status by being rooted to the soil which calls
him to perform his two bounden duties to the Fatherland: supply it with food; supply it with men. The agricultural-economic
linkage divides the labour, so that some may specialise on raising
" food for others " while maintaining themselves—the regular
peasantry—and others may specialise on the production of goods
or for their distribution to others while supporting themselves
at least in part from the soil.

But, the shrewd Nazis argue, the soil will nourish not only
the bodies of the faithful amongst Aryan men. It will likewise
feed their souls. The man, peasant or labourer, who works on
the land will draw therefrom a new " world point of view " and
a new set of values in which not " material " things count, but
only those things which the " leaders " alone are competent to
determine he shall believe in, think, and feel. Thus is a revamped
system of fixed and rigid feudal status to be wedded in
a morganatic alliance to a decentralised industrial system in
common service to a capitalist-military state.

In theory the helmsman is " Der Führer," Adolf Hitler, and
he alone knows the course which he must steer. In practice,
" Der Führer " concerns himself with spiritual things only,
leaving it to his numerous lieutenant-" leaders " in fields,
factories, and workshops to " guide " the " followers " in the
" duties " it is their allotted function to conscientiously perform.

It is, in short, the bounden " duty " of the labourer, riveted
to the land, to do whatever the employer tells him. He must
work without murmur or complaint, for whatever wage or other
terms this self-appointed " leader " may establish. Add chattel
slavery, feudal serfdom, and the individual contract wage
system, and divide the sum by three. The quotient is the Nazi
bucolic paradise !

CHAPTER IX

Economics: Business Men, the Born Élite, Should Rule

EVERY member of the Advisory Council of the National Economic Chamber must take the following pledge: "I bind myself as follower to The Leader and National Chancellor with unalterable faith. In fulfilment of the National Socialist will, I will dedicate all my power to the upbuilding of the Third Reich, and I will direct all my thoughts and energies so that in my own activities and those of my co-workers, and through all the functions and authorities entrusted to me, only the highest aims will be pursued, the work of The Leader promoted, and an enduring and true people's community assured."[1]

Business men, said the National Economic Minister, Dr. Schacht, at the opening of the National Labour and Economic Council in Nuremberg, must serve the state. "The time is past," he asserted, "when the notion of economic self-seeking and unrestricted use of profits made can be allowed to dominate. To be true, no individual enterprise, no less than the national economy, can exist without making a surplus, but the *gains must once again be applied in the sense and in service to the total community*. The economic system must serve the nation."[2] Business must, if he could have used the words of the American philosophers of capitalism, Mooney and Reiley, make "profits through service, profit in this sense meaning the compensatory material gain or reward obtained through service."

Similar to the ideas of Gerard Swope—one of the spiritual fathers of the N.R.A.—the United States Chamber of Commerce, and other similar spokesmen for "self-government in industry," "the ideal held up to us by The Leader is a new system of self-administration with the emphasis laid on the responsibility of every individual."[3] In this theory, business men must be allowed so to organise themselves as to avoid the "bureaucracy' assumed to be inherent in state control and to give free play to "ethical" private initiative in business.

"We cannot dispense with the economic willing of individual business leaders and workers," Schacht said. To do so, he held, would be to destroy the "creative power" of the people. The function of business enterprise is to release this creative power on behalf of the nation. "Under no circumstances," he continued, "shall we destroy the multifarious individual character of our economic system. For all time to come we shall need the independent employer who, for better or worse, is connected with his enterprise."[4] In other words, business men in the new Germany are to be given free rein to function as before, except now they must be "honest" in the sense that they must not resort to "unfair" tactics to achieve corporate ends.

This is no more and no less than the idea of "self-regulation" to ensure "fair competition." "We cannot," Schacht said, "get along without an honest struggle of competition."[5] Racketeering, to use a much-overworked Americanism, must be eliminated, and honest business given a chance. The *intent* and the *drive* of this programme is identical with that of the N.R.A.[6]

The purpose of the new economic organisation in Germany is, then, merely that of implementing the programme for giving "honest business" a chance to make profits by "serving the community." To this end, the enabling law for the Preparation of the Organic Reconstruction of Germany's Economic System (February 27, 1934) was said to "serve the purpose of eliminating the excessive organisation of German business hitherto prevailing, with its resulting inactivity, as well as the obstruction and disturbances caused by the rivalry of individual organisations. It is planned to carry out a comprehensive, strict, and uniform organisation of all parts of industry."

In the words of Dr. Schmitt, predecessor to Dr. Schacht, "our task is the limited one of *co-ordinating* with the present idea of national government the organisation of *the enormous field of German business administration.*" With a slight change of phraseology these might have been the words of General Johnson, acting as official spokesman of N.R.A. at the Washington, D.C., "field day" sessions, March 1934—at almost exactly the same time that Schmitt was busy proclaiming the new law for Germany.

Likewise as with the N.R.A., the new German economic organisations are supposed not to engage themselves with "economic planning," since, according to the Nazis, planning can lead only to "bureaucratisation." "Free economy, private initiative, and personal responsibility are not demands of employers on us, but our demands on the employers,"[7] as a Nazi Party spokesman expressed it. But this is only to assert that the totalitarian powers of the new state can and will be used to see that no one escapes whatever the majority of the more powerful German business men decide to do. Membership is compulsory in the new " self-administered " organisations. Nobody is to be allowed to stay outside and spoil the game. All must follow where they are " led " by the *state-recognised spokesmen* for their respective groups.

If all this be true, then there would seem to be small reason to expect any very significant or far-reaching changes from those in vogue when the Nazis came to power. The changes one should expect would be those which would give greater effect to decisions made, rather than those which would indicate any real redirecting of the bulk of business activity. The changes would be in machinery, not in the purposes for which business activity is conducted; in methods of enforcement, not in policy. Such, in fact, is exactly the case.

The machinery for the co-ordination of business policy has, so to speak, been " streamlined." The figure is bad if it conveys the idea of simplicity and clarity of outline, but it will serve the purpose if it is understood to mean more smoothly functioning and better co-ordinated machinery for achieving the objectives business men in Germany have so long been seeking to reach. There is still a great deal of confusion, of duplication and overlapping of functions and fields of authority, of conflict of opinion and warring of factions. But in the main the changes have been well along the major lines of development which have characterised German monopoly-tending business growth over the last three-quarters of a century.

Under the Nazis the machinery for co-ordinating business enterprise is ranged in three separate, but closely intertwined, hierarchies of control. The first, the National Economic Chamber, is primarily a *policy-debating and opinion-forming* body. The second, contained within the structure of the National Economic Chamber, but functionally quite different from it, is the Co-operative Council of the Chambers of Industry and Commerce. This body possesses all the really effective *policy-enforcing* power.

The third hierarchy is made up of separately organised but closely dovetailed central trade associations for the various lines of industry and trade in Germany. Each industry has some such body, with a central headquarters, some sort of regional and local system of sub-division of authority, and a series of methods for making its influence felt wherever its interests are at stake. These latter are perhaps best characterised as *policy-pressure* hierarchies.

This way of speaking of present German business organisation should not lead one to imagine that the three hierarchies are in any wise separate and distinct from each other, or that they represent different and competing lines of interest. It is, rather, that all business men are represented in a policy-debating and opinion-forming hierarchy, a policy-enforcing hierarchy, and a policy-pressure hierarchy. The differences lie in the functions to be performed, not in the interests represented.

The three hierarchies of business organisation will be taken up in the order given. The first and most important of these—which contains the second and third hierarchies as co-operating bodies —is the National Economic Chamber.

1. THE NATIONAL ECONOMIC CHAMBER: POLICY-FORMING HIERARCHY FOR GERMAN BUSINESS

As can be clearly seen from Chart IV at end of book, the new National Economic Chamber includes all phases of economic activity lying outside the fields of agriculture and labour. Complex as the Chamber appears to be from the chart, the new organisation provides, in reality, not much more than a re-shuffling of pre-existing organisations, considerable simplification of former fields of control, and a marked increase in the degree of centralised direction from above.

Were space available, it would be possible to show the lines of transition from predecessor organisations in considerable detail. However, the four principal changes brought about under the Nazi regime may be briefly summarised.

(1) The old Central Committee of German Employers' Associations was dissolved, its anti-labour activity transferred to the

Labour Front, and its more purely economic functions fused
with those of other central business organisations. The changes
effected in carrying through this reorganisation meant a broaden-
ing of function combined with simplification of structure, not
a change of direction or " duties " as might—and, in fact, as
was by a good many observers—at first be supposed.

In the main, the old line of organisation was kept, as can be
seen from comparison of the subdivisions of the original Central
Committee and its successor body:

Central Committee of German Employers' Associations[8]	The National Economic Chamber
National Federation of German Industry	National Group Industry
Commerce (3 sub-groups)	National Group Commerce
Banking (2 sub-groups)	National Group Banking
Insurance (2 sub-groups)	National Group Insurance
Handicrafts	National Group Handicrafts
Transportation	National Group Power
Agriculture	
Miscellaneous Associations	

In the new set-up, agriculture was split off as a separate
organisation (National Food Estate), transportation is separately organised under the Minister of Transport, and the miscellaneous groups are brought together in subdivisions of the
National Group Industry. The one innovation is the National
Group Power, which brings together for the first time all the
" energy " producers of gas and electricity.

(2) With the exception of the National Committee of German
Agriculture, all the more purely central trade associations and
industrial federations (really federations of trade associations)
were brought under the direct and formal administration of the
National Economic Chamber. The most important of these
previous central business associations so " co-ordinated " were
the following: The National Federation of German Industry
(now the National Group Industry); the National Federation of
German Handicrafts (now the National Group Handicrafts); the

Central Association of German Retail Trade and the National Association of German Wholesale and Overseas Trade (now the National Group Commerce); the League of German Industry and Commerce (now the Co-operative Council of the Chambers of Industry and Commerce); the Central Association of German Banks and Banking (now the National Group Banking); and the National Association of Private Insurance (now the National Group Insurance).

(3) These central business organisations were previously quite independent of each other, except in so far as they co-operated in the various divisions of the Central Committee of German Employers' Associations, and as they might co-operate through dual membership with each other. In each case the former constituent members were regrouped, their structure somewhat simplified, and their more purely policy-forming functions considerably clarified.

The results of this shake-up can be seen in a considerable reduction in the number of previously and more or less independently functioning, central headquarters. For example, the old National Federation of German Industry consisted of 19 main or semi-independent groups. Some of these, such as the Stone and Earth group, included a number of sub-groups (e.g. Stone and Earth, Ceramics, Glass). The main and sub-groups together totalled 32 in all. In the new Group Industry, as can be seen from Chart V (at end of book), there are now only seven main groups; the balance (29 in number) are all subsidiary to these seven.

(4) Membership in the new National Economic Chamber and in the special Groups and Chambers is no longer voluntary, election of officers of the leading organisations has given way to appointment from above, and a strict line is drawn between the functions of the member bodies and those of the Labour Front on the one hand, and the various types of marketing organisations (cartels, etc.) on the other. The entirety of all functions delegated are brought under the formal control of the National Economic Minister.

The National Economic Minister appoints the Leader of the National Economic Chamber. This Leader is responsible singly and solely to the Minister, and can be removed by him at any time and for any reason whatsoever. The powers of the Minister permeate, via the office of the Leader, all functional and regional offices. In this capacity he has complete control over all nominations for office, appoints his own deputy officers, the Council members and the Leaders of all the Main and Functional Groups, and can remove any officer appointed by himself or by any of his functionaries entirely at his own discretion.

The Minister has the right to request reports and to make investigations at any time and concerning any matter, can call together any national, provincial, or local council or assembly at his choosing, and has general supervision over finance and the conduct of all organisation activities. The Leader normally exercises the most of these powers, and as such he can be regarded as the immediate deputy of the Minister. The same holds for the relationship of the Leaders of the larger to the Leaders of each of the smaller subsidiary groups. Appointment, removal, and complete control is from the top down; responsibilities and duties are from the bottom up.

The National Economic Chamber is organised along two main lines, *functional* and *regional*. The first is a purely vertical division, including all enterprises and business associations falling into any trade or industrial group. These are known, technically, as " National Groups." There are six of these altogether (see Chart V at end of book): Industry, Commerce, Handicrafts Banking, Insurance, and Power. A seventh group, Transportation, has, as was pointed out above, been segregated and brought directly under the control of the Minister of Transportation.[9]

Pursuing this *vertical* division a little further, we find that each of the *National Groups* is in turn subdivided into, first, *Economic*, and then into *Functional* Groups. In the single case of the National Group Industry, there is an intermediate step between the Economic and the National Groups, known as " Main Groups."[10]

Taking all the National Groups together, we find a total of 43 Economic Groups, 393 Functional Groups, and 6 Independent Groups, divided as follows:

NATIONAL GROUPS	ECONOMIC GROUPS	FUNCTIONAL GROUPS	INDEPEN-DENT GROUPS
Industry:			
Main Group Mining, etc. . .	4	18	
Main Group Machine Building, etc.	6	63	
Main Group Iron, etc. . .	1	4	
Main Group Stone and Earth, etc.	6	53	
Main Group Chemicals, etc. .	3	31	
Main Group Leather, etc. . .	3	28	
Main Group Food Products .	5	25	
Total: Industry Groups .	28	222	
Handicrafts	0	50	
Commerce	5	92	6
Banking	6	16	
Insurance	2	13	
Power	2	0	
Total: All Groups . .	43	393	6

Examples of these different groups are given below to make clear the way the functional lines are drawn:

NATIONAL OR MAIN GROUP TO WHICH ATTACHED	ECONOMIC GROUPS	FUNCTIONAL GROUPS (TRADE)
Mining, Metal Ore Production	(A) Mining	Coal mining, Lignite mining, Iron-ore mining, etc.
Chemicals	(A) Chemical Industry	Sulphuric acid, soda, alkaline electrolysis, and by-products, Dyes, Pharmaceutical products, etc.
Commerce	(B) Retail Trade	Tobacco, Shoes, Radio, Musical goods, Paper, etc.
Banking	(E) Credit Co-operatives	Agricultural Credit Co-operatives, Industrial Credit Co-operatives

The second line of organisation is regional or provincial (by geographic provinces). Here several combinations are possible. To follow these down in detail would make the picture seem very complex. In actuality, the lines of regional organisation are comparatively simple, the reader having no more to do in order to understand how the system functions than by imagining it possible for each of the three gradations of economic organisation—the National (or Main), the Economic, and the Functional (or Trade) groups—having the right to organise on a provincial basis. There are 14 of these geographically marked-out provinces.

Taking examples of the different types of groupings given above, the rule is that each of the " Groups " in each of the columns may organise itself in as many of the 14 geographic provinces as may appear to be justified in the opinion of the Leaders. In some cases, as with the National (or Main), the Economic, and the Functional (or Trade) Groups falling into the field of Commerce, it is obvious that every one of the 14 provinces would have need for separate organisation. The only exception that might possibly be called for would be in the event that in some locality nobody bought or used radios, or musical instruments or some other definite line of goods sold through stores specialising in their sale.

A contrary example is offered by the case of mining activity. In certain of the 14 provinces there is very little mining activity. Because of this fact there might be no regional division of the National Group in these provinces at all, and probably none in the subsidiary Economic and Functional Groups. But if what little mining there were in such provinces were concentrated, let us say, in the Functional (or Trade) Group " Lignite Mining," then there might be a provincially organised Functional (or Trade) Group " Lignite Mining."

Between these two extremes most of the other groups are to be found. In some cases each separate group is provincially organised; in others the majority; and in some others practically none.

At this point the Nazi economic " Leaders " have carried through a very interesting innovation. They have gathered together all the provincially organised groups, whether associated with National (or Main), Economic, or Functional (or

Trade), into Provincial Economic Chambers. In four areas, the
volume of economic activity was so extensive that the province
was represented by two instead of one Provincial Economic
Chamber. There are, hence, 18 Provincial Economic Chambers:
one each for ten provinces; two each for the remaining four. The
regional subdivisions and the headquarters for the separate
Provincial Economic Chambers are as follows:

ECONOMIC PROVINCE	HEADQUARTERS OF CHAMBER
East Prussia	Königsberg
Silesia	Breslau
Brandenburg	Berlin
Pomerania	Stettin
North Mark	Hamburg
Lower Saxony	Bremen and Hanover
Westphalia	Dortmund and Düsseldorf
Rhineland	Cologne
Hessia	Frankfurt-on-the-Main
Central Germany	Magdeburg and Weimar
Saxony	Dresden
Bavaria	Munich
South-West Germany	Karlsruhe and Stuttgart
Saar	Saarbrücken

To these newly constituted Provincial Economic Chambers
they have added all the local bodies of the second hierarchy of
economic organisation mentioned above, the resident Chambers
of Industry and Commerce.[11] Membership in the Provincial
Economic Chamber, then, comes from duly accredited representatives of all the locally organised national groups and all the
resident Chambers of Industry and Commerce.[12]

Each of these 18 different Provincial Economic Chambers is a
more or less exact replica of its parent body, the National
Economic Chamber. There is only this difference, that while in
all cases the Leader of the National Economic Chamber may be
appointed from at large by the National Economic Minister, in
the Provincial Economic Chamber the Chairman of the Chamber
of Industry and Commerce in which the headquarters of the
Provincial Chamber is located automatically becomes Leader
of the provincial body.

From here on the system of organisation is much the same. The Leader has two Deputies, one of whom is the Provincial Handicraft Master; the other is appointed by the National Economic Minister. The Leader is also assisted by an Advisory Council, made up of the Leaders of the various Provincial Groups (National, Economic, or Functional), the Chairman of the various local Chambers of Industry and Commerce and of the Handicraft Chamber, the Leaders of the National (or Main) Groups who happen to reside in the local area, representatives of local government authorities (not more than three), one representative of the National Food Estate, and one representative of the Transport organisation.

The eighteen Provincial Economic Chambers are brought together in the National Economic Chamber, where they participate—as a separate (regional) grouping of the same economic interests—along with the representatives of the various National (or Main) Groups, and the central organisation of the second hierarchy of economic control, the Co-operative Council of the Chambers of Industry and Commerce.

So much for the form and structure of organisation of the National Economic Chamber. With respect to the scope and nature of its powers, it represents, as previously indicated, all German business and industrial activity, domestic and foreign, and in all relationships excepting only agriculture, labour, and the police. Since the organisation has been in existence in its present form but slightly over one year, it is difficult to generalise about its functioning other than to make clear the purpose and intent of the enabling acts. The decree of the National Economic Minister of May 3, 1935, is sufficiently explicit and brief to be worth duplication here in full:

Par 1 : The National Economic Chamber is the general representative of the functional and regional organisations of industry, the Chambers of Industry and Commerce, and the Handicrafts Chambers.

The National Economic Chamber is located in Berlin, includes the entire Reich area, and is legally competent.

Par. 2: Members of the National Economic Chamber are the National Groups of business economy, the Economic

Chambers, the Chambers of Industry and Commerce, and the Handicrafts Chambers.

A Co-operative Council of the Chambers of Industry and Commerce is established in the National Economic Chamber. The National Economic Minister determines its rules of order.

Par. 3: The National Economic Chamber operates, (a) as an organ of self-management for the general affairs of the National Groups, the Economic Chambers, the Chambers of Industry and Commerce, and the Handicrafts Chambers; (b) performs duties laid upon it by the National Economic Minister.

Par. 4: The Leader of the National Economic Chamber and his Deputy Representative are appointed by the National Economic Minister. The Leader and his Deputy must discharge their activities honourably.

The Leader, and in event of inability his Deputy, represents the National Economic Chamber judicially and extrajudicially. He has the position of a legal representative.

Documents which legally obligate the National Economic Chamber are to be signed by the Leader or his Deputy, and by one of the Business Leaders.

Par. 5: The Leader is responsible for seeing that the co-operative work, necessary for the fulfilment of the duties of the National Economic Chamber, between the members in both functional and regional respects is carried through, and can investigate the members in order to carry through the necessary measures. He can delegate definite tasks to his Deputy.

Par. 6: The Leader can regulate the conduct of the business of National Economic Chamber through the issuance of ordinances.

Par. 7: The National Economic Chamber has an Advisory Council. Members of the Advisory Council are:

(a) The Leader, his Deputy, and the Leader of the Co-operative Council of the Chambers of Industry and Commerce.

(b) The Leaders of the National Groups and of the Main Groups of Industry.

(c) The Leader of the Economic Chambers.

(d) Members appointed by the National Economic Minister, specifically:

A representative of the National Food Estate proposed by the National Peasant Leader;

A representative of Local Governments proposed by the National Minister of the Interior;

Miscellaneous persons active in business life or persons especially entrusted with its relations.

The persons designated under (b) and (c) as Advisory Council members can designate, in the event of temporary inability to act, deputies to represent them.

Par. 8: The Leader of the National Economic Chamber calls the Advisory Council together at the wish of the National Economic Minister, who determines the issues upon which advice is sought, leads the discussion or is represented therein.

The Leader of the National Economic Chamber can call the Advisory Council together for advice on affairs concerning self-management.

The Leader of the National Economic Chamber shall give the Advisory Council an opportunity to discuss all order of business which is of especial importance to the members, especially, (a) the budget, (b) assessments, and (c) fundamental questions of the organisation of business economy.

Par. 9: In preparing the work of the National Economic Chamber for particular purposes, special committees, made up of persons from the Advisory Council and especially trusted people from industry fields, may be established.

The Leader appoints the members of the committees and determines the chairman.

As in the case of the Co-operative Council of the Chambers of Industry and Commerce, the German Handicrafts Business Chamber Assembly (*Gewerbekammertag*), the National Groups, and the Economic Groups must take care that the work of the Committees is supported by expert advisers from their own businesses.

Par. 10: In the conduct of the business of the National Economic Chamber, the Leader may, with the consent of the

National Economic Minister, name one or more administrative officers. The Leader regulates the division of labour amongst them.

The miscellaneous labour required for handling the business is employed either by the Leader or by his duly authorised business leaders.

The conditions of employment of the business leaders and of all other employees are regulated by the Leader.

The conduct of business is carried out according to instructions issued by the Leader of the National Economic Chamber. As in the case of the administration of the Co-operative Council for the Chambers of Industry and Commerce, the administrative staff of German Handicrafts Business Chamber Assembly, the National Groups and the Economic Chambers can be called upon by the Leader of the National Economic Chamber for the performance of tasks.

Par. 11: The Budget of the National Economic Chamber requires the approval of the National Economic Minister. Within this budget plan a special budget should be set up for the Co-operative Council of the Chambers of Industry and Commerce.

The budget requirements of the National Economic Chamber shall be covered half by the National Groups, half by the Co-operative Council of the Chambers of Industry and Commerce and the German Handicrafts Business Chamber of Assembly, as designated by the Leader of the National Economic Chamber.

The budget requirements of the Co-operative Council of the Chambers of Industry and Commerce shall be raised by the Chambers of Industry and Commerce.

Par. 12: The first business year of the National Economic Chamber begins on April 1, 1936.

These extensive and all-inclusive powers are divided between three groups, the Ministry of Economics, the Co-operative Council of the Chambers of Industry and Commerce, and the various Groups and their subsidiary organisations. Aside from those decisions the Minister of Economics may cause to have carried out by its various agencies, and the specific powers given to the

Co-operative Council, neither the National Economic Chamber, nor any of its nationally organised Groups, Provincial Groups, or Provincial Economic Chambers, possess any real authority at all. That is to say, all real power is lodged in the hands of the Minister on the one hand, and the Co-operative Council on the other.

The functions of the Groups and the Provincial Chambers are, hence, purely advisory and consultative. They are, in short, *policy-debating and opinion-shaping* organisations. It is in these bodies that policies proposed by the Minister of Economics, by trade association and other important business executives, or by political leaders are taken up. Local and trade applications are discussed, suggestions and criticisms are made, and general ideas are formulated. These ideas run the gamut of much more than " business-as-usual." In addition to problems of " fair competition,"[13] monopoly, price regulation, production control, foreign exchange, labour conditions, and such ordinary business topics, they are given plenty of opportunity and encouragement to formulate policies on the entire range of political, social, and cultural matters affecting nation, locality, industry, or individual business.

Krause, a well-recognised Nazi authority on the subject, seems to be very certain that the Provincial Economic Chambers, for example, have no legal authority whatsoever. " The tasks of the Economic Chambers," he writes, " are not definitely stated by law. They constitute working confraternities of business activity in the Province in which the natural conflicts of interests of individual members can be worked out."

Apparently, likewise, they are allowed considerable latitude in the detailed management of the duties which they see fit to perform within the limits of the general powers granted them as local representatives of the National Economic Chamber. Krause cites the case of the Provincial Economic Chamber located at Düsseldorf, where functions are divided between the different members Chambers of Industry and Commerce on the one hand, and the various provincially organised member Groups on the other. " . . . the Düsseldorf Chamber of Commerce took over the handling of tax questions, and matters affecting money, banking, the exchanges, and foreign trade;

the Duisburg Chamber of Commerce: transportation and statistics; Essen: social politics, bankruptcy and comparative law, and the Commercial Register; Krefeld: the National Food Estate, planning problems, and problems of expert counsel; Munich-Gladbach: raw materials and management of foreign exchange; Solingen: settlements, activities of the Honour Courts, the Chamber of Culture; Wuppertal: retail trade, vocational education, cartel and syndicate problems. Handicraft problems were taken care of by the Düsseldorf Handicraft Chamber, while the specialised problems of industry were handled by the Functional (or Trade) Groups of the individual Economic Groups."

Wide as is the range of issues included in such a recital of activities, the Provincial Economic Chambers in and of themselves appear to lack authority to go beyond general discussion and policy clarification. Their members, when grouped as Chambers of Industry and Commerce, have powers, as will be demonstrated shortly, which go far beyond the point of discussion and debate. But in their capacities as members of the Provincial Economic Chamber they are active in the former, not the latter sense.

The Provincial Economic Chambers, accordingly, serve more as " ideological clearing-houses " for a united business front in the several Provincial areas rather than as agencies for specifically implementing policies decided upon by the various Leaders above. At any rate, there is no evidence that either the Leader or the organisation at his command has any power to coerce any constituent or subsidiary group, and it is clear that no decisions made here dare run contrary to those of the various National (or Main), Economic, and Functional (or Trade) Groups.

But these latter possess powers no different in kind than those of the Provincial Economic Chamber. The differences which exist between them are matters of specific industry and trade groups included on the one hand, and of the national as against the local emphasis on the other. But the differences are in the *direction* and not in the *manner* in which interests are focused.

Actual and effective economic power lies in the hands of the second hierarchy of control, the Co-operative Council of the Chamber of Industry and Commerce.

2. THE CO-OPERATIVE COUNCIL OF THE CHAMBERS OF INDUSTRY AND COMMERCE: POLICY-ENFORCING HIERARCHY FOR GERMAN BUSINESS

The Co-operative Council exists as a separate and constituent body in the National Economic Chamber. It is, in effect, charged with the " duty " of promoting the interests of business, i.e. the interests of the " community " and the " Fatherland " through co-ordination of all " exchange of experience " according to a " unified point of view." Specifically, this means making a general programme for all business enterprises in the entire Reich of a practice which had grown up amongst business men and business associations during the years preceding the Nazis —a practice of " exchanging experience " in all matters relating to the establishment of a common front on all policies vitally affecting trade and general business interests.

This practice took many forms, not the least interesting of which were the numerous " Committees for the Exchange of Business Experience." Originally set up for the purpose of exchanging business experience concerning such things as organisation of plant, methods of bookkeeping and the allocation of costs, and various other minutiæ in the conduct of business enterprise, they led first to a considerable pooling of informational material, and then to the growth of nuclei for the promotion of common policies on the larger social and political issues of the day.

More significant than their own direct committee work was the idea which they were able more or less dramatically to present to the business world: the idea of a " united front " against growing " control of government " over business, and the threat of revolution from the workers. In this they represented merely another factor promoting the consolidation of the business point of view regarding social and political events. The active agents for the massing of business power, however, were the local Chambers of Industry and Commerce with which every German city above the size of a village was equipped.

Under the Nazi set-up, all the local Chambers have been brought into the Co-operative Council of the Chambers of

Industry and Commerce, established as a permanent body in the place of the previous rather amorphous Assembly of German Industry and Trade. The new body is presided over by a Leader appointed directly by the National Economic Minister. The Leader must be the president of some local Chamber of Industry and Commerce. In the event that the Leader of the National Economic Chamber is the Chairman of some such local Chamber of Industry and Commerce himself, he becomes automatically the Leader of the Co-operative Council *ex officio*.

The Leader is supported by deputy representatives, by an Advisory Council, and is aided by a series of special committees. The Council consists of not more than 30 members drawn from Leaders of the various Local Chambers. Especial emphasis is laid upon representation on the Council of presidents of medium-sized and small chambers. The tasks of this organ are purely advisory, being that of supporting the Leader in all his decisions on the one hand, and seeing to the execution of his dicta on the other.

In pursuance of his powers, the Leader may review the Council budget, all membership assessments, and all problems of organisation. The practical work of the Co-operative Council is carried out under his guidance by a series of standing committees, to whom may belong representatives of other organisations not normally included in the membership of the various chambers. Amongst these may be " representatives of the N.S.D.A.P. (National Socialist Party), the German Labour Front, and the Hitler Youth."

From time to time the Leader may call together a National Assembly, made up of all members of the Co-operative Council and its own Advisory Council. The Assembly " . . . is the organ in which, at certain regular time intervals, all Chambers can exchange experience and points of view on fundamental questions."

The Co-operative Council, in addition, represents " all recognised foreign German Chambers and economic federations of German industrialists and merchants abroad." Attached to it are several other special service bodies. Of particular importance amongst these are the " . . . Co-operative Council of the Foreign Trade Office (*Aussenhandelsstelle*), the Central Office of the

German Public Auditors, and the German Group of the International Chamber of Commerce in Paris."

Finally, the Co-operative Council of the Chambers of Industry and Commerce supplies the National Economic Chamber with its principal working staff. The Leader of the National Economic Chamber possesses no special apparatus for the conduct of the detailed functions of his office. His reliance upon the Co-operative Council for this purpose offers further proof of the dominating role played by the Chambers of Industry and Commerce in the conduct of the economic affairs of the country.

All policies and programmes formulated by the Co-operative Council are implemented through the machinery of the local Chambers of Industry and Commerce. In this capacity, the local Chambers are possessed with legal authority to act on behalf of the state. One author, for example, lists among the " obligatory functions whose fulfilment the state demands " the following: giving expert advice on local business trends; eliminating local cut-throat competition; exercising control over the activities of the local stock exchange; co-operating in the naming of commercial judges; registering commercial and co-operative concerns; guaranteeing of commercial honesty; licensing of firms doing a foreign business; giving advice on allocation to individual concerns of available foreign exchange; attesting to the worth of different types of local products; co-operating with the foreign trade control offices (*Überwachungsstellen*); and co-operating with local authorities in the enforcement of national and local legislation.

Thus, from top to bottom, the Chamber of Industry and Commerce organisation is possessed of really effective economic power. Its most important activities possess legal validity, and its decisions have the weight of law. In effect, what happens is something of this order: business men are compelled by law to belong to (1) some division of the various Groups, and (2) to a local Chamber of Industry and Commerce. They cannot belong to one to the exclusion of the other; membership is required in both. As member of some Group, they discuss and formulate their policies with respect to labour, markets, production totals, and so forth. The conclusions they come to, and the policies

284 THE CO-ORDINATION OF STRUCTURE

they endorse, are rendered effective through the Chamber organisation.

If the policies relate solely to local matters, they will be implemented, under the grant of broad powers of control by the Minister of Economics, directly by the local Chamber of Industry and Commerce. But if the policies relate to industry or trade-wide matters, or if they affect super-provincial and national interests, they will be given effect through the Co-operative Council of the Chambers of Industry and Commerce. In the former case the contact is between some local Group and the local Chamber of Industry and Commerce; in the latter case it would be between the National (or Main) Group and the Co-operative Council.

It is this second hierarchy, then, which exercises the real deputised legal authority of the National Minister of Economics. This authority is exercised over all phases of the work of the National Economic Chamber and its subsidiary organisations.

The National Economic Chamber provides a forum where national economic policies may be formulated and discussed, and, through the Co-operative Council, supplies the machinery for the implementing of all policies decided upon. It is in the National Economic Chamber that policies are clarified, differences in application worked out, and co-ordination to achieve results secured. As such, its official status is that of a legally competent body possessed with power to levy such assessments upon its membership as may be required for organisation expenses, but it has no legal authority to levy taxes on its own members. The same holds for the different regional, economic, functional, and other subsidiary Groups.

The Chambers of Industry and Commerce, on the other hand, are Corporations of Public Law, and, as such, have the right to legally represent the state in all activities delegated to them, and to levy taxes upon their membership. Since membership in the Chambers of Industry and Commerce is compulsory, the possession of legal authority converts the chambers into political bodies within the more common meaning of the term. The Chambers are, in fact, politically competent bodies.

This power is further enhanced by the fact that the Chambers of Industry and Commerce supply the principal organisation cement for all stages in the economic hierarchy of control. (a) Compulsory membership ensures complete control over all local business. In addition, the National Economic Minister can compel any local representative of the Functional, Economic, or National Groups to join the resident Chambers of Industry and Commerce in this special capacity. (b) The leading role occupied by the local chambers in the Provincial Economic Chambers assures them equal control over all economic affairs within each of the fourteen districts, since the Provincial Chambers represent all business activity within these areas, regardless of how organised. (c) Any conflicts that might arise between the Provincial Economic Chambers and the National Economic Groups, or any of their subsidiary Economic or Functional Groups, can be resolved through the National Economic Chamber in which, again, the Chambers of Industry and Commerce possess predominant control.

This way of stating the case should not, however, be interpreted to mean that final legal control lies in the hands of the local Chambers of Industry and Commerce acting through the instrumentality of the National Economic Ministry. The " Leader Principle " operates from the top down, not the reverse. Neither the National Economic Minister nor the Leader of the National Economic Chamber is in any wise legally responsible to their constituencies, whether the latter be considered in their capacities as individual business men, or as represented in the Chambers of Industry and Commerce.

There are only two ways in which the business men can exercise control over economic affairs: by effective control over the National Economic Minister himself, and by having delegated to their " self-managed " business institutions—Chambers, etc.—the powers which they wish to exercise on their own behalf.

The machinery which has been set up, in other words, can be used to achieve any purpose. The business men can be controlled, lock, stock, and barrel, even to the point of complete and final expropriation of all their properties. There are no longer any formal obstacles to such action, should the National Economic Minister see fit so to proceed.

By the same token there is nothing to prevent them from

286 THE CO-ORDINATION OF STRUCTURE

doing exactly as they please in all things if they have any means for " controlling the controller." Because the business men of Germany have been able to do precisely this thing, the organisation of economic life in Germany is best described as that of a " business dictatorship." In other words, they have achieved in the National Economic Chamber, the ultimate for Germany in the process described in the final chapter as the " centralisation of policy-forming power," and they have succeeded in endowing this central authority with formal political power.

That this is no exaggeration of the facts can be seen from consideration of a few outstanding facts.

In the first place, the sanctions on which capitalistic business enterprise rests have not been disturbed in any significant sense. As has been pointed out, the " rights " of property, free contract, pursuit of profit, and the exercise of individual business initiative have not been at any place seriously abridged. The official literature, in fact, approves of these " elemental rights " as the foundation-stones for the new economic system of the Third Reich. The simple rule laid down that no business man shall behave " dishonourably " with respect to business and marketing policies means nothing more than that " fair competition " shall be the rule, not the exception. No one, in other words, shall be allowed to " spoil the market " by " unfair " or " dishonest " methods. And, so long as business and all its policies are " fair," the principle holds good that all are exercising their talents on behalf of the " common good." No business man in Germany, nor any important governmental official, is to be found who doubts that " good business " is identical with " service to the common good," and that " good business " means profitable business.

Not only have the fundamentals of capitalistic economy not been disturbed, but, in the second place, none of its organisational forms have been seriously altered. The combines have not been broken up, the trade associations have not been dissolved, and the cartels function as before. All of the big combines of industry and trade continue to function as usual. Siemens and Halske and the German General Electric have remained intact and undiminished in size or influence. The gigantic United Steel

Works was reorganised, its capital written down, and certain properties separately segregated.

All this, however, involved nothing more than a " rationalisation " of internal structure. The Krupp Company has expanded its activities in proportion with the rearmament programme. The same is true with the huge chemical and dye trust, the I.G. Farbenindustrie, A.G. The two great shipping companies, Hamburg-American and the North German Lloyd, have been, for all practical purposes, merged into a single operating corporation. Concentration of control in internal shipping, amongst the electric power and gas companies, and numerous other types of enterprise has not been halted. Not even the big department stores, such as Wertheim and Leonard Tietz, have been broken up. In fact, with few exceptions the combines have not only not diminished in number and importance, but have either held their own or considerably expanded their influence. This holds, whether one has in mind control over costs, prices, markets, production, or any other more or less strictly economic function.

The same picture holds for the various types of trade and industrial associations which make up the third, or *policy-pressure*, hierarchies in German business referred to above on p. 279.

3. THE NATIONAL TRADE ASSOCIATIONS: POLICY-PRESSURE HIERARCHIES FOR GERMAN BUSINESS

National Trade Associations are to be found in practically every field of trade and industry in Germany. Since the coming of the Nazis they have in no wise nor at any time had any of their significant powers curtailed nor their influence diminished. Quite the reverse, in fact. No longer compelled to occupy their time with troubling labour disputes, and functioning under a regime which considers them essential to the conduct of " organic business," they have to all intents and purposes grown in strength and importance.

A recent jubilee volume published by the Federation of German Iron Founders, for example, makes only incidental reference to the new regime. This association embraces almost the entirety of the German iron and steel industry, and includes in its activities all technical, economic, and social work of all its members. The volume referred to, published as a special number of *Steel and Iron (Stahl und Eisen)*, finds the policies introduced by the Nazis no more than a logical fulfilment and a crowning achievement of seventy-five years of hard co-operative work within the industry. Now that the Nazis have given them what they have been working for over this long period of time, of what have they to complain ? Precisely nothing !

Such associations, in fact, are recognised, not only as legitimate business forms, but are closely intertwined with the various offices, divisions, and sub-divisions of the National Economic Chamber. Along with the cartels, they are represented directly in the machinery of the various National Economic Groups.

The National Group Industry, for example, has a special Department of Marketing Organisations and Business Economy which is concerned solely with dovetailing the work of the cartels with the formal machinery previously described. A leading author on the present status of cartels in Germany lays it down as a principle of the new system that " *cartels are only means to the end* of securing a better organisation of production and market relationships in the interests of all parties."

In conformity with this view, all the previously described agencies of the National Economic Chamber are expressly forbidden to enter into price and market regulation. These are reserved especially for the trade associations, cartels, and other market regulating bodies. The same business men belong to the two types of organisation, but neither shall trench on the field of activity reserved to the other.

The words of Hecker, Leader of the National Group Industry, are explicit on the relationships that must be observed: " A close and confiding co-operative work between the Groups and the Cartels is commanded and necessary. It is to be observed in the carrying through of such co-operative work in the field of market organisation problems that the Leader Principle and Compulsory Membership of the Cartels to the Groups is not to be applied, and that, further, the decisions of the Law for the Supervision of Cartels are to be respected. The cartels must limit themselves to measures for the regulation of markets. Cartels do not need to be organised in the line with Group membership.

The Groups, however, shall co-operate in market regulation questions in observing, advising, and trustful work, and should take a definite position with respect to all cartel measures."

4. THE LOCATION OF POWER

Not only have the old organisation forms been kept substantially intact, but it is also true that none of the new central policy-forming machinery is new in principle. Most of it is not even new in form. How relatively slight most of these transitions have been was shown in several instances above. Such changes as have been made are in line with previous development, and enjoy the enthusiastic support of the majority of the business men, both large and small.

Careful examination of the records will show that the complaints which the business men make from time to time have to do almost entirely with awkward functioning, not with either the new machinery nor the underlying principles on which it was established. Some, it is true, fear that the elaborate controls provided for will inevitably lead to complete regimentation of business routine. Most of the business men do not seem to worry about this prospect so long as money can be made out of it. Those that do are assured that the system is not " bureaucratic " —an official utterance which, in a country where opinions are made to order, appears to satisfy many dissidents—and that it allows them much more latitude than before.

Aside from the fact that such latitude as is allowed is permitted mainly as a product of their own choosing—so that complaints against the restrictions it imposes are mostly complaints against their own decisions, as was commonly the case with the N.R.A. in the United States—the principle of " self-management" does appear to allow the business men to do pretty much what they wish. The cartels and market organisations remain, and have, in fact, been considerably strengthened in many cases. These are the most important organisations from the point of view of profits. The larger machinery is, as previously indicated, primarily designed to *co-ordinate policy on threats to the underlying tenets of the capitalistic system.* The fact that the new system is called " socialism," and that " capitalism " has been

KF

repudiated, does *not detract from* this generalisation in the slightest. The changes made are such as worry compilers of dictionaries and experts in etymology, not economists. For the realities of " capitalism " has been substituted the word " socialism "; for the realities of " socialism " has been substituted the word " Marxism "; " Marxism " has, then, been completely repudiated. By reversing the word order one arrives at the truth, i.e. " socialism " in all its forms has been repudiated, and capitalism has been raised into the seventh heaven of official esteem.

Since the whole Nazi philosophy necessarily calls for this apotheosis of bourgeois and capitalistic virtues, it is only natural that when they were presented with an opportunity to shape organisation more nearly after the pattern of their hearts' desire the business men should also be able to name their controlling staff of " Leaders." And such has been the case. In all the literature published by business organisations, and of all the dozens of business men personally interviewed in Germany, regardless of their industrial, trade, or financial origin, not a single criticism has been found of the *type* of " Leaders " placed in command. There is a great deal of complaint about individuals and policies, but these are uniformly the pleadings of minority groups who are being discriminated against, or else against the specific incidence of policies which economic facts compel them to endorse.

Further, the leadership has been entirely that of men enjoying the confidence of the business community. This holds for the Chambers of Industry and Commerce, the Provincial Economic Chambers, the various National, Economic, and Functional (or Trade) Groups, and the National Economic Chamber and its various subdivisions. The first Leader, Schmitt, was a well-known German business man, and thoroughly acceptable to the business community at large. The second Leader, Dr. Schacht, has been so completely acceptable, and his dicta so readily enforced throughout the country, that he is commonly known as the " economic dictator of Germany." Under the leadership of these men, the appointment and removal of inferior " leaders " through the system has been, with minor exceptions, entirely to the satisfaction of the business communities affected.

A final reason for supposing the new set-up to be entirely satisfactory to the run of German business is found in the nature of the division of labour between the National Economic Chamber and the other " estates."

With respect to the National Food Estate, the division has affected two areas of control. On the one hand, the marketing of agricultural commodities after these have left the land, and the manufacturing of agricultural products beyond the first processing stage are typically under the administration of the National Economic Chamber. Up to this point all agricultural activity is entirely within the control of the National Food Estate. On the other hand, the whole settlement programme, both rural and suburban, is tied up with a programme for industrial decentralisation and labour " neutralisation " which is of direct moment to all divisions and subdivisions of the National Economic Chamber.

As is indicated in the run of business literature, every large factory, every Chamber of Industry and Commerce, every Provincial Economic Chamber, a good many of the National, Economic, and Functional Groups, and many of the special interest trade associations have been continuously concerned with questions of factory settlements. The division of labour between the two " estates " in this respect appears to be purely " functional," and to vary considerably from instance to instance. But there is no evidence that any decisions have been made at any time which run counter to the wishes of the business men who desire to have an agriculturally rooted, industrially bound, and " ideologically neutral " proletariat.

The same picture holds for the relations between the National Economic Chamber and the organs of local government. As Frielinghaus has put it, " The new structure of economics recognises no differences between public and private economic activity. . . ." Not only are representatives of the various local governments to be found on both the national and regional organs of the National Economic Chamber, but it is even true that local government is co-ordinated to the end that economic activities pursued by them shall enjoy no non-economic advantages over private enterprise.

The literature on this point is perfectly explicit, being of a nature with which the general American public is familiar through numerous utterances of business leaders on the " dangers of government competition with private enterprise." Under pressure of this sort the Reich government and many of its subsidiary bodies have begun to dispose of their properties to private enterprise, or to cease " competition " with private enterprise where no properties are at stake. Thus the Reich, the states, and the communes have already disposed of much of their holdings in the iron and steel industry (notably the United Steel Works), coal, and electric power. Similarly, support is being withdrawn for loans to individuals wishing to construct private dwellings wherever private enterprise can possibly make any money out of the transactions. True, the government has been expanding its activities in some directions, but mainly where there is no talk of " competition with private enterprise," and with an eye to providing business men with effective guarantees against losses.

Relations with the Labour Front are somewhat more complicated, but no less satisfactory to the business men. As will be shown later on, the Labour Front possesses control over all employer-employee relations for the entire Reich. Under the famous Leipzig Agreement between Schacht of the National Economic Ministry, Ley, Leader of the German Labour Front, and Seldte, of the National Labour Ministry, March 26, 1935, the National Economic Chamber was, similar to the procedure of the National Food Estate, entered as a corporate body in the German Labour Front. Simultaneously there was created a National Labour and National Economic Advisory Council, made up jointly of representatives of the Advisory Council of the National Economic Chamber and the Labour Council of the National Labour Front. To this body was delegated all problems of labour relations affecting the functioning of the two " estates." In effect, the agreement delegated to the National Economic Chamber authority over all labour problems of an " economic " character, while reserving to the Labour Front all labour issues of a social, political, or cultural character.

The Labour Front was, thus, left with two primary functions, that of adjudicating all disputes through the instrumentality of the " Trustees of Labour," and of providing for the cultural regimentation of workers through the programme of Strength through Joy. The latter is partially under the direct control of the Ministry for Propaganda and People's Enlightenment (operating through the fourth " estate," the National Chamber of Culture), whereas the Trustees of Labour are under the joint control of the Economic and Labour Ministries. Furthermore, the regional organisations of the Trustees and of the National Economic Chamber are identical. For each Provincial Economic Chamber district there is a regional labour Trustee office. It is thus apparent that the Labour Front is more or less completely under the control of the National Economic Chamber. At any rate, there have been no complaints from the business men that the new division of labour was not entirely to their own liking.

Two additional considerations serve to greatly reinforce this impression. In the first place, as was pointed out above, the new National Economic Group division of the National Economic Chamber is almost identical with that of the pre-existing Central Committee of German Employers' Associations. The earlier organisation existed as a body for the purpose of co-ordinating all anti-labour union activities of all German employers. When it was dissolved, a portion of its functions were transferred to the National Economic Chamber, and the balance to the German Labour Front.

Since the unions and all their political affiliates were simultaneously dissolved, it follows that to argue that the German Labour Front now " represents " the interests of labour is a mild euphemism at the very best. This is especially true, as was shown in an earlier chapter, since no self-elected organisation of the working men exists in fact, and since the functions now performed by the Labour Front deal almost exclusively with " spiritual " and " cultural " issues.

In the second place, the whole plan for the " co-ordination " and " neutralisation " of labour, as laid out in the programme of the German Labour Front, is no more than an expansion on a national basis of the earlier programme of the German Committee for Technical Education and Training. This committee was organised in 1926 in the offices of the United Steel Works in Düsseldorf. By 1933 its " cells " had been established in several hundred of the largest plants in Germany. Its executive officer, Dr. Arnhold, has subsequently been placed in charge of all vocational education under the control of the Labour Front.

Even here the control of the National Economic Chamber does not cease, since this vocational training is typically carried out under the direct auspices of individual enterprises such as Siemens and Halske or Krupp, local Chambers of Industry and Commerce, and the several National and Functional Groups of the National Economic Chamber. Every National and Main Group, in fact, has a special committee concerned solely with the task of " co-ordinating " the education of those permitted to serve as apprentices to the industry or trade in question.

Finally, it is worth recalling that the National Economic Chamber is thought of as an organ integral to the new " corporate " or " estate " society, and that every person or class of persons brought under its control is being duly " fitted " and " bound fast " to that task to which " nature " has ordained his talents shall lead him. It is in this sense that the word *Fach* (in connection with Functional or Trade Groups), translated above as *functional*, should rather be rendered as *professional*, or perhaps even better, *occupational*. The business men have the " professional duty " of " leading " labour; labour has the " professional duty " of " following " the " business leaders " in those occupational tasks for which they are, according to Nazi theory, each and severally best adapted.

Herein lies the basis of a further division of labour between the National Economic Chamber and the National Chamber of Culture. It is the " duty " of the latter so to guide and control the " people's spirit " (*Volksgeist*) that all the rest shall seem the natural " German " thing to do. In general this means to do as you are told, with no questions asked; in the economic sphere it means to follow where you are led, with no kicks made.

And the " Leaders " are the business men.

CHAPTER X

Self-Government in Business: The Goal

" THE century of expansion," Reithinger writes,[1] " is past—at least for the European industrial countries." The twentieth century is a century of *planned organisation.* " One cannot expect to push organisation and rationalisation of the individual economic unit to its maximum without being drawn into a corresponding rationalisation and organisation of the entire economy."

It is idle, he feels, to talk any longer of a " free " and unfettered economic system; the age of ordering, organising, and co-ordination is already upon us. " The public commercial policies of nearly all countries have established control which provides a regulatory basis for the exchange of all goods between their own and foreign countries; national and international cartel bonds have long been used for the purpose of regulating markets of important basic raw materials; the development of the tariff system in transportation has served similar purposes, and in the new branches of our economy developed during the twentieth century, such as power supply, aviation, and radio, a free economy in the nineteenth-century sense of the term no longer exists at all. At the present time no less than a third of the more important raw materials of the world is bound up by international production and market agreements, while another third is controlled by the market regulations of individual states."

But the issues raised thereby, Reithinger proceeds to explain, are not those of collective versus individualistic society, of state or private enterprise. The " either-or is false," because it is a mistake " to believe that a planned organisation of the national economy makes private initiative superfluous." Rather is it true that the degree of freedom or control must be adjusted to the role each economic form plays in the total economic structure. The state must " oversee " all that which lies beyond the competence of the individual enterprise. It may do this directly, or through a " suitable representative of the individual economic or professional estates (*Stände*)." The state, in other words, must regulate inter-enterprise, inter-association, inter-trade, and inter-national relations, but business enterprise is the unit of reckoning, and competition the life of trade.

This view—which is not basically dissimilar from those expounded on behalf of the numerous governmental regulatory authorities which have sprung up over the past forty or fifty years in practically every capitalistically organised country, and which is to be found in a more advanced stage in such programmes as those of the American N.R.A. and A.A.A. plans, the British Marketing Acts, and the Belgian De Man plan—accepts the entire structure of capitalistic economy as worthy of salvage at all costs.

Looking through the literature with considerable care, it is possible to classify all the Nazi programmes along this line under two heads. *First*, are all those *programmes designed to eliminate the self-destructive tendencies inherent in business practices and changes in business organisation. Second*, are all those *programmes designed to eliminate the left challenge to the social, political, and cultural foundations of the capitalistic system itself.* The second has already been dealt with in the early chapters of this book. The first will be taken up somewhat more in detail in this chapter in order to show how organisation forms have been adjusted to specific " business rationalisation " proposals, and how these dovetail to promote the "co-ordination of spirit" which constitutes the crux of the second.

It was pointed out in the preceding chapter that the primary purpose of the National Groups was the " co-ordination of business policy." The programme has four phases: (1) determination of policy, (2) gathering and assembly of the necessary information, (3) organising for control, and (4) implementing to secure results in line with policies. Under the Nazi system all these must bear in upon and be adjusted to the requirements of (a) the individual business enterprise, and (b) the business system at large.

According to the Nazis, these two sets of requirements are met simultaneously by maintenance of the conditions of " fair competition." In the words of the Leaders of the National Group Industry: " Competition is necessary in order to stimulate increase in efficiency. Efficiency competition is to be greeted favourably; speculative competition, on the contrary, is to be cut off. Unfettered freedom in the play of financial and economic power leads to an unlimited and unbridled competition on the market to the advantage of individuals at the expense of others. Setting aside degenerate competition is necessary in order to co-ordinate the advantages of the individual to those of the total economy. In order to link the competitive struggle to sound and becoming practices, principles and rules must be established for the organisation of the market."[2] The task is to bring harmony and efficiency (profitability) into the economic system without disturbing the *status quo*.

A number of highly significant assumptions underlie this conception of " business planning."

It is first assumed that there is a fundamental harmony— a sort of Golden Mean—underlying all conflicting interests within the state. This harmony relates not only to relations between the state and individual business enterprise and between capital and labour, but also to relations amongst all individual businesses. There is, in this view, no fundamental conflict between small and large enterprise, between loosely and compactly organised businesses, between manufacturer and distributor, and between producer and consumer.

A proper combination of all these forms and interests constitutes what the Nazis call an " organically integrated " economic society. Such a society will be achieved the instant that, to use an American term, all business is made " fair." It can be made " fair " if the state will " trust " business to be " honourable " and responsible, and will use its powers " helpfully " to punish all those who refuse to abide by the rules laid down.

It is assumed, secondly, that there are no long-run tendencies which are operating to destroy what might at any given time appear to be an " organically integrated " economic society. For example, competition is upheld, monopoly is condemned, and freedom of contract is endorsed. Individual initiative is declared to be the foundation of economic efficiency, the profit incentive to be indispensable, and private property to be the right of all men. Yet the state and business enterprise concur in the need for regulation of all phases of production, marketing, and price formation. For example, the whole organisation of the National Economic Groups promotes exercise of monopoly powers.

But the significance of these contradictions lies not in the fact of conflict alone, but in that there has been no change visualised which tends in any material way to decrease the element of centralised regulation, or to slow down the growing concentration of power to make and enforce policy. In other words, while assuming that long-run tendencies do not exist powerful enough to destroy current notions of a harmonious balance, the entire organisation of economic society in the Third Reich is built directly on structures whose primary purpose was the destruction of the elements out of which the assumed balance was to be contrived.

In the third place, it is assumed that whatever weakness the economic system showed before can be removed by allowing the business community to " regulate itself." The state, in this view, does not regulate; rather it lends its power of coercion to business organisation in the hope that business will " restore " the conditions which it defines as " sound," i.e. profitable. It is taken for granted in Nazi Germany that a nation is economically " sound " when business is profitable. That is to say, that whatever is good for the business community at large is to the advantage of the general community.

Finally, it is assumed that all these problems can be " solved " by organising. The line of thought runs: harmony can be achieved, structural stability can be maintained, self-regulated business can be made " honest " and " fair," and proper organisation will take care of the details.

A little reflection will show that this programme is almost identical with that of the N.R.A. in the United States. The two were co-terminous in time, officers of each kept in constant contact with developments in the other, and the basic programmes were in principle the same. This holds for both guiding ideas and the general structure of organisation. The American N.R.A. programme was, in short, a " Fascist " programme in idea, in principle, and—in the main—in structure. What differences there were between the two lie, in the main, in variation in types of industry most vitally affected in the scale of industrial

operations, in the degree to which preceding organisation could
be built upon, in the consistency with which plans were carried
out, and in the degree to which powers could be enforced. In
these respects the principal contrasts are found in the fact that
the preceding organisations in Germany were much more highly
developed, the plans were more consistently and ruthlessly
carried through, and the state lent its authority more whole-
heartedly to the task. Germany's " New Deal," in other words,
came earlier because centralisation had proceeded further in
that country.

That this is descriptively accurate so far as business plans
were concerned—the labour side has already been dealt with—
can be seen from a brief review of the specific programme of
the new organisations outlined broadly in the preceding chapter.
For sake of clarity these will be dealt with under several headings.

1. WHAT CONSTITUTES " FAIR COMPETITION " ?

In the " Fundamentals of Market Organisation " (*Marktordnungsgrundsätze*), published by the National Group Industry
for the benefit of its member bodies, a series of propositions
are laid down. These may be regarded as valid for German
business under the Third Reich—a careful sampling of a considerable mass of German business literature, and conversa-
tions with several dozen German business men ranging in
importance from National Leaders to shopkeepers, having
shown that the " Fundamentals " outlined by the National
Group Industry can be taken as representative of the general
business point of view.

According to this brochure, " fair competition " lies at the
heart of the problem of price fixing. Three rules are said to hold:
goods shall be sold at set and non-discriminatory prices, prices
shall not be unduly advanced, and sales shall not be made below
reasonable cost. Under the first rule it is held that " *basically all
orders shall be filled only to set prices without the right of subsequent
change* " on behalf of privileged persons. " Exceptions are to be
made only in unusual cases, in particular with large orders with
extraordinarily long delivery dates."

The second rule is even more reminiscent of the words of

President Roosevelt and General Johnson during the early days of N.R.A.: " Foresight and restraint should be used in setting prices. The measures of the National Administration for supplying labour with jobs and for stimulating advance from the low level of production should be supported by avoidance of price advances." Every effort should be made to secure profitability through decrease of costs and more efficient management, not by cutting labour expense or by raising prices.

The third rule deals with the most difficult problem of all, " fair price." As a general principle it is declared that " . . . prices should be so adjusted that the deliverer is in a condition to meet his obligations to the public authorities and to his private creditors (followers—labour—financial creditors, those who have delivered supplies to him)."

This does not mean any abstract " just price," such as was once declared by the Provincial Court of Krefeld,[3] nor a prohibition against " selling below cost " under all circumstances. Fashion goods and other seasonal commodities remaining unsold at the end of the season may, for example, be then sold below cost without damage to anybody. Nor, further, is there any desire to prevent price lowering due to superior efficiency as such. But where distinct damage is done to the *competitive positions* of business rivals, or where such prices tend to " endanger an entire industry," they may be enjoined. To this end all sales " below cost " of a speculative character are condemned. In the main the rule is to hold that *goods shall not be sold below " reasonable cost," qualities being given due consideration.*

All policing is to be entrusted to neutral bureaux, set up by the various groups, which will be empowered to enforce compliance through control over costs, prices, and employment elements. The bureaux shall pay particular attention to that type of unfair competition which results in the spread of the control of a particular enterprise or class of enterprise into other commodity fields, or where sale of commodities by one division of a vertically organised combine to another division of the same company below prevailing prices results in a final price of the second division below that of the general market price for the final product.

Supplementary to these general rules are a number of more routine guides.

(1) " Contracts made should be punctually fulfilled." This is because " contractual good faith is the basic principle of all commercial trade." Once a contract is made, neither party shall have the right to alter it to his advantage. If payment cannot be made punctually, interest must be paid on the advance. Payment made by draft or other internal exchange media shall not be regarded as equal to cash, and the costs of encashment of the same shall be borne by the person so paying. Shift of purchase from one supplier to another because of the imposition of interest charges for delayed payment will be regarded as unfair competition.

(2) Commercial credit extended shall earn an interest in proportion to the bank rates and bank costs involved.

(3) The length of the payment period need not be the same for all commodities, nor for all sections of the country. But there shall be no discrimination between classes of buyers of particular commodities.

(4) Orders for delivery should not be made on such short notice as to require overtime.

(5) The practice of dividing orders between several suppliers, thus burdening the latter with many small high-cost deliveries, should be discouraged.

(6) No firm should be allowed to bring pressure on suppliers to buy its own commodities. The result of this practice is usually to split up orders into uneconomically small allotments.

(7) An attempt should be made to unify conditions of sale and delivery in each of the Functional and Economic Groups.

It requires no discerning eye to see that this series of major assumptions and guiding rules for the conduct of business-as-usual under Nazi domination are identical in type, content, and tone with those long familiar to American readers who have kept up with the trends of legislation and court decisions in the United States having to do with " fair competition " and " trust-busting." More significant still, the issues, the methods of handling them, and the conclusions reached are those employed in the drafting and attempted enforcement of N.R.A. Codes.

2. WHAT SHALL BE THE RELATIONS BETWEEN THE GROUPS AND THE CARTELS ?

This is almost identically the same question which might have been asked in the United States, substituting for " Groups," " Code Authorities," and for " Cartels," " Trade Associations." As previously pointed out, apparently none of the important cartels or trade associations in Germany has been disbanded. Cartel agreements are at least as common as before the coming of the Nazis, and probably more so. None of the previous special interest trade associations has been broken up—the case of the German Iron Founders has been mentioned. As near as can be discovered, the Functional (or Trade)—*Fachgruppen* —are the effective administrative groups, and are organised similarly to the Code Authorities, with the addition of compulsory membership. The Economic and National Groups are more or less similar to industries covered by so-called " Blanket Codes."

Furthermore, the activities of none of the cartels nor the special interest trade associations seem to have been seriously curtailed. The offices exist as before, the outline of functions and duties remains similar to that which preceded, and no officer of such associations has been found able to supply examples of undesirable " arbitrary interference." As with the case of the Code Authorities, the interleaving between the leading special interest trade association or associations in each field and the new " self-administered " bodies is so close in terms of offices, officers, and outlines of functions that in many cases they can be considered the same for all practical purposes.

Descriptively the relation between the Groups and the other types of business organisation seems to be about as follows: Within each field, represented as an Economic or Functional (or Trade) Group in the National Economic Chamber, there exists a central trade association which is primarily concerned with problems of policy of special interest to their own memberships. The leading trade association in the Economic Group " Machine Building," for example, is the National Association of the German Machine Builders. The dominant association in the Economic Group " Steel and Iron Making " is the Federation of German Iron Founders.

These associations or federations are apt to be organised both nationally and regionally and they may be established as central bodies for a number of more specialised trade associations. However set up, they are the leading bodies in the national, economic, functional, and regional groups of the National Economic Chamber.

The members of these trade associations—simultaneously represented in the provincial Chambers of Industry and Commerce on the one hand, and in one or more of the Groups on the other—may or may not be subscribers to cartel agreements. The cartel agreements may be " free " or " compulsory " of the " lower " or " higher " order, and local or national in scope.

" Free " cartels are those which are established voluntarily by business men, and subject only to the terms of contractual obligations entered into. The agreements, however, must be in writing, and must not contravene established law. To this end they must be registered with the state: no unregistered agreement is legally valid or enforceable in any way whatsoever. " Compulsory " cartels are those in which terms, membership, or administration are under the complete or partial control of the state.

Cartels of the " lower " order merely limit the activity of the individual enterprise with respect to markets, prices, or production. These are of several types. The *Conditions Cartel* provides for uniform regulation of sales conditions but does not concern itself with price fixation. The *Price Cartel* is concerned—usually —with fixation of minimum prices. The *Calculations Cartel* does not fix prices, but determines solely the methods of calculating or computing costs and prices. The *Regional Cartel* divides market areas amongst its members. *Customer Protection Cartels* protect members against buyers. *Production Cartels* limit production, through agreements not to expand plant, to not increase plant efficiency, to close down certain plants, to shorten hours of labour, etc. *Submission* or *Contract Cartels* determine which members shall submit lowest bids for given contracts. *Specialisation* or *Production Cartels* may concern themselves with agreements allocating commodities to some one or more specialised plants, general promotion of efficiency of production, or similar plans. *Patent Cartels* involve the exchange and pooling of patent and copyright holdings.

All or a portion of these cartel types may be combined in a single cartel agreement. But, for each cartel of the " lower " order, there may be constructed a cartel of the " higher " order by addition of the *syndicate feature*, i.e. centralised administration and control. Where a cartel takes the syndicate form, all individual members surrender enterprise identity for the terms of the agreement. For example, when prices are centrally controlled, deliveries are made to the cartel, the cartel in turn makes all the sales, and so forth.

Either the lower or higher order of cartels may be organised on a regional or a national basis or both.

How many of the different types fall into one or the other classification is difficult to say. Estimates vary a great deal. Metzner, Leader of the Cartel Bureau of the pre-Nazi National Federation of German Industry, estimated the number of cartels in the Federation's Functional Groups to be 1,543 in 1926, divided as follows[4]:

Mining	51
Iron making	73
Metal smelting and semi-mfg. goods	17
Machine building	147
Iron and steam boilers and apparatus	48
Railway rolling stock building	1
Automotive and bicycle	8
Iron and steel ware	234
Electric mfg., fine mechanical and optical	56
Metal wares	78
Wood	44
Leather	46
Stone and earth	30
Building industry	—
Ceramic industry	10
Glass industry	20
Chemicals	91
Oils and fats	36
Paper	107

Textiles	201
Clothing industry	71
Brewing, malt and milling . . .	97
Sugar and food products . . .	24
General and luxury foods . . .	49
Shipping and forwarding	4
Total	1543

In the year 1925 a government report estimated there to be 2,500 cartels in industry, 400 in wholesale trade, and 150 in retail trade. The handicraft cartels were not included in this survey. The differences in the estimates are accounted for by differences in definition, the percentage of local cartels included, exclusion of certain trade groups, and the years of reckoning. There are unquestionably more cartels in existence to-day than at the time either of the two above-mentioned estimates were made.

The Nazi state regards cartels as necessary and indispensable. Müllensiefen[5] regards the change made from the pre-existing state attitude to be a change from hostile tolerance to positive approval. According to his formula, " anti-cartel policies = Liberalism. Positive cartel policies on the basis of the compulsory cartel law = National Socialism." The " positive cartel " policy has two phases, " positive " and " negative."

Under the first, traceable to the original " Law concerning the Establishment of Compulsory Cartels " of July 15, 1933, the state possesses the power to compel outsiders to join the cartel in the event that " market regulation by voluntary agreements is defeated by too strong an emphasis of individual over collective interests . . ." and likewise the power to " forbid the establishment of new enterprises and the expansion of existing establishments."

Specifically this means *legal authority* to do a number of things: control investment, whether by establishment of new plants or expansion of old; control borrowing on the market or increase in capital by self-financing; fix prices, quotas, and penalities; protect small enterprises, etc. Under these authorities, for example, construction of new plants was forbidden in the chalk industry. For differing periods of time, production was limited

and new *plant construction* was forbidden in the following industries: jute weaving, paper and pulp, textile goods, cement and
hollow glass, cigar and cigar-boxes, high-tension electric cable,
zinc-rolled products, clocks and watches (with exception of
wrist-watches), nitrogen, superphosphates, stone objects and
materials, peat moss, radio, smoking tobacco, horseshoe, hosiery
dyeing, rubber tires, white lead, red oxide of lead, litharge, white
zinc, lithophone, staining and earth dyes, pressed and rolled
lead products, tubing, and insulation tubes.[6] Legal control over
prices of market conditions was exercised in a number of cases,
notably in such industries as cement, hollow glass, zinc rolling,
paper, paper-cartons, and stone objects. In the smoking-tobacco
industry measures were taken to protect small producers by
preventing expansion of the large.

Under the " negative " phase of the new ordinances the
cartels, along with all other types of associations directly or
indirectly engaged in price fixing, are brought under the control
of the National Price Commissioner (*Reichskommissar*). The
Commissioner is legally endowed with power which " . . . includes
all goods and services with the sole exception of salaries and
wages." How extensive the formal powers designated to this
office are can be seen from the comments of *News in Brief*.[7]
" An ordinance of November 13 [1934] against price-combinations, decrees in its first paragraph that corporations and other
organisations of public or civil law may fix, agree upon, recom-
mend, or change to the disadvantage of the retail customers'
prices, minimum margins, maximum reductions, and minimum
increases, only with the approval of the National Price Commissioner or his representatives.

" Par. 2 forbids producers and wholesale dealers to fix or
change retail prices to the disadvantage of customers without
the consent of the National Price Commissioner. This makes
impossible the unlimited issue of new standard articles. New
standardised articles will be approved by the National Price
Commissioner only if the goods show an adequate quality for
trade-mark protection and if the prices are fair in every respect.

" Par. 3 forbids to make more difficult, slow, or expensive the
course of products from the producer to the consumer by means
of economically dispensable middlemen of any kind. As a

matter of course, legitimate trade will not be interfered with. Only such intermediary agencies are to be attacked as are dispensable and no longer possessing a justified and useful effect on national business. The National Price Commissioner reserved disputable cases for his personal decision so as to avoid uncertainty in practice."

Subsequent ordinances have been issued " to make possible an adequate examination as to whether price-combinations are compatible with the common weal." In theory, these ordinances confer upon the National Price Commissioner plenary powers which he may exercise entirely at his discretion. In reality, all action is taken through the machinery, and by and with the counsel, of the various local Chambers of Industry and Commerce. The Functional (or Trade) Groups of the National Economic Chamber are authorised to establish Supervisory Offices (*Überwachungsstellen*) dealing with price problems, but not to exercise direct powers over price formation.

Foreign-exchange control is somewhat more rigid, coming as it does under the direction of the National Economic Ministry. The Exchange Control Offices (*Devisenüberwachungsstellen*) are set up along regional lines, with a separate bureau for each foreign country or geographic area with which Germany has important trade relations. They have final control over all imports and exports through effective pooling of exchange payments and allocation of exchange for payments abroad. With variations as to detail these offices work about as follows: payments for exports are poured into a book-keeping pool in the form of foreign exchange. Payments from the pool to individual firms selling the goods abroad are then made in German marks. The foreign exchange resulting is then allocated to individual importers upon presentation to the government of a statement from the supervisory office in question authorising the purchase. The purchaser pays the government in marks the amount required at the established rate.

The Exchange Control Offices also manage the payment of export subsidies. The amounts required for payment of the subsidies are, typically, levied *en masse* upon the industrial Groups in rough proportion to the percentage of total foreign exchange they will require for necessary imports. For example, the machine industry may be asked to raise a certain sum of money in marks in order to finance subsidies to machine companies selling goods abroad. The goods sold abroad are disposed of at prevailing world prices, or in competition with protected domestic products. The difference between the domestic and the foreign prices determines the subsidy margin. In the case of medium-priced automobiles this sum has for some time amounted to 400 Rm. per car. This money is paid from the subsidy fund. The proportion of the fund allocated to the machine industry is approximately that which has been raised by the machine industry for this purpose; the total raised is in proportion to the ratio of machinery sales abroad to all other sales. The amount of exchange arising from foreign sales determines, in the main, the amount of exchange which can be used for payments of imported raw materials required by the industry.

To promote the supervisory work of the National Price Commissioner, the various price and exchange offices, and several groups, and the Chambers of Industry and Commerce, extensive information is required. According to the dicta of the National Group Industry, all business and trade associations, federations, and cartels should keep currently compiled statistical data on production and markets. They are further encouraged to keep comprehensive and precise information on costs, and if possible to compile such data reduced to a " unified cost scheme " in order to facilitate exact cost comparisons. Supply of such information is not, however, compulsory except in cases involving price supervisory offices, the cartel courts, and similar legal controls.

A special injunction is laid upon cartels to observe " discipline." " Cartels are agencies of mutual protection. It is their business to bring order and sanity into the market. Their recognition is bound up with assumption of duties and tasks on behalf of the people and the state. . . . Every member is obligated to exert his best energies on behalf of the protective association. Among his duties are regulator participation at conventions and meetings, and in the supply of association statistics and business data. . . . All violations and evasions of agreements must be, in order to protect the faithful cartel members, made known. . . . Every member must give proof that he has fulfilled his cartel tasks. . . . Every violation or evasion of cartel obligations will be punished."[8]

Finally, among the relations involved between the various Groups of the National Economic Chamber and marketing organisations which deserve comment here, is that of defining functions and fields of operation. For example, an agreement between the leading organisations of wholesale trade on the one hand, and of industry on the other, offered the following guides to proper performance of the " wholesaling function "[9]:

" Wholesalers are such merchandising concerns, entered into the Commercial Register, who perform the following commercial functions to the full extent:

1. Purchase in quantity from producers, warehouses or importers and sell in a free market to those who purchase for resale and for purposes of continued manufacture.

2. Advertise and seek markets; that is, search out new methods for selling already known commodities, and market possibilities for new goods.

3. Take and distribute goods at their own risk.

4. Maintain warehouses supplied with the variety of commodities customary in the trade.

5. Order ahead; that is, place their orders as far in advance as possible in order to promote uniform employment in industry.

6. Supply additional credit out of their own resources and distribute credit taken up from creditors to credit dependent purchasers for commercially customary terms.

7. Bring about equalisation of supply and demand with respect to local, temporal, price, and quantity factors.

8. Appraise all market information concerning adaptability of commodities, quality of goods, use of warehouses, techniques of marketing, advertising, etc.

9. Fulfil social tasks through maintenance of the independent existence of numerous self-managed individual enterprises, and the education of a younger generation of

merchants imbued with a sense of responsibility and entrepreneurial joy."

The meaning of all this is, of course, perfectly clear. The business men of Germany are attempting to cut out the " chisellers " who undermine " fair " trade and " spoil the market " for many by making business unprofitable. None of the associations, cartels, or groups is designed to do anything more than just that. What has been offered above as evidence could be expanded into several volumes of direct citations. All else is superfluous. Particularly the generalisations about the role the individual enterprise must play in the state, and all the talk about the " common before the individual good." The business men are to be filled with " entrepreneurial joy " by being given a chance to make such rules for " managing themselves " as they may see fit in their quest for profits while engaged " responsibly " in " serving the community " !

3. HOW MUCH AND WHAT TYPE OF MONOPOLY SHALL BE ALLOWED ?

Fascism and Nazi doctrines are sometimes thought of as " the revolt of the little business man." Revolt against encircling monopoly, revolt against the surrender of individual initiative to coercive and predatory business organisations, revolt against the crushing domination of the giant concern. Those who followed the course taken by the Nazis in their rise to power will remember particularly the virulent threats and bitter words hurled against chain and department stores. The same tactics were employed, on behalf of small manufacturers and handicraftsmen, against encroachments of the mass-production methods employed by large concerns.

What, then, have the Nazis done about this phase of their programme ? The answer is, nothing. Or, perhaps, not quite *nothing* at all, since the policy they have pursued of letting the business community make all its own decisions on this score has resulted in, *not less, but more monopoly*. What exceptions must be made to this generalisation are to be explained not in terms of opposition to monopoly, but on entirely different grounds. Most important amongst these are plans for decentralising industry and thereby neutralising labour unrest and the war plans of the military.

But monopoly tendencies have not been turned back, nor even challenged. How true this is can be seen from a brief review of the facts pertaining to economic activities operating under varying degrees of monopoly influence.

(a) " *Natural Monopolies* ": By natural monopolies is here meant all effective monopolies, regardless of how achieved, or on what grounds justified. This definition may seem highly capricious, but so far no exception has yet been found to the rule that *once monopoly has been achieved, it is commonly defended on " natural " grounds completely regardless of how the activity was characterised prior to addition of the monopoly element.* " Natural " monopolies, in other words, are " effective " monopolies.

Most of these monopolies in Germany are of the public-utility type. Most of them are owned and operated by the government. The outstanding examples are the National Railways, and the National Post. The first owns and operates practically the entirety of all the railway lines and facilities in the entire country, and is the largest single-operating corporation on the European continent. The National Post has a complete monopoly of the entire postal, postal check, postal savings, telephone, telegraph, and radio systems of the country. A similar monopoly is held by the *Lufthansa*, which, with its two affiliates, dominates the entire aviation industry of Germany.

But the significance of monopoly in these fields is to be found in neither the fact of exercise of monopoly power itself, nor in state ownership and control. Far more important is the power which monopolies possess to prevent threat to the exercise of monopoly powers by compulsory " co-ordination " of competition. In this respect, no line can be drawn between public and private enterprise under the Nazi regime.

With respect to publicly owned enterprises, the new regime has been almost completely successful in its promotion of monopoly. Each of the three enterprises mentioned above comes under the control of a separate Ministry—the National Railways under the National Transport Ministry, the National Post under the National Postal Ministry, and the *Lufthansa* under the

National Aviation Ministry. In so far as competition existed between any of the separate services operated by each of the corporations in question, such has been almost entirely eliminated by compact and agreement. The control of the National Post over telephone and telegraph, for example, eliminates competition between the two services. Competition between the three corporations in passenger service has been eliminated by a series of compacts. A uniform schedule of passenger rates has been worked out between the *Lufthansa* and the National Railways. The rural mail-passenger omnibus services of the National Post are non-competitive with the National Railways, schedules and time-tables have been dovetailed, and service made continuous throughout.

The principal threats to these three have come through growth of inter-urban bus and trucking services, expansion of canal and river traffic, and the " cut-throat " competition of local bus, trucking, and forwarding companies. Before the coming of the Nazis numerous attempts have been made to unify schedules, adjust rates, and dovetail services in these fields. A history of developments in each field over the post-war period would show rapid advance of plans for further centralisation and co-ordination of services. It would likewise show, in detail and at large, that the new inter-traffic organisation under the control of the National Transport Ministry is in line with the basic monopoly tendencies within the industry which were clearly discernible long before the coming of the Nazis.

The chart gives a pretty clear picture of the organisation of the National Transport Council. It is directly parallel in every important feature with the National Economic Chamber. It is organised both functionally and regionally, it includes all the important classifications of national and local freight and forwarding services competing with the three above-mentioned corporations in any respect whatsoever, and its duties and responsibilities are identical with those of the several Groups of the National Economic Chamber. Membership is compulsory within each National Transport Group, offices are held by appointment from above, duties are supervisory, informational, and advisory, and effective detailed authority is exercised by the Chambers of Industry and Commerce. As the chart shows, the

Council is made up of the Services and the Customers. The former include the Leaders of the several Groups, representatives of the National Railways, the National Post, and the *Lufthansa*, and the General Inspector of Roads. The latter includes representatives of the National Food Estate, Industry, the National Chamber of Culture, Municipalities, and the German Labour Front. The Provincial Transport Councils are patterned after the National Council in every important detail.

The " advisory " role of this new body should not be misunderstood. The Council does not, it is true, possess authority to act. Nor has it operated to exclude all competition. But it does do the following things: it provides a medium for unifying each of the several services throughout each significant geographic area. It provides machinery for negotiating divisions of traffic by types and regions, as, for example, between local and long-distance hauls, bulky low-value and high-value freight, full and part car-load lots, etc. It operates so as to prevent, and probably so as to eventually exclude entirely, duplication and overlapping of services, discriminatory rates, and the rise of new competitors. Under its general supervision compacts are made for interchange of traffic at given points and at fixed rates. The new highway networks and the services thereon are largely under the direct control of the National Railways. " Cooperative work," in other words, means unification, interleaving, and " co-ordination," and these terms mean expansion of effective monopoly powers within each respective field and outward from the national transport agencies to include more and more phases of all other nominally " competing " services.

This does not imply, however, " socialisation." The Nazi government has leaned over backwards here, as elsewhere, in favour of private enterprise. This is particularly well illustrated in the electric-power field. While no national monopolies exist in power distribution within given supply areas, duplicate facilities are very rarely met with. The bulk of the companies supplying either local municipalities or large geographic areas are publicly owned in whole or in part. But the Nazi authorities have resisted all attempts to expand public at the expense of private networks. Simultaneously, they have eased the way for continued growth of local and regional monopolies.

"The most important entrepreneurial changes since the National Socialist revolution are the founding of the Provincial Electrical Association of Oldenburg for the purpose of merging 32 public corporations (Law of April 29, 1933), the setting up of a ' Community of Work of the Large Electric Power Enterprises of the Rhine-Main Economic Area ' under the leadership of the Hessian Railways, Inc., the Municipal Electric Works of Frankfurt-on-the-Main, and the Main Power Works (October 1933), the founding of the Electric Power League of North-West Saxony—which has meanwhile come under control through purchase of a capital stock majority of the Power Corporation of Leipzig (February 1934)—and finally, in March 1934, the unification, on the initiative of the state of Württemberg, of the Württemberg Provincial Electric Power, Inc., and the Württemberg Bill Collection Corporation for purposes of power transmission under state control. It is remarkable that these changes in organisation have been brought about essentially through co-operative work of the participating companies and groups rather than through capital transactions and the extension of the power of individual entrepreneurial groups."[10] Since these lines were written, further changes along the same lines have been going on steadily.

An interesting example of how the state lends its authority and aid for the promotion of private enterprise in the electric power and electrical supplies fields is to be found in the "Fronts." These are organised locally for the purpose of promoting the electric business, and may include, in addition to electric-power interests, gas utilities, electric and gas equipment supply concerns, and numerous other affected business groups. The *Westdeutsche Wirtschafts-Zeitung* for January 1934, for example, contains a public announcement of the formation of a local "Community of Work of the Gas-Electric Front." The list of member bodies is very interesting:

The District Leadership of the National Socialist Party
The Chamber of Industry and Commerce
Federations of Landlords and Real Estate Owners
Wholesale and Retail Trade
Municipal Gas and Electric Works

Labour Trustees
The Handicrafts Chamber
Installers of Electric and Gas Equipment
The Electric and Gas-Supply Industries
The Rhine Power Company, Inc.

The purpose of the Front is to encourage consumption of gas and electricity, and promote the installation of appropriate appliances. To this end the Front offers special discount, credit, and rate terms for new installations and new customers.

A somewhat similar organisation has been set up to cover such " co-operative " work for the entire Reich: the National Electric Power Supply Federation (Reichsverband der Elektrizitäts Versorgung-R.E.V.). Organised in 1934 as the " sole federation of the German power industry " for the purpose of an " active electric-power front," its controlling membership is drawn more or less equally from both public and private power concerns. Its purpose is to promote electric power consumption, the electric supply industry, electric installations, the retail of electric equipment, and the electric handicraft industries.

Nothing could show more clearly the intent of Nazi control in economic affairs than the make-up of the active management of this organisation. Despite the fact that better than three-fourths of all German electric power is owned or controlled by public bodies, the directing heads of the National Electric Power Supply Federation are drawn almost exclusively from the ranks of private enterprise. Its first Board of Directors was presided over by two chairmen, both representative of private power companies: Hellmuth Otte, General Director of the Hamburg Electric Works, Inc. (controlled by the Siemens-Schuckert combine, largest manufacturers of electric equipment and supplies in Germany), and Dr. Wilhelm Lühr, member of the Board of Directors of the Gesellschaft für Elektrische Unternehmungen-Ludwig Löwe & Co. A. G. (the largest holding company in the private German electric-power industry, the company likewise controls several electrical supply manufacturing concerns).

This organisation, again, is dominant in the Power Group of the National Economic Chamber, discussed in the last chapter. The Leader of the Group is likewise associated with the

Gesellschaft für Elektrische Unternehmungen-Ludwig Löwe &
Co. holding company, thus giving the private electric-power
companies a leading position in the new power " advisory "
body to the National Economic Ministry.

(b) *Partial or Incomplete Monopolies:* In this group fall
practically all the so-called " heavy industries," some specialised
manufacturing and a few of the " service " industries. The giants
in this field are: Steel: the United Steel Works and Krupp;
Chemicals: the Dye Trust (I.G. Farbenindustrie, A.G.); Electric
Manufacturing: The Siemens-Schuckert combine, and the
German General Electric; Oceanic Shipping: the Hamburg-
American–North German Lloyd combine; Machinery: Demag;
Potash: the Wintershall-Kalliindustrie combine. There are
dozens of smaller concerns associated fairly closely with the
large combines though not directly under their control.

One will search the economic and propaganda literature of the
" New Germany " in vain for proof that these concerns are being
broken up, or their power diminished in any way. Not only do
mergers, communities of interest (*Interessengemeinschaften*),
combinations, cartel agreements, etc., continue to be made
daily, but also with apparently the complete approval of the
administration. None of the large business leaders consulted in
Germany seemed to have any apprehensions on this score; in
fact the attitude of the Nazi government towards them was almost universally greeted with approval and satisfaction. This generalisation holds whether reference be had to social or economic
problems. Amongst the latter, the attitude of the government
towards further combination is regarded as entirely " friendly."

Even more significant is the dominant role played by the
Leaders of the big corporations in the Groups, the Chambers of
Industry and Commerce, and in the leading special interest trade
associations. The Communities of Work (*Arbeitsgemeinschaften*),
so strongly emphasised in all the Nazi literature, serve as means
for the filtration of monopoly powers of the big combines
throughout their respective industries. The new organisations
change nothing of importance, except as they promote further
centralisation of policy-forming power. And the centralisation
of policy-forming power is the first and most significant step in
the expansion of monopoly influence throughout all types and

segments of industry. Competition, in other words, is not being defended, since in these fields nobody in a position to do anything about it believes competition a goal worth striving for.

(c) *Where Competition Prevails:* Competition is said to be the rule, monopoly the exception, in the manufacture of consumer goods, trade and commerce, the catering and personal service fields, and in handicrafts. Yet, so far as Nazi Germany is concerned to-day, the word " competition " is being bent so far from its original meaning in these lines of economic activity as to be more or less meaningless. For one thing, none of the monopoly tendencies in these fields is being counteracted. The big chain and department stores continue to function as before. Combines in the brewing, textile, food products, and allied fields are as strong as they ever were. Furthermore, the new machinery of functional and regional Groups has been built upon previous organisations for the purpose of strengthening the grip of centralised business control. Changes in policy have been, on the whole, inconsequential.

Likewise, as with the cases cited above, the very existence of the old central trade organisations and their successor bodies is indicative of the fact that significant monopoly influences permeate these fields of economic activity as well. In them is concentrated power to determine policy; with them are associated bodies—principally the Chambers of Industry and Commerce and the local Handicraft Chambers—endowed with power to act. The extension of the " authoritarian " principle into these fields changes nothing fundamental, but it does indicate clearly the fact that policy-forming powers are being siphoned off, concentrated, systematised, and co-ordinated with other phases of economic and cultural activity.

In Germany, as elsewhere, no industry, no trade, no social or political activity can any longer escape this trend towards centralisation of control. All compact interest groups require organisation; organisation leads to hierarchies of control, and this by definition to centralisation of power to make and enforce decisions. That there are no possible backward steps in this process can be seen by tracing through the stages of development in any trade or industrial field leading to the centralised bodies over the past 75 years. That no field can escape the tendency can be seen from examination of the nature of the centripetal forces which have led to such coagulation of economic power even where, not " monopoly," but " competition " has commonly been regarded as the only " natural " state.

A glance at the organisation of the National German Handicrafts Estate (Chart IV at end of book) will show how far this co-ordination has proceeded in the most extreme case that can be imagined. But it is still more important to realise that even in this case the new organisation is " new " to only a minor extent. The Guild Associations and the Handicraft Chambers, both national and local, existed before. The predecessor to the German Handicrafts Chamber was the German Handicrafts and Trade Chamber Assembly, divided regionally into 26 divisions with 59 Handicraft Chamber and 8 Trade Chamber member bodies (Handicraft and Trade in this usage mean the same thing). With it were combined five Provincial and five " Economic Region " Assemblies of Handicrafts and Trade.[11]

Every significant change wrought in this pre-existing machinery has tended to eliminate competition, destroy " individual initiative " and to promote the exercise of monopoly influence. The changes have been four in number: (1) the system of Handicraft Masters (" Leader principle ") has been added; (2) the regional organisation has been developed; (3) the co-ordinated new central body, the National Group Handicrafts, has been placed under the National Economic Chamber; (4) the national and provincial bodies have via the Masters (Leaders) been given effective legal powers to act. The set-up here is, hence, identical with that of the National Economic Chamber. As such it is directly in line not only with preceding tendencies within handicraft organisations themselves, but also with those dominant in the economic system at large. The transformation has been continuous, unidirectional, and persistent. The former tenuous gossamer threads of influence are now being transformed into steel webs of control; the controls now range over practically all areas of activity, and the power to coerce is exercised by dominant nuclei of interests within the handicraft trades themselves.

All the same generalisations are valid when applied to the Group Trade, or the Group Banking. The same forces have long been at work, the same coagulation of interests and powers had taken place, and the same type of cap-stone has been placed on them by the Nazi state. The ideal of a completely " organised " state is, at least on paper, close to fulfilment. And that idea is one which rests upon the assumption of complete centralisation of power to determine policy and enforce compliance with decisions arrived at from on top.

Neither the idea of " self-government " in business, nor that of either or both regional and functional decentralisation of management militate against this generalisation. " Self-government " in reality means the acquisition of legal and quasi-legal power to decide economic questions according to the " business point of view." Managerial decentralisation is the almost inevitable corollary to centralisation of power to form policy. It becomes more thorough-going and uniform in application the greater the centralisation. Thus it has become more complete in such firms as the American Telephone and Telegraph Company, the General Motors Corporation, the German Dye Trust, and the German General Electric Company than elsewhere in the capitalistic world. So close and rigid is this connection between managerial decentralisation and policy centralisation that it can be taken as almost axiomatic that growth of the former is a necessary function of expansion of effective monopoly-type power to enforce uniform compliance with policy decisions from the apex of the pyramid down through all layers to the base.

4. FOR WHAT PURPOSE IS BUSINESS SELF-GOVERNED ?

From what has been said above it is perfectly clear that " planned organisation " should be understood not as social-economic planning in the socialist sense of the term, but as " business co-ordination " with a view to exercise of monopoly powers. There is nothing in the literature which permits a discerning reader any other interpretation. By the same token, the expression—interlarded through the endless stream of propaganda and explanatory newspapers, brochures, books, and reports—*Gemeinnutz geht vor Eigennutz*, requires transliteration into English patois in order to be understood properly. *Gemein* means " common," or " public," or " general "; *nutz* means " fruits," or " emoluments," or " returns." The expression

Gemeinnutz, as used by the Nazis, means " return to the community," or, more precisely, " service to the community." *Eigen* on the other hand, means " individual " or " own." *Eigennutz,* then, means " returns to the individual," or " profits." The exact meaning of the whole expression is " service to the community before profits to the individual "; the American wording is " profits through service."

This interpretation is in line with an old distinction, running back through several generations of German economic and business literature, between *Privatwirtschaft* and *Gemeinwirtschaft,* on the one hand, and *Gemeinwirtschaft* and *Sozialwirtschaft* on the other. *Privatwirtschaft* has always been taken to mean an *economy of private enterprise* in the English, liberal, *laissez-faire* sense. *Gemeinwirtschaft* was used to mean a *profits economy from the public point of view,* or, in other words, a *profit economy supplying a service to the community. Sozialwirtschaft,* on the contrary, has long meant *socialisation.* All the Nazi literature emphasises the present economic system as a *Gemeinwirtschaft.*

What this means specifically can be seen from the following generalisation by Callman, taken from his monumental commentary on German Common Law, in which he summarises— year 1934 !—the purposes of economic activity: " The economic man of the exchange economy is dominated by the striving for gain. The gain incentive of the individual is the steady effective basic factor of world economy; out of it comes for economic men the end purpose of professional activity. All other objectives set are only means to the attainment of this final goal, are only intermediate aims whether considered as aims of phases of economic activity or as independent but partial objectives. Thus the acts of equipping an enterprise in technical and commercial respects or of eliminating industrial competition are simultaneously ultimate and intermediate goals. In practical activity they are the final goals of professional effort in a link within the total activity. But in respect to these they are no more than means to the reaching of a dominating ultimate objective: *making profits.* It is a question of temperament and of general economic conditions whether the striving for gain is explained as *maintenance of profits* or *increase of profits.*" (Italics by Callman.)[12]

The objective, in short, is profits. If in an organised economy the community must be made to believe that service comes first, it can be argued that profits are no more than the just reward for success in this labour of public love. But for the initiated there can be no confusion; the single, sole, and dominating purpose is necessarily profits. The public relations departments of German business, in other words, have put it across !

SUMMARY AND SOME INTERNATIONAL COMPARISONS

CHAPTER XI

The Looming Shadow of Fascism Over the World

THAT Fascism exists is now a matter of common knowledge. Every man on the street has some familiarity with its insignia and phrases. Every daily paper carries news of its successes or failures abroad, of its newly won adherents or opponents at home. A rapid succession of dramatic events—the persecution of the German Jews, the Italian conquest of Abyssinia, the bitter and fratricidal civil war in Spain—have served to pose its programmes to both the humble and the proud. In millionaires' drawing-rooms and wretched tenements its slogans are being discussed. In academic halls and on the public forum its progress is being charted, and its issues analysed.

As a flame or age separates chemicals in a retort, so some major divisive forces in modern society seem to be slowly separating the people of every nation into warring camps. Left and right, Popular Front and Fascist, red and reactionary, capital and labour—the terms vary with time and circumstance, but the cleavage remains the same. Remains the same, but for ever widens, for ever deepens, for ever sharpens the edge of hatred and brings nearer the threat of war, civil and international. However the divisive forces may be analysed, the fact that this cleavage runs, like a widening geological fault, through all the layers of society is beyond question.

Beyond question, likewise, is the fact that this line of cleavage runs through the social structures of every people and every nation. Italy and Germany are the major exponents of Fascism. But only less so are Portugal, Hungary, Austria, Greece, Roumania, Brazil, Bolivia, and Japan. In England, France, the United States, the Argentine, and in all other non-Soviet lands the issues of Fascism are being bitterly debated, the slow coagulation of warring political factions is taking place, and first skirmishes of fighting outposts are matters of daily occurrence.

What can be the meaning of all this ? Why, in the long toil-worn and battle-scarred history of the human race, should there be no other present world for the people of Spain than terror by night and death behind barricades by day ? For what reason should the events in Spain seem no more than tragic episodes fitted into a long chain of events which appear to lead up to an impending struggle that may engulf the world—a struggle which may, as many experts believe, succeed in destroying much, if not all, of what we term " modern civilisation " ? What lies behind ? Why does the issue turn on " fascism," and not on something else ? Or, does the issue really turn on " fascism " at all ?

Knowledge of the facts and a little reflection will show that the issue does not turn on " fascism " *per se*, but on that form of capitalism of which it is no more than the politically conscious phase. For better or worse, the deeper issue now being squarely faced is whether *capitalism as a coercive political and economic system* should be allowed any longer to survive. Left and right to-day recognise this to be true, and correspondents are correct in speaking of the Spanish rebels as *fascists* and the loyalists as Popular Front.[1] A little more clarity in conception would have led them to describe events in the revolutionary upheavals of Germany, Greece, Chile, Brazil, and Portugal in a similar fashion. It will not be long before the struggles between political parties in other countries will be recognised in the same way for what they are at bottom.

There is nothing new in principle between the civil war in Spain and the struggles which take place almost daily between massed employer and labour groups elsewhere. Only in Spain the issues are *now* more clearly drawn, and the action has passed from the " peaceable " to the overtly warlike plane. On this ultimate, and apparently inevitable level, the struggle is san-guinary, and all hope of further compromise gone. As all parties realise, the end result will be either the triumph of reaction and a new lease on life for capitalism, or else a victory for socialism and the extermination of the rich and powerful of bank, factory, bivouac, and cloister. On the Iberian Peninsula both elements are *politically conscious; it is this fact, and this fact alone, which makes the Spanish struggle a war to the death between fascism and people's rights.*

There is, however, no more magic in the word " capitalism " than in the term " fascism." People are not fighting wars over terms but over actualities. It is not " capitalism " as a turn of phrase that is at stake, but the effects, the intent, and the results of capitalism. It was widespread poverty and mass privation, leading to mass revolutionary action, which caused Italian financial and industrial interests to underwrite Mussolini's bought-and-paid-for Fascism. It was mounting unemployment and decline in standards of living which led to steady growth of the revolutionary left, and caused German capital to strike its bargain with Hitler. It was an attempt to recover lost property and class privileges which provoked the union of right—fascist—forces in Spain against the growing strength of the champions of peasant and worker claims. And it is the challenge of the poverty-stricken labourers and farmers of England, France, and the United States which is activating the consolidation of fascist forces within their own frontiers.

The issue is not alone that poverty is next door neighbour to plenty. This in itself has always constituted a latent threat to the status of the leisure classes throughout all recorded history. The famous slave revolts of the ancient world (particularly those of Sicily and Rome), the Peasant War in the early sixteenth century, the Jacobin phase of the French Revolution, and the almost world-wide cycles of revolutions in 1848 and immediately after the World War, arose out of the immediate juxtaposition of extreme poverty and superabundant wealth.

The advance of civilisation has done nothing to change the picture. The extremes of wealth have never been greater in the history of the world than they are to-day. Only in the orient or the disease-infested squalor of the outskirts of the great ancient cities is such poverty to be found as one may meet at random in the East End of London, the vast desolate waste of the English Midlands, the mining districts of Wales, the East Side of New York, or the share-cropper[2] districts of the American South. All of these districts exist within sight of munificence as great as the world has ever seen. In such contrasts lie to-day, as always, the seeds of mass revolt. But far more than this lies behind the contemporary wave of mounting unrest.

Present-day mass poverty exists not alone because the privileged have squeezed all there is to have out of the system, but *because the system itself has broken down.* To employ an analogy, for close on to a quarter of a century no more than four out of the six cylinders have been working; for short periods of time four out of the six have been running idle. In the best of times the economic system at large does not produce more than two-thirds of which it is capable, and during the current depression the proportion is probably not more than one-third.

This occurs at precisely the time when the peoples of all the earth have through day-by-day contact with their realities or their fictions been won over to implicit belief in the *fruitfulness of modern science and technology,* and to acceptance of their *implied promise of a minimum of material comfort and plenty for all.* The poorest ploughman and the most under-nourished vagabond on the street share alike the view that modern methods are productive beyond the fondest dreams of earlier man. All stand alike in the immediate presence of unleashed forces and of idle productive capacity. Those who have not lived from a miserable dole in the shadow of some idle factory, or walked hungry and disconsolate along some ruined fertile field, have read or heard of the protean powers of industrial production and of the material blessings it is able to confer upon the formerly disinherited of all cultures and lands.

Not only have the rank and file come to believe that they *might receive,* but they have in effect been *promised* that they *will receive.* For the past century and a half it has been universally taught in classrooms and the public forum that " equal opportunity," " individual initiative," and industrial methods must naturally and inevitably distribute the fruits of production according to individual merit and individual contribution to output.

It is in the face of commonly recognised potential productive capacity, and this " promise " of its enjoyment by the mass of the people, that the economic system has broken down, and that instead of plenty and security, growing percentages of the population have been compelled to lead a tenuous and precarious existence, balanced day by day on the edge of starvation and vagrant wandering. In the changed modes of life which the industrial system has compelled, and under which increasing masses of people are herded together within the confines of giant cities, the old security reserves of family and return to the land are denied to all except the occasional few. There is nothing left for those who remain except idleness, privation, and the charity dole. Nothing else except revolt.

Furthermore the mass of the unemployed threatens the wages and status of those with jobs, and tends, in the absence of effective organisation, to drive them down to the economic levels of the out of work. In so doing, however, it not only spreads the general ruination of life and adds to the psychological malaise so characteristic of modern times, but it also destroys the markets on which capitalism feeds for the gathering of profits without which it cannot exist as a system. It not only destroys the markets by cutting off mass purchasing power at the source, but it is compelled thereby to further curtail production in order to restore the balance of " supply and demand."

At this point mass protest constitutes a direct threat to the system, and something must be done about it. The alternatives to revolt are economic recovery or some combination of the dole and work relief. Under present conditions, which do not permit full restoration of international division of labour nor the free and unhampered expansion of activity at home (largely on account of exercise of monopoly influences), economic recovery becomes primarily *business* recovery, and this need not call for the re-absorption of any considerable percentage of the unemployed. In fact, it is quite possible at the present time that the rate of technological advance will approximately keep pace with with growth in output, and by so doing prevent any considerable re-employment at all. At least this seems to be the experience of England and the United States to the present date.[3]

The dole and " public works "[4] result in an accumulation of debt obligations which must eventually be paid. But payment means future shifting of income from the people at large to the holders of government bonds, for unless economic recovery increases the paying capacity of the general population, the only effect is that the revolution-charged situation is temporarily

relieved by a levelling down of real income through dis-
bursing of borrowed money to the out-of-work as a condition to
a later scaling up by way of tax levies upon the whole community
in order to secure funds with which to pay off the rich who
bought the bonds. The crisis which will then ensue is bound
to be much more serious than the present one unless new borrowing possibilities are opened up at that time. And, if these are
discovered, the issue is only delayed one point further. Sooner
or later the economic system must give work to the growing
army of unemployed or it will collapse.

In the long run, it can only do this by a reversal of the tendencies leading to growth in the army of unemployed. The pros-
pects for such a change of direction in the next decade or so are
not very promising. In view of the way both international and
domestic affairs are set up at the present time, there seems little
hope of any type of recovery, which means elimination of the
mass of the unemployed for either short or long time periods,
and there is absolutely nothing in the picture—not even in the
most optimistic forecasts of business leaders—to prevent recurring and equally catastrophic depressions in the future.

So long as business leaders offer no better prospect than this,
they must face a situation in which the threat of mounting social
unrest and revolutionary action is bound to increase, not
decrease. But this unrest is not only explosive in and of itself;
it possesses now, as it never has before, *direction* and *organisation*. It is directed by belief that industrial methods can produce
and that the *system* is at fault if it does not; and it is organising
to gain its stated ends. It makes no difference how the case is
stated, whether the charges take the emotional form of hatred
of " Wall Street " or the " money trust," or the calculated argument of left-wing and Marxian writers. It suffices that the public
which feels the pinch believes that something is fundamentally
wrong in the economic system for which the business men can
be held to account, and that the only way to gain concessions
from capital is to organise and take what it wants by pressure
or overt force.

But, in its struggle for power to enforce its demands, trade
unions and other forms of organised political, social, and
economic unrest run full tilt into a fact of enormous portent for

the " shape of things to come "—that *business itself is organised and politically conscious.* Business already possesses predominant influence in the counsels of every capitalistically organised state. If the challenge of the forces arrayed against it prove sufficiently serious, capital will no longer remain a " silent partner " to government. Rather than surrender power it will resort to the *coup d'etat* and reach out for the mantle of sovereign power. It will seek, in short, to establish a fascist regime.

For this change of phase the business community possesses enormous resources, and has at its disposal an elaborate network of finely meshed business organisation. This network has not been used for the purpose of *planning* the economic future of the country—this type of planning is, in fact, foreign to the very nature of the business system itself. It has, on the contrary, been devoted to promotion of the interests of business enterprise— the prime " beneficiaries," as Mr. Kennedy, first Chairman of the Securities and Exchange Commission, so blandly expresses it, " of a preserved profit system." [5]

These organisations range all the way from the tightly bound together trust or combine to the looser federations of business such as trade associations and the Chamber of Commerce. Of primary importance in the present connection, however, is not the mere fact of concentration of property control which these organisations promote, but the ease with which they may be used for the *centralisation of the power to formulate and direct business policy. It is this very centralisation of policy-forming power which has turned these central co-ordinating bodies into politically active and fascist-inclined agents.*

The variety of these *central business policy-forming agencies* is very great. The more common types—cartels, trade associations, communities of interest, pools, trusts, syndicates, etc.— are to be found in some form or other in most industrial countries before the turn of the past century. Some of them go back to even earlier times. Beginning about 1880, they start to become important as means for the promotion of some degree or other of monopoly influence. Thereafter they have grown steadily in importance. Decade by decade they have increased in number, widened their influence, expanded the range of business activity over which they exercise some form of control, and have become more *politically conscious* of the powers for coercion which lie within their grasp.

This has meant a steady erosion of the individual initiative of the business entrepreneur; a steady erosion of the necessary conditions for the maintenance of *free competition* and *laissez-faire*. This can be shown by the history of any single type of policy-control body. Take, for example, the most common European form, the cartels. Originally the cartels pooled business control over such things as prices, " legitimate " costs, conditions and terms of delivery, patent and copyright holdings, and allocation of market areas. Originally cartel agreements were of very short duration; like the early English and American pools, they existed primarily to promote some special line of interest for but a short period of time.

But from promoting control over one line of business interests they have expanded to control related lines; from purely " emergency " and short-time bodies, they have expanded into long-term—and in some cases " permanent "—organisations. Those that began by attempting to control some market were shortly led to attempts to control prices. From this they were led insensibly to control over other closely related phases—production, market areas, the conditions and terms on which business was transacted, and so on. With whichever activity they began, they were led step by step to expand control into other fields, to organise more carefully and for longer periods of time, and steadily to increase the rigour of the powers which they were established to exercise.

To-day scarcely a field of business activity in any capitalistic country is without its central business association. All lines of manufacturing, of wholesale and retail trade, of domestic and foreign shipping, of finance and banking, possess their own trade associations, cartels, syndicates, pools, or other alliances. This is true of England, France, and the United States as well as of Germany.

It makes no difference which way the process runs—whether local organisations are brought together in regional and finally on a national basis, or whether a skeleton national organisation is first set up and then local and regional sub-divisions organised and attached thereto. In all cases the tendency is for centralisation of power to form policies with regard to prices, wages, labour union, markets, imports and exports, and other matters to be unitary and national in scope.

The number of trade associations, to take only one type, in the United States to-day is variously estimated to run from 3,000 to 5,000. Approximately one-third of the total number have some form of national office; five or six hundred of them have fixed central headquarters, with paid staff and secretariats.

A government report in 1925 estimated the number of German cartels to be around 2,500. The number has since materially increased. A large percentage of these are national in scope. The same picture holds for England, France, Japan, and all other countries. Levy, writing in 1927, found England " overrun with monopolist organisations." Even before the war, some 114 international cartels were functioning in some fashion or other.

Simultaneously, these various associations began to group themselves in special interest blocks or federations. These tended to be of two general types. First are those representing any particular line of business, as e.g. manufacturing, or distribution, or transportation, or finance. Examples in the United States are the National Association of Manufacturers and the American Railway Association. In England they have the Federation of British Industries, in Germany (pre-Nazi) the National Federation of German Industry.

The second type may be either national or local, but, on whatever basis of organisation, it tends to include all business enterprise within the area. The most common form is the Chamber of Commerce. To-day practically every town, city, and state in the United States has such a chamber. At the peak of the pyramid is to be found the United States Chamber of Commerce. Similar organisations are to be found in all foreign countries. A common variation of this type of organisation is central federations of employers' associations.

The same process has been going on within these combinations of business associations; i.e. they have gone from temporary to permanent organisations. They have proceeded from loose discussion or " get-together " bodies to associations wielding wide influence and in some cases coercive powers. Local organisations have been united into regional and national pyramids of control, or national bodies have reached their tentacles of authority into all business and localities connected by any genuine bands to the national economic system.

Every capitalist country, then, tends to become overlaid with a vast network of business organisation. Layer after layer of these webs of control are spun with each passing decade, and with each decade these networks are gathered together and knitted into the national economic framework. And, as the lines of central control become more numerous, the gossamer threads of influence tend to change into ribbed frames of authority to command.

Laissez-faire capitalism, in other words, *has been giving way to control capitalism*, with the clear and unmistakable implication of ultimate exercise of deliberate, formal, and all-inclusive monopoly powers. *Power to control policy* relative to wages, unions, prices, markets, production, investment, and other features of business strategy *has been, is being, and gives every indication of continuing to be centralised throughout the entire business world, and in every capitalist country. The tendency is to all intents and purposes wellnigh universal, unidirectional, and quite irresistible.*

The forces arrayed in opposition to this tendency have not been able to make their protests very effective through government action. Government, in fact, has been too directly under the influence of the business community to be able to stem the tide. In the case of the United States, it is doubtful if the anti-trust legislation had even the effect of slowing up the tendency. Oriented as it was against the superficial facts of formal business combination, its trust-busting tactics had little more effect than to compel either more rational or more subtle forms of control. But trust-busting did not set back the trend. At any rate, the N.R.A., hailed as a programme for " regulating free competition," had no other effect than to accelerate the process of centralisation. When finally cast aside, the final result of N.R.A. was that it had served as a partial catalyst in forcing the pace of development along this line.

The same holds for similar attempts in all other industrial countries. In fact, the governments of both England and Germany, despite national differences in tradition, general economic organisation, and types of political machinery, have devoted considerable effort to promoting phases of this centralising trend. The laws in Germany covering cartels, trade associations, chambers of commerce and industry, and associations of employers have long been almost uniformly favourable to such centralisation.

As for England, next to no legislation impeding monopoly tendencies has ever been in effect. In more recent years, when such centralising forces were beginning to get into full swing, the government took an active interest in the formation of such quasi-monopolies as the Central Electricity Board, the London Passenger Transport Board, the " Big Four " railroads, and the amalgamation of competing shipping lines. In one administration after another it has been willing to aid and guide programmes for reorganising coal, steel, and textile industries which would have led to governmentally uncurbed centralised business power to determine policy for all member enterprises and associations.

In one form or another—ranging from the closed and rigidly organised combinations to the looser forms of cartels—this process was practically complete in Germany before the advent of the Hitler regime. The governments of democratic Germany did no more to halt the process than did the Hohenzollern regime before, nor the Hitler regime after, its stay of power. There was in Germany by 1933 only one railroad system, one postal system, one telephone and telegraph system.[6] One chemical company dominated the chemical field; two oceanic shipping; two steel. One cartel controlled the entire potash output; another controlled both coal and lignite. The Federation of German Machine Builders dominated nine-tenths of the machine industry. The National Federation of German Industry acted as a central co-ordinating body for all branches of German industry.

An analogous picture holds for the United States.

Far more important than the mere fact of centralisation, however, is the truism that *control over business policy means central command, and central command means massed strength*. It matters little whether the controls exercised relate to mere formation and focusing of opinion, or to the enforcement of decisions as though they had the effect of law. The principle is the same.

And the principle is that *massed strength is political strength.*
Power to influence legislation is political power; power to coerce
trade unions is political power; power to enforce price policies is
political power; power to command more or less exclusive use of
media for manipulating public opinion is political power.

Under modern conditions this power persistently and cumu-
latively grows in volume, flows over into more and more fields,
and acquires increasing singleness and directness of purpose as
these business organisations reach full growth. This coagulation
of *business sentiment* and this *mobilisation of the arrayed resources*
of the business community involve directly, inevitably, and
inescapably a reaching out for control over the effective and
organised powers of the state. *States within states* already, all
the facts of modern history, even without any direct threat or
challenge to the capitalistic system, are operating to stimulate
continued federation, with the only possible ultimate result being
an attempt to take over direct control of the government
itself.

How much stronger, then, the incentive to capture the state
machinery when faced with compactly organised ranks of
farmers and labourers—growing rapidly, able to command the
attention of increasing percentages of the unorganised, inflamed
by chronic mass privation, angry, interest-conscious, and
steadily drifting to the left in both doctrine and method. Like
organised capital, organised labour is engaged in the struggle
for power, and its political consciousness grows in direct proportion as it acquires strength, confidence, and centralised
interest-oriented authority. And it grows steadily more militant
as it becomes aware of the full implications of the system with
which it is face to face: as it becomes aware of the prodigal
wastage of the people's natural resources, of the vast armies of
rootless millions sinking down into the wretched misery of slum
and dump-heap, and looking hungrily for any snatch at a job
however poorly paid, of the loss of security to job, family, and
home, of the lack of futures for the children and the yet unborn,
of the crushing and all-destroying black madness of endlessly
impending wars.

In the face of growing labour militancy and its stated or
implied thrust at the heart of the capitalist system, what sort

of a politico-economic system can the business men be expected
to promote ? The answer is inescapable by all the logic of the
past quarter century. *Fascism.* And fascism is a term applied
to the wedding of a *condition* and a *myth.* The *condition* represents no more than formal extension, via employment of the
machinery of the state, of the leading principles of business-as-
usual to encompass the entire population. And the *myth* is that
interpretation of the business case which is designed to gain
popular support. With regard to this latter, it may be laid down
as an indispensable condition that, without some measure of
popular support, fascism—even with the aid of the military—
becomes next to impossible to put across at the beginning.

With respect first to the condition, it has been pointed out in
the first chapter of this study, and illustrated in subsequent
chapters, that the German business community did not depart
one iota from tried and true " business principles " when they
underwrote the Nazi programme. Every business practices towards its own staff the " leader " and the " authority " principles, and it undeviatingly aspires towards the " total " principle. That is to say, all officers and staff members are appointed
and removed from on top entirely at the discretion of management (*leader* principle), and authority is from the top down,
responsibility from the bottom up (*authority* principle). And
every employer attempts to control so far as humanly possible
the attitudes, beliefs, and points of view (*Weltanschauung*) of his
employees and every section of the public with which he comes
in contact (*total* principle).

Every business establishment is, in other words, completely
autocratic and completely undemocratic in structure, ideology,
and procedure. It is, by the same token, completely intolerant of
all opposition within or without, or of any criticism which does
not redound to the advantage of the profit-making possibilities
of the enterprise. The enterprise may be compelled, it is true,
to make important concessions on all points, but it should not
be forgotten that these are *concessions, not departures from
principle.*

Furthermore, every employer regards the gradation of pay
and authority amongst the staff over which he presides as being
essentially just and sound, because each indicates the relative

ability he or she possesses by the position occupied. The criteria are not productive, but acquisitive. Each is paid according to his ability to acquire or " get ahead," not according to his contribution to output. If the two—contribution to output and contribution to acquisition—happen to go together, well and good. If they do not, it matters little, since their juxtaposition is a matter of accident, not of interdependence.

The condition of society in which the business men would rule would be that one which is *natural to them*. It would, as a matter of course, be centralised, autocratic, and intolerant, and it would be so constructed that each would get exactly what he deserves for the simple reason that according to the rules he deserves whatever he can get. It is the well accepted business view that most, if not all of the unemployed are shiftless, worthless, irresponsible, and undisciplined. It is taken as axiomatic that the lowest wage-earner receives all that " is coming to him," since if he could get more by any means which does not disturb business routine it is obvious that he would. His failure is the measure of his incompetence, and with that all has been said about it that may be mentioned by gentlemen of good breeding and respectable station !

This *condition* is one that would normally appeal to the conventional army officer. The military is the only other completely undemocratic,[7] completely autocratic, and completely intolerant —completely " leader," " authoritarian," and " totalitarian "— organisation in modern society. Provided due allowance is made for recognition of the military hierarchies of " authority " and " duty " in the fascist state, it can be fitted into the pattern of the business man's *ultima thule* without a single tonal jar. The moods, attitudes, points of view, values, and appraisals of human worth are fundamentally the same.

It is for this reason that it seems so easy for the military and business hierarchies to get together as they have in Italy, Germany, Portugal, Hungary, and many other places. But the significance of this *natural* alliance is that the military holds the key to political power. Once the alliance takes place, *fascism is here* unless the elements arrayed against it—as in Spain— possess superior force. It does not follow that the army rank and file will follow their officers any more than it does that labourers will follow their employers. But, if they do, fascism is practically certain to gain the ascendancy.

With the aid of the officer corps the conditions of business may be maintained as valid for all members of society (fascism) provided some way can be found for neutralising or completely eliminating organised opposition. It is here that business forces attempt to build up a *myth*. The myth is designed purely and simply as a means for circumventing opposition, and its propositions are regarded as equivalent to " true " and undeniable facts if they can be successfully put across, since, as is usual in business, success is the measure of " truth " as well as of ability.

It is important to realise the purpose and quality of the *myth* that fascism builds up, since failure to do so will lead to the type of naïve confusions so common to those writers who find all departures from " democracy," as found in England and America, to be without fundamental difference in form, purpose, or mass support. Mass support for fascism is obtained, not by promotion of the group interest of the rank and file—which programme fascists call " Communist "—but by diversion of popular attention towards " causes " and ideologies the fulfilment of which means direct renunciation of their previous claims. Fascism attempts, in short, to put across to the people a " self-denying ordinance " through conversion of the disinherited to the theology of their self-confessed betters.

In all the complicated, confused, and myth-charged experiences of the human race, there can be no more curious spectacle than that which is taking place along this line before our very eyes in every capitalistic land to-day. Here we have the business enterprise, perhaps the most completely amoral and materialistic single-purpose institution the human mind has yet devised, governed by a class of men who may be ever so sentimental with their children and ever so " kind and gentle with their wives," but who, in order to maintain their position unimpaired as the prime material beneficiaries of economic activity, are compelled to resort to the wholesale promotion of one of the most incredibly jejune, intellectually and emotionally shallow, and crudely primitive " faiths " known in the iridescent annals of myth and fable.

The doctrinal position of business evangelism has two faces, an inner and an outer. The first is that which business men believe concerning themselves and their human kind. The second is that which they wish the remainder of the population to believe about the business—military hierarchy—the " leaders " —on the one hand, and about the proper role each and every member of the rank and file should expect to play in this " best of all possible worlds " on the other.

Both these propaganda faces are the same in all nations ordered on a capitalist basis. There is a veritable mountain of literature obtainable in every one of these countries which could be used to illustrate the close parallels in the programme, the doctrine, and the mood of their respective business communities. The variations which one will find are in the form of adaptations of the same doctrinal positions to local or national circumstances; they do not indicate differences in doctrine. As was shown in many different places in the preceding chapters, almost the entirety of the German Nazi programme and line of argumentation is identical in content and point of view with that of the American business community. Such elements as the persecution of the Jews is different, not in *intent*, but only in the fact that such persecution could serve Nazi ends in Germany in the particular circumstances of the years 1933–36. When the American situation has ripened to that of Germany in 1933, there will be race terror in the United States as well, and it will be anti-negro, anti-Jew, anti-Mexican, and anti-Japanese.

The inner face of fascism considers man as a beast of prey. Scientists, artists, the rank and file of the people, may recoil from this doctrine; the leading figures in the business world of Italy, Germany, England, France, and the United States do not.[8] In 1933, Spengler, then approved by the Nazis as a prophet of the New Germany, wrote:

" Man is a beast of prey. I shall say it again and again. All the would-be moralists and social-ethics people who claim or hope to be ' beyond all that ' are only beasts of prey with their teeth broken, who hate others on account of the attacks which they themselves are wise enough to avoid. Only look at them. They are too weak to read a book on war, but they herd together in the street to see an accident, letting the blood and the screams play on their nerves. And if even that is too much for them, they enjoy it on the film and in the illustrated papers. If I call man a beast of prey, which do I insult: man or beast? For remember, the larger beasts of prey are noble creatures, perfect of their kind, and without the hypocrisy of human morale due to weakness."

In this view man is arrayed against man. The only code of behaviour which has any real meaning for the species is that " might makes right." Where only strength counts, the strong are those who have taken; who have the power to have and to hold. The weak are those without holdings—of station, or property, or power. It is a doctrine that human society is nothing but organised " piracy." Is there any fundamental difference in appreciation of human values or in general outlook on life between a stockbroker and a pirate? So far as the specific activity is concerned there is no difference, not even in the methods of sharing the spoils. What on the open seas is thought of as an outlaw and " piratical " raid of group on group, is in another setting played as a legitimate game in which each man is pitted against every other man for all he can " get by with " short of a snarl with criminal law.

That business men in the United States hold this view is beyond question. They hold it axiomatic in describing the character of their own kind, and they hold it to be valid for the human race at large. Anyone who has taken the trouble to interview stockbrokers, captains of industry and finance, advertisers, public relations counsellors, or other participants in, and apologists for, the business system will soon learn that this view of human nature governs their actions and their behaviour in practically all things, and that it is regarded as so obviously true as to require no comment, explanation, or justification.

Thus there is not the slightest objection to using all the armed forces of the state in a war on India, on Morocco, on Manchuria, on Abyssinia, on Nicaragua, Spain, or Mexico. If you are big enough, strong enough to take it, the rule is: take it. Take the country, take its resources, take its wealth, take the lives, health, and happiness of all its inhabitants. " Realities rule "; the justification can be concocted later.

Nor, on the other hand, is there the slightest objection to using the troops against strikers, hunger-marchers, share-croppers, or any other group which for any reason whatsoever wants a little of what the insiders may have. All the emphasis on war, all the promotion of the army and the navy, of " national defence," of that curiously bellicose frame of mind commonly known by the euphemistic term " patriotism," is born of the same view of life, of human nature, of civilisation and culture.

The other face of fascism—the other side of the fascist *point of view*—is that which it presents to the public. It is a programme which might be characterised by the expression Veblen once employed in characterising the " ethic " of the advertising " profession "—*suppressio veri, suggestio falsi*—were it not for the over-simplification implied. The only valid criterion in the programme for the public is this: What is effective ? What will succeed ? What will suppress, or deflect, or undermine opposition ? What will create a favourable attitude ? If this means to suppress the truth and suggest the false, the same will be done. If it means, however, to tell some portion, or on occasion all, of the truth, this in turn will be done. And if it means to so re-define the meaning of " truth " that it becomes whatever is told by those able to enforce compliance with doctrine, then " truth " will become, *ipso facto*, whatever is told the people.

Propaganda—meaning the *propagation of doctrine*—which supports the business system, is the mental-emotional diet which must be ladled out to the public. This propaganda is based upon the *conquest of attitude, of belief, of point of view*, and it proceeds on two levels. The first might be called the *persuasive*, or " educational," level; the second is the *coercive* level. The second does not dispense with persuasion, but it adds thereto the compulsion to conform.

On both levels it seeks to instil in the popular mind belief that the " leaders " of economic and political affairs are endowed with inspired vision, wide humanitarian interests, and the highest type of acceptable social ethics.[9] On both levels, business propaganda attempts to inculcate in the public the attitude it expects from paid employees: (1) belief in the " rights " of those in possession to own, to enjoy superior emoluments, and to command in all things; (2) unquestioning obedience, respect, and a proper degree of servility and abnegation; (3) belief that each has his allotted function, graded to his talents, which he must perform, and from which alone he may obtain his due meed. The first promotes the need for myths of leadership, of authority, and the nature of life values. The second promotes emphasis on discipline and loyalty. The third promotes the formation of a class or caste hierarchy. The first is theological in stamp, the second military, the third medieval or caste.

If the analysis being given here is correct, the only difference between fascist and non-fascist capitalist states—between Italy, Germany, Portugal, Austria, Hungary, Brazil, etc., on the one hand, and England, France, the United States, the Argentine, Belgium, etc., on the other—is to be found *not in the content, but in the level* on which the propaganda is promoted. The non-fascist, as in England and the United States, are still *mainly on the persuasive level*, while the fascist, as in Italy and Germany, are fully oriented on the coercive level. To adopt simpler terms, in the United States business is still trying to " sell itself to the public," while in Germany this is no longer necessary—it has sold the public to itself, and those who do not believe, who do not accept, and who do not conform, are branded as " traitors " to the state and treated accordingly.

Keeping in mind the data supplied on each point for fascist Germany in the preceding chapters, it may be of interest to cite here a few leading examples of the types and elements of fascist arguments now being widely advocated in non-fascist countries, and the nature of some of the leading institutions especially established for the purpose of promoting the propaganda. In most cases these refer to the *persuasive level*; in a few cases these have already passed over into the *coercive* or *overtly fascist level*:

(1) *The doctrine of unity.* Argument: There is no conflict between capital and labour, only misunderstanding. There is a real harmony of interests among employers, employees, and the public. There is no such thing as the " class struggle."

Examples: Programme of the N.R.A.; the Swope Plan; Mondism (British); the " Middle Way " of the Swedish co-operatives; Mr. Filene's plan for consumers' co-operatives; the company union idea and " welfare capitalism";

British Whitley Councils; various plans for "planning under capitalism " such as that of de Man the Belgian; and the C.G.T. (France). *Literature* such as books of Link, *The Return to Religion*; Aldous Huxley, *Eyeless in Gaza* (Positive Pacifism); Tugwell, *Industry Comes of Age*; Carver, *The New Industrial Revolution*; President Roosevelt's Triborough Bridge Speech; Smuts, *Holism and Evolution*; Koffka, *Gestalt Psychology*. *Movements* such as the Oxford Movement; the Catholic Church Militant; the National Youth Administration.

Typical statements of argument:
" The head of a large industrial corporation does not perform his whole duty if he narrowly holds himself to trying to make profits for his stockholders. He is not the representative of the stockholders and neither is he simply their head man. He cannot serve the stockholders unless also he serves the workers, and he can serve neither unless he serves the public. There are no well-defined dividing-lines, even in a single corporation, between the stockholders, the workers, and the consuming public " (Samuel Crowther, *Private Business and Public Relations*, 1934).
" Our American plan of living is simple. Its ideal is the greatest good for the greatest number—and it works. You, and every one of you more than 127,000,000 fellow-citizens, are members of a firm. No matter whether you are a doctor, lawyer, merchant, farmer, clerk or machinist . . . you— whether you know it or not—are a partner of the United States Inc." (National Association of Manufacturers— National Industrial Council publicity release of late summer, 1936).
" Then in a God-controlled nation, capital and labour would discuss their problems peacefully and reach God-controlled solutions. Yes, business would be owned by individuals, not by the state, but the owners would be God-controlled " (Dr. Buchman, leader of the Oxford Group, *New York World Telegram*, August 6, 1936). " It [the Oxford Movement] bridges the gulf that separates master from man, class from class and nation from nation " (James Watt,

former Communist organiser for Fifeshire, Scotland, now member of the Oxford Movement, *New York Times*, May 31, 1936).

" Yes ! Apprentice boy and corporation president, sinewy shop mechanic and dynamic sales manager—all of the 38½ millions in industry [U.S. Census, 1930] are fellow-workers, rewarded for individual achievement, and increasingly conscious that each individual prospers when the entire group of employees and investors prospers. . . . An essential . . . is loyalty to the company, to the products, and to the group with whom one works shoulder to shoulder in a common cause. Such loyalty is very profitable to all concerned . . . there is need for even greater co-operation between the manufacturers and the public, a closer understanding, a sharper definition of the responsibilities of each " (C. M. Chester, President, National Association of Manufacturers; Chairman, General Foods Corporation, *The Responsibilities of Corporate Management*, release of the General Foods Corporation, July 10, 1936).

" We believe in ' one big union ' in which all have an interest, whether it is those who furnish the labour or those who furnish the capital " (Arthur Pound, *Industrial America*, Boston, 1936: in March 1st issue of the Goodyear Rubber Company factory paper, *Wingfoot Clan*).

(2) *The function of business is service.* Argument: The purpose of business is not to make profits, but to serve the public; profits come before, not after, service. Business men are no more than trustees of public property on behalf of good to the general community.

Examples: Public relations vice-presidents of corporations (perhaps two-thirds of those in U.S. appointed in the past two years); public relations counsellors; " good will " and institutional advertising; public relations campaigns such as that of the National Association of Manufacturers. *Literature:* Mooney and Reiley, *Onward Industry!*; Crowther, *Men and Rubber* (Harvey Firestone), *Moving Forward* (Henry Ford), and *My Life and Work* (in collaboration with

Henry Ford); Tead, *The Art of Leadership*; articles of Merle Thorpe; advertising campaign literature of *Nation's Business*; special issue of *Factory, What Industry Means to America* (August 1936).

Typical statements of argument:

" The purpose of business is to get wealth to people—to produce and to distribute to all humanity the things which humanity, with its new-found power, can now be organised to make only if it can be organised to buy and use them " (Filene, *Successful Living in this Machine Age*).

" The employer who assumes the responsibility of giving work to other people, of providing the necessary weekly payroll, of entrusting larger responsibilities to his subordinates as the business grows, of meeting the risks of competition, labour problems, manufacturing difficulties, and the thousand and one griefs that go with almost every business, manifests daily a high order of unselfishness. Through his energy and leadership, he improves the lot of his employees far beyond the point which their personal efforts would have made possible. The fact that he may benefit, materially, more than any other one individual, is inevitable in the situation and not an indictment of his character " (Link, *The Return to Religion*, pp. 80–81).

" The objectives of industrial organisation have . . . been defined as profit through service, profit in this sense meaning the compensatory material gain or reward obtained through service " (Mooney and Reiley, *Onward Industry!* p. 342).

" The spread of the Oxford Group would substitute stewardship for greed as the driving force in our economic life, and easily produce enough wealth to satisfy the legitimate needs of all classes and enrich our common life beyond anything the world has ever seen before. . . . Stewardship is the key word of the economics of the future, you have to become stewards of your material wealth, your time and everything you have " (Vrooman, Assistant Secretary of Agriculture under President Wilson at a meeting of the Oxford Group, *New York Times*, May 31 and June 2, 1936).

" Remington Rand has been run, throughout the depression, *for the benefit of its employees only* " (advertisement of Remington Rand, Inc., *Syracuse Journal*, May 25, 1936: italics in original).

(3) *People who object to business are ignorant, incompetent, or malicious.* Argument: On the tolerant level, argued that the discontented are neurotic, pathologic, frustrated, or ignorant; on the intolerant level, that they are " red," " communist," " alien," etc., and in all cases malicious.

Examples:

Tolerant level: All the personnel and occupational institutes and associations, such as the British Institute for Industrial Psychology, the Personnel Research Federation, the National Occupational Conference, Industrial Relations Counsellors, the Taylor Society, and the American Management Society. *Literature:* Mayo, *The Human Problems of an Industrial Civilization*; Miles, *The Problem of Incentives in Industry*; Lasswell, *The Psychopathology of Politics*. Pamphlets such as the " foremanship " series of the United States Chamber of Commerce.

Intolerant level: American Legion " red-hunting " campaigns; teachers' oath; vigilante committees such as those organised by the Associated Farmers of California; "shirts legionaires " such as the Silver Shirts; Liberty League; Crusaders of America; National Civic League. *Literature:* Link, *The Return to Religion*; Dilling, *The Red Network*; Ortega, *Revolt of the Masses*; Dennis, *The Coming American Fascism.*

Typical statements of argument:
Tolerant level:
" One of the most common symptoms of an inferiority complex or of personal failure is the desire to change the social order, usually in one's immediate environment, often in the world at large. The youngsters, suffering from personal failure, often want to change their families, not themselves. The student who fails in his studies wants to change his

teachers or the marking system, not himself. The employee who fails to get the desired salary wants to improve his employer, not himself. The worker, unable to get or hold a position, wants to change the system generally " (Link, *The Return to Religion*, p. 130).

" It is known that an adult of insufficient social experience will not be merely socially maladjusted; he will also be found using inferior logical techniques " (Mayo, *The Human Problems of an Industrial Civilization*, p. 163).

Intolerant level:
" America, the world's greatest industrial nation, industrialised itself under private capitalism for use *and* for profit. . . . America's suffering started only when capitalism took sick. Like a sick horse, the decrepit economic system on the back of which we are now crawling along is not Capitalism himself, but a Capitalism loaded down with Socialism. . . . What have socialistic experiments ever achieved except deficits or failure ? . . . If capitalists and capitalism are a blight to humanity, then Egypt should be a happy spot. But the happiest event which has befallen Egypt in many centuries came with the British ' imperialism ' and ' capitalism ' which built the Assuan Dam. . . . If capitalism is ' greed ' and a blight to humanity then why are the savage and miserable lands which have no capitalism not blessed ? . . . Why is the standard of living of the *whole* people in any land raised in proportion to the success and development of its capitalistic enterprises ? . . . As Bernard Shaw put it: ' Compulsory labour with death the final punishment, is the keystone of socialism.' . . . *The National Republic*, Dec. 1933, under the heading *The Failure of Socialism* states: ' Persons socialistically inclined often point to the present world-wide depression as " a failure of the capitalist system " . . . but the present world-wide breakdown could more properly be charged to a collapse of the socialist system. Every important power in the western world to-day, except the United States, is under either socialist parliamentary control, or that dictatorship to which socialism leads as in Italy, Poland, Germany and Russia.' " (Elizabeth

Dilling, *The Red Network*, Caspar Co., Milwaukee, Wisconsin, 1934, pp. 92–93).

(4) *What we need is a New Age of Faith:* Argument: The trouble with society is its materialism, its mammonism, its confidence in science, engineering and industrial productivity, its belief in knowledge, etc. Science proves nothing, and is reconcilable with religion. We need to study and improve men, not society.

Examples: All the associations and books mentioned above under " The doctrine of unity," the growing trend in the Catholic and Protestant Confessions along this line; programmes of the various Churches, American Legion, and other bodies for the youth and the women. *Literature:* Eddington, *The Nature of the Physical World*; Jeans, *The Universe Around Us*; Nichols, *The Fool Hath Said*; Irving Babbitt.

Typical statements of argument:
" He [the Leader] at least must cherish the firm convinction that *the effort is worth while*. And this conviction is an un-reasoned or non-rational one as often as it is logically demonstrable. . . . The leader has to be willing to trust people. He has to act on the assumption that when they are committed genuinely to appealing purposes they will on the whole tend to carry on toward their realisation. Implicit in this is his faith that people want to be soundly led and can be influenced in the direction of their own best aims.

" Human problems aren't economic. They're moral, and they can't be solved by immoral measures. They could be solved within a God-controlled democracy, or perhaps I should say a theocracy, and they could be solved through a God-con-trolled Fascist dictatorship. . . . I thank heaven for a man like Adolf Hitler, who built a front line of defence against the anti-Christ of Communism " (Dr. Buchman, leader of the Oxford Group, *New York World Telegram*, August 26, 1936).

" The non-logical response, that, namely, which is in strict conformity with a social code, makes for a social order and discipline, *for effective collaboration in a restricted range of activity*, and for happiness and a sense of security in the individual " (Mayo, *The Human Problems of an Industrial Civilization*, pp. 164–65).

" If the influence of American churches in the furtherance of socially wholesome and forward-looking movements, in the spread of conscientious and unselfish living of all sorts, were to be eliminated, it is my belief that our democracy would in a few years become so corrupt that it could not endure. . . . Finally, if the growth of modern science has taught anything to religion and to the modern world, it is that the method of progress is the method of evolution, not the method of revolution " (R. H. Millikan, *Living Philosophies*, Simon & Schuster, New York, 1931).

" Democracy is ever eager for rapid progress, and the only progress which can be rapid is progress downhill. For this reason I suspect that all democracies carry within them the seeds of their own destruction, and I cannot believe that democracy is to be our final form of government. . . . If I think of democracy as a juvenile ailment, I think of socialism as a definite disease. . . . The truth seems to be that no socialist state ever endures for long as such. Thus, I do not picture the future government of the world as either socialistic or democratic " (James Jeans, *Living Philosophies*, Simon & Schuster, New York, 1931).

(5) *What we need is discipline.* Argument: It is lack of proper training, it is an excess of ease and material things, it is the breakdown of parental and other similar authorities which accounts for the " irresponsibility " of the rising generation and of labour. All these are soft, unmannerly, disrespectful, critical, disorderly, rebellious. These things must be counteracted by training to instil the sense of duty, loyalty, instantaneous and uncomplaining obedience, and the habits of hard work.

Examples: Propaganda of the Army and Navy; military and war movies; programme of the Reserve Officers' Training Corps, the Civilian Conservation Camps, the Citizens' Military Training Camps.

Typical statements of argument:

" The men who emerge from the rigid discipline of these camps [C.C.C.] ... have not only experienced an abundant life, but are better equipped to achieve a more abundant life. Through their enforced contacts they have learned to respect and like people whom they would never voluntarily have chosen as friends. Having learned, often, to think more highly of their fellow-workers, they have also acquired greater confidence in themselves—the latter is a by-product of the former. Through the pressure of mass action they have come to appreciate a day's work at jobs which, left to themselves, they would have spurned at three times the pay. Life in the barracks, in tents, and on army fare, has given them an inkling of the fact that the more abundant life lies, not in the American standard of living or in $2,500 a year, but in themselves. Under a discipline which did not consult their whims, they have learned that action is more satisfying than introspection, physical exhaustion sweeter than self-indulgence. They emerge from those camps better equipped to *give* their energies and attention to others, and therefore more likely to *receive* a satisfying compensation for themselves. In short, they have become extroverted " (Link, *The Return to Religion*, pp. 171–72).

(6) *The " élite " should rule:* Argument: Mankind is graded in a hierarchy of innately given, not environmentally acquired, capacities. Each should " stick to his last." Those at the top, the " born *élite* " should rule; the less capable should each be given that to do for which he is ideally adapted by nature; none should aspire to the nature-determined station of others.

Examples: All the associations, institutions, and literature listed under (3) above. All publications and organisations promoting the idea that the negroes, the Jews, and the Mexicans or other racial groups are inferior, that woman's place is in the home or that she should be paid less on the job, etc. *Literature:* Grant, *The Passing of the Great Race*; Stoddard, *The Rising Tide of Colour*; Wiggin, *The Fruit of the Family Tree*; Dennis, *The Coming American Fascism*;

350 SOME INTERNATIONAL COMPARISONS

Pareto, *Principles of Sociology*; Ortega, *Revolt of the Masses*; miscellaneous writings of H. L. Mencken; Carver, *The Religion Worth Having*.

Typical statements of argument:
" The laws of natural selection are merely God's regular methods of expressing his choice and approval. The naturally selected are the chosen of God. (That nation, or that people, whose average individual character and conduct and whose social institutions and customs are such as to make them strong in competition with other peoples and able to spread over the earth and subdue it and have dominion over it, becomes by the very fact the chosen people, whatever their name, language, or religion.) " (Carver, *The Religion Worth Having*).

" There is great social significance in the fact that the *élite* of exceptional natural endowment, who, as a matter of course, become the *élite* of power and influence, actual or potential, are a fairly constant percentage of the total population. From this fact it follows that no social system can long survive, once it tends strongly to declass more and more of the *élite*. . . . The *élite* may be defined roughly and arbitrarily as including capitalists deriving most of their income from property, business enterprisers and farmers, the professional classes, and, generally, the employed whose salaries are considerably above the average, or, say, above $3,000 a year for the entire country. . . . A wise social philosophy, such as that of fascism, strives to make a place for all the members of the *élite* " (Dennis, *The Coming American Fascism*, pp. 229, 231, 237).

" The next question is, How scarce do jobs have to be ? The answer is, Just scarce enough so that labourers are not likely to get uppish, make unexpected demands, and get away with them. Just scarce enough, in other words, so that wages are definitely under the control of the employing class, at least so far as abrupt fluctuations are concerned. And under what circumstances can the labouring class be depended upon to sit tight, lick the hand that feeds them, and make no unexpected demands ? The answer is when they are all strictly up against it, with just barely enough wages to make ends meet—almost, and distress staring them in the face if they should lose their jobs. And this condition can obtain only when there is a reserve army of unemployed sufficient to keep those who do have jobs in abject fear of losing them " (Finney, " Unemployment, An Essay in Social Control," *Journal of Social Forces*, September 1926).

" . . . most well-mannered debaters carry on with the White Lie of Democracy; and thus they reach worthless conclusions. A land swarming with tens of millions of morons, perverts, culls, outcasts, criminals, and lesser breeds of low-grade humans cannot escape the evils all such cause. . . . So long as we have an underworld of 4,000,000 or more scoundrels willing to do anything for a price, and a twilight world of fully 40,000,000 people of profound stupidity or ignorance or indifference, and a population of nearly 70,000,000 who cannot support themselves entirely and hence must think first of cost, whenever they buy things, we shall have a nasty mess on our hands . . . " (Pitkin, *Let's Get What We Want*, pp. 72, 283).

This listing is necessarily quite incomplete, and at the best does no more than indicate the *type* of argument, the *orientation* of the elements, the *nature* of the institutions, and the *attitude* of mind out of which Fascism compounds and by the use of which it implements the *efficient propaganda required to gain popular support for its concrete programme of action.* None of these has any significance of itself. Their importance in the present connection lies solely in the observation that, within every capitalistic country to-day, (1) these doctrines enjoy an enormous and rapidly expanding vogue, particularly among business men, middle-class people in general, and the world-weary intelligentsia, (2) that expert counsellors for business men are becoming increasingly aware of the uses to which they can be put and are, consequently, organising for their definite promotion, and (3) that all the available evidence shows that such promotion quickly, easily, and irresistibly passes from the *persuasive to the coercive level.*

All such promotion shows another and exceedingly interesting change in approach as soon as it becomes organised and direction-conscious; it couches its programme in the language of the man on the street and it cradles its argument in the specific values and prejudices of each cross-section of the population to whom it appeals. It speaks in many languages, and it becomes " all things to all men." To the rich it speaks of dividends and business stability. To the poor, it speaks of jobs and security. To the religious it promotes spiritual values and love of God.[10] To the patriotic it speaks of discipline, heroism, loyalty, sacrifice, the Fatherland (or the Empire, or the Constitution). To the youth it speaks of opportunities to become rich, or wise, or great, or powerful. To the women it whispers the values of mother and child, or of the subtle influence of women on the minds of men throughout the world.

These lines of development all parallel those briefly discussed in the first pages of this chapter. In every country they will be found keeping step throughout all phases of their growth with the slow coagulation and centralisation of business policy-forming power, with the interlacing between business and military interests and the fusion of their minds, with the growing political cast of the bulk of the issues discussed and decided upon, and—above all, the most important—with the mounting of social unrest which expresses itself in organised and systemised form. Along none of these lines has there been any significant backward step since the close of the world war. There have been lulls and periods of relative stagnation. But with the beginning of the depression in 1929 the pace has been quickened, and the issues brought starkly into view. Now there is no possibility of turning back; the forces set in motion must work out to their conclusion. Either the world will turn fascist, or fascism will be destroyed. The issues are now drawn; no nation, and no people, can any longer hope to evade the conflict which looms across the pages of every newspaper, and which is written darkly in the uneasy mind of every man or woman who thinks.

There is no forecasting the outcome. But of this much we can be certain; if and when fascist forces seize power in England, the United States, or other still technically non-fascist countries, they can do no more than control the power of the *national* state. As with Germany and Italy, there is no higher political power to acquire. Because this is true, any important future fascist triumphs will carry with them some exceedingly sinister possibilities. These are of so terrifying and disastrous a character as to seem utterly fantastic even to a generation which can remember the shambles of the World War, the revolutions of Russia, Germany, Austria, and Spain, and the paralysing effects of the greatest depression of all times.

Fascism requires the full mobilisation—*militarisation*—of all the national resources. It attempts to expand over all layers of the population the autocratic controls of the business establishment and the barracks. It both figuratively and literally *puts the nation in arms*. It expands the army, navy, and aerial forces on the one hand, and on the other it clamps down the routine compulsions and the idea patterns of the commandant on all layers of the " peaceful population." It " solves " the problem of unemployment by the uniform (expansion of recruitments, military and labour camps), and of dissent by propaganda implemented with coercion.

The nation, under these circumstances, becomes, like the people who command it, " beasts of prey." Even non-fascist countries and peoples must arm and mobilise their resources. And in this environment two possibilities present themselves. Either the fascist or fascist-inclined nations fall to fighting amongst themselves, or they combine against those which are anti-fascist. Either means a world war, and on a hitherto unprecedented scale, and with a hitherto undreamed-of ferocity —a ferocity but dimly forecast by the last barbarous depths of the World War, and mirrored in microcosm by the terror of the current Spanish civil war.

In either case, anything short of a quick and decisive victory by a single or a combination of fascist powers is almost certain to be interrupted or followed by revolution. It is probably safe to say that no important statesman in any of the capitals of Europe to-day believes that a major war could possibly last for more than a year without an internal smash-up in the form of a revolution in one or more of the belligerent countries. Should

MF

fascist countries, combining against non-fascist—the Soviet Union and France, for example—lose, revolution from their own ranks is certain to follow.

Should conflict, by any chance, be drawn out, most, if not all, that we describe as modern civilisation will certainly be destroyed. As every man on the street knows, modern war is no longer a matter of army against army, but of people against people. When real interests of fighting forces and populations seem to be at stake, particularly when class is arrayed against class, all the rules of warfare are off. This is the testimony of all history, from the ancient slave revolts of Sicily and Rome (gladiatorial) to the class wars of the French Revolution, the Bolsheviki in 1917, and the Spanish civil war of 1936. The World War, despite its nameless brutalities, lacked the necessary fanatical and hatred-driven bitterness to turn it into war of slaughter-bent reaction against slaughter-bent people. That element fascism supplies, since its very existence is dependent upon the ruthless crushing of all opposition.

Does this run counter to the statement that fascism attempts to deny, or to eliminate the idea of class war? Not in the least, for the very reason that it makes no attempt to remove the very foundations of class division. On the contrary, it attempts to crystallise these lines into hard-and-fast class, or caste, divisions. And the very attempt to do this leads to the wholesale militarisation of the state. It is this very militarisation, pledged to the maintenance at all costs of exploitive class status, and coupled to the fact of completely autocratic control, which brings about the conditions described.

Here we have the modern parallel to the ancient story of the hero, Cadmus, who, in the quest for the Golden Fleece, slew the fiery dragon. Following the voice of an unseen oracle, he sowed the dragon's teeth in the soil where the battle took place, and from thence sprung a race of warriors who rose and fought each other to death. When the business forces of the world openly sow the dragon's teeth of discord amongst otherwise peaceful peoples, they prepare, if not themselves, coming generations for the waste-land shambles; for ten to fifty or a hundred years of sanguinary war and terror-ridden struggle in what may be the growing darkness of a fading and broken civilisation.

They condemn, likewise, the arts and sciences. In the stifling atmosphere of fascism, no originality of mind, no creative powers, can flower. The writer must drop his novel or his poem for the bitter propaganda tract. The natural scientist must search for that which promotes the ends of those who command what he shall know, think, and believe. The social scientist must, like a high-school debater, supply proof for arguments advanced by those who have no interest in the truth.

There is no hope against all this, except that of sweeping away the very foundations on which fascism constructs its brittle edifice. If the world-wide fascist trend of things is to be reversed, what is left of democracy must be reinforced, and the sweep of the tide turned. But this means an erosion of fascist foundations, not by humanising business enterprise, but by arraying together all those forces whose face is turned the other way.

Against an opponent who believes singly and solely in force and guile, force must be massed. The hope of the people of the United States is to be found, not in giving free reign to monopoly-oriented and fascist-inclined capitalism, but in turning back its fields, factories, and workshops to those who fought its war of freedom against a tyrannical power, and who built, with their muscles and brains, all the real wealth and all that there is in America which deserves the name of culture. But it will not come to them as a " gift "; they must learn that the only solution to recovery of their heritage lies within themselves.

And the solution is no different for any other people or nation in the world.

NOTES

Chapter I

1. " The Treaty of Versailles deprived Germany of 13 per cent of her territory (European), 13 per cent of her population, and 14·3 per cent of her arable land. In terms of her 1913 production, Germany surrendered 19 per cent of her coke, 74·5 per cent of her iron ore, 26·6 per cent of her blast furnaces, 19·2 per cent of her raw iron and steel, 15·8 per cent of her rolling mills, 68·5 per cent of her zinc foundries, 12 per cent of her livestock, her entire ocean-going merchant marine, 5,000 locomotives, 40,000 waggons, and other miscellaneous equipment. More serious still, the Treaty and the subsequent decision of the League of Nations following the Polish Upper Silesian Plebiscite of 1921, split wide open two of the three major industrial centres of Germany, the Lorraine-Rhine-Westphalian and the Upper Silesian districts. In the former and more important of these two centres, one section was placed under a temporary French mandate pending a plebiscite at a later date (the Saar), another section was removed entirely from the German customs union (Luxemburg), two small sections were given to Belgium (Eupen and Malmedy), and a final and highly important section (Lorraine) was ceded outright to France. The principal losses were coal (Saar and Upper Silesia) and, especially, iron ore. Lorraine ore had supplied about 75 per cent of the needs of the Ruhr iron and steel industry before the war. In Upper Silesia practically all the iron ore and about 75 per cent of the coal were transferred to Poland. In both areas the Treaty settlements destroyed the whole internal balance of the heavy industries remaining under German control. Coal pits were separated from cokeries, cokeries from blast furnaces and steel mills, steel mills from rolling mills, and so forth."—Robert A. Brady, *The Rationalisation Movement in German Industry*, Berkeley, 1933, pp. xiv–xv.

2. The two " groups " were balanced against each other in power, not in numbers. The right never had mass support of any sort. It represented caste privilege, vested interests, property. Then, as now, the left stood for the people's rights, for democratic principles, for the mass of mankind. Such popular support as the right was, later, able to muster came via clever and misleading propaganda, not via identification of real interest. See Chapter XI, p. 323.

Chapter II

1. Max Planck, " The Origin and Effect of Scientific Ideas," *Research and Progress*, Vol. 1, No. 1, 1/35, p. 4.
2. Eduard Spranger, *Wilhelm von Humboldt*, Vol. 1, No. 3, 7/35.
3. W. Frank, " Zu neuen Ufern deutscher Wissenschaft," *Völkischer Beobachter*, 20/10/35.
4. B. Rust, *New York Times*, 30/6/36.
5. W. Frank, op. cit.
6. W. Frank, op. cit.
7. W. Frick, quoted from *L'Europe Nouvelle*, 4/6/35, p. 320, by Chas. A. Beard, " Education under the Nazis," *Foreign Affairs*, Vol. 14, 4/36, pp. 437–52.
8. Madison Grant, *The Passing of the Great Race*.
9. *Völkischer Beobachter*, 9/8/35.
10. W. Gross, Speech at Reception for the Foreign Press, 3/35.
11. *Why the Aryan Paragraph?*
12. W. Frick, Reich Minister of the Interior.
13. E. Krieck, *Nationalpolitische Erziehung*, Leipzig, 1933.
14. A. Rosenberg.

15. R. W. Darré, *Das Schwein als Kriterium der Nordischen Rasse*, München, 1933.
16. George Norlin, quoting.
17. R. Thurston, "The Nazi War on Medicine," *The New Republic*, 4/12/35.

Chapter III

1. It apparently has not occurred to Mr. Barton that however satisfactory he may find his illustration for purposes of explaining variations in human ability, it is completely inverted when applied to the facts of relative economic opportunity. There is a handicap system in business life, but it is a handicap scheme not for offsetting the advantage of the strong, but for underwriting it against the weak. To make his illustration stick, Mr. Barton would need a golf club where the players in the seventies were given the handicap advantages, and the players in the hundreds had handicaps assessed against them. That a situation analogous to this obtains in business life is so notoriously true that Mr. Barton will find no one, left or right, prepared to deny it. If the initial argument regarding ability gradations is no more than naïve, the implications drawn from it are directly contrary to indisputable fact.
2. *Deutsches Kulturrecht*, Hamburg, 1936, p. 5.
3. Ibid., p. 11.
4. Ibid., p. 9.
5. Ibid., p. 18.
6. Ibid., p. 10.
7. Ibid., p. 11.
8. Ibid., p. 12.
9. Ibid., p. 13.
10. Ibid., p. 13.
11. Ibid., p. 13.
12. Ibid., p. 64.
13. Quoted by F. Schumann, op. cit.
14. Bruce Barton, op. cit.
15. *Deutsches Kulturrecht*, p. 18.
16. Ibid., p. 18.
17. Charts—Ministry of Propaganda and People's Enlightenment.
18. *Deutsches Kulturrecht*, p. 65.
19. Ibid., p. 72.
20. Ibid., p. 69.
21. Ibid., p. 74.
22. Ibid., p. 67.
23. Ibid., p. 24.
24. Ibid., p. 66.
25. Ibid., p. 64.
26. *Völkischer Beobachter*, 1/12/35.
27. Karl Künkler, *Hochschule und Ausland*, March 1935.
28. *News in Brief*, Vol. 3, No. 23/24.
29. *News in Brief*, Vol. 2, No. 17.
30. Karl Künkler, *Hochschule und Ausland*, p. 15.
31. *News in Brief*, Vol. 2, No. 5.
32. *News in Brief*, Vol. 2, No. 17.
33. *Völkischer Beobachter*, 28/11/35.
34. *Völkischer Beobachter*, 22/1/36.
35. *News in Brief*, Vol. 2, No. 15.
36. *News in Brief*, Vol. 3, No. 18/19.
37. *News in Brief*, Vol. 3, No. 16/17.
38. Miscellaneous mimeographed material.
39. *News in Brief*, Vol. 2, No. 10.
40. *News in Brief*, Vol. 2, No. 23/24.

41. Miscellaneous mimeographed material.
42. *News in Brief*, Vol. 4, No. 1/2.
43. See Chapter V, p. 173, for a more complete description of the programme for the Hitler Youth.
44. See Chapter V, p. 163.
45. I. Kandel, " Education in Nazi Germany," *Annals American Academy of Political and Social Science*, Vol. 182, pp. 161–62.
46. Outline for a Model Course in Modern History, Recommended by No. 42, 1934, of the *Nationalsozialistischer Erzieher*, the official pedagogical journal as translated in *The Yellow Spot*, the Extermination of the Jews in Germany, London, 1936, p. 255.
47. " . . . the head of the *Deutsche Studentenschaft* is the Reich Leader of the students, who is at the same time the Reich Leader of the professional group of German students at universities and professional schools. Subordinate to the Reich Leader are the leaders of the various chief offices."— M. Gärtner, *The Organisation of German Students*, mimeographed literature from the Propaganda Ministry.
48. See Chapter V, p. 163.
49. M. Gärtner, *The Organisation of German Students*.
50. *Der Angriff*, as reported in the *New York Times*, April 24, 1936.

CHAPTER IV

1 This title, employed here to summarise the Nazi programme, is taken, significantly enough, not from German but from American sources. Answering the question, How can the led be brought to serve the ends which the leaders of society map out as objectives to be pursued? the two American authors Mooney and Reiley reply, " The answer . . . is *co-ordination*, but what is here meant is a real *co-ordination of the spirit* based on the common knowledge of the common purposes and *ingrained* through the doctrine of the organisation itself" (*Onward Industry!* Harpers, London; italics by R. A. B.).
2. Adolf Hitler, on " occasion of the second German Labour Congress," quoted in *News in Brief*, Vol. 2, No. 10, pp. 2–3.
3. The Purport of the Act for the Organisation of National Labour, *Herausgegeben vom Reichsarbeitsministerium*, Berlin, 1934, p. 22. (The full quotation reads: " The principle which at one time made the Prussian Army the most wonderful instrument of the German Nation must, in the future, in a figurative sense, be the principle for the construction of the Constitution: Authority of every leader downwards and responsibility upwards.")
4. Par. 2 of the Act for the Organisation of National Labour, dated January 20, 1934, reads: " Article 1. The leader of the establishment shall make decisions for his followers in all matters affecting the establishment in so far as they are governed by this Act. Article 2. He shall promote the welfare of his followers. The latter shall be loyal to him as fellow-members of the works community " (*Herausgegeben vom Reichsarbeitsministerium*, Berlin, 1934, p. 3).
5. Dr. Luer, leader of the Reich Group Commerce, " The Employer as an Administrator of Public Property," quoted in *News in Brief*, Vol. 3, No. 11.
6. Idem.
7. Address delivered by Dr. Ley, Leader of the German Labour Front, to the representatives of the Foreign Press in Berlin, in the Hotel Kaiserhof, March 7, 1935: " The History and Aims of the German Labour Front," " New Forms of Community Work," *Herausgegeben vom Reichsarbeits- und Reichswirtschaftsrat*, Berlin, 1935, p. 15.
8. Hitler, *My Struggle*, quoted in the Purport of the Act for the Organisation of National Labour, op. cit., p. 4.
9. " New Forms of Community Work," op. cit., p. 3.
10. Cited from Hitler by Krause, op. cit., p. 56.

360 NOTES

11. See the section pp. 141–43 dealing with the Schacht-Seldte-Ley Leipzig Agreement.
12. See, especially, Selig Perlman, *History of Trade Unionism in United States.*
13. G. H. Miles, *The Problem of Incentives in Industry*, Pitman, London, 1932, pp. 19–32. An advertisement for this book announces that the author " discusses the root problem of industry—how to supply adequate incentives so that the maximum energy of each worker, from the managing director to the office boy, may be *aroused and directed in the best interests of the firm* " (italics by R. A. B.). It would be difficult to find a more succinct summary of the whole Nazi labour philosophy than this.
14. Elton Mayo, *The Human Problems of an Industrial Civilisation*, Macmillan, London. There is scarcely a line in this book which the Nazi labour " leaders " would take exception to.
15. Along the same line see, Mathewson, Leiserson, Morgan, Dennison, *Restriction of Output among Unorganised Workers*, Antioch College, 1931, where experiments showed that the normal " withdrawal of efficiency " of routine day labour certainly averaged no less than 50 per cent of the amount of work possible without strain.
16. It is not surprising, considering the great stress being laid on labour productivity there—as in the Stakonov movement—to find an enormous amount of attention being paid to non-commercial incentives in the Soviet Union. The Institute for the Defence of Labour, the central and regional psychotechnical research institutes, and the vast system—organised by industries and covering practically all phases of economic life in the Union—of personnel testing agencies is easily the most advanced and extensive in the world. It is scarcely necessary to add, however, that in the Soviet Union wage increases go hand in hand with increased labour productivity. In the Soviet system there is nothing else, alas, to do with wages but to give them to labour.
17. Mooney and Reiley, op. cit.
18. " New Forms of Community Work," op. cit., p. 19.
19. See p. 140.
20. Ley, op. cit., p. 20.
21. J. W. E. Thelwall, *Economic Conditions in Germany*, 1934, H.M.S.O., London.
22. Thelwall, op. cit.
23. Krause, p. 57.
24. Ibid., p. 28.
25. The Law reads: (1) The number of Confidential Men shall be as follows:

In establishments employing 20 to 49 persons .. 2
,, ,, 50 ,, 99 ,, .. 3
,, ,, 100 ,, 199 ,, .. 4
,, ,, 200 ,, 399 ,, .. 5

(2) The number shall be increased by one for each additional three hundred persons employed, and shall not exceed ten. (3) An equal number of substitutes shall be appointed (Act for the Organisation of National Labour, January 20, 1934).
26. All quotations from Krause, pp. 28–37.
27. Quoted by Krause, p. 34, from an " Official Announcement given out by the Trustee for Labour for the economic district Brandenburg " (italics by R. A. B.).
28. " New Forms of Community Work," op. cit., p. 23 (italics by R. A. B.).
29. American readers, who may be shocked at this cynical combination of simulated concern for the public well-being, maintenance of the husks of representative government, and complete subjection of labour to the power of employers, may well be interested to note that the entire Nazi labour programme is identical in effect with one of the earliest arguments on behalf of company unions; the Industrial Creed announced by John D. Rockefeller, Jr., in an article on Industrial Co-operation prefacing a collection of his addresses—most of which were delivered before or during the war. The

Industrial Creed contains the following points: (1) " Capital and labour are partners, not enemies ... their interests are common, not opposed "; (2) " The community is an essential party to industry "; (3) " The purport of industry is quite as much to advance social well-being as material prosperity " (interests of community considered, well-being of employees guarded, management recognised, and " capital justly compensated." Loss of one is " loss to all four parties "); (4) " Every man is entitled to an opportunity to earn a living "; (5) " Service is the only justification for the possession of power "; (6) Grievances should be promptly settled; (7) " Industrial harmony and prosperity " depends upon " adequate representation of the parties in interest "; (8) " The most effective structure of representation is that which is built from the bottom up " (Mr. Rockefeller means the *company union*); (9) " Attitude and spirit are all important ... forms are wholly secondary "; (10) " Greatest social service " is to co-operate to promote self-development of all, The Nazi programme for conquering the " soul of labour " would agree with this " creed " in its entirety.

30. Ley, " New Forms of Community Work," p. 23 (italics by R. A. B.).
31. The disposition of the money collected from such fines is not clear. Presumably the money goes into the party coffers.
32. Quoted by Krause from " official correspondence of the N.S.B.O. and the D.A.F.
33. Decision No. 4358 of the Arbitration Senate of the National Insurance Office, quoted by Krause, p. 31.
34. Act for the Organisation of National Labour, op. cit., pp. 7–8.
35. R. Ley, " Aims of the German Labour Front," " New Forms of Community Work," *Reichsarbeits- und Reichswirtschaftsrat*, Berlin, 1935, p. 27.
36. Act for the Organisation of National Labour, op. cit., pp. 7–8.
37. " New Forms of Community Work," p. 27.
38. Act for the Organisation of National Labour, p. 11.
39. Krause, p. 40.
40. Ibid., p. 43.
41. Ibid., p. 45.
42. Ibid., p. 53.
43. Act for the Organisation of National Labour, p. 14.
44. Krause, p. 159.
45. Quoted from Ley by Krause, p. 165.
46. Quoted by Schuman, *The Nazi Dictatorship*, p. 136.
47. Geiger, Leader of the Propaganda Office of the Arbeits Front, quoted from the *Völkischer Beobachter*, July 9, 1935.
48. *Abschrift, Jahresbericht der N.S.-Gemeinschaft " Kraft durch Freude,"* January 1936.
49. Ley, " New Forms of Community Work," op cit., pp. 20–21.
50. *Abschrift, Jahresbericht der N.S.-Gemeinschaft " Kraft durch Freude,"* p. 3.
51. Hitler, quoted by Schuman, op. cit.
52. Ley in *Völkischer Beobachter*, op. cit.
53. Local *Kraft durch Freude* house organ of the Werksgemeinschaft der I.G. Farbenindustrie, A.G., pp. 2 and 3.
54. *Völkischer Beobachter*, op. cit.
55. *Der Angriff*, July 8, 1935.
56. Circular from the " Amerika-Institut." Ideas and data culled from the booklet, *Leibesübungen mit Kraft durch Freude*.
57. *Abschrift, Jahresbericht der N.S.-Gemeinschaft " Kraft durch Freude,"* op. cit.
58. The reader should, for sake of clarity, be very sure to distinguish here between *form* and *intent*. The Nazis have borrowed Soviet *forms*; the *intent* in borrowing is exactly the reverse of that which dominates the use of these forms in the Soviet Union.
59. *Abschrift*, op. cit.
60. Ibid.
61. Mimeographed circular, *Winter Help Campaign 1934–35*, sent out by the Propaganda Ministry.

62. Quoted by Konrad Heiden, *A History of National Socialism*, Methuen, London.

CHAPTER V

1. See *Jugendland* (*Youth Land*), a publication for children of factory workers put out by Dinta, for May 1930, p. 8.
2. C. Arnhold, *Der Betriebsingenieur als Menschführer*, Berlin, 2/3/27, p. 3.
3. Ibid., p. 3.
4. C. Arnhold, "Mensch und Arbeit," *Verkehrswissenschaftliche Lehrmittelgesellschaft M.B.H. bei der Deutschen Reichsbahn* (1934), pp. 20, 30.
5. C. Arnhold, *Der Betriebsingenieur als Menschführer*, Berlin, 2/3/27.
6. C. Arnhold, "Mensch und Arbeit," *Verkehrswissenschaftliche Lehrmittelgesellschaft M.B.H. bei der Deutschen Reichsbahn* (1934), p. 33.
7. C. Arnhold, *Grundlagen der Berufserziehung und Arbeitsführung*, 1935 (mimeo.).
8. C. Arnhold, "Mensch und Arbeit," *Verkehrswissenschaftliche Lehrmittelgesellschaft M.B.H. bei der Deutschen Reichsbahn* (1934), p. 19.
9. M. Gärtner, *National Trades Competition* (mimeo.).
10. *Jugend an der Werkbank*, Presse- und Propagandastelle des Reichsberufswettkampfes.
11. "The Second Rural Year," *News in Brief*, Vol. 30, No. 13/14, 7/35, p. 17.
12. Ibid.
13. Kretzschmann und Edel, *Der Reichsarbeitsdienst im Wort und Bild*, Deutscher Verlag für Politik und Wirtschaft G.m.b.H., Berlin (1935), p. 63.
14. H. Schmeidler, *Compulsory Labour Service in Germany*, Wirtschaftspolitische Gesellschaft, 1936, p. 2 (mimeo.).
15. Ibid., p. 3.
16. At present (spring of 1936) the activity of the Labour Service is distributed as follows: 53 per cent agricultural work; 15 per cent construction of field and country roads; 5 per cent settlement work; 12 per cent forest work; the balance is devoted to special work, such as the construction of dams across valleys for the purpose of water regulation and storage or the provision of protection from catastrophes, etc.—From *Compulsory Labour Service in Germany*, mimeographed Wirtschaftspolitische Gesellschaft, Berlin.
17. A. Krüger, *Aufgabe und Sinn des Arbeitsdienstes*, Verlag Deutscher Arbeitsdienst (1935), p. 39.
18. Ibid., p. 29.
19. A. Krüger, *Der Deutsche Arbeitsdienst als Baustein zum Dritten Reich*, Leipzig, 1935, chapter vii.
20. Ibid.
21. J. Goebbels.
22. Kretzschmann und Edel, *Der Reichsarbeitsdienst im Wort und Bild*, Deutscher Verlag für Politik und Wirtschaft G.m.b.H., Berlin (1935), p. 81.
23. *Youth in a Changing World*, Terramare Office, 4th ed., 1936, Berlin, p. 12.
24. Ibid., p. 18.
25. *Der Reichsjugendführer an die Amerikanische Öffentlichkeit*, Eine Unterredung mit dem Vertreter der Associated Press, I. P. Lochner.
26. *Youth in a Changing World*, Terramare Office, 4th ed., 1936, Berlin, p. 18.
27. B. von Schirach, *Völkischer Beobachter*.
28. *Völkischer Beobachter*.
29. C. Arnhold.
30. Ibid.
31. Werner Haverbeck, "Aufbruch der jungen Nation," *Nationalsozialistische Monatshefte*, Heft 35, p. 81.
32. *Hitler Jugend im Dienst*, Verlag Bernard & Graefe, Berlin (1935), p. 180.
33. Ibid., p. 181.
34. Otto Tolischus, "Nazis Draft into Youth Army," *New York Times*, 5/1/36.

35. *Die Jugendschaft, Blätter für Heimabendgestaltung im Deutschen Jungvolk*, Berlin, 2. Maiausgabe, Folge 10.
36. *Youth in a Changing World*, Terramare Office, 4th ed., 1936, Berlin, p. 8.
37. Ralph Thurston, " Under the Nazi Christmas Tree," *New Republic*, 25/12/35.
38. Ibid.

Chapter VI

1. Hitler, Address at Nürnberg Party Convention, 8/9/34. F. L. Schuman, *The Nazi Dictatorship*, New York, 1936.
2. *Völkischer Beobachter*, 12/6/34. F. L. Schuman *The Nazi Dictatorship*.
3. Rudolf Hess's statement in *New York Times*, 26/5/36.
4. *Das Wissen der Nation*, August 1934. F. L. Schuman, *The Nazi Dictatorship*.
5. Lydia Gottschweski, " Von Nordischem Frauentum," *N.S. Frauenbuch*, München, 1934.
6. Hitler's Speech before the Women's Congress at Nürnberg, September 1934.
7. Ibid.
8. Toni Saring, *Der Deutsche Frauenarbeitsdienst*, Berlin, 1934.
9. Gertrud Scholtz-Klink, " Weg und Aufgabe der Nationalsozialistische Frauenbewegung," *N.S. Frauenbuch*, München, 1934.
10. Tony Sender, " Fear of Spies Rules Nazi Homes," *New York Evening Post*, 2/6/36.
11. Toni Saring, *Der Deutsche Frauenarbeitsdienst*, Berlin, 1934.
12. Tony Sender, " Fear of Spies Rules Nazi Homes," *New York Evening Post*, 2/6/36.
13. *Economist* (London), 8/2/36, p. 303.
14. G. Scholtz-Klink, *The Position of Women in the New Germany*, Lecture given in London, 7/35 (mimeo.).
15. Maria Burgstaller, " Der Deutsche Frauenarbeitsdienst," *N.S. Frauenbuch*, München, 1934.
16. Elfrieda E. Pope, " When Girls Volunteer," *Germany and You*, Berlin, Vol. 5, No. 5.
17. Toni Saring, *Der Deutsche Frauenarbeitsdienst*, Berlin, 1934.
18. *Völkischer Beobachter*, 22/1/36.
19. *News in Brief*, Vol. 2, No 19, October 1934, Berlin, pp. 10–11.
20. G. Scholtz-Klink, *Deutsches Frauenschaffen*, 1934, p. 10 (mimeo.).
21. *Völkischer Beobachter*, 22/1/36.
22. *The Fight vs. Unemployment among the Female Youth in Germany*, p. 2 (mimeo.).
23. Stefan Heym, " Youth in Hitler's Reich," *The Nation*, New York, 27/6/36.
24. *The Household Year for Girls* (mimeo.).
25. Ibid.
26. *Das Hauswirtschaftliche Jahr* (leaflet).
27. *The Board for Women within the German Labour Front* (mimeo.).
28. Ibid.
29. G. Scholtz-Klink, *Deutsches Frauenschaffen*, 1934 (mimeo.).
30. G. Scholtz-Klink, *The Position of Women in the New Germany*, Lecture in London, 7/35 (mimeo.).
31. Else Vorwerck *Die Deutsche Hausfrau in der Volkswirtschaft*.
32. G. Scholtz-Klink, *The Position of Women in the New Germany*, Lecture in London, 7/35 (mimeo.).
33. *Arbeitsplan für die Durchführung des Hilfswerks "Mutter und Kind,"* 2. Auf. 1935.
34. Marie Tscherning " Die Erziehung unserer weiblichen Jugend," *N.S. Frauen-Warte*, München, April 1935, Heft 21.

Chapter VII

1. Hitler quoted in 3. Reichsbauerntag in Goslar, Berlin, 1935, p. 7.
2. Hitler quoted in *Das Buch des deutsches Bauern*, Berlin, 1935.
3. Herman Gauch, *Die germanische Odal oder Allod Verfassung*, Goslar, 1934.
4. To settle lands inalienably on a person and his descendants or a certain line of descendants. *News in Brief*, Vol. 2, No. 10, May 1934, p. 5.
5. Sering mentions the following as the leading reasons for this situation: weakened productivity incidental to the war and the compulsory measures which accompanied it; lack of operating capital following change from inflation to the new fixed exchange; the necessary transformation of accounts current and exchange credit to high interest-bearing gold obligations; raising of taxes in gold even before the stabilisation of the currency; the decreased purchasing power of agricultural produce because of increased taxes, wages, and social burdens; success of propaganda by landlords and credit lenders, aided by state credits in part, in promoting borrowing; and disproportionately high interest rates charged for all credit extended. To these might be added several other factors, such as the continuously high level of prices of goods—particularly machinery, equipment, and fertilisers—which farmers paid for; the growing inability of German agriculture to compete with foreign specialised mass production crop areas; and the disastrous fall in agricultural prices which accompanied the world economic depression.
6. See, in particular, R. W. Darré, *Neuadel aus Blut und Boden*, op. cit.
7. Law of September 30, 1933; October 1, 1933.
8. The best exposition of this phase of this incredible doctrine—a doctrine which I have attempted to condense here in a few paragraphs—is to be found in *Neuadel aus Blut und Boden*, by Reichsbauernführer Darré, Munich, 1934.
9. Throughout the discussion of the Inheritance Law, I am following a publication of Dr. Wilhelm Saure, *Das Reichserbhofgesetz*, Berlin, 1934. This is regarded as an official clarification of the law in all its details and applications.
10. Ibid., p. 59.
11. *News in Brief*, Vol. 2, No. 22, November 1934, p. 6. This statement is a condensation from Reischle-Saure, *Aufgaben und Aufbau des Reichsnährstandes*, Berlin, 1934.
12. Classes *a* to *d*, idem. Class E from *Jahrbuch für Nationalsozialistische Wirtschaft*, 1935, p. 85.
13. See chart of organisation, III and IIIa.
14. Dr. A. B. Krause, *Organisation von Arbeit und Wirtschaft*, Berlin, 1935, pp. 122–23.
15. Ibid., p. 125.
16. Max Sering, *Deutsche Agrarpolitik auf geschichtlicher und landeskundlicher Grundlage*, Leipzig, 1934, p. 96.
17. Krause, op. cit.
18. *Jahrbuch*, op. cit., p. 88.
19. Reischle-Saure, op. cit., p. 90.
20. Reischle-Saure, op. cit., pp. 97–98.
21. Idem.
22. Ibid., p. 144.
23. Dr. Hans Merkel, " Bäuerliche Marktordnung," *Jahrbuch*, op. cit., pp. 92–93.
24. Institute for Business Cycle Research.

Chapter VIII

1. J. W. Ludowici, *Das deutsche Siedlungswerk*, Heidelberg, 1935.
2. *Der Angriff*, 2. Juli 1935.

NOTES 365

3. Gärtner, " Landdienst " in Germany—Mimeo. Wirtschaftspolitische Gesellschaft.
4. See *Richtlinien für die Neubildung deutschen Bauerntums* vom 1. Juni 1935.
5. *Führer Durch die Essener Wohnsiedlungen der Firma Krupp,* Sommer, 1930, p. 6.
6. Ibid., p. 8.
7. See, in particular, Karl Burhenne, *Werner Siemens als Sozialpolitiker.* Munich, 1930.
8. See, in particular, Ludowici, op. cit., p. 33.

Chapter IX

1. Cited by Krause, op. cit., p. 75.
2. Cited idem.
3. *News in Brief*, Vol. 3, No. 7, April 1935, p. 5.
4. *News in Brief*, Vol. 2, No. 5, March 15, 1934, p. 2.
5. Idem.
6. It cannot be too strongly emphasised here that the N.R.A. was in no significant fashion " imposed " on business by government. The original idea itself was very old, and was to be found scattered throughout the business and trade literature for a decade previous to the inception of N.R.A. The writings of Swope are, in this connection, particularly noteworthy. The original draft of N.R.A., as is now well known, was drawn up in the United States Chamber of Commerce, and that body was uniformly and enthusiastically behind it until certain monopolistic practices, promoted under the apparent protection of N.R.A., raised so much of a hullabaloo amongst some of its own constituents. But all the codes were drawn up by and for business men; they did not proceed to disown it until they obtained from it what they wanted—the right to pool information and present united fronts on policy. Nothing can be more " inevitable " in modern times than that American business men will return to a future and much stronger N.R.A., and that, when they do, it will embody all the salient features of the German National Economic Chamber—not by way of imitation, but because the same basic forces are at work in the promotion of both.
7. Cited by Krause, op. cit., p. 80.
8. *Jahrbuch der Berufsverbände im Deutschen Reiche, herausgegeben vom Reichsarbeitsministerium,* 1930, p. 43.
9. The reason for this special treatment of all Transportation is found in the fact that approximately 80 per cent of all such facilities are publicly owned, and hence under the direct supervision of the Ministry of Transport. Close cooperation with the National Economic Chamber and its various Economic Groups is, however, provided for.
10. There are seven of these altogether: (1) Mining, Iron and Metal Ore Production; (2) Machine Building, Technical, Optical, and Fine Mechanical Industries; (3) Iron, Plate, and Metal Wares; (4) Stone and Earth, Wood, Building, Glass, and Ceramics Industries; (5) Chemicals, Technical Oils and Fats, Paper and Paper-Making; (6) Leather, Textiles, and Clothing; (7) Food Products Industries. Each of these " Main Groups " is then divided into Economic Groups as described above. The division thereafter into Functional Groups follows the standard pattern.
11. The Handicraft Group is organised, both nationally and regionally, on a slightly different basis than with other Groups. In each of the 14 Provinces they are organised into Handicraft Chambers of the Provincial District. These are then represented in the Provincial Economic Chambers on the same basis as the provincial organisations of each of the other separate groups.
12. Krause, op. cit., p. 99.

13. Karlrobert Rengel, *Entwicklung, Einrichtungen und Aufgaben der Preussischen Industrie- und Handelskammer für das Rhein-Mainische Wirtschaftsgebiet*, Mitteilungen der Preussischen Industrie- und Handelskammer für das Rhein-Mainische Wirtschaftsgebiet, No. 18, September 1933, p. 226.

CHAPTER X

1. A. Reithinger, *Jahrbuch für Nationalsozialistische Wirtschaft*, op. cit., pp. 106–109.
2. Krause, op. cit., p. 100.
3. Heinz Müllensiefen, *Von der Kartellpolitik zur Marktordnung und Preisüberwachung*, Berlin, 1935, p. 8.
4. Cited by Horst Wagenführ, *Kartelle in Deutschland*, Nuremberg, 1931, p. xiv.
5. Cited by Müllensiefen, op. cit., p. 67.
6. *News in Brief*, Vol. 2, No. 21, Nov. 1934, pp. 6–7. See also Müllensiefen, op. cit., p. 33.
7. *News in Brief*, Vol. 2, No. 23/24, Dec. 1934, p. 8.
8. Müllensiefen, op. cit., p. 15.
9. *Marktordnungsgrundsätze der Reichsgruppe Industrie*, pp. 28–29.
10. *Die Elektrizitäts Wirtschaft im Deutschen Reiche*, Berlin, 1934, p. 438.
11. *Jahrbuch der Berufsverbände im Deutschen Reiche*, 1930, p. 49.
12. Rudolf Callmann, *Das Deutsche Kartellrecht*, Berlin, 1934.

CHAPTER XI

1. The Loyalists of Spain are not, of course, all socialists. They range from moderate republican to communist and anarchist factions. But one element they all have in common—they are popular, mass, and people oriented. With minor exceptions they are anti-property (private property in productive equipment), anti-clerical, anti-royal, anti-grandee. As a single collective noun, the phrase " Popular Front " expresses the basic popular and interest drive better than any other. The anarcho-syndicalist factions of Barcelona are as fundamentally Popular Front in sympathy as the various socialist and communist groups in programme and plan.
2. Share-cropper: a type of tenant farmer common to the Southern regions of the U.S. Unlike the usual tenant farmer, the share-cropper owns neither tools nor livestock and therefore receives these and his food on credit from the owner who customarily also runs a shop to supply these. The share-cropper therefore receives a much smaller share of the crop, being forced to live on a sub-subsistence level.
3. It has been confidentially stated by persons in close touch with the longer-range plans of the present administration in Washington, D.C., that the minimum chronic unemployment for the United States is not expected to drop below the 8,000,000 figure. With an average of $3\frac{1}{2}$ members per family, this means 28,000,000, or more than one-fifth of the entire population, on a *permanent relief basis*. The situation is not greatly different in England, France, and Germany. One must not be misled by the statistics. Economically, the army and navy, the members of the C.C.C. and the Labour Service Camps, and the percentage of part- to full-time employment—to cite a few outstanding examples—are unemployed.
4. The " public works " type of programme is not new, either as a method of work creation or as a method of neutralising the danger of revolt. The Great Pyramids of ancient Egypt, the public buildings of Rome and other ancient cities, and many of the great medieval structures—castles and cathedrals—were erected with the aid of unemployed labour which, idle, represented a direct challenge to the prevalent social order. A similar role

has been played by the army throughout all history. One of the most interesting stories yet to be written will centre around the expansion of armies and empires as a solution of the problem of what to do with the unemployed. This is not, of course, the only, or perhaps even the most important, cause of the growth of military power—but it is evidently a much more significant factor than has been heretofore realised.

5. Commenting on the " New Deal," Mr. Kennedy adds: " . . . there is scarcely a business man, large or small, who should not be with Roosevelt, and this for selfish reasons. It is the business man, large and small, who has chiefly prospered through the policies of the President . . . for reasons of dollars and cents the business men of America, the beneficiaries of a preserved profit system, should be with Mr. Roosevelt . . . the wealthy have been the chief beneficiaries of the New Deal policies, as witness the financial pages of any paper. There existed at the time of the inauguration a tremendous antagonism against the rich and powerful, natural enough in view of the growing destitution of the masses . . ." and so on (*New York Times*, September 6, 1936). Mr. Roosevelt, he says, " never condemned wealth as such, but only the ignoble, the selfish, the irresponsible wealthy "—a perfect Nazi-type argument which should be taken to read, " only those who were caught with the goods were bad " !

6. These three are governmentally owned. But what brought them together in single systems was not the fact of governmental ownership, but the nature of the services which they performed. The same forces were at work here as elsewhere, except, perhaps, that they came to the fore somewhat earlier and in a somewhat simpler form. At this point it is worth pointing out that fascism can be just as strongly in favour of " nationalisation " of certain key industries as may socialism, though not for the same reasons. It is no more a violation of good business principles to have the government own the railroads than to have the city own the waterworks. Much has been made out of the " nationalisation " of certain heavy industries in Italy, as though such action involved a serious step on the road to socialism. Far from it; the purpose is to provide common carrier and common supply services without undue discrimination against any given business *bloc*. Nor is the effect the same, since such " nationalisation " tends not to compromise, but to strengthen, the system. The same generalisation applies to " government regulation " under capitalism. See, for example, the argument advanced by Professor Copland, of the University of Melbourne, at the Harvard Tercentenary Conference of the Arts and Sciences, as reported in the *New York Times*, September 9, 1936, in which the " hope of capitalism " is found in " regulation " by the state. A particularly naïve example of this line of reasoning is to be found in Ware and Means, *The Modern Economy of Action*, New York, 1936 (see, in particular, chapter xi, " The Role of Government ").

7. The War Department of the United States Government sponsors the following definition of democracy: " Democracy—a government of the masses. Authority derived through mass meetings or any other form of ' direct ' expression. Result is mobocracy. Attitude towards property is communistic —negating property rights. Attitude toward law is that the will of the majority shall regulate, whether it be based upon deliberation or governed by passion, prejudice, and impulse, without restraint or regard for consequences. Results in demagogism, licence, agitation, discontent and anarchy."—*Training Manual No. 2000-2025 for the Reserve Officers' Training Corps.*

8. Many of them would, of course, recoil from such a doctrine stated thus badly and in this form, just as some of them object to the employment of the term " profit motive " in business literature—not because the truth is otherwise, but because so to state the facts " gives a bad impression." But they do not object, except in the occasional and unusual case, to the realities. The rules of the game set it up thus, and hence nobody can be held to blame—such is the typical account given if any objections are

raised. And is not that which is good for business good for the whole community ? Object to this way of stating the question and any run-of-the-mill business man will regard you with righteously indignant horror. Even though every man is set against every other man, with the strongest (within the recognised rules) the victors, this is justified as " competition," the " life of all trade " and the secret of all " efficiency." But it will never do to forget that this " efficiency " relates not to production, but to acquisition; not to co-operation, but to the act of garnishee; not to growth, but the act of " prey " (reaping, taking, " making profit " from growth).

9. The outlines of the best-approved picture are thoroughly familiar. The stance is firm, the shoulders square, the jaw courageously fixed, the eye clear and ready. Broad-visioned and heavily weighed with care, this Jason becomes Hercules cleaning the Augean stables, or one of the genii of Aladdin's most wonderful lamp—he rubs the lamp, and lo, the fruitful earth blossoms with the hope of his visions, express trains crisscross the land heavy laden with pleasure-goers, and mother and child stand entranced by the good fireside, their faces turned in gratitude to smile acknowledged thanks to this giver of all life—this guider and controller to whom God, in His infinite wisdom, has given over the goods of this world in trust !

10. It would be exceedingly interesting to trace through some of the current literature to show how these doctrines are intellectualised to make them palatable to the " intelligentsia " on the one hand, and vulgarised to make them acceptable to the philosophically illiterate on the other. The same process is going on here which the Romans of the imperial period witnessed in the case of Christianity. In one redaction—Luke and John—Christianity was amalgamated with Greek philosophy, particularly Platonism, Neo-Platonism, and Stoicism. The modern parallel here is Aldous Huxley's " Positive Pacifism " and, in a somewhat weaker form (more like Epicureanism), the Oxford Movement. In another redaction—Matthew, Mark, and the Book of Revelation—it was amalgamated with the mystery cults of Isis and Osiris, Mithra, Mazdaism, and others to appeal to the broad masses of the empire. The modern parallels here are the Strength through Joy, the Dopolavoro (Italian), and the programme of the Father Coughlins and Huey Longs. Can fascism find a " Petrine Rock " and a " Council of Nicea " to bring these together—the stuff being the same, but the language different ? See Chapters II and III above.

INDEX

Folk customs, as culturally useful, 148
Food scarcity, 241
Forced Labour, *see* Concentration Camps, Labour Service Camps, Work Camps, *etc.*
Foreign Department, curriculum for, table showing, 112
Foreign exchange, when solely procurable, 239
Frank, Dr. W., on German Historical Science, 52
Frederick the Great and rooting of men to the soil, 255
" Free Art," co-ordination of, methods of, 101–2
Freedom, the new German, 234; true, and Nazi, 51
" Freedom of the press " under the Nazi regime, 95, 96–7
Frick, Dr., programme of, for writers of History, 53–4
Frielinghaus, —, *cited*, 291
Functional Groups, 302

GÄRTNER, M., *cited*, 161
Gas and electricity energy producers, grouping of, 269
Gas-Electric Front, Community of Work of, member bodies, 314–15; purpose of, 315
Galileo, fate of, 51; and others, mathematical-mechanical " world-view " of, how conditioned, 48
" *Gemütlichkeit*," revival of, 18
General National Socialist Women's Student Federation, work of, 205
German and alien mating, alleged results, 55–6, 60, 62
German boasts, 160
German Dye Trust, house organ of, and Hitler, 145; pooling by, of research, 74
German Economic System, law for Preparation of Organic Reconstruction of, 266
German Evangelical Church, Law for Preservation of, working of, 104–5
German General Electric Co., pooling research, 74; unchanged position of, 286
German Hop Trading Company, working of, 235

German Labour Front, a euphemism concerning, 293
German mothers, what they should pray for, 181
German peasant laws, the new, theory behind, 219 ff.
German peasants, conditions of, when Nazi power began, 215 ff.; stratification of, 216–17
German Students' Union, function of, 255
German superiority, early inculcation of, 182–3
German Young Folk Year, a proposed object of, 179
German Young Folks League, age of entering, 179; divided functions of, 176
German Youth Hostels, 180, 181
Germany, growing internal strains of, 143; pre-Roman, attempt to revive, 220
Girl-students, department helping, 205
Girls, German, Union of, 176
Girls, a Household Year for, 150, 199–200; Peasant Leader schools for, curriculum of, 113–14; scant reference to, in books on Hitler Youth, 192, *see also* Federation of
Girls' camps, 192
Girls' division of Hitler Youth, 176, 191–2
Gobineau, Count de, 57
Goebbels, Dr., 165, 170; *cited*, 42, 116; and control of the Culture Agencies 90; ministry of, 103; powers of, 116 ff.
" Godmother work," 151
Government, influence on, of the business community, 332
Government [trade] regulations, 296
Grant, Madison, *cited*, 57–8, 59 ff.
Great Divide, the, parallel to, in Nazi culture programme, 39
Great German Youth Movement, 173
Grouping, examples of different types of, 273
Groups and Cartels, relations between, 288, question of, 302 ff., formation of, 125; functions and fields of operation, defining of, agreement illustrating, 309–10
Gymnastics, object of, 109

INDEX

Peasants as balance against urban
proletariats, 253
" Picked number " for leadership,
training of, 177
Pig, the, attitude to, of Jew and of
German, 61
Planck, Max, *cited*, 45; and others,
myths believed in by, 75
Planned organisation, twentieth cen-
tury, Reithinger on, 295–6
Planning, Nazi objection to, 266
Plato, society envisaged by, 123–4
Policy-pressure hierarchies, 268
Political faith, unanimity in, com-
pulsory, 43
Politics, trend to the left in, 28
Pooling of scientific information, 74
Pound, Arthur, *cited*, 343
Poverty, revolution and Fascism, 325
Power, economic, location of, 289
Pre-Nazi Groups and Cartels, non-
interference with, 302
Press, the, freedom of, Hitler on, 96
Preysing, Konrad, Graf von, Bishop of
Berlin, 105
Price-fixing, 300; and fair competi-
tion, 299
Prices, agricultural, increased, 239;
retail, and attempts to keep down,
240, 241; stable, 241
Private enterprise, fields open to, 313 ff.
Private ownership, scope of, 41
Producer-users, Communist ideal of,
123
Production, means of securing, 158
Productive capacity lying idle, 326
Productivity, industrial, and the
" attitude to life," 123
rofessors, political, Rust on, 53; selec-
tion of, 110
Profits and " service," the former the
chief aim, 321
Propaganda, 42; level of, persuasive
and coercive, 341, 342; tools of, art
and education, 78 ff.; German and
American, 87–8
Propaganda Ministries, the three, 103 ff.,
and People's Enlightenment, Ministry of, 103; scope and activities of,
116 ff.
Prosecutions by Labour Trustees, 136
Protection of German Blood and German Honour, law passed to afford,
62–3

Provincial Economic Chambers,
organisation of, 273 ff.; activities of,
280; Krause on, 279–80
Provincial Transport Councils, model
for, 313
Pseudo-Aryan mysticism and magic, 45
Public opinion, Hitler on, 86
Public Relations Counsellors, U.S.A.,
87
Public utility type of monopolies,
311 ff.
Public works, as relief, 327

QUASI-MONOPOLIES, British, Government interest in, 333
Questionnaire, monthly, of factory
cells, 135

RACE, German claim to superiority of,
59
Race suicide, 247, 252
Racial differences, German exploita-
tion of, 69; purity, 59; science, 47,
56 ff.
Ramlow, Dr., *cited*, 98
Rationalisation, twentieth century, 295
Raw materials, agreements, etc., con-
cerning, 295
Recreational facilities for boys, 156
Reich, the, future divisions of, 263–4
Reichsbank, the, 239
Reischle-Saure, —, *cited*, 234
Reithinger, —, *cited*, 295
Religious bodies, political adherence of,
30
Renteln, —, *cited*, 145
Reparations, 23; scaling down, 23–4
Research and practice, former liaison
between, ruptured, 73; results of
pooled, 74
Responsibility, working upwards, 119
Resurgence of the German People,
20; dread underlying, 20–1, 35
Revolution, post-war, 17, 21
Rhineland, industrials, support of, to
Hitler, 32
Ricardo, David, 221
Right, the, Ebert and, 29; Conserva-
tism of, 29
Right and wrong in Nazi-ism, 115
Roads, military, Labour Service used
to make, 169

INDEX 381

Tobacco, imported, indictment of, 70
"To-day's spring" in new Germany, Schirach on, 185
Totalitarian state, Nazi references to, 39
Tours, as rewards, 146–7, 156–7
Toys, military form of, 183
Trade and the flag, 81
Trade associations in U.S.A., Britain, and Germany, 331
Trade or occupational groups, 294
Trade Unions before Marx, utility of, perversion and destruction of, 41, 120; the drive against, 105, 118, 140; membership of, fluctuations in, 27–8, 30; militancy of, 30
Transportation, authority dealing with, 269, 271, 313
Trilke-Gut, girls' Leader School, curriculum of, 113–14, 115
Trustees of Labour, 127, 130, 131 ff.
Truth, irrelevant in Germany, 88
Tugwell, —, 342

UNEMPLOYED PERSONS, number of, growth of, reversal of causes of, 328; and suburban settlement, 257, 258
Unemployment, Fascist solution of, 196, 353; long-range plan for, 258–9; and productive capacity lying idle, 326–7; and small families, 252
Unemployment Services, 150 ff., 167–8
Union of German Girls, divided functions of, 176
U.S.S.R., German statements on, and attitude to, 69
United Steel Works, present position of, 286–7; Technical Education Committee organised at, 293
Universities, limitation of women in, 205
University students working on the land, 254–5
Unrest, social, causes and potential consequences, 324 ff.
Urban youth life-organisation to be as that of the peasant, 163

VACATIONS, annual, proposed for German women, provision for their absence, 197–8
Values worth preserving, 155

Varus, 220
Veblen, —, naïve ideas of, 74
Versailles, Treaty of, 21, 35; alleged Jewish responsibility for, 66; real significance of, 27; symbolism of, 22, 27
Vögler, —, and the Dinta, 153
Völkischer Beobachter, the, 116
"Voluntary," Nazi meaning of, 173

WAGE-RATES, regulation of, 136–7
War, the Great, aftermath of, 17; German defeat attributed to the Jews, 66; ignorance of its causes, 21
War, modern, without rules, 354; revolution as certain to intervene, 353
Washington Naval Conference, 25
Watt, James, cited, 342
Wealth and poverty, extremes of, revolutions due to, 325
Weimar Constitution, compromise and inconsistencies in, 28
Weimar Republic, 66
Welfare Capitalism, U.S.A., and the Nazi Labour Front, 121
Welfare technique, firms employing, 121–2
Wettkampf, meaning of, 177–8
Whitley Councils, 342
Wholesaling function, proper performance of, 309–10
Wiggin, E. A., writings of, 57
William II, Kaiser, militarism of his days, 20, found faulty, 21; flight of, 21; on his indifference to public opinion, 86
Wilson, President W., and his Fourteen Points, 21, 22
Winter Help Campaigns, 151
Women, co-ordination of, agencies for, 191; duties and loyalties of in the Nazi state, 186, 187; emancipation of, repudiated by Nazism, 188; German, intrinsic superiority claimed for, 189; how convince that Nazi views are best for them? 190–1; Nazi attitude to, 209–10; Nazi programme for, 114–15; new German ideal of, 185, 186 ff.; Red Cross Department of, 205; and the soil, 186, 218; wages of, relative to men's, 136–7; withdrawal of, from men's work, 136, 190, 196, 247, 258 ff.

Women's Activities, Committee of groups composing, 207–8; functions of, 205 ff.; main task of, 206; organisation of, 206
Women's Labour Service, 191, 192; compulsory organisation of, 164, 166; labour camps for, 114, 192 ff.; hard work at, and superiority of the city girl, 194–5; teaching at, 196; work and propaganda of, double purpose of, 193 ff.
Women's Work, organisations included in, 201; departments of, 202, supplementary, 205
Work camps, 165
Workers, demands of, Arnhold on, 154; and employers, relations of, summarised, 151–2; examinations of, 157; making happy in their jobs, 158; training of, according to type, 157–8; welfare of, 156 ff.
Working hypotheses, German equivalent of, 49, 51
Working masses, needs of, Hitler on, 143

Workless, the, division of, 151
Workman, Workmen, Aryan, male, insistence on, 150; as a fighting man, object of his fight, 160, 161; invalids, facilities for, 158–9; wives of, training for the post, 158
Works Ordinances, 128

Young Folks League, the, 174
" Young Germans," scope of the term, 164
Young Girls, the, 176, 191
Young Plan, 24
Youth, culture directed to, 102; militarisation of, 172, 177
Youth Committee of the Nazi Party, 173
Youth Movement, 108, 145
Youth organisations, 108, 144–5, 151; " agreements " of, with other party organs, etc., 176; co-ordination of, 174
Youth Press, chauvinism of, 180